INSURANCE
LAW AND PRACTICE

Third Revised and Enlarged Edition

C.L. Tyagi
Madhu Tyagi

ATLANTIC
PUBLISHERS & DISTRIBUTORS (P) LTD

Published by

ATLANTIC

PUBLISHERS & DISTRIBUTORS (P) LTD

7/22, Ansari Road, Darya Ganj, New Delhi-110002
Phones : +91-11-40775252, 40775214, 23273880, 23275880
Fax : +91-11-23285873
Web : www.atlanticbooks.com
E-mail : orders@atlanticbooks.com

First Edition 2007, 2010, 2013
Second Revised and Enlarged Edition, 2016
Third Revised and Enlarged Edition, 2022

Printed & bound in India by Atlantic Print Services

Preface to the Third Edition

The third revised edition of the book could not be brought out on anticipated time due to COVID-19 pandemic. Now, it is ready for the students with all the updates and new opportunities in insurance sector. The pandemic has provided a short of booster to the health insurance with over 500 new products launched during the period. This segment has overtaken motor insurance to become the largest business for non-life companies. However, there is a protection gap (between ailments and claims) in smaller cities which remains a concern. The 'Corona Kavach', a standardised basic health insurance cover specific for treatment of COVID-19 has been designed by IRDA.

Chapter 10 on 'Protection of Policyholders' Interests and Foreign Exchange Management (Insurance) Regulations' has replace the old one. Pradhan Mantri Fasal Bima Yojna and Corona 19 in health insurance are the new topics covered in this edition. Additions have been made in Rural Insurance, Fire Insurance, and Accident Insurance.

Lastly, legal cases on different types of insurance are a novelty of this edition.

Any suggestions for improvement are welcome.

C.L. Tyagi
Madhu Tyagi

Preface to the First Edition

Insurance is a fast growing services sector in India since a decade. Gone are the days when it was difficult to sell insurance. Today insurance sector is significantly contributing towards economic growth of Indian economy. Many foreign insurance companies/insurers have opened their branches in India, after denationalisation of insurance in 1999. Insurance Regulatory Development Authority was set up to improvise, regulate, and develop insurance sector. Many varieties of insurance products, particularly life insurance, are being offered these days thereby enabling the people to make a choice according to their preference and suitability. At the university level, courses are offered in insurance at the graduate and post-graduate level. Students opt it either as a major or minor subject. The present book is written primarily for students of Insurance. However, professionals in financial sector will also find it useful. The book comprehensively presents the details of the subject in a lucid style.

The book covers life, fire, and marine insurances as well as Employees State insurance, motor vehicle insurance, fidelity guarantee, home insurance, and personal liability insurance. Other forms like personal accident, professional indemnity, shopkeeper's insurance, Mediclaim, Air travel, and students safety have also been explained. Main provisions of Deposit Insurance and Credit Guarantee Act and Insurance Regulatory Development Authority Act have been summarily given. Above all, various types of life insurance products now offered have been explained separately.

The book does not claim originality and at places matter has been drawn from various authors and newspapers, and we owe thanks to them. We particularly acknowledge Bajaj Allianz for providing printed material for their products. Our heartfelt thanks go to Dr. K.R. Gupta, Chairman, Atlantic Publishers and Distributors (P) Ltd., for bringing out this edition without whose erudition and cooperation the book would not have seen the light of the day.

C.L. Tyagi
Madhu Tyagi

Contents

1

Concept of Risk

Introduction

The dictionary meaning of the word 'Risk' is "the possibility or chance of meeting danger, suffering loss, or injury". Risk traditionally has been defined in terms of uncertainty. Risk may be defined as uncertainty concerning the occurrence of a loss. Risk is a measure of the potential to cause damage. Risk is the probability of harmful consequences or expected losses (deaths, injuries, property loss, loss of livelihood, disruption of economic activity or environment damage) resulting from interaction between natural or human induced hazards and vulnerable conditions. Conventionally, risk is expressed by the notation:

$$\text{Risk} = \frac{\text{Hazards} \times \text{Vulnerability (extent of effect)}}{\text{Capacity to manage or reduce hazard}}$$

In insurance, "Risk is uncertainty concerning loss and uncertainty is incidental to life". Risk is costly.

Chance of loss and risk are not the same thing. Risk may or may not result in loss.

Types of Risks

On the basis of frequency and severity, risks may be of four types:

(a) Risk of low frequency and low severity.

(b) Risk of high frequency and high severity.

(c) Risk of low frequency and high severity.

(d) Risk of high frequency and low severity.

Firstly, risks can also be classified into (1) Pure risk (static) and (2) Speculative risk (dynamic). In pure risk, there is uncertainty that loss will occur like loss by fire. In speculative risk, there may be gain or loss. Pure risk is static, while speculative risk is dynamic. Dynamic risks arise in a situation where there is a possibility of loss coupled with the possibility of a gain, e.g. dealing in shares in a stock market. Such risks are two-way risks, i.e. possibility of downward or upward potential. Pure risk or static risk refers to possibilities that can result in only loss or no change. Nothing good can come from an exposure to pure risk. A fire may break out or may not break out, is an example. In case of pure risks, the upside potential is absent. If a certain risk materialises, there is a loss, but if it does not materialise, there is neither gain nor a loss. They can be measured statistically. Pure risks may further be divided into three types: (a) personal risks like illness, accident, riot, weather, earthquake, floods, etc., (b) liability risks, e.g. fidelity of an employee, liability under any law (Employee's State Insurance or Workmen Compensation Act), and (c) property risks.

Speculative or dynamic risks are not mostly insured and may be divided into (i) management risks like marketing risks of goods and services, financial risk due to trade cycles or strikes, etc. or production risks, (ii) political risks like change in government, war or nationalisation, and (iii) innovation risks, e.g. innovation or change in technology, etc.

A second-way risks may be classified as (a) Fundamental risk and (b) Particular risk. Fundamental risks are those risks that arise at MACRO level, e.g. natural disasters (Tsunamis or earthquake). All the dynamic risks that arise due to political, social or economic factors are included in the category of fundamental risks. The origin of such risks and their impact is impersonal in nature. Particular risks are those risks that arise out of more localised causes, e.g. fire or theft. Their impact can also be far-reaching. Such risks arise at MICRO level.

All the above risks may affect a person, a business, a society or country. To sum up risks may be financial or non-financial, static or dynamic, fundamental or particular and pure or speculative risks.

A third-way to classify risk is whether it is objective or subjective. Objective risk can be observed. Subjective risk arises from the mental attitude of a person and can't be so easily observed.

Sources of Risk

The sources of risks are in a hazard. A hazard is a dangerous condition or event. It is either natural or manmade. It could cause an injury, loss of life or damage to property, livelihood or environment. The examples of natural hazard are earthquake, volcanic eruptions, tsunamis. Man-made hazards are generally associated with industries and factories. Examples are explosion, leakage of toxic waste, pollution, dam failures, war and civil strife, terrorist attack are also manmade. Some hazards may be caused by both natural or manmade reasons, e.g. landslide, floods, droughts and fire. Drainage or groundwater extraction leads to drought and destruction of mangroves may make storm strong.

Hazards can also be divided into three other types: (a) physical hazard, (b) moral hazard, and (c) occupational hazard. Physical hazards like loss of property or injury or death, water contamination or pollution. They are verifiable and can be evaluated in terms of their risk in a standardised form. Moral hazards cannot be seen in physical form and relate to ethics and morals, e.g. suppression of facts about the subject matter or willful misconduct or dishonesty and carelessness. Occupational hazards, as the name suggests, arise due to inherent causes in occupations, e.g. electric risk (for electricians), infection or irritation (in mines), lung problem (cotton textile). Physical hazards like injury or illness can be known by medical report, moral hazards by information given in insurance proposal form and occupational hazards by medical reports.

The cause of loss is called "PERIL". Insurance covers specified perils. Loss caused by any hazard may be either for tuitions, i.e. by chance or catastrophic, i.e. by Act of God. The latter is called "DISASTER" or "CRISIS".

Risk Management

Risk management is a specialised function. The objective of risk management is to minimise the cost of risk. Traditionally, risk management was considered to be synonymous with insurance management. The appropriateness of handling risk and strategy has to be decided on the basis of expected costs and benefits associated with each alternative. The details of risk management would vary from organisation to organisation. But the basic framework of corporate risk management remains the same. The objectives of risk management should be clearly defined.

Following are the steps of risk management:

(1) Risk Identification. This concept means identifying all significant types of risks and their sources. The uncertainty connected with each activity being developed or implemented to be found. One has to define the risk in terms of "what it includes and what it excludes". The elements at risk, the causes of risk and the root causes of vulnerable conditions are to be identified. This involves taking into account physical, geographical, social, political, and psychological factors that cause the hazards. In insurance proposal form, medical/agents/value report may be a source of risks. They must be properly checked.

(2) Risk Measurement/Assessment. This step involves analysis of risk and its evaluation. The analysis may operate at different levels, e.g. at learning level, at policies level and at top management level. Those risks which affect other risks are to be analysed as well. It is the vulnerability of hazard that is to be assessed, i.e. the probability or chances that losses will occur.

(3) Risk Control. The risk may not be fully controlled or prevented. Some risks may be reduced or eliminated, while some may be transferred or avoided. Some risks can be pooled or absorbed. A record must be kept of fast risks to help in controlling them. The handling of risks may be done in following ways: (i) Risk may be avoided. Some risks are inherent in life and cannot be avoided. Avoidance is possible only where choice is available, (ii) Risk may be assumed. Risk are accepted either in ignorance or advertently or sometimes intentionally, e.g. driving without a belt or helmet, and (iii) Risk may be reduced.

(4) Risk may be Reduced, i.e. Monitor the Outcomes. This is done by taking preventive measures, e.g. fire extinguishers installed in buildings or using materials that resist earthquake. Chances of illness can be reduced by regular medical check-ups. Such steps reduce the risk and hence losses may be reduced, i.e. PREVENTION and MITIGATION reduce risks. Mitigation means taking steps that reduce risk impact, e.g. such steps may involve structural and non-structural measures.

Structural mitigation involves use of medical or architecture or engineering techniques. Non-structural mitigation involves legal provisions by government, land planning, incentives, training, and education of the people. Thus, loss prevention may take the form of preventive, protective, mitigating, and salvage measures. Risk reduction has three components: (a) preparedness. It may be either avoided or retained, i.e. risk may be absorbed, (b) mitigation, i.e. reduction, and (c) prevention. Prevention is better than cure.

So risk can either be tolerated or treated or transferred or terminated.

Risk can be Transferred

The risk is shifted by various methods in business such as (a) Hedging, (b) Sub-contracting, (c) Surety bond, (d) Limiting liability, (e) Insurance, and (f) Creation of contingency fund.

Hedging means taking a position in two or more financial assets that are taking opposite trading positions to reduce risk i.e., buying as well as selling at the same time the same financial asset. Sub-contracting means transfer of a part contract to some other person. In insurance, this is done by reinsurance of a part of the subject matter and 'retaining' a part with oneself. A surety guarantees the payment in case of a default by debtor through a legal agreement called "surety bond". Risk can be limited by limiting the liability like in a limited partnership or a company with limited liability.

Insurance is a contract of 'pooling of risks' and the loss caused is distributed over many people (insured). A contingency fund is created by the government alone or along with states or insurance companies or individuals to meet any disaster or crisis.

Note: It is mandatory for all insurance companies to have a risk committee of directors under IRDA rules.

Classification of Risk: Risks may broadly be grouped in business under following heads:

(a) *Industry and Services Risks*:

(1) Economic risk i.e., dependent on person or product or industry.

(2) Services risks: Business dynamics, market structure.

(3) Competition risks affecting tariffs prices, costs, revenues, and customer preferences.

(4) Customer relations risks.

(b) *Management and Operations Risks*: These risks relate broadly to the company's organisation and management such as planning, monitoring, and reporting systems in the day-to-day management process, namely:

- Risks to property.
- Clear and well-defined work processes.
- Changes in technology/upgradation.
- R&D risks.
- Agency network risks.
- Personnel risks such as labour turnover risks involving replacement risks, training risks, cost risks, skill risks, etc. There are also unrest risks due to strikes and lockouts. These risks affect the company's business and earnings.
- Environmental and pollution control regulations, etc.
- Locational benefits near metros, railway stations, ports, cities, etc.

(c) *Market Risks*: These risks relate to market conditions, namely:

- Raw material rates.
- Quantities, quality, suppliers, lead time, interest rates risks and forex risks, namely fluctuation risks and interest rate risk in respect of foreign exchange transactions.

(d) *Political Risks*: These risks relate to political uncertainties, namely:

- Electrons.
- War risks.

- Country/area risks.
- Insurance risks like fire, strikes, riots, and civil commotion, marine risks, cargo risks, etc.
- Fiscal/monetary policy risks including taxation risks.

(e) *Credit Risks*: These risks relate to commercial operations, namely:

- Creditworthiness risks.
- Risks in settlement of dues by clients.
- Provisions for doubtful and bad debts.

(f) *Liquidity Risks*: These are financial risk factors, namely:

- Financial solvency and liquidity risks.
- Borrowing limits, delays.
- Cash/reserve management risks.
- Tax risks.

(g) *Disaster Risks*: These risks relate to disasters from following factors:

- Natural risks like fires, floods, earthquakes, etc.
- Man-made risks factors arising under the Factories Act, Mines Act, etc.
- Risk of failure of effective disaster management plans formulated by the company.

(h) *Systems Risks*: These risks relate to the company's systems, namely:

- System capacities.
- System reliability.
- Obsolescence risks.
- Data integrity risks.
- Coordinating and interface risks.

(i) *Legal Risks*: These risks relate to the following:

- Contract risks.
- Contractual liability.
- Frauds.
- Judicial risks.
- Insurance risks.

Note: Pricing risk, actuarial risk, and life expectancy risks are specific risk to insurance companies. Broadly, insurance companies face operational risk (sales, technological risks), financial risk (assets-liability mismatch) and market risks (interest rate and equity risks).

Risk Management Process

Risk management is no longer discretionary but essential for managing business entities in this dynamic corporate world. It takes commitment from the top, a sound methodology and

* Institute of Company Secretaries of India, "Corporate Governance" 6th Ed., p. 270.

discipline in its application to obtain the maximum benefit. Risk management must become imbibed into the organisation's culture.

Model Risk Management Policy for a Company

Risk

Risk may be defined as the possibility that an event will occur and adversely affect the achievement of the company's objectives and goals. A business risk is the threat that an event or action will adversely affect an organisation's ability to achieve its business objectives/targets. Business risk arises as much from the possibility that opportunities will not be realised as much from the fact that certain threats could well materialise and that errors could well be made.

Risk Management

Risk management is a structured, consistent and continuous process, applied across the organisation for the identification and assessment of risks, control assessment and exposure monitoring.

The objectives of the company's risk management framework comprise the following:

- To identify, assess, prioritise and manage existing as well as new risks in a planned and coordinated manner.
- To increase the effectiveness of internal and external reporting structure.
- To develop a risk culture that encourages employees to identify risks and associated opportunities and respond to them with appropriate actions.

Initiatives undertaken by the company to achieve its risk management objectives comprise the following:

- Identification and assessment of key risks in the context of the company's risk appetite.
- Accurate, complete and timely escalation of risk information to support management decisions-making at all levels.
- Active involvement of all employees in the risk management process within their own areas of responsibility.
- Continuous monitoring and management to an acceptable level of the potential impact.
- Integration of risk management into the company's day-to-day operations.

Risk Management Framework

The key elements of the framework include a risk management strategy, risk management structure, risk portfolio management and risk measuring, monitoring and optimising. The implementation of the framework is supported through a criteria for risk assessment and categorisation, a risk escalation matrix, risk forms and MIS.

Risk Management Strategy

Formal authority, responsibility and accountability for designing, implementing and sustaining effective risk management processes rest with the Company's Board of Directors. The Audit Committee, Risk Management Committee, Chief Risk Officer, other risk officers. Management and employees assist Board of Directors in fulfilling this risk mitigating responsibility.

At the company, this priority is allied to an ongoing risk measuring discipline. Business heads periodically review risks facing their areas of responsibility and implement an effective system of internal controls to manage them; they designate responsibilities and provide for upward communication of any significant issues that could arise.

Risk Management Structure

The company has a formal risk management structure with defined roles and responsibilities.

(i) *Risk Committee*

The Audit Committee ordinarily reviews risk management on a quarterly basis, or earlier when required for urgent matters. The Audit Committee monitors the progress of risk management initiatives and updates the Board of Directors with respect to changes in the company's key risk portfolio.

(ii) *Risk Management Committee*

The Risk Management Committee is responsible for broadening and strengthening the Company's risk management; it comprises Business Heads, Presidents, Chief Financial Officer, Chief Information Officer and Chief Compliance Officer.

(iii) *Chief Risk Officer*

The Chief Risk Officer provides inputs and insights in the establishment, monitoring and structuring of controls and assists management in identifying, assessing and managing risks.

Risk Portfolio Management

The risk portfolio management cycle begins with risk identification; followed by risk assessment, risk categorisation and finally the recording of risks in the risk registers.

Risk Management Cycle

(i) *Risk Identification*

Risk identification involves identifying potential events that may have an adverse impact on the achievement of business objectives. The process of risk identification involves an understanding of the objectives of the company and strategies adopted to achieve the same as well as potential events, past events and trends and possible future exposures. An event with a positive impact represents an opportunity while one with a negative impact represents a risk.

(ii) *Risk Assessment*

Risk assessment involves the quantification of the impact of risks to determine potential severity and a probability of occurrence. Inherent as well as residual risks are considered in the process of risk assessment. Each identified risk is assessed on a five-point scale with respect to the following criteria for determining their inherent and residual exposure: likelihood of the occurrence of an event and impact if the event occurs.

Both inherent and residual risks are to be considered in the process of risk assessment. An inherent risk is defined as the risk faced by the organisation in the absence of any actions (controls) that management might implement to alter the risk's impact or likelihood. The combination of an inherent likelihood of event occurrence and inherent impact represents the 'inherent risk exposure'.

The components of gross risk i.e. the probability of occurrence and magnitude of impact are sought to be reduced through the institution of adequate controls, the remaining risk being termed as residual risk. The combination of residual likelihood and residual impact represents the 'residual risk exposure'.

Risk exposure can vary from low to high as depicted in the following risk table.

(iii) *Risk Categorisation*

Risk categorisation assists in the assessment and prioritisation of risk. The company categorises risks into the following categories:

Table: Risk Exposure

Strategy risk	Operational risk	Financial risk
Business segments Substitution risk Competition risk Concentration risk	Force majeure Cost competitiveness Quality Obsolescence risk Proprietary risks/contingencies	Funding risk Foreign currency risk Receivables management risk Working capital cycle risk
Legal, regulatory and compliance risk	Human resource risk	Technology and information systems risk
Contractual risk Compliance and regulatory risk	Performance and attrition risk	 Storage and safety risk

In addition, there are external risks i.e. risks arising out of the external environment. Generally, the company exercises minimal or no control over such risks.

Risk Recording

Risk recording is done to record identified risks and related information in a structured manner. Reports drawn from the register are used to communicate the current status of all-known risks and are vital for assessing management control. The risk register constrains the following information with respect to each identified risk: risk description, risk owner, root causes, risk category, inherent risk evaluation, controls to mitigate the risk, residual risk evaluation, action plan, owner, timelines and status of action plans.

Measuring and Monitoring

Control assessment: The purpose of control assessment is to assess the effectiveness of risk minimisation procedures implemented by the process owners.

Evaluate control design

↓

Evaluate operational effectiveness

↓

Identify and remediate deficiencies

(i) **Risk reviews:** A risk review involves re-examination of all risks recorded in risk register to ensure that the risk assessment as currently recorded remains valid. The risk review is conducted to monitor the effectiveness of the risk assessment framework.

Risk reviews also involve the following:

- Assessment of completeness and validity of risks recorded in the risk register.
- Assessment of changes in the business processes; operating and regulatory environment since the last risk assessment and corresponding changes required in the risk profile, risk appetite and risk management procedures.
- Reviewing efficacy and implementation status of action plans for identified risks and consequent revision in action plans.

(ii) **Risk escalation:** The risk escalation matrix specifies the levels in the organisation to which risks with different magnitudes are to be escalated based on the significance arrived at as part of the risk assessment process. Risk escalation is critical for prompt communication, timely follow-up of specific issues and for effective risk management. The communication of key risk information is also important to ensure that all significant risks identified in a department are considered in the context of the overall operations of the company in a co-ordinated and consistent manner.

(iii) **Risk optimisation:** Risk optimisation involves the management of various risk line with the risk appetite of the company.

Overall Risk Management Process

Risk management at the company begins with the approval of a risk management strategy. The overall responsibility for insuring compliance with the risk management policy and policy guidelines is the responsibility of the CRO. In addition to providing an overall guidance and monitoring risk management procedures, the CRO also provides quarterly updates to the Board of Directors/Audit Committee. Heads of departments are responsible for identifying risks, preparing and executing action plans within their own areas of responsibility. They are also responsible for reviewing and escalating risks.

Management's Assessment of Risk—An Example*

A study on Enterprise Risk Management (ERM) was published in 1999 by Colquitt, Hoyt and Lee. They surveyed 397 risk managers. Indian companies do not take a comprehensive approach towards ERM. ERM provides a framework for risk management.

Strategy and Governance Risk

It involves those risks, which threaten the achievement of the company's objectives or the goals, which support the vision and mission of the organisation.

* Extracts from a company's corporate governance policy.

Competition risk

Spiraling costs in an inflationary environment could blunt the company's competitive edge. The company derives a large part of its revenues from outside India. The proportion of domestic revenues is expected to decline following the proposed capacity expansion, which will direct it towards uncharted geographies. Within India, the company's product ranges address the product-price-quality matrix supported by a dedicated dealer network.

Globally, the company enjoys a significant presence in USA and EU, the most competitive markets. The market in these geographies is dominated by large retailers, specialising in all lifestyle areas. The company is optimistic that its competitive cost structure, contemporary technology, quality-led, cost-effective manufacture and proximate customer relations will enable it to enhance its presence in chosen markets.

The businesses of the company are vertically integrated, which enables it to maximise value addition with the potential to protect it in the face of cyclical downturns.

The initiation of Kaizen and small group activities (SGA) were undertaken to curtail costs. Further, the vertical integration of the textile business, commissioning of state-of-the-art equipment, consumption of in-process waste and the modernisation of existing/outdated equipment reduced human intervention and improved productivity.

Concentration risk

A high dependence on any particular client or geography could be detrimental in the event of client attrition or geographical instability.

Exports accounted for about 56 per cent of the company's revenues, derived from more than 37 countries across five continents, with the US contributing a major share. Within US, the company enjoys a diversified presence in all its geographical segments through retail chains.

The company is pursuing a multi-pronged risk minimisation strategy: Revenues from key customers increased on an absolute basis but declined as a proportion of overall revenues through a widening of the client base.

The company is concentrating on diluting its geographic concentration to capitalise on opportunities, serve a rationalised customer base, develop raw products from existing/new facilities and cater to a specialised and satisfied client base as an effective counter to a large unorganised presence. The company is moving to a wider number of customers across unexplored geographies.

Within India, the company enjoys a major presence in all geographical segments; North India contributed a major part of the company's revenues on account of the sheer size of the market and logistical convenience. Following the introduction of a uniform value-added tax, the competitive advantage in favour of the organised sector will increase and the company expects to benefit from it.

Operational Risk

Risks arising from the normal processes/activities of the company fall in this category.

Force majeure

The company established four different manufacturing facilities within a 10 km radius in Punjab. Their interdependence and geographic proximity could be detrimental in the event of a regional disturbance.

The plants are located close to raw material sources. The company has built residential colonies for employees adjoining its plant premises. These dwelling units accommodate most of its workforce ensuring that operations at the plant can be sustained even in challenging circumstances. For protecting its other assets including investments, the company has taken adequate insurance cover. However, revenue loss due to a probable disruption in manufacturing activity cannot be quantified.

Cost competitiveness

The company may not be able to retain its cost advantage. The company has invested in larger, world-class plants to encash economies of scale; apart from establishing vertical integration in its textiles business from yarn to terry towels, it enjoys synergies between its paper and textile business; from the generation of steam and power with the view to reduce costs. A large and centralised purchase function also leads to enhanced efficiencies; the company sources material from international suppliers to rationalise costs. Therefore, it is confident of retaining its competitive edge and remaining profitable.

Quality

A marginal drop in product quality can lead to client attrition, dampening the company's performance.

Quality adherence is an obsession with every member of the company. The company maintains strict quality control measures to ensure that the customer consistently gets what has been asked for. The company created a quality management team across each division to check quality across the process flow from the input stage to the end product prior to dispatch. The company commissioned sophisticated equipment, increased automation, initiated Kaizens and SGAs to ensure that internal quality benchmarks consistently meet the international standards.

Obsolescence risk

Obsolete technology could hamper productivity and product quality.

The company has positioned itself at the forefront of emerging technologies across each of its businesses through ongoing upgradation and fresh investment. These ensure that the company's products are contemporary and its processes competitive. The company's dedicated team of technocrats concentrates on quality enhancement and customisation while stressing eco-friendly manufacture.

Proprietary risks/contingencies

The company has initiated adequate insurance covers to hedge against natural risks in the business. These are assessed on a regular basis and the company takes the best possible coverage of insurance from the well-established sovereign enterprise at minimal costs.

Financial Risk

This comprises all risks with a financial implication such as adverse movements in foreign exchange, capital expenditure and interest rates, etc.

Foreign currency risk

Being a large exporter, foreign currency fluctuation could dampen the company's profitability. About 56 per cent of the company's revenue is derived from foreign exchange, any fluctuation in which could have an impact on the company's top line as well as bottom line.

The company has created a forex management team; more than 50 per cent of the export earnings are hedged; the remaining export position is kept open in line with the risk appetite of the company. The company manages this position through an ongoing risk analysis of every forex transaction; it outsources expert forex advice from a number of international banks. In addition, the company has laid down standard operating procedures to de-risk itself from currency volatility. It enjoys a natural hedge as a major part of its paper project is to be expensed off in foreign exchange; the company could indeed benefit from a strengthening in the domestic currency against the US dollar.

Funding risk

The company may not be able to put together adequate low-cost resources to finance its growth plans, dampening profitability.

Over the years, the company has ploughed back earnings into the business, creating a strong financial statement. The company maintains a history of timely repayments of all external liabilities. These factors allow it to collect funds at rates, which are better than industry standards. The company has leveraged these factors to its advantage.

Receivables management risk

An untimely receipt of funds could bloat the working capital cycle. The locations of the textile and paper units are geographically dispersed with a majority of the customers accounting for a small financial exposure. Any default or downgraded credit worthiness of the customers could affect profitability.

The company has documented credit policy for its customers, which is periodically reviewed and approved by the management. The policy dictates that dispatch is made only against adequate collateral from the client. In addition, the credit period is only extended on a selective basis, which is approved by the management.

The company's investment in SAP has facilitated a real-time monitoring of its debtors' position, which was a constraint. This system has a three-level check and a multitude of MIS reports that highlight old debtors along with other details. This has facilitated in reducing the level of debtors and liquidating the company's receivables from old debtors.

Human Resource Risk

Risks (like attrition) that are part of the personnel-related process of the company such as recruitment and performance measurement.

Performance and attrition risk

The company initiated a change management programme to focus on ownership, leadership and team building, ensuring that management succession is seamless and beneficial.

The company enjoys a fair blend of youth and experience; it has a prudent mix of a competent and experienced Board as well as young and energetic operational team. A meticulous disaster management plan prevents the possibility of hazardous operations being managed by unskilled persons.

Legal, Regulatory and Compliance Risk

Risks arising out of non-fulfilment of/non-compliance with applicable compliance, legal and statutory requirements.

Contractual risks

The company is exposed to possible liabilities that could arise from the non-performance of certain contractual conditions. To protect itself from these, the company has established a review and documentation process for contracts. Each contract to be executed by or on behalf of the company requires vetting from the company's legal and secretarial department before execution. While vetting contracts, the department evaluates the legal risks involved and ascertains legal responsibilities.

Compliance and regulatory risk

The company is committed to being a responsible corporate citizen and respects the laws and regulations of the countries in which it operates. The company has an informed and proactive legal cell, which ensures compliance with various statutes. Besides, it also takes advice from reputed law firms from time to time. The legal cell advises the company on various compliance issues and ensures their alignment with the laws of jurisdiction as well as to the territory where the company operates. The Board reviews the detailed compliance report on quarterly basis. The company also recognises the need for sustainability with a minimal impact on the ecology and environment. In view of this, the company makes continuous investments in generating green energy and treating effluents. These investments result in compliance with the most progressive global standards.

The company has taken a Directors and Officers (D&O) Liability Insurance to protect its Directors' or officers' personal fortunes against the consequences of their personal liability for financial losses arising out of their unintentionally wrongful acts.

Technology and Information Systems Risk

Risks pertaining to storage, safety, reliability obsolescence and retrieval of information and data.

Storage and safety risk

To avoid possible disruption during any contingency situation, a disaster recovery site has been commissioned. This site is tested twice a year by a simulation with realistic failure of servers and all probable technological recovery site to have business resumption within the shortest possible time.

Users can add programmes, copy data or modify local security policy of their computers only after requisite clearances are obtained from the Information Systems Team, as a part of the company's security policy.

Risk Evaluation and Prediction

It is not possible to predict the crisis or disaster, yet it is possible to know the chance of loss of many risks. The earthquake in Gujarat and in Nepal, Kolkata fire of January 2008, death due to heat wave in May 2003 in Andhra Pradesh, terrorists attack in Mumbai in September 2001 and Nov. 2008, Bhopal Gas tragedy in Dec. 1984 and Tsunamis were such crisis that could not be predicted. Though many scientific methods are there which give early warning like of tsunamis or earthquake, but none of them is fool proof. Some are manmade like traffic accidents, fires and terrorists attacks, some are natural. However, preventive measures can be taken to mitigate the loss.

The premium charged by insurers, mainly the price of the risk, is calculated on the statistical estimates of future claims on the insurance company arising out of obligations. All these estimates are based on long-term averages. There is a possibility of significant deviations from such expectations.

Following methods are available for handling risks, their assessment and management: (1) Reserves, (2) Reinsurance, (3) Performance of assets, (4) Pricing methods, (5) Statistical Techniques and models.

First, reserve (also called contingency fund) is a buffer which helps to bridge such gaps that may arise due to such adverse unforeseen events. Second tool for risk management is reinsurance (risk transfer). Third is performance of assets. Banks have risk-based capital calculations which is not available to insurance companies. A general insurance company needs capital for three main reasons—for meeting growth needs, for meeting unforeseen claims and meeting investment losses. Retail insurance like health and motor insurance require higher minimum capital as compared to fire. Fourth is "option pricing method" instead of tariff rates. Fifth probability distribution, measure of standard deviation and variation are statistical methods used to evaluate risk. Some statistical models are also used such as (a) expected loss ratio method, (b) chain-ladder method, (c) average cost per claim method, (d) Bornhuetter-Ferguson method, and (e) pure premium method.

Note: The claim settlement passes through three stages: (i) Event occurred for claim, (ii) Claim reported, (iii) Claim paid. The claim is paid after some time when claim is reported. This may be in the end of year in which policy was taken, i.e. in a future claim year. But the claim relates to the year when policy was taken. So insurer needs RESERVE to cover future payments from claims that (i) have been incurred but not yet reported (IBNR) and (ii) have been reported but not yet paid. This figure can be estimated by following statistical methods. An estimate from data of claims for a portfolio taking into account the year that policies were taken and the year they were settled. These data are summarised in what is called a "RUN-OFF TRIANGLE" or "DELAY TRIANGLE". Calculations in all these methods can be adjusted for inflation.

(A) Expected Loss Ratio Method

Accounting Year	*Estimated Premium*	*Expected Loss Ratio (ELR)*	*Ultimate Developed Loss*
2005	400	75%	300
2006	500	75%	375
2007	600	75%	450
2008	800	75%	600

Hints: (1) 400 × 75% = 300

(2) Amount in thousands (₹)

Actual loss ratio is divided by ELR to find a percentage change in loss.

The advantage of this method is that it is simple. But the drawback is that it is not easy to determine the ELR. It is also difficult to adjust the method as the losses develop and show the ELR to be more and more unlikely.

Loss Development

Accident year data: Accident year losses are losses that happened during a 12-month period. Policy year losses mean the losses associated with policies written during a 12-month period. Calendar year losses mean losses paid or made during a calender period. We shall take cumulative accident year paid losses.

Cumulative Paid Loss Triangle

Year	*Lag (in months)*			
	12	*24*	*36*	*48*
2005	100	200	300	300
2006	125	250	375	–
2007	150	300	–	–
2008	200	–	–	–

For accidents that happened during 2006, ₹ 250 was paid in total by year end 2007.

(B) The Traditional A.H.A. Chain-Ladder Method

This method proposes predictors of the ultimate cumulative losses. Every predictor is obtained sequentially by multiplying the current cumulative loss by the chain-ladder factors. These factors are certain link ratios from the run-off triangle.

Chain-Ladder Method

- **Some terminology:**

  Origin year: Year policy is taken in order to cover an event.

  Delay year: Number of years until payment from a claim is made.

- **Presentation of claims data (run-off triangle):** We can present claim payments per year in a run-off triangle or delay triangle. In the following example, we assume the table is compiled at the end of 2009, and the amounts are in thousands Rupees.

Table 1

		Delay year			
		0	1	2	3
	2006	300	250	100	65
Origin	2007	400	350	160	
year	2008	500	360		
	2009	700			

The 'diagonals' in the ® direction give payments for a particular year. Alternatively, we can present cumulative claim payments in each row as in Table 2 for the claim payments as given in Table 1.

Table 2

		Delay year			
		0	1	2	3
	2006	300	550	650	715
Origin	2007	400	750	910	
year	2008	500	860		
	2009	700			

- **Objective:** To estimate the entries in the lower right triangle of Table 1, which represent the future payments from policies written over the origin years in the table, i.e. project the future development of the run-off triangle.
- **Projections using delay (development) factors:** We assume that payments will emerge in a similar way in each origin year. However, the observed proportionate increases in cumulative payments will differ with the origin year as illustrated in Table 3 for the data in Table 2.

Table 3

		From year – year		
		0-1	1-2	2-3
	2006	1.83	1.18	1.10
Origin	2007	1.88	1.21	
year	2008	1.72		
	2009			

For example, for 2006 origin year, cumulative payment to delay year 2008 is 1.18 times that for 2007 (delay years 1 to 2) (650/550 × 100) and for year 1999 (715/650 × 100) is 1.10.

The increases vary within each column of Table 3, so what single value should we use to represent the increase in each column (i.e. as we change from one delay year to the next)?

The quantity is the delay (development) factor for the cumulative payments from year 0 to year 1. The development factors for all of the data in Table 2 are:

Table 4 From year – year

0 - 1	1 - 2	2 - 3	
$\frac{2160}{1200}$	$\frac{1560}{1300}$	$\frac{715}{650}$	(1) 750 + 910 + 500 = 2160
			(2) 300 + 400 + 500 = 1200
			(3) 650 + 910 = 1560
= 1.80	= 1.20	= 1.10	(4) 550 + 750 = 1300

Note: Delay factors are calculated for cumulative payments rather than the original yearly payments as they are generally more stable for the former.

For origin year 2008, we can similarly obtain cumulative claims for years 2 and 3:

Delay year

2	3
860×1.20	1032×1.10
= 1032	= 1135.2

Then similarly for origin year 2007. Table 5(a) summarises the projections of cumulative payments. We can then calculate the projected payments per development year; these are given in Table 5(b).

Table 5(a)

		Delay year			
		0	1	2	3
	2006				
Origin	2007				1001.0
year	2008			1032	1135.2
	2009		1260	1512	1663.2

Table 5(b)

		Delay year			
		0	1	2	3
	1997				
Origin	1998				91.0
year	1999			172	103.2
	2000		560	252	151.2

- **Model checking:** This is to check whether the method of projection is reasonable. We start with the actual claims in year 0 and project them using the delays factors. Table 6 shows the results for the cumulative claims in Table 2 using the delay factors calculated for these data in Table 4.

Table 6	Delay year :	0	1	2	3
	Factor :		1.80	1.20	1.10
	2006	300	540	648	712.8
Origin	2007	400	720	864	
year	2008	500	900		
	2009	700			

Table 7 shows the resulting estimated claim payments assuming the cumulative claims shown in Table 6 and compares them with the actual claim payments given in Table 1.

Table 7		Delay year			
Origin year		0	1	2	3
2006	Actual	300	250	100	65
	Estimate		240	108	64.8
	Error		10	–8	0.2
2007	Actual	400	350	160	
	Estimate		320	144	
	Error		30	16	
2008	Actual	500	360		
	Estimate		400		
	Error		–40		

However, we still need to decide whether an 'error' is too large—we could look at 'relative error' but a better approach is to use statistical modelling and to look at residuals.

The advantages of chain ladder method are that it is objective. It does not work off a subjective expected loss ratio. Regulators and insurers may prefer methods with less "actuarial judgement". Unlike expected loss ratio method, as losses develop and time passes the estimate gets closer to reality.

But if suffers from the disadvantages also. The relationship between loss at different development periods may not be multiplicative. It will be distorted by changes in claim payments, e.g., if claims for losses are paid faster, then this method overstates the developed loss. If in above table in the year 2008 in 12 months lag the loss is ₹ 2.50, then it will be ₹ 500, 700 and 720 in subsequent lag periods.

(C) Average Cost Per Claim Method

This method also takes into account the number of claims made and estimates of the number of future claims. Then the average costs per claim per development year can be obtained for the claims fully processed and estimate; obtained for the future years.

For the data presented in Table 1, suppose the claim amounts were from the number of claims shown in Table 8.

Table 8

		Delay year			
		0	1	2	3
	2006	300	150	13	5
Origin	2007	380	200	20	
year	2008	450	215		
	2009	650			

Estimates of the future number of claims in the bottom part of the run-off triangle in Table 8 can be obtained using the basic chain-ladder method. The development factors based on the cumulative numbers of claims (not shown) are:

Table 9

From year – year		
0 - 1	1 - 2	1 - 3
$\frac{1695}{1130}$ = 1.500	$\frac{1063}{1030}$ = 1.032	$\frac{468}{463}$ = 1.011

Hence, after estimating the future cumulative numbers of claims, estimates of the future numbers of claims are shown in Table 10. Estimates of the future claim amounts, obtained by multiplying the entries in Table 10 by the average claim amounts for each delay year above are shown in Table 10.

Table 10

		Delay year			
		0	1	2	3
	2006				
Origin	2007				6.48
year	2008			21.31	7.41
	2009		325	31.24	10.86

Table 11

		Delay year			
		0	1	2	3
	2006				
Origin	2007				84.24
year	2008			167.90	96.33
	2009		552.21	246.13	141.18

From Table 11, an estimate of the reserve needed to meet outstanding claims from these policies is 1287.99.

(D) Bornhuetter-Ferguson Method

This method proposes predictors of the outstanding losses. Every predictor is obtained of the expected ultimate cumulative loss by an estimator of the percentage of the outstanding loss with respect to the ultimate one. The main important difference of this method and chain-ladder method is that later method proceeds from current losses and this method from expected ultimate losses. The fact that these methods aim at different target quantities since predictors of ultimate losses can be converted into predictors or vice versa.

This method has advantages of both the chain-ladder and the expected loss ratio method. The basic idea of this method is—The developed losses = that is actually paid + what we would expect to develop if the expected loss ratio is correct.

The advantages of this method are that it is combination of above two methods. The expected loss ratio is less important as experience develops.

But disadvantage is that it is affected by faster claim payment period.

A naive estimate of reserve for each origin year could be made by multiplying the premiums received for that year by the expected loss ratio, where the loss ratio for a given year is the ratio of ultimate claim losses to the total premium received.

This approach requires knowledge of the loss ratio expected for each origin year. This method combines the prior expectation of losses provided by simple loss ratio estimates with the actual rate of emergence of claims.

For example, using the claims amount given in Table 1 and assume an initial loss ratio of 80% along with the total premiums (in 000's) in the second column of Table 13. The claims data in Table 1 provide the expected development pattern of claims through the development factors (see Table 4). We will need the proportion of ultimate claims paid off by the end of development year j, denoted earlier by r_j. The calculations of these is shown in Table 12, where the ultimate year is year 3. The final row in Table 13 gives the r_j's.

Table 12	Delay (Development) Period	0 - 1	1 - 2	2 - 3
	(Development) factor	1.80	1.20	1.10
	Delay (Development period)	0 – ultimate	1 – ultimate	2 – ultimate
	Cumulative factor	2.376	1.32	1.10
	Inverse	0.4209	0.7576	0.9091

Table 13

Origin year	Total premium	Naive estimate of ultimate claims	Estimated proportion outstanding $1 - r_j$	Estimated reserve
1997	1300	1040		
1998	1400	1120	0.0909	101.82
1999	1600	1280	0.2424	310.30
2000	1800	1440	0.5791	833.94

From the sum of the entries in the last column of Table 13, an estimate of the reserve needed to meet outstanding claims from these policies is 1246.06.

(E) Pure Premium Method

A combined ratio [commission ratio plus loss ratio plus expenses ratio] is calculated.

$$\text{Loss} = \frac{\text{Loss amount}}{\text{Amount of earned premium}}$$

i.e., premium written + reinsurance premium minus premium ceded.

Expense Ratio = Operating Expenses divided by net premium written i.e. after adjustment of increase or decrease of company's liability for unearned premium during the year.

The method depends upon reliability of historical data.

Note: I.R.D.A. has laid down norms for providing "mathematical reserve" and I.B.N.R. (Reserve for claims incurred but not reported) negative reserve, MAD (margin for adverse deviations) and reserves in respect of linked business. This helps to manage the risk's.

Approach Proposed by Credit Rating Agencies

With the ever-growing importance of risk management credit rating agencies over a period of tune have been laying great emphasis on risk management practice of companies. They suggest following areas to look at:

(a) (i) Setting a framework and culture towards risk management in an insurance company. The board and senior management should be involved in risk management, (ii) Establishing and communicating risk management objectives, (iii) Setting risk tolerance and key risk matrices, and (iv) Setting roles/responsibilities and oversight.

Risk Evaluation Map

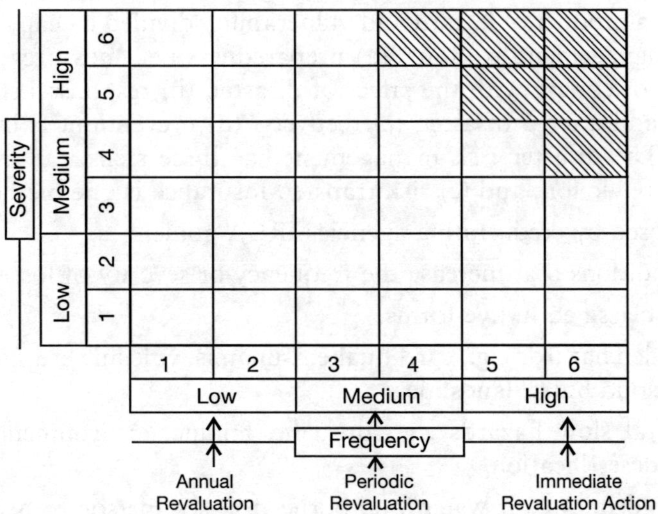

(b) Risk Identification and Management Rating agencies recommend working on defining traditional risks and having exception reporting with action plans in place of exception items. A risk register must be kept, which helps to aggregate common risks and to analyze and manage those risks effectively.

(c) Two approaches (a) Top down and (b) Bottom up may be employed for risk identification. However, risks can be mapped in a frequency severity matrix, given below:

Nowaday Indian Insurance Companies are following what is called 'Capital modeling'. Capital modeling is a tool which enables the organisation to evolve towards measuring returns board on risk allocated capital. Allocation of capital is done based on risk adjusted returns for each line of business IRDA has issued guidelines on economic capital, a first step towards capital modeling.

IRDA Guidelines for Risk Management

IRDA in August 2009 issued guidelines on corporate governance for the insurance sector. Apart from laying emphasis on the importance of governance in the insurance sector, the circular laid out the importance of risk management and need for control functions. Accordingly, every insurance company was mandated to form a risk committee as well as appoint a Chief Risk Officer. The guidelines stated that sound management of an insurer is dependent on how well risks are managed; and emphasized the need to lay down the risk management strategy and monitor all risks across lines of business.

Solvency Margin Regulations 2000 prescribed by IRDA (see p. 225) and guidelines of mathematical estimation of IBNR claims provision (see p. 233) are also step towards risk management. IRDA has created Indian Motor Third Party Declined Risk insurance pool on 1-4-2012. It is a measure towards risk reduction by motor (insurance companies who are suffering loses (see chapter on Automobiles).

Disaster Management

A disaster is a manmade or natural event which results in widespread human loss. It is accompanied by loss of livelihood or property causing human suffering and loss in a definite area. Disaster risk is a product of hazard and vulnerability divided by capacity. The components phases of disaster management are four: (a) preparedness i.e., measures that community and services are capable of coping with the effect of disaster, (b) response i.e., the measures taken in advance, during and after a disaster, (c) recovery, (d) prevention. It includes planning and mitigation of loss. The disaster risk management has three steps: (a) risk identification and assessment, (b) risk reduction, and (c) risk transfer. Insurance is one method of risk transfer.

Approach proposed by credit rating agencies IRDA guidelines.

Hazards are conditions that increase the frequency or severity of losses.

Hazards can be classified in five forms:

(a) Natural sudden hazards e.g., earthquake, tsunamis, volcanic eruptions, floods, cyclones, avalanche, cloud burst, landslide.

(b) Environmental slow hazards e.g., drought, famine, environmental degradation pest, infestation, desertification.

(c) Pandemic/Epidemics e.g., water/food-borne diseases, person-to-person diseases, vector-borne diseases, birds flue, etc.

(d) Industrial/Technological accidents e.g., systems failure, fire, explosion, chemical leakage/ spoilage.

(e) Manmade e.g., war and civil strife, transport accidents, terrorists attacks, Fraud—such hazard may be moral hazard or morale hazard. Moral hazard results from fraud e.g., insured may exaggerate a loss. Morale hazard results from carelessness or indifference to loss created by purchase of an insurance contract e.g., remaining in hospital to collect health insurance claim without any ailment or not caring in case of fire.

To mitigate the loss caused by above hazards, strategies to be adopted depend upon the type of hazard, as given below:

(i) Earthquake: Engineered structures, public awareness.

(ii) Landslides: Preservation of grassland, retaining walls, surface drainage control and engineered structures, increasing vegetation.

(iii) Floods: Land use control, flood control, engineered structures and cyclones.

(iv) Fires: Proper electric wiring, safety measures for combustible materials and firefighting appliances.

Most important of all strategies is community awareness and preparedness. Approaches to disaster management may be engineering approach (using protecting device), human approach or behaviour. A Loss Prevention Association of India has been set up in 1978, as a company limited by guarantee, engaged in promotion of safety and loss control through education and training of people. It has branches at Delhi, Kolkata, Chennai, Hyderabad and Cochin. Its members are like GICI, New India Assurance Co., The Oriental Insurance Co. and United India Insurance Co. A terrorism port, managed by G.I.C., set up in 2002 by general insurance companies, which covers loss for a company up to ₹ 750 crore due to terrorism.

Essentials of Insurance Risk

All risks cannot be insured. There are certain legal, commercial and moral considerations which make it impossible to insure every kind of risk e.g., an octogenarian or robbers or just a pencil cannot be insured. In insurance, an insurable risk must have following requisites:

1. There must be large numbers of similar risks. Insurance is based on law of large numbers. The risk will be high if the insured group is small and vice versa.

2. The loss caused by the risk must be definite, measurable and of sufficient of severity. These must be certainty of loss if the event happens. The loss may be very little or more.

3. The occurrence of loss must be accidental and beyond insured's control. There must be either uncertainty whether the event will ever happen or not. If the event is such which must happen at any time, there must be uncertainty as to the time it will happen. Depreciation of machinery is not loss because it is not accidental and so it is not insurable.

4. The loss must be large enough to cause hardships. The peril insured must be capable of producing a loss large enough that the insured cannot bear himself without economic problem. The minor risk if insured, the cost of its protection will be high.

5. The cost of insuring must be economically feasible. The cost of insuring must be within reach of common man. The cost of insurance includes the cost of management, agents commission and cost of risk. The insured will not take a policy if he has to pay ₹ 2 to recover a loss of ₹ 1.

6. It must be possible to calculate the chance of loss.

7. The insurance should not be in the nature of gamble, against public policy or a wagering contract.

2

Insurance: An Introduction

Insurance is a fast growing sector. This sector is significantly contributing towards economic growth of the country. Dr. Mohd. Arif Khan writes that insurance came into being as a result of revolt by travelling salesmen 5000 years ago in Euphrates Valley. The salesmen were robbed in countries they travelled. As a result of compromise between businessmen and salesmen, called '*Code of Hammurahi*'* in 2250 B.C. security of transactions was provided. The sailors were responsible as bailees like insurers of today. Insurance has assumed the status of one of the world's leading economies. Its motto everywhere being "Yogaksheman Vahmyaham" i.e., "*Your welfare is my responsibility*". In 18th century, there was insurance against going to hell (*T.O.I.* 31-9-2010). Mr. James Dadson, a fellow of Royal Society, gave the more reliable mortality tables. EQUITABLE Insurance Company (1762) is forerunner of today's life insurers. Let us begin with the definition of insurance.

Definition

Some popular definitions by famous authors are reproduced below:

1. Insurance is a contract by which the one party, in consideration of a price paid to him adequate to the risk becomes security to the other that he shall not suffer loss, damage, or prejudice by the happening of the perils specified to certain things which may be exposed to them.

   —*Justice Lawrence*

2. Insurance is a social device for reducing risk by combining a sufficient number of exposure units to make their individual losses collectively predictable. The predictable loss is then shared proportionately by all those in combination.

   —*Prof. Robert Mehr*

3. Insurance is a social device whereby uncertain risks of individuals may be combined in a group and thus made more certain, small periodic contributions by the individuals providing fund out of which those who suffer losses may be reimbursed.

   —*Riegel R.* and *Miller J.S.*

* *Theory and Practice of Insurance*, Mohd. Arif Khan P.I.

4. Insurance is a method of spreading over large number of persons a possible financial loss too serious to be conveniently born by an individual borne.

—Maclean J.B.

Nature of Insurance

Insurance is an economic activity that helps to reduce the risk of loss. It is a contract of indemnity where the indemnifier (called insurer/assurer), agrees for consideration (called premium) to indemnify the loss caused to the indemnified (called insured/assured). It is in writing and the insurance deed is called policy. The period for which policy is taken is called "term of policy".

Insurance is one of the aids or auxiliaries to business. There are various hindrances that come in the way of trade and business. These hindrances are of person, place, time, finance, knowledge, information and risk. They are removed with the help of trade, transport, storage and warehousing, banking, advertising and insurance. Insurance removes the hindrances of risks by insuring the risks of loss or damage due to theft, fire accidents, etc.

The basic idea of insurance is to give protection against losses. The Indian customs of giving money, clothes or gifts on the birth of a child or on the marriage or death are primarily based on the idea of insurance.

Insurance is all pervasive. All the human activities need umbrella of insurance, e.g., goods may be damaged during transit or stolen or damaged by fire, weather or while in godown. A person may be injured by accident or may fall ill. Insurance covers all these risks.

Insurance is "the law's attempt to socialise responsibility." Insurance has proved to be available and reliable means of carrying the benefits of social security to the people, e.g., employees state insurance is to insure industrial workers against various hazards of life and to protect them from economic insecurity. The list is endless since every conceivable aspect of human activity is being insured in advanced countries.

Insurance is a service. It is difficult to sell insurance service as compared to other services. "One who can sell insurance can sell everything" is an old saying. Once an insurance agent rang the doorbell of a prospective customer. The man opened the door and on telling by the agent that he is an insurance agent, the man shut the door by saying, 'I am not interested'. Again the agent rang the doorbell and got the same reply. Third time again the same was repeated. The prospective customer filled a bucket of water to be thrown on the insurance agent if he rings the bell fourth time. The insurance agent rang the doorbell and the man threw the water on the agent. The agent with a smile said, "Please now get yourself insured". The man purchased the insurance. A Chinese saying "Don't open a shop without a smiling face" applies cent per cent to insurance business.

Insurance contract is a species of general contract. A contract of insurance is a species of general contract. It is governed by the same principles of law as other contracts. Section 10 of the Indian Contract Act, 1872 states that an agreement made by free consent of parties who are competent to contract for a lawful consideration and with lawful object and not expressly forbidden by law is a contract.

For insurance contract, the following requisites are essentials:

(a) Offer and Acceptance: an agreement in writing (policy).

(b) Competent Parties: parties should be competent to make a contract (not a minor, idiot or lunatic).

(c) Free Consent: no fraud, coercion, undue influence, mistake or misrepresentation (good faith).

(d) Legal Object: no illegal purpose.

(e) Consideration: fair and equitable payment (premium).

Insurance contract is not a **gamble** or **wager.** An insurance contract looks like a contract of gamble or wager. A wager or gamble depends upon the happening or not happening of an uncertain event. In insurance contract, the liability of the insurer also depends upon happening or not happening of an uncertain event (except death). The contract of insurance is an aleatory contract, but is not a wager. Following are the differences between insurance and wages or gamble:

1. Indemnity. A contract of insurance (except life, sickness and personal accident insurances) is a contract of indemnity. The insured is indemnified for the loss suffered by him on the happening of an uncertain event. In case of wages, the parties do not intend to cover the risk hence are not contract of indemnity.

2. Object. The object of the insurance contract is to protect the insured against losses. The object of a wager contract is to earn speculative gains.

3. Insurable interest. The insured has insurable interest in the subject matter. In wager, there is no insurable interest of the party except the pecuniary interest created by the contract.

4. Utmost good faith. Insurance contract are contracts based on good faith i.e., no concealment of facts or fraud. In wager, no such thing is to be observed.

5. Validity. Wagering agreements are against public policy and are void *ab-initio*. An insurance contract is a valid contract. A contract of insurance by way of wager is void.

6. Risk calculation. In insurance, risk premium is calculated scientifically by actuarial science. In wager, no such calculation is made.

7. An insured event may cause varying degrees of loss or damage. A wager is either won or lost.

Types of Insurance

Insurance business is divided into three types under Insurance Act, 1938:

(1) Life Insurance, (2) Health, (3) General Insurance. General Insurance means fire, marine or miscellaneous insurance business, which is carried on singly or in combine action with one or more of them. Miscellaneous insurance includes casualty like personal accident, motor insurance, theft and others. Section 2(13B) of the Insurance Act, 1938 days down that miscellaneous insurance business is other than fire, life and marine insurance.

The above classification is not rigid. In "*others*" insurance of many types are included, e.g., vehicle insurance, riot insurance, crop insurance, credit insurance, or fidelity insurance, special weather risk policy, limb insurance, glass insurance, etc. The term 'social insurance' covers workmen's compensation insurance and employees state insurance. Social insurance is done by government. Further, insurer may be the government organisation or a private company.

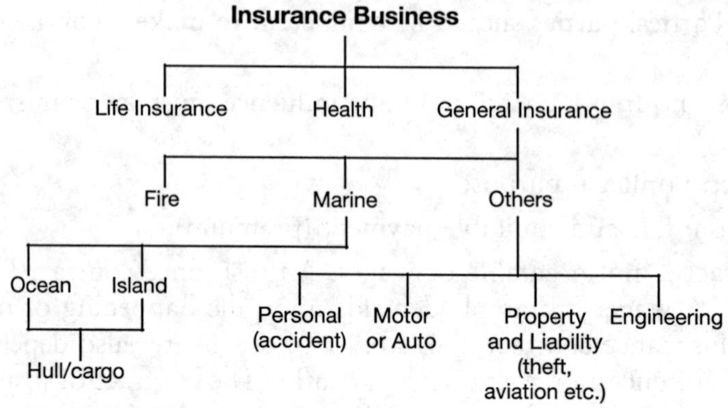

Note: For details a general insurance see Chapter 10.

Note: Technically, the word "Assurance" is used for life and word insurance is used for remaining types of insurance. But usually this distinction is not made.

According to IRDA regulations, life insurance has been divided on the following basis:

(1) **Classification:** Business within India and total business.

(2) **Category:** Linked and non-linked.

(3) **Division:** Individual and group.

(4) **Sub class:** Life, general annuity, pension, health and micro (Life and General).

(5) **Group:** With or without guarantee. Both may be with or without participation of profits (also called par or no par policies).

Individual business means individual insurance contracts issued on single or joint lives.

Group business means those insurance contracts issued on a group, usually persons less than 50.

Linked business means life insurance contracts or health insurance contracts under which benefits are wholly or partly to be determined by reference to the value of underlying assets or any approved index (e.g., cost of living index).

Non-linked business means life insurance contracts or health insurance contracts which are not linked business.

General annuity business means the business of effecting contracts to pay annuities on human life but does not include contracts under pension business.

Pension business includes business of effecting contracts to manage investment of pension funds or superannuation schemes or contracts to pay annuities that are approved.

Health insurance business or health cover means effecting of contracts which provide sinkness benefits or medical surgical or hospital expense benefit, whether in-patient or out-patient, on an indemnity, reimbursement, service, prepaid, hospital or other plans basis, including assured benefits and long-term care.

Micro Insurance. It may be general micro insurance product or life micro insurance product. General micro insurance product means any health insurance contract, any contract covering the belongings, such as hut, livestock or tools, or instruments or any personal accident insurance contract, either on individual or group basis as per terms in schedule I of the IRDA regulations.

Life micro insurance product means any term insurance with or without return of premium, any endowment insurance contract or health insurance, with or without accident benefit rider, either an individual or group basis as per terms stated in schedule II of the IRDA regulations:

Par or No Par (also called policies with or without participation) policies means which are entitled or not entitled for any share in surplus or profits respectively. Policies with deferred participation in profits share the profits after a certain period from the commencement of policy.

In case of non-linked life or health insurance INDIVIDUAL business, the sub-group may be with or without or deferred participation of profits under DISCOUNTED BONUS system. In case of non-linked life or health GROUP insurance business, with or without participation of profits the sub-group is based on PREMIUM GUARANTEED separately for more or less than one year.

The sub-group, in case of general annuity or pension, whether individual or group business, are based on immediate or deferred annuities either with or without participation in profits (for further details see the chapter on Micro Insurance).

Principles of Insurance

There are certain fundamental principles and elements common to all classes of insurance and are based upon common law of England. They are: (a) Economic, (b) Actuarial, and (c) Legal. Economic principle is based on principle of sharing risk and loss. The actuarial principle lays down that premium should be calculated on scientific basis. Following are the legal principles:

1. Utmost Good Faith. A contract of insurance is a contract of '*uberrimae fidei*' (Latin word), i.e., based on utmost good faith. If the utmost good faith is not observed by either party, the contract may be avoided by the other. Since insurance shifts risks from one party to another, it is essential that there must be the utmost good faith and openness between the insured and the insurer, i.e., the whole truth must be told about the subject-matter of insurance and all circumstances surrounding it in order that the underwriter may know the extent of his risk and how much he must charge for the insurance of it. The wilful or innocent withholding or misrepresenting of any relevant information is a serious matter, and the underwriter can declare the contract void on discovering it.

The duty to make a full and true disclosure continues, till the contract is concluded and it is not a continuing obligation. Thus, any material fact coming to the knowledge after the conclusion of the contract need not be disclosed, but the duty to disclose revives with every renewal of the old policy or alterations in the existing policy. The rule of 'Caveat Emptor' does not apply to insurance.

It is to be noted here that no policy of life insurance shall after the expiry of two years, from the date on which it was effected, be called in question by an insurer on the ground that the statement made was inaccurate or false, unless the insurer shows such statement was on a material matter or suppressed facts which it was material to disclose and that it was fraudulently made by the policyholder. This provision is called "INCONTESTABLE CLAUSE" (Refer p. 52).

"An applicant for the insurance policy was asked to state whether he has applied to any other company and whether such application was rejected. The applicant stated that he was insured with two companies but did not disclose the fact that his application was rejected by many other companies." Held, there was material concealment of the facts and the policy was liable to be set aside. *London Insurance Company* vs. *Mansel.*

"In a proposal form, the proposer, in answer to a question if he had consulted any physician in the last five years said "*none*". In fact, he had consulted a doctor who prescribed tonics, but he had never been away from his work. The insurer's doctor said he would have still recommended the case at the ordinary premium even if the proposer had answered the question in the affirmative." Held, there was no material concealment of facts and the policy could not be avoided. *Mutual Life Insurance Co. of New York* vs. *Ontario Metal Products Co.*

The following are the types of facts are which not required to be disclosed in the proposal, i.e., the non-disclosure of them shall not affect the contract:

(i) Any fact which diminishes the risk; or any fact that comes to the knowledge of the insured after the contract is made; or

(ii) Any fact which is known or presumed to be known to the insurer; e.g. habits, personal and family history and occupation, disease or injury history; or

(iii) Any fact which relates to the nature of public knowledge or which relate to the law of the country; or

(iv) Any fact as to which information is waived by the insurer.

If the utmost good faith is not observed by either party, the contract becomes voidable at the option of the party not at fault, irrespective of whether the non-disclosure was intentional or innocent. Of course, in case of innocent misrepresentation the premium is refundable on the avoidance of the contract.

2. Indemnity. Indemnity means to make good the actual loss caused to the insured. It is indemnified to the extent of the loss and it should not be more than the actual loss. Therefore, in the contract of insurance the insurer agrees to make good the losses to the extent they are caused. Insurance company does not agree to pay for the loss of profits.

Except life assurance, health (sickness or medical), a contract of insurance of fire, marine, burglary or any other is a contract of indemnity. This means that the assured, in case of loss against which the policy has been issued, shall be paid the actual amount of loss not exceeding the amount of the policy. Indemnity is the controlling principle in contracts of fire, marine, and burglary insurances. The object of very contract of insurance is to place the assured in the same financial position, as nearly as possible, after the loss as if the loss had not taken place at all. Under no circumstances the insured is allowed to benefit more than the loss suffered by him. This is because, if that were so, the temptation would always to be insure of high amount and thus to obtain the policy amount. This would obviously be contrary to the public policy.

Contracts of fire or marine insurance cease to be contracts of indemnity when they provide for the payment of a fixed sum of money in the event of Total LOSS or destruction by the peril insured against. This is so in the case of 'VALUED POLICIES'. However, in such policies as well, if PARTIAL LOSS is there, then the insured is only indemnified, because no body is allowed to make a profit of his loss.

A contract of life insurance or insurance of human body against sickness or accident is not a contract of indemnity. In this case, the insurer is liable to pay the sum mentioned in the policy upon the happening of the contingency (death or expiry of a certain period, whichever comes earlier specified in the policy). Some health insurance companies may have a rider. The company may pay full amount of critical illness. The health insurance is not a contract of indemnity.

However, in case of life insurance 'Keyman insurance' is a contract of indemnity.

"'A' insured his house against fire and, therefore he agreed to sell his house to 'B'. However, before the sale could take place, the house was damaged by fire. 'A' received the compensation from the insurer as well as sale price from 'B' under the contract." Held, the insurer could recover from 'A' the money paid by them (*Castellain* vs. *Preston*).

3. Double Insurance and Reinsurance. It can be explained by an example. 'A' has a building and he insures it against fire with Oriental Insurance Company for ₹ 1,50,00,000 and with Tata Insurance company for the same amount. This is a case of double insurance, i.e., the subject matter is insured with two insurers. If the loss by fire is ₹ 50,000, 'A' can recover it half from Oriental Insurance and half from Tata Insurance. If he recovers the full amount from Tata Insurance, then Tata Insurance can claim from Oriental Insurance for half contribution, the share of Oriental. So the loss is paid according to indemnity principle. Double insurance is beneficial only in case of life insurance. The insured can recover from all insurers the amount in the ratio of the sum insured. There can be over insurance also, i.e., more than the value of the subject matter. In that case average clause (explained in fire insurance) will apply.

In the above example, if 'A' insures his property with Oriental for ₹ 1,50,00,000 and then Oriental insures the same property with other company, it is a case of reinsurance. This happens when the first insurer feels that the amount of insurance is too much and it cannot bear such risk. If Oriental insures the property with Tata Insurance for ₹ 50,00,000 then in case of loss Oriental can recover the loss in the ratio of 3:1 from Tata Insurance but not more than ₹ 50,00,000. In this case the insured is not concerned at all with Tata Insurance because there is no privity of contract between them. Further all the conditions that apply to original insurance with Oriental shall apply to insurance policy with Tata Insurance. Reinsurance has following advantages:

1. Increases underwriting capacity of the insurer.
2. Stabilises profits.
3. Reduces unearned premium.
4. Provides protection against catastrophic losses.

Some other terms relating to reinsurance are "Cession, Facultative, Retrocession and Retention."

The word "*Cession*" means the unit of insurance passed to a reinsurer by the insurer which issued a policy to the original insured. A cession may be the whole or a portion of single risks, defined policies or defined divisions of business, as agreed in the reinsurance contract. The percentage cession of the sum assured on each general insurance policy to be reinsured with the Indian reinsurer is 10%.

"*Facultative*" means the reinsurance of a part or all of a single policy in which cession is negotiated separately and that the reinsurer and the insurer have the option of accepting or declining each individual submission. "*Retrocession*" means the transaction whereby the reinsurer cedes to another insurer or reinsurer all or part of the reinsurer if has previously assumed. "*Retention*" means the amount which an insurer assumes for his own account in proportionate contracts, the retention may be a percentage of the policy limit. In excess of loss contracts, the retention is the amount of loss. The arrangement between insurer and reinsurer is called 'treaty' and two or more usurer or reinsurance may jointly underwrite operation of insurance and is called '*Pool*'.

The reinsurance programme must be guided by following objectives:

(a) Maximum retention within the country,

(b) Develop adequate capacity,

(c) Secure the best possible protection for reinsurance costs incurred,

(d) Simplify the administration of business, and

(e) It should be proportional reinsurance rather than non-proportional.

The IRDA, with previous approval of Central Government and in consultation with Insurance Advisory Committee, under Section 114A of the Insurance Act, 1938 and under Section 25 of the IRDA Act, 1999, has constituted a Reinsurance Advisory Committee. The committee has a chairman, secretary and two or more members.

Under Section 101A of the Insurance Act, 1938, every insurance shall reinsure with Indian reinsurer who carries on EXCLUSIVELY reinsurance business and is approved by Central Government. The IRDA will specify the percentage of the sum on each policy in respect of general insurance business to be reinsured, but not more than 30% of the sum assured. It shall also specify the proportions in which the said percentage shall be allocated among Indian reinsurers. In case of a fire insurance, the insurer is allowed such amount out of first surplus in respect of that business as he thinks fit.

But the aggregate amount of premiums payable by him on such reinsurance in any year in not less than the said percentage of the premium income (without taking into account premiums on reinsurance ceded or accepted). The Indian insurer shall place their reinsurance business outside India with only those insurers who for the last five years enjoyed a rating of not less than BBB (with Standard and Poor) or equivalent. They may place reinsurance with Loyds syndicates also. Indian insurers shall organise domestic pools for reinsurance surpluses in fire, marine, hull and other insurers. For inward re-insurance business the insurer should have well-defined underwriting policy. He shall also make outstanding claims provision and provision on/BNR on its reinsurance. General Insurance Corporation undertakes mainly reinsurance business and a bit of aviation insurance. (The bulk of general insurance is taken by its four subsidiaries.) This corporation is our national reinsurer arrangement.

Reinsure or Retain. The extent of retentions depend upon following factors:

1. Solvency margin regulation
2. Underwriting capacity
3. Financial strength
4. Willingness to take on risks
5. Portfolio composition i.e., ratio of direct insurance and reinsurance
6. Market conditions
7. Practice and tradition

8. Retention policy
9. Cover capacity
10. Technical backup
11. Rating considerations.

Business Net retention represents the percentage of a company's gross policy writings, excluding policy writings by its affiliates, that are retained for its own account.

4. Insurable Interest. 'Insurable interest' is an essential prerequisite in effecting a contract of insurance. The insured must possess an insurable interest in the subject-matter of the insurance at the time of contract, otherwise the contract of insurance will be a wagering agreement which shall be void and unenforceable. Every person is presumed to have insurable interest in his own life and health. A wife has insurable interest in her husband and vice versa. An employer has insurable interest in his employee's life and health. In case of marine insurance insurable interest must be present at the time of the loss of subject-matter and it is not essential for the assured to have an insurable interest at the time of effecting the insurance. **In life insurance, insurable interest must be present at the time when the insurance is affected. In fire insurance, it must be present both at the time of insurance and at the time of loss of the subject-matter.**

Insurable interest means some pecuniary interest. The object of insurance is to protect the pecuniary interest of the insured in the subject-matter of the insurance and not the material property as such. A person is said to have an insurable interest in the subject-matter insured where he will derive pecuniary benefit from its existence or will suffer pecuniary loss from its destruction. Insurable interest is thus a financial interest in the preservation of the subject-matter of insurance. A purely sentimental interest or a non-monetary benefit will not cause an insurable interest. Accordingly, a creditor has an insurable interest in the life of the debtor not a debtor in the life of creditor. In fire or marine insurance, it is not the owner alone but all those persons who run a risk having something at stake or something to lose by the loss or damage to the property or goods insured. Hence, a person who has advanced money on the security of a house has an insurable interest in the goods pledged. The charterer of a ship has insurable interest in the ship because he runs a risk of losing his freight if the ship is lost or damaged. Thus, insurable interest may arise due to ownership, possession or contract of subject of matter in fire and marine insurance. It is presumed to exist in life insurance.

It is the existence of insurable interest in a contract of insurance that differentiates and distinguishes it from a WAGER OR GAMBLING CONTRACT. But it is essential that the insurable interest must be actual and real and not a mere expectation or an anxiety. It must be pecuniary interest, a purely sentimental interest would not be enough. Thus, a contract of insurance effected without insurable interest is void. A life policy cannot be transferred. The insured can assign it to someone only to receive the amount.

5. Causa Promixa. Section 55 of the Marine Insurance Act, 1963, lays down that unless the policy otherwise provides, the insurer is liable for any loss proximately caused by peril insured against. 'Proximate' does not mean the 'nearest in time'. The cause which is truly proximate is that which is proximate in efficiency. If the loss is the result of this efficient cause, it will be regarded as having been caused by the 'proximate cause'. An insurer is liable to make good the loss only if the loss is proximately caused by any of the risk insured against. It is called the Doctrine of Causa Proxima. According to it, when the loss is caused by a number of successive causes, we have to look to the nearest cause to ascertain the liability of the insurer, although the loss would not have happened without the remote cause.

In a case, a ship was insured against collision. The ship collided and the cargo of oranges was mishandled, resulting in delay. Consequently, the oranges deteriorated. Held, the damage to the cargo was not proximately caused by collision but was remotely caused by delay and mishandling which were not insured. Hence, the insured could not recover the loss.

In another case, a ship was insured against damage by seawater. The cargo on the ship was destroyed by seawater flowing in the ship through a hole made by rats in a bathroom lead pipe. Held, the underwriter was liable as the cargo was proximately destroyed by the seawater.

In this case, it should be noted that there are two successive causes. One is rats making the hole and the second is water entering the ship. Making of the hole is a remote cause (i.e., distant cause) and water is the nearest cause because water has destroyed the cargo, although water would not have entered the ship unless rats had made the hole. The loss is, therefore, caused by seawater, and accordingly, insured can recover the loss.

Thus, in deciding whether the loss has arisen through any of the risks insured against, the proximate or the last of the causes is to be looked into and other causes are rejected. If a loss is caused by the occurrence of more than one peril simultaneously and if one of the perils is an uninsured one, the insurer shall be liable to the extent of the effects of insured peril if it can be separately ascertained. The insurer shall not be liable at all if the effects of insured peril and uninsured peril (or expected peril) cannot be separated.

A ship was insured against damage by enemy action. It was damaged by passing over a torpedoed ship. Held, no damages could be recovered as the loss in this case was not due directly to an enemy action but to torpedoed ship.

In another case, a ship carrying meat was delayed by storm in consequence of which it became decomposed and had to be thrown overboard. It was held that the loss of meant was not a loss by the perils of the sea.

Although the principle of Causa Proxima applies mostly in the case of marine and fire insurance, it is applicable in health and the life insurance as well because in 'personal accident policies' the proximate cause of the death should be accident or hospitalization expenses will be reimbursed only if the disease has been insured against.

6. Risk must Attach. A contract of insurance can be enforced only if the risk is attached. If the risk is not run, the consideration fails. The underwriter receives a premium for running the risk of indemnifying the assured, and if he does not run the risk, the consideration for which the premium was put into his hands fails and, therefore, he must return it. While a policy does not attach till the risk begins, it can equally not attach after the risk is determined one way or other, except in those special insurance where both parties being ignorant of the position of the thing insured, contract to insure it lost or not lost.

The risk also does not attach where a policy is declared to be void *ab initio* account of some defect, e.g., assured being minor. The premium cannot be recovered where the policy is avoided by the insurer on ground of fraud by the insured.

7. Mitigation of Loss. According to this principle, an insured must take all reasonable steps to mitigate the loss, i.e., to minimise the loss. He must act as if his property were not insured. For example, a person gets his house insured against fire. His house catches fire. He should act as if his house were not insured. At the time of fire he should take only such steps as a man of ordinary prudence will take in his own case. He is not expected to wait and watch until the fire is extinguished. He should call neighbours and fire brigade to help him to extinguish the fire.

8. Principle of Subrogation. The doctrine of subrogation is a corollary to the principle of indemnity and applies only to fire and marine insurances. According to it, the insurer, on making good the loss, is entitled to succeed to all the ways and means by which the assured might have protected himself against the loss. Therefore, an assured has received full indemnity in respect of his loss, all rights and remedies which he has against third persons must be held and exercised for the benefit of the insurer until he (the insurer) recoups the amount he has paid under the policy. In simple words, the insurer steps into the shoes of the assured when he has paid the amount of the policy to the assured or he is entitled to every right of the assured.

Lord Cairns, defines subrogation as: "a right founded on the well-known principle of law that there one person has agreed to indemnify another, he will, on making good the indemnity, be entitled to succeed to all the ways and means by which the person indemnified might have protected himself against or reimbursed himself for the class."

The principle of subrogation is subject to the following limitations:

(a) The insurer is subrogated only to the rights and remedies available to the assured in respect of the thing to which the contract of insurance relates.

(b) The insurer's right of subrogation arises only when he pays the loss for which he is liable under the policy.

(c) The insurer is not entitled to the benefit of what is recovered until the assured has recovered a full indemnity.

9. Doctrine of Contribution. In cases where there are two or more insurances on one risk, the principle of contribution applies as between different insurers. The aim of Doctrine of Contribution is to distribute the actual amount of loss among the different insurers who are liable for the same risk under different policies in respect of the same subject-matter. In case of loss, any one insurer may pay to the assured the full amount of the loss covered by the policy. Having paid this amount, he is entitled to contribution from his co-insurers in proportion to the amount which each has undertaken to pay in case of loss of the same subject-matter. A contribution clause reads as follows:

"If at the time of any other subsisting insurance or insurances effected by the assured or by any other person or persons on his behalf covering such property, either alone or together with any other property this company shall not be liable to pay or contribute more than its rateable proportion of such loss or damage."

Example: 'X' insured car for ₹ 80,000 with 'Y' and for ₹ 60,000 with 'Z'. He suffered a loss of ₹ 42,000, 'X' cannot recover ₹ 42,000 each from 'Y' and 'Z'. He can receive only ₹ 42,000. 'Y' and 'Z' will bear this loss in the ratio of 80,000:60,000, i.e., 4:3. 'Y' will pay ₹ 24,000 and 'Z' will pay ₹ 18,000. If 'Y' pays the whole amount of loss of ₹ 42,000, then he can recover ₹ 18,000 from 'Z'.

The right of contribution arises when

(a) there are different policies which relate to the same subject-matter,

(b) the policies cover the same peril which caused the loss,

(c) all the policies are in force at the time of the loss, and

(d) one of the insurers has paid to the assured more than his share of loss.

Difference between Subrogation and Contribution

1. Number of Contracts. There is only one contract in subrogation. The question of contribution arises only when there are more than one contract. Thus, there is no contribution in subrogation.

2. Object. The object of contribution is to distribute the loss among the different insurers in rateable proportion. In case of subrogation, the object of substitution of one person in place of another so that the one who is substituted succeeds to the rights and remedies of the other person.

3. Recovery. In case of contribution, the insurer, after having paid the amount to the assured, recovers the amount which he had paid in excess of his share from the other co-insurers. In case of subrogation, the insurer after having paid the amount to the assured tries to recover it from the person who would have been liable to pay if there had been no insurance.

Insurance is based on Theory of Probability and Law of Large Numbers. The theory of probability refers to the fact that most phenomena, called chance, becomes defined and understood if sufficient observations are made of a particular result over a period of time and a sufficient number of events are taken into consideration. On the basis of this theory, the rates of premium are calculated. The law of large numbers is based on the regularity of the occurrence of an event through it the losses of a few are spread over many. The law of large numbers is the principle that the reliance upon a given probability is increased when a series of observation is increased. For example, if 100 houses are insured against fire, the probability is that only one house may get fire. The loss suffered by that house owner is spread over remaining 99 house owners. Actuaries apply probability theory which can be measured by central tendency and dispersion. The central tendency is measured by mean or expected value. **Dispersion** is measured by standard deviation and variance. They employ both actual loss and theoretical loss based on probability.

Rule of Estopple

Estopple is a legal term. Estopple prevents a person or organisation or a company from adopting a position, action or attitude inconsistent with an earlier position if it would result in an injury to another person. It is a rule of fair play. Estopple may arise by following reasons:

(1) Estopple by record: This frequently arises as issue of cause of action estopple or judicial estopple where the orders or judgements made in previous legal proceedings prevent the parties from relitigating the same issues or causes of action.

(2) Estopple by deed: It occurs where rules of evidence prevent a litigant from denying the truth of what was said or done.

(3) Estopple by silence: Estopple that prevents a person from asserting something when he had the right and opportunity to do so earlier, and such silence put another person at a disadvantage. A tells B that he is agent of C in presence of C. C keeps silent. B deals with A. Later C is estopped from denying that A is not his agent. (Agency by estopple)

(4) Reliance-based estopples: These estopples involve one party relying on something the other party has done or said. The party who did/said the act is the one who is estopped. In above example A cannot deny later. Under English law estopple may take three following forms:

(a) *Estopple by representation of fact*: Where one person asserts the truth of a set of facts to another.

(b) *Proprietary estopple*: Where the parties are litigating the title to land.

(c) *Promissory estopple*: Where one person makes a promise to another, but there is no enforceable contract.

Example in Insurance

1. An insurance company had a history of accepting late payments from policyholders. A policyholder's policy was cancelled due to late payment. The court estopped the company from cancellation of policy because it has misled its policyholder into thinking that sending late premium payments was acceptable.

2. An insurance company has routinely mailed its policyholder's a notice when each premium was due. It suddenly stops sending premium notices, without warning or explanation. The insurance company was estopped from asserting that policyholder's policy has lapsed because premium payment was late. The policyholder was misled into thinking a premium notice would always be sent before policy would lapse for nonpayment of premium. The insurance company had created a reasonable basis for the insured to rely in the premium notice.

3. Policy is a *prima facie* evidence of title to the insurance. If any clause or statement is untrue, whether intentionally or accidentally, any person acting on it (e.g. advanced money on it) can compel the insurance company to make good its statement and pay compensation for any damage caused by reason of any statement.

Negligence

Negligence is defined as failure to take due care and as a result of which injury ensures. Negligence excludes wrongful intention, since they are mutually exclusive. Carelessness is not culpable or ground of legal liability except in those cases in which law has imposed a duty of carefulness. Carelessness depends upon the degree of skill and knowledge which a profession professes and is expected to have.

Contributory negligence means negligence by the effected or aggrieved party himself. A patient not taking care himself to follow up the treatment or tampering with plaster put on a fracture.

The injured or aggrieved party can sue the person guilty of negligence in a civil court as well as in a criminal court.

Negligence in Insurance

Negligence may be on the part of the insured, insurer or a third party.

(1) Negligence of the assured. In case of fire policy, fire due to negligence of the assured (e.g. not providing precaution against fire) will not hold underwriter liable. In case of accident, the plea of contributory negligence on the part of the assured will not debar him to claim. Under Employees State Insurance Act, a worker, guilty of contributory negligence that caused his accident or death, will not debar him to get accident or death benefit. In case of property insurance against theft, insured will not be entitled to benefit if he is negligence of not providing safety measures.

(2) **Negligence of insurer.** An insurer shall be liable for damages for his negligence under **Contract Act and Consumer Protection Act** e.g. issuing policy in a wrong name or amount.

(3) **Negligence on the part of third party.** In Cargo insurance, either by sea or air, mishandling will make the carrier liable for loss to the insurer. In health insurance, a doctor guilty of negligence in treating insured patient, will make him liable to the insurer (see p. 375 liability insurance).

Insurance and inflation. For those who take long-term life insurance policy, inflation will affect the future value of the present savings in coming years. The amount which insured receives in future will not have same purchasing power. In some countries, not in India, policies are issued under which benefit can vary from time to time with cost of living.

Advantages of Insurance

Life insurance "assures" our tomorrow, general insurance 'secures' our today.

1. Transfer of Loss. The purpose of insurance is to transfer the financial loss to insurer who spreads it over large numbers (policyholders). So the loss suffered by one person is distributed over many. It is called substitution.

2. A Social Security Tool. Insurance provides social security to people. It is generally considered that the responsibility of providing social security to its citizen lies with the government. Developed countries have gone far ahead in this direction by providing unemployment allowance, old age pension and subsistence allowance to the destitutes. However, in developing countries, the progress is slow but satisfactory, i.e. LIC maintains social security fund on behalf of the government for various schemes e.g. Jana Shree Bima Yojna for slow poverty line persons or landless agricultural labourers group insurance scheme. Social security is treated at par with national pension scheme and annuities: Premium on social security schemes are exempted from tax.

3. Tax Concession. In India, the government has floated many of its schemes, though the benefits thereunder are quite low. However, in an indirect manner the government has been furthering the cause of social security by giving income tax concessions, rebate on savings effected through life insurance, provident fund etc., under Section 88DD of the Income Tax Act. The proceeds of a life insurance policy are also fully exempt from income-tax under Section 10(10D) of the Income Tax Act, 1961. Under new Direct Tax code deduction on account of deduction premium will be redundant under new law ₹ one lakh investment in specified pension plans is exempted for tax. However, it may not be true, see table next page.

4. Development of Economy. Insurance mitigates the financial losses of the insured people, due to theft, fire, loss of goods or other hosts of eventualities. Imagine the plight of a factory owner in the event of fire, if there were no fire insurance policy. Same is the case in every sphere of human activity. Thus, insurance provides continuity in trade and commerce which ultimately helps the economy to grow.

5. Investment of Insurance Funds. Insurance companies collect huge funds from public which they invest in various instruments in the economy of the country. A large chunk of these funds are invested in government securities and other public debts. Every country lays down rules for investment of insurance funds depending upon the economic condition so that the government is able to embark upon a programme of nation building. A classic example is the nationalisation in 1956 of life insurance business in India. The main objective then was to harness vast amount of insurance funds for financing Five-Year Plans. Since then LIC have been contributing to the socially-oriented sector of the economy in a big way.

6. Protection and Investment. Life insurance affords both protection against risk and is good investment. The insured gets his money back with interest/profit/bonus and so provides financial security. Other insurances afford protection against risk of loss. However, it may not be true, see table.

7. Other Benefits

(a) It develops the habit of saving money.

(b) It facilitates loan on policy.

(c) It generates employment by giving work in insurance companies.

(d) It provides economic security to workers against sickness disablement, maternity and accident. Employees State Insurance is the agency for this purpose.

(e) An insurance makes business people secure. So business flourishes and foreign trade increases.

Insurance is not an Investment

Insurance plans offer poor returns and insufficient life cover

Why traditional plans don't make sense

Premium payable by a 35 year old male for 20 year plan

Traditional Endowment Policy	Term Plan + PPF Combo		Term Plan + ELSS Combo	
Annual Premium ₹ 50,000	Term Plan	PPF	Term plan	ELSS Premium
	Annual Premium		Annual Premium	
	₹ 4568	₹ 45.43	₹ 4568	SIP of ₹ 3750
Insurance Cover ₹ 25 lakh	Insurance Cover ₹ 25 lakh		Insurance Cover ₹ 25 lakh	
On maturity after 20 years ₹ 17.5 lakh as tax free corpus	On maturity after 20 years ₹ 23 lakh as tax free corpus		On maturity after 20 years ₹ 36 lakh as tax free corpus	
Our Assessment Low returns of less than 5% insufficient life insurance cover	**Our Assessment** Five times higher cover and 30% bigger benefits as insurance plan		**Our Assessment** Five times higher cover and more than double the corpus with same tax benefits as insurance plan	

Term plan example is HDFC click on line plan assumes 8% returns for PPF and 12% for ELSS funds.

Insurance is also Bot the Best Tax Saver

Life insurance plans give lowest returns among all Section 80C investment of options

Tax Saving Option	% Returns	Liability of Corpus	Liquidity
Life insurance plans	4.5–5	Tax free	Term of Plan
Bank FDs	7–7.25	Invest taxable	5 years
NSCs	8	Invest taxable	5 years
PPF	8	Tax free	15 years (but partial withdraws allowed in sixth year
Sukanya Samriddhi Yojna	Market linked	40% tax free	Sixth year
Nation Pension Plan ELSS	Market linked	Tax free	3 years

Source: TOI, dated 6-03-2017, p. 18.

Insurance and Economic Development

There is a difference between economic growth and economic development. Economic growth is gradual, while economic development is discontinuous and a spontaneous change. Economic development is measured by increase in industrial sector, agricultural sector, economic welfare of people and standard of living. There is no unanimity of opinion among economists about the indices that are to be considered for measuring qualitative economic development or economic growth. The increase in GDP is taken a major yardstick to measure them. GDP depends upon increase in all resources like human resources, natural resources, capital resources and technological resources. The capital formation (increase in inventory and fixed assets) is one important indice to measure industrial development.

Economic development needs investment in profitable sectors. Investment depends upon savings. Insurance inculcates the habit of saving among the insured. The funds collected by insurance companies are available for investment in the economy for its development. IRDA has laid down norms for investment of life insurance funds e.g., at least 50% be invested in government and approved securities. In India, the investment avenues are many like fixed deposit with banks, provident fund, bonds and equity, mutual funds, estates, jewelry, post office schemes and life insurance. Very few people would like to invest in life insurance, though people are becoming more health conscious and take insurance products.

The objectives of making investment are many e.g., to meet a long-term or short-term liability, to take benefit at retirement, for child education or marriage, to meet medical expenses and lastly to earn high returns. Last one is more popular. Most of the other objectives are met by insurance.

Business Environment and Insurance

Business environment is classified either as (a) internal environment or (b) external environment.

Internal environment, by and large, is controllable, while external environment is non-controllable. External environment may be microenvironment or macroenvironment.

Internal environment is effected by management structure, production finance, R&D, human resources and marketing capabilities of a business.

The micro external environment is affected by customers, suppliers, competitors, public, financiers and intermediaries. The factors that affect macroenvironment are economic factors, social factors, demographic factors, political factors, natural factors, technological factors and global factors. Any of the above factor or factors together may create a risk, e.g., human resources have the risk of death, illness or accident and physical assets may be destroyed by fire or there may be a theft. Similarly, political factors threaten takeover of business, natural factors cause loss due to earthquake or floods and social factors may result in loss due to strike, arson or protests from public (like creation of special economic zone in Bengal or metro rail constructed near colonies). To overcome any risk caused by any external or internal factors, business and industry need protection which is provided by insurance.

The role of insurance in business can be grouped into three heads:

(a) Insurance is a hedge against risk-personal or property.

(b) Insurance is an alternative to investment products.

(c) Insurance can be offered as a collateral security. Let us discuss them one by one.

Insurance as a Hedge against Risks

Insurance is a hedge for changing the person's or firm's risk exposure. Insurance is to society "what scalpels are to surgery". Insurance covers are available even against political risks associated with exports and foreign investments e.g., Export Credit Guarantee Corporation of India (ECGC) provides covers against risk involved in foreign trade or deposits with banks or World Bank Multilateral Investment Guarantee Agency provides insurance cover against risks involved in foreign investments. ECGC also provides cover against foreign exchange rate fluctuations.

A man has to face risk at every step. It may be related to human body or property (movable or immovable) and financial or nonfinancial. Human body has the risk of untimely death or accident or illness. Property has the risk of theft, embezzlement, fire, damage, looting, or natural calamity (like Tsunami), or to meet future liability (like marriage, child education). Insurance provides hedge against all these risks by indemnifying the loss except death. In case of death of a person, the survivors are assured of monetary help by insurance.

Insurance thus is "POOLING of Risks" at one place and the loss caused by any risk is distributed over many insured.

Insurance as Collateral Security

A debtor can give insurance policy as a collateral security against a loan taken from a bank or any other person. Even the insurance companies offer a facility of loans on the life policies on which a number of premium has been paid. The loan is granted on the security of policy and is limited by surrender value of policy. It may be paid back within a certain period. If it is not paid during the period of loan, the amount due can be recovered at the time of maturity.

It should be noted that ALL types of policies can be assigned, since policy is an actionable claim. It can be attached by court as well. Loans are given only against life policy and not against any other type of policy.

Insurance as an Alternative to Investment Products

"Life insurance is both an investment and protection." Other types of insurance afford only protection against loss. In India, people were not insurance conscious and preferred investment in jewellery, fixed deposit in banks or post offices and lastly in securities. At present, with the expansion of insurance sector in India, people need not be convinced about insurance. Many attractive life insurance products in the nature of safe and income yielding investments are available nowadays with insurance companies e.g., SBI offers lifelong pensions, Bajaj unit or invest gain, Kodak safe investment, HDFC single premium whole life, Birla flexi life line, INGVYSYA rewarding life and Max investment plans.

IT and its Use in Insurance

IT is being used in every aspect of business. In insurance, IT helps in the following areas:

- To store the data of policyholder and scanned documents (Application Form, etc.).
- To centeralise the database, so that the policyholder can visit any branch for his policy related queries.
- To get automatic periodic information related to premium dates both to policyholders and agents in physical, web or in SMS form.
- To get commission/targets related details of agents.
- For online training of agents.
- To share the details of uninsurable persons among other insurers.
- To fast processing of claims by quickly transferring the documents by web.

E-commerce and its Use in Insurance

E-commerce helps in getting online policies without visiting any branch or agents. A number of companies are offering online policies. In this, an application form is filled online on the insurer's website and the payments are made electronically. The documents, if required, are sent in the soft form.

After satisfying the risk taken, the insurer issues the policy to the insured. This policy document can be sent my post only.

E-payment and its Use in Insurance

People in India are increasingly shifting to pay their insurance premiums online. All the insurance companies are facilitating to pay premium electronically. The procedure to pay premium online is very simple. It can be accomplished by visiting insurer's website. This premium can be paid by credit card or net banking. Insurers are offering discount or gifts for paying online as it helps in saving a lot of manpower. Also policyholder is benefited as he does not need to visit an agent or a branch.

Also, insurance companies are paying the maturity benefits or survival benefits directly to the policyholder's saving bank account with the help of ECS (Electronic Clearing System). It helps in cost-cutting as the postage of sending a physical cheque is saved.

Factors Effecting Insurance Business

In any economy, insurance business can flourish only on certain factors. It is not easy to sell insurance products in less-developed country because it is not easy to get money out of pocket of someone when you are not giving any tangible product like in insurance. Following are the factors that affect insurance sector in any country:

(1) **Demographic Distribution:** The entire market area where insurance company to launch its business must have breakup of population—old, young and children, men and women, married and unmarried, age distribution of each of above.

(2) **Mortality and Morbidity Rates:** Statistics about the death rate of people of different ages and the state of sickness of persons, rate of accidental death, should be studied. This will help the company to issue life insurance products accordingly.

(3) **Literacy:** To convince educated people to buy insurance is more comfortable than the less educated or illiterate persons.

(4) **Investment Opportunity:** The insurance funds—shareholders fund as well as policyholders funds—are to be invested in different sectors by an insurance company e.g. mutual funds, securities, real estates, etc. In a developing country, such opportunities exist.

(5) **Income Distribution:** The different policies can be marketed according to income distribution of people—rich, middle class, lower middle, poor and below poverty line people.

(6) **Competition:** Have there other competitors in the field. Till 2000, LIC and GIC did not have any competition. Now many private players are in the field.

(7) **Legal Requirements:** The laws relating to insurance and other legal formalities must be complied with. IRDA, in India, regulates the working of insurance companies.

(8) **Financial Institutions:** Banking, NBFC, mutual funds help to expand insurance. Even post offices can be of great help to reach insurance facilities in remote areas.

(9) **Communication Facilities:** In India, communication facilities like telephones, e-mail, E-business mobiles, couriers have helped insurance sector to expand.

(10) **Other Factors:** Inflation, interest rates, industrialisation and urbanisation, social environment and political environment are other factors affecting insurance.

Insurance Company Evaluation

Insurers' evaluation by the insured should be formed on following four criteria:

(1) Financial soundness and performance, (2) Product availability (3) Service quality, and (4) Ethical behaviour. Any evaluation should begin with complete identification of the company, its rating done by any agency, surplus adequacy, financial analysis, asset quality, profitability, investment yield and leverage. It should be noted that there are no completely satisfactory means of comparing the financial condition and operational performance of an insurance company.

Corporate Governance Reporting to the Insurance Regulator (IRDA)

The items include:

(1) A brief statement on company's philosophy on code of governance.

(2) Information about the Board of Director:

- The composition and category of the Board of Directors of the company. For example: promoter, executive, non-executive, independent non-executive, nominee director, etc. and which institution represented as lender or as equity investor.
- Attendance of each director at the Board meetings and the last Annual General Meeting and information relating to the number of Boards or Board Committees in which he/she is a member or chairperson.
- Number of Board meetings held dates on which held.

(3) Information about Audit Committee:
- Information with brief description of terms of reference given to the Audit Committee.
- Composition, name of members and chairperson of the Audit Committee.
- Details of the meetings of Audit Committee held and attendance of the members during the year.

(4) Remuneration Committee:
- Brief description of terms of reference of the Remuneration Committee.
- Composition, name of members and chairperson of the Remuneration Committee.
- Details of attendance of the members of Remuneration Committee during the year.
- Remuneration policy and details of remuneration to the directors (as per format in main report).

(5) Shareholders Committee:
- Name of non-executive director heading the committee.
- Name and designation of compliance officer.
- Number of shareholders' complaint received so far.
- Number not solved to the satisfaction of shareholders.
- Number of pending complaints.

(6) Information relating to the General Body meeting:
- Location and time, where last three Annual General Meetings held.
- Whether any special resolutions passed in the previous three Annual General Meetings.
- Whether any special resolutions passed last year through postal ballot—details of voting pattern.
- Whether any special resolution is proposed to be conducted through postal ballot.
- Procedure for postal ballot.

(7) Various disclosures required from the insurers:
- Disclosures on materially significant related party transactions that may have potential conflict with the interests of company at large.
- Details of non-compliance by the company, penalties, strictures imposed on the company by Stock Exchange or SEBI or any statutory authority, on any matter related to capital markets, during the last three years.
- Whistle Blower policy and affirmation that no personnel has been denied access to the Audit Committee.
- Details of compliance with mandatory requirements and adoption of non-mandatory requirements of this clause.

(8) Information to be given about General Shareholders:
- Details of Annual General Meeting—date, time and venue.
- Financial Year.
- Date of Book Closure.
- Dividend payment date.
- Listing on Stock Exchange.

- Stock Code.
- Market Price Data: High, Low during each month in last financial year.
- Performance in comparison to broad-based indices such as BSE Sensex, CRISIL index, etc.
- Register and Transfer Agents.
- Share Transfer System.
- Distribution of shareholding.
- Dematerialization of shares and liquidity.
- Outstanding GDRs/ADRs/Warrants or any convertible instruments, conversion date and likely impact on equity.
- Plant locations.
- Address of correspondence.

Risk Management

(A) Disclosure about Risk Management

Like involvement of:

(a) Risk relating to various policies/Political Risk;

(b) Business Risk

  (i) Client Construction

  (ii) Credit Control

  (iii) Geographical Risks

  (iv) Economic Risks

  (v) Technology Risks;

(c) Financial Risks

  (i) Liquidity

  (ii) Leverage

  (iii) Foreign Currency Fluctuation;

(d) Legal and Statutory Risks

  (i) Legal and Statutory Risks

  (ii) Contractual Risks

  (iii) Statutory Compliance;

(e) Management Risks

  (i) Human Resources Management and Enhancement

  (ii) Internal Upgradation

  (iii) Internal Control System

  (iv) Disaster Recovery Plans.

(B) Risks and Concern and Risk Mitigation

The company has built up a risk inventory of all the identified risks cutting across its various business units. The risks have been prioritized through a company-wise exercise. Members of senior management have undertaken the ownership of the top risks of the company and work on mitigating the same.

All the Indian general insurers need to fulfill IRDA's specific directive to them—"The Authority advises that a Chartered Accountants firm, who is not the Statutory or internal or Concurrent Auditor of the concerned insurer and having a minimum of three to four of experience of IT systems, risk management and process controls of Banks or Mutual funds or Insurance Companies, shall certify that the Investment Risk Management System and Processes envisaged by these guidelines are in place and working effectively."

3

Life Assurance

The Life Insurance business in India was nationalised on January 19, 1956. On September 1, 1956, Life Insurance Corporation of India came into existence. But in March 2000, the exclusive privilege of LIC to carry out life assurance business in India has ceased. Under the Insurance Regulatory and Development Authority Act, 1999, the Insurance Regulatory and Development Authority (IRDA) of India was set up to protect the interest of policyholders and to promote, regulate and ensure orderly growth of insurance industry. The law relating to business of insurance is governed by Insurance Act, 1938, which contains 120 sections and eight schedules. Only an Indian insurance company is permitted to do insurance business in India. It includes a company registered under Companies Act, 1956 in which total equity share holding by a foreign company (including subsidiaries and nominees) do not exceed 26% of the paid up equity capital of the Indian company. It must obtain a certificate from IRDA.

Section 2(II) of the Insurance Act, 1938 defines 'Life Insurance business' as the business of effecting contracts of insurance upon human life. It includes:

(1) any contract whereby the payment of money is assured on death (except death by accident only) or the happening of any contingency dependent on human life; and

(2) any contract which is subject to payment of premiums for a term dependent on human life; and shall be deemed to include:

   (a) the granting of disability and double or triple indemnity accident benefits, if so provided in the contract of insurance;

   (b) granting of annuities upon human life; and

   (c) granting of superannuation allowances and annuities payable out of any fund applicable solely to the relief and maintenance of persons engaged or who have been engaged in any particular profession, trade or employment or of the dependent of such persons.

A life insurance contract is a contract in which one party agrees to pay given sum on the happening of particular event contingent upon the duration of human life, in consideration of the payment of a sum by another. Thus, insurer pays a sum assured on survival upto a certain specified period or death. The word assurance is used for life insurance.

Difference between Life Assurance and Fire/Marine Insurance

1. Indemnity. The contract of fire, marine and property accident insurance is contract of indemnity. The insurer is liable to pay the actual loss caused to the subject-matter or the amount insured if loss is more than the sum insured.

In life assurance, the insurer pays the sum insured on the death of the insured or after the expiry of fixed period for which insurance is taken. This is because human life cannot be evaluated in terms of money.

2. Certainty of event. In fire, marine or property insurance, the event may or may not happen, i.e., fire may or may not break out. In life insurance, death is a certain event that is bound to happen.

3. Insurable interest. In life and personal accident insurance, insurable interest must be proved at the time of contract. In marine and property accident insurance, it must be present at the time of loss. In fire, it must be present both at the time of contract and at the time of loss. It cannot be measured in money in life insurance, but can be measured in terms of money in fire or marine insurance.

4. Period. Fire insurance is only for one year and so is vehicle accident insurance. Marine insurance is for a period or for a particular voyage. Life insurance can be for a period or till the insured is alive.

5. Surrender value. In life insurance, if insured surrenders the policy after a particular period, he gets back some amount called surrender value. In other types of insurances there is no such value. In case of property accident, some rebate may be allowed in the amount of premium if there was no claim in past period.

6. Nomination. In life insurance, the insured may nominate any person as nominee who is entitled to receive the amount at the time of death of insured, whereas in other insurance it is not so.

7. Loan facility. Life insurance policy can be given as a security for a loan, whereas other policies cannot be given as a security.

8. Premium. In life insurance, premium is determined according to age of the insured and the period of policy. Premium is generally paid in installments. In other insurances, premium is determined according to the nature and extent or risk involved and the premium is paid in lump sum.

9. Subject matter. In life insurance, it is the life that is insured while in other insurances it may be property, ship, cargo and freight.

Insurable Interest

The main motives for effecting life assurance is either making provision for self in old age or for family in the event of death or children's education and 'start in life'. It means the insured is interested in continued life for him or his family members. He is also so placed that he is going to suffer a pecuniary loss in the event of the death. Thus, the interest the insured possesses in the life of any person (life is the subject-matter of insurance here) or in his own life is called insurable interest. Insurable interest is presumed if a person takes life insurance for his wife. Insurable interest must be present at the time of taking the policy in life insurance.

Suicide. Insurance policies usually contain a clause that no payment will be made in case of suicide by an insured. Therefore, insurance company cannot refuse payment if insured commits suicide unless there is a specific clause to that effect in the policy. [*Northern India Assurance Co. Ltd.* vs. *Kanhaiya Lal*]

Nature. In insurable interest, the following conditions are necessary:

(i) There must be a monetary benefit if the insured remains alive and if the insured dies financial loss to the person who takes insurance;

(ii) The amount of insurance should not be excessive to the interest of the insured;

(iii) It should involve legal liability;

(iv) It must be present at the time of taking the policy.

Existence. Insurable interest exists in the following cases:

Every person has insurable interest in his own life. A husband or wife has insurable interest in the life of his or her spouse. Non-relatives may also have insurable interest, e.g., creditor in the life of his debtor, surety in the life of the principal debtor, partner in the life of other partners and employer in the life of his employee.

Life Insurance Documents and Procedure

The various insurance documents involved in life insurance contract are:

1. Proposal forms
2. Consent letter
3. Declaration about health
4. Income tax assessment order
5. Copy of marriage certificate
6. Premium receipt
7. Policy

Each type of policy envisages different benefits. Also the cover for risk of death varies from policy to policy. In the case of non-medical proposals, some extra information such as height and weight of the life assured is called for. Depending upon the requirements, different proposal forms are devised. A few types of such forms are given.

1. Various forms for proposals

(i) Proposal for insurance on own life.

(ii) Proposal for assurance on the life of another person.

(iii) Proposal on the lives of minors.

(iv) Proposal for Annuity.

(v) Proposal for Capital Redemption Assurance Policy.

(vi) Proposal for Pensionary Plans (Immediate type).

(vii) Proposal for Pensionary Plans (Deferred type).

(viii) Proposal for female child with provision also to cover husband after marriage.

(ix) Proposal for pensionary benefits for self and spouse.
(x) Proposal for farmers, containing special provisions for unpaid premium.
(xi) Proposal for insurance (see Chapter 10).

Other related forms

(i) Personal statement regarding health for a new policy on own life.
(ii) Personal statement regarding health for a new policy on another life.
(iii) Agent's confidential report.
(iv) Queries regarding occupation.
(v) Addendum to proposal form for policies under Payment Wages Act, 1936.
(vi) Addendum to proposal to be financed through income of HUF to be completed by the Karta of HUF.

2. Consent letter. It conveys the affirmations of the assured to the imposition of some restrictive clause or lien or extra premium. It is duly signed by the assured. This consent letter forms the basis of contract.

3. Declaration of good health. It is a self-declaration by the assured in which he/she declared about the "Status" of his/her health on the date of declaration. It is required to assess if the life assured continues to be in good health since the date he submitted proposal for assurance.

4. Income-tax assessment order. In proposals for very large sum-assured, it becomes necessary to ensure that premium falls within the financial capacity of the assured. It is because of this that in some cases income-tax assessment orders for last three years are called for. If the assessment of income is pending with the Income-tax Department, the Chartered Accountant of the assured is asked to submit a letter showing the income for which return has been filed. A authority letter for deduction of premium out of the salary of the assured is obtained duly signed by the assured in salary savings schemes cases.

5. An authorisation letter from the provident fund authorities. It is required if the premia are desired to be financed out of provident fund account of the assured.

6. Copy of marriage certificate. A copy of marriage certificate or letters from two persons who attended the marriage of the female life assured in support of her having changed the name. A female's pre-marriage name in the school certificate may be different from what she has stated in the proposal form.

7. First premium receipt. As explained earlier, an insurer first evaluates the risk under a proposal and then determines the terms on which to accept the risk. The assured signifies his consent by paying the premium in full. The insurer then issues the first premium receipt (FPR) which is called Acceptance-Letter-cum-First Premium Receipt. It acknowledges that the proposal for assurance for a specified sum has been accepted on the terms specified from the date of the said receipt and that the insurer shall be at risk subject to the conditions laid in the Policy Bond which it promises to send shortly. It also advises the policyholder to write to the insurer for delivery of the Policy Bond if the same is not received within 40-50 days from the date of First Premium Receipt. FPR is the document on the strength of which the life assured can compel the insurer to issue the Policy Bond which is treated as Evidence of the Contract of Life assurance.

Note that date of commencement may be different from risk date of a policy. The former is when proposal for insurance is made. The later date is when first premium is received and cover note is issued.

Renewal premium receipt. In majority of cases, the assured is required to pay premium for a specified number of years. The premium falling due subsequent to the first premium is called Renewal Premium and the receipt issued in lieu of its having been paid is called Renewal Premium Receipt. It is a proof of the assured having discharged his duty of paying the renewal premium specified in the receipt.

Renewal servicing. Once the policy is issued, the important servicing work that has to be undertaken by the insurer is the collection and issue of renewal premiums until the policy becomes a claim.

To safeguard that full years' premium is recovered in death claim cases, it is condition that in the year of death, any unpaid installments due for the policy year will be deducted from the claim amount. This rule applies to all cases.

8. Policy contract. In order that mutual rights and obligations of the insurer and the assured are formalised as a document in proof of the contract a Policy Bond or Policy Document is issued. It is an evidence of the contract of life assurance. The Policy Bond is prepared by the insurer who incorporates the terms of the contracts therein. It is stamped as per Section 47 of the Indian Stamp Act and is required to be delivered to the policyholder within one month of the acceptance of the first premium.

Form of policy. The policy document is prepared on a printed form instead of a "narration" policy. The format of a policy bond can be as follows:

(i) *Heading*. It shows in bold letters the name of the insured.

(ii) *Preamble*. It states the circumstances leading to the insurance contract and expresses that:

   (a) Proposal and declaration submitted by the life assured and also statements contained therein are to form the basis of contract.

   (b) It has received the first premium.

(iii) *Operative clause*. It refers to the mutual obligations of the two parties i.e., payment of premium by the assured and insurer to pay the claim when it arises as per the agreed terms.

(iv) *Proviso*. It declares that the policy shall be subject to conditions and privileges printed on the back of the policy.

(v) *Schedule*. It is usually in a graphic (cage) form and gives details of the insurance such as type of policy, sum assured, premium amount, and date of maturity, extra premium and nominee, etc.

(vi) *Attestation*. It testifies to the company having entered as a party to contract.

(vii) *Date*. It is the date on which policy bond is signed on behalf of the insurer.

(viii) *Conditions and privileges*. These are printed on the back of the Policy Bond.

Note: Matters to be stated in life insurance policy (see Chapter 10).

Delivery of policy bond. As per Section 66 of the Indian Stamp Act, the insurer is bound to deliver the duly stamped policy bond to the policyholder within 30 days of the acceptance of proposal.

Incontestable clause. As pointed out earlier, this clause states: "The policy shall be incontestable after it has been in force for a period of two years from the date of issue." It means that insurance company cannot revoke the policy on ground of alleged misstatements by the insured after two years. But this clause does not apply in case of fraud committed by the insured.

Alterations

Life assurance being a long-term contract, often requires the assured to ask for alteration in the terms of the contract. Alteration which increases the risk of insurer is not allowed.

Need for alterations. If assured has some compelling reasons or financing difficulties, alterations are generally allowed.

(a) Alteration should not increase the risk to the insurer such as increase in term of policy from 10 years to 20 years.

(b) Alterations necessitated on account of mistakes in the preparation of the policy, or due to age discrepancy. These occur due to mistake on the part of the office.

(c) Alterations relating to mode of payment of premium or reduction in sum assured arise due to financial difficulties of the policyholder and are usually accepted.

(d) Other types of alterations such as reduction in term, conversion from 'non-profit' to 'with profits', are also agreed to.

(e) Splitting of a policy into two or more because of:

   (i) the financial difficulties in paying the premium under the policy, say, for ₹ 10 lakh. By splitting into two policies of ₹ 5,00,000 each, the assured surrenders the one policy and continues the other.

   (ii) The necessity to appoint different nominees—e.g. two children.

Endorsements

Endorsement is an authenticated noting on the back of the Policy Bond and forms part of the contract.

Endorsements, if due to paucity of space, are on separate sheet of papers, need to be kept attached to the policy. If an alteration has the consequences of changing many conditions and benefits, a new policy is issued for which cost is to be borne by the life assured.

Renewal Notice

It is an intimation sent by the insurer, conveying to the life assured that a particular premium is going to fall due. It is a matter of courtesy and business ethics that renewal notices are issued. The insurer is otherwise under no obligation to issue to renewal (premium) notice.

Bonus Notice/Card

After the declaration of valuation results, insurer issues to every policyholder of a participating policy, a letter/card showing the amount of total bonus vested in his policy. It is also called bonus card. This notice or card has the information value for the assured. The assured does not require its production at any level of policy servicing. The notices are sometimes used by the insurer as a publicity tool by incorporating same typical information for the interest of policyholder.

Other Documents

The other special documents required in some of the specialised products of life insurance are:

Keyman Insurance (refer to p. 140)

(i) Special questionnaire from the employer as to how:
   (a) the proposed life assured is determined as a Keyman;
   (b) the contribution of the Keyman to the profits of the company; and
   (c) the basis on which sum assured is determined.

(ii) Copy of the Board's resolution approving the purchase of Keyman Plan.

(iii) Article and Memorandum of Association of the company.

(iv) Profit and Loss Account and Balance Sheet of the company for the last year.

(v) Letter from the company agreeing to the condition that in the event of assured employee leaving the services/employment, the policy will be either surrendered to the company or assigned to the employee life assured only.

Partnership Insurance

(i) Whether all the partners or some are insured.

(ii) Profit and Loss Account and Balance Sheet of the firm for the last year.

(iii) Deed of variation, allowing purchase of life assurance policy.

(iv) A copy of the Deed of Partnership which should contain a clause that in the event of death of a partner the other partners have the option to purchase his share or not.

Jeevan Griha (Triple Benefits) of LIC. Since this policy is granted only to cover the housing loan, a copy of the loan approval letter must be attached with the proposal.

Cover Note

It is a document issued by an insurer (underwriter) on receiving a proposal pending the execution of the policy. It covers the risk between the date of contract of insurance and actual issue of policy. If a cover note was issued on 18-6-2003 and which covered risk from by mistake 15-6-2003. The goods are destroyed on 16th June unknown to both the parties. The defence of mistake is of no use. The company shall be liable to pay the loss.

Age Admission

Verification of age on the basis of some documentary evidence is done by insurer. The following are considered standard are proofs:

(i) Certified extract from municipality or other government record made at the time of birth.

(ii) Copy of certified extract from school or college record if date of birth is stated therein.

(iii) Copy of certified extracts from Service Book in the case of Government Employees or Public Limited company.

(iv) Passport.

(v) Voters Identity card.

Any other document where the date of birth or age has been proved on the basis of one of the standard age proofs such as domicile certificate, naturalization certificate, etc.

It should be noted that even Section 45 of the Insurance Act, 1938 makes it mandatory for the assured to get age admitted by the insurer. The importance of his obligation on the part of the life assured can be felt by the fact that the condition of age admission is printed on the back of the policy bond and hence forms part of the policy contract.

Payment of Premium in Advance

All premiums are payable in advance as per Section 64 VB of the Insurance Act, 1938 which states:

(i) no insurer shall assume any risk in respect of any insurance unless and until premium is received in advance.

(ii) risk may be assumed not earlier than the date on which premium is received.

(iii) if after utilising the full premium, some amount is left to the credit of the life assured, the same shall be refunded by the insurer to the policyholder only.

(iv) if the agent collects the premium from the policyholder, he shall deposit the same with insurer within 24 hours excluding bank and postal holidays.

Revival of Policy

Revival means bringing back to life an assurance policy which has lapsed due to non-payment of premiums.

Revival is possible:

(a) only by payment of the arrears of premium in full with interest and production of satisfactory evidence of health if required by insurer's rules.

(b) only during the lifetime of the life assured and before the date of maturity.

(c) after six months, insurer usually asks for a medical report, along with full arrears of premiums with interest.

(d) within six months of lapse by payment of outstanding premiums with interest without medical examination of the life assured.

You should note here that revival is treated as a fresh contract. Insurer may decline or modify the earlier terms of acceptance.

Types of Revival Schemes

There are many schemes of revival with every insurance company. Some of them are:

1. Revival by installments. Full arrears of premiums with interest up to the date of revival are spread over two to three years so as to give relief to the policyholder who remains covered under the policy for full protection.

2. Revival by raising loan from the insurer. Loan amount is calculated by treating the policy in force and revival dues are deducted out of loan and policy made up-to-date.

3. Special revival scheme. If the policy is not eligible for revival under installment scheme and life assured is not in a position to pay arrears in lump sum, the insurer may agree to revive the policy by advancing the date of commencement of the policy by period for which the lapsed policy was in force. This arrangement reduces the revival dues considerably. It is practiced by LIC.

"Backdating"

Backdating refers to the practice of predating the time at which the policyholder bought the policy. Suppose A buys a policy on, April 5, 2008.

The policy is said to have been backdated if the insurance company and A (parties to the contract) together agree to officially show that the policy was purchased on, say, January 5, 2008, Backdating is legally permissible, and is used to lower the premium commitment or time the incidence of outflow.

Backdating cannot be effected on a policy more than once. A policy can be backdated at the time of purchase or within a particular time.

A policy can be backdated up to the first day of the accounting year in which the policy is purchased; that is, a policy bought any time between April 1, 2011–March 31, 2012 can be backdated up to April 1, 2011 and not after that.

Is backdating useful?

Backdating is useful in certain situations. A life insurance policy is not the best way to save tax and there are better; more flexible and lucrative options to do so. Even so, millions of taxpayers buy life insurance to save tax. If a taxpayer needs to exhaust his Section 80C limit through a life insurance policy this year but wants to pay the premium on a monthly or quarterly basis from next year; he will find backdating useful. He can pay the premiums for this year at one go, and from next year; he can pay them whenever they are due.

It is also useful in case the buyer has just crossed the minimum age for buying a certain policy.

There are also sentimental reasons for backdating. Sometimes, buyers want their insurance policies to be issued on an important date during the year. It could be a birthday, wedding anniversary or any other date with emotional value. This also ensures that the maturity of the policy coincides with that important date. It also sets a reminder for the premium.

Look before you leap

Going back in time also reduces the waiting period for the policyholder: If you buy a money-back policy in March 2014, you will get the first tranche (which is 20% of the sum assured) after five years in 2019. However, if you backdate the policy to April 2013, you will get the money in four years and one month, in April 2018.

Before you are led into believing that this is a great way to get your money back faster; do the math. The next premium becomes due in a month in April 2014. Also, you are charged a 10% interest on the premium you pay for the backdated policy. "It makes little sense to pay 10% interest on a policy that earns you only 6-7%," says a Delhi-based insurance expert.

If the backdate is more than one month away, the buyer is charged a 10% annual interest on a pro-rata basis. So, if you want to backdate a policy by three months, be ready to pay an interest of 2.5%. The Anand Money-back package, a combo of two money-back plans and an endowment policy, being hawked by LIC agents, has one plan dating back to April 2013. The premium will be due next month.

Incidentally, the interest on the backdating kicks in only after 30 September. Till this cut-off date, the LIC does not charge any interest even if the policy any interest even if the policy is backdated by 5-6 months. There is also no charge if the back-dating is for less than a month.

Zero sum game

Insurance agents use backdating to lure buyers. Insurance companies base their premiums on the policyholder's age. LIC, for instance, goes by the last birthday of the buyer. If the policy dates back to before your birthday, the premium will be lower. However, this is a zero sum game. In your quest for a lower premium rate, you will end up paying extra premium. This is why backdating works only in endowment and money-back plans. Backdating a term plan is an exercise in futility because the coverage for the entire backdated period effectively goes waste.

Five Facts on Backdating

1. Backdating is possible only in endowment and money-back policies. Market-linked plans cannot be backdated.
2. Insurance companies charge an interest on backdating policies. LIC charges 10% per annum on a pro-rata basis.
3. Usually, no interest is charged if the policy is backdated by less than a month or before September 30.
4. Backdating lowers the premium if the issue date is before your birthday. But you also end up paying an extra premium.
5. Backdating reduces the policy term, but advances the premium payment. The next premium becomes due faster.

Advantages: Backdating can be considered for the following reasons:

(1) Premium contributions are, among others, a function of age. The older a person grows the higher the premium. Insurance company determines premium rates on the basis of 'age nearer last birthday'.

Suppose a person is 51 years, and he has not crossed six months after his 51st birthday. However, company will base premiums on 52 years if he is 51 years and 7 months. By backdating his policy three months, he can effectively reduce his total premium contribution.

(2) By backdating, premium contributions can also be timed.

For example, those running independent businesses or self-employed, with receivables subject to seasonal inflows, control over funds can be correlated with certain time periods every year.

If a farmer takes a policy in December, but his funds position is comfortable just after the harvest, in late September, the policy can be backdated so that premiums are paid every September.

(3) If the policy applicant is unable to furnish proof of age, and the company asks him to provide proof of age after a year, the insurer will allow backdating the policy, to bring it in accordance with the age declared.

This would remove the burden of having to pay additional premium plus interest charges.

(4) A policy can be backdated to let its maturity coincide with any special day, such as birthday or wedding anniversary.

(5) Insurance companies frequently allow policies to be backdated as it means potential business opportunities to them. The loss in premium (due to lower age) is not important compared to the business gained.

When backdating a policy, the premium will have to be paid for the backdated period together with interest charges.

(6) Backdating also reduces the policy's effective term. For instance, if a 20-year term life cover bought on January 1, 2009 is backdated to April 1, 2008, the policy would mature on April 1, 2028 instead of January 1, 2029.

The policy matures earlier than it normally would. In endowment policies, this could be an advantage as survival benefits accrue earlier.

In a term assurance policy, however, the effective coverage period is lost to the extent the policy is backdated, though the policyholder still pays premium on the entire term.

Assignment of Policy

The insurance policy may be assigned by the policyholder to meet his financial requirements such as to raise loan from the bank or he may otherwise, transfer his interest in the policy to his blood or other relation.

A policy can be assigned (e.g. marine policy) if the assignee has insurable interest in the subject-matter.

Procedure. Section 38 lays down the procedure of assignment:

(i) An assignment can be made by an endorsement on the policy or by a separate deed called Deed of Assignment. Separate deed of assignment attracts stamp duty.

(ii) A notice of assignment in writing is necessary to be submitted to the insurer along with either the policy document duly endorsed or Deed of Assignment.

(iii) The insurer has to register the assignment and has to give a written acknowledgement of receipt of such notice.

(iv) As a result of assignment all the rights and liabilities under a policy are transferred to the assignee.

(v) It is possible to make an assignment which is conditional.

(vi) Agents are prohibited from being assignees under the policies of others, except those on the lives of their relatives.

(vii) Assignment specifying shares of assignee may be held void under law. It should be avoided.

(viii) A transfer or assignment of a life policy whether with or without consideration, can be made only by an endorsement upon the policy itself or by a separate instrument. The endorsement or the separate instruments must be signed by the assignor, and attested by at least one witness.

(ix) The assignment shall be binding upon the insurer after a notice in writing and endorsement on the instrument or a certified copy thereof is delivered to him.

(x) In case of more than one assignment, the priority of the claims of the assignee shall be governed by the order in which the notice to the insurer is delivered.

(xi) On receipt of the notice, the insurer shall record the facts of the assignment together with the date and the name of the assignee. The insurer on request and on payment of the prescribed fee by the assignor or assignee, is bound to acknowledge, writing the receipt of such notice.

(xii) Subject to the terms and conditions of the assignment, the insurer shall from the date of the receipt of the notice, recognise the assignee named in the notice as the only person entitled to the benefit under the policy.

(xiii) An assignment in favour of a person made with the condition that it shall be inoperative or that the interest shall pass to some other person on the happening of a specified event during the lifetime of the person whose life is insured, and an assignment in favour of survivor or survivors of a number of persons, shall be valid.

(xiv) It is important to note that a valid assignment is irrevocable and cannot be cancelled subsequently.

Conditions for a Valid Assignment

(i) The assignor must be major and a person competent to contract.

(ii) The assignor must not be subject to any legal disqualifications, such as insane, insolvent, etc.

(iii) Assignment must be supported by consideration which may be either

(a) valuable consideration—money or money's worth, or

(b) natural love and affection which a person may have towards those who are related to him/her by blood or marriage or by way of gift in favour of them.

(iv) Assignment must be in writing and it must be very clear in the operative part of the endorsement that interest in the policy has been transferred and has transferred and has become vested in the assignee.

(v) Assignor must affix his signature to the assignment. The signature must be attested by at least one witness.

Types of Assignment. Assignment is of two types:

(a) Absolute—for valuable consideration—or gift,

(b) Conditional—for natural love and affection.

Conditional assignment made by a Muslim is valid and Muslim Personal Law does not make it absolute.

Until a notice of assignment is received by the insurer the assignment will not be operative as against the insurer. Therefore, it is important for the agent to note and advise the policyholders that the notice of assignment should be submitted promptly.

If the assignment is in favour of a minor, in the event of claim, policy money cannot be paid to him as he cannot give a valid discharge. It is, therefore, desirable that where the assignee is a minor, guardian should be appointed.

Not stamp fee is required on the document appointing the guardian.

If conditional assignee dies, the benefits revert to the life assured.

If absolute assignee dies, then the benefits would go to the estate of the assignee.

An assignment automatically cancels nomination. Therefore, after reassignment a fresh nomination should be made.

Assignment in favour of insurer. If policy is assigned to the insurer, for raising loan, then nomination made earlier will stand even after loan is repaid and policy re-assigned to the life assured.

Nomination. Nomination assumes a special importance in life assurance policies because it is governed by Section 39 of the Insurance Act, 1938. The effect of appointing a nominee is that in the event of death of the life assured, claim money is paid to the nominee. It facilitates the insurer in paying the claim money under the life assurance policy.

Section 39 of the Insurance Act, 1938 lays down:

(i) A holder of policy on his own life can affect nomination. Under children deferred policies, nomination can be made by the child on his attaining the age of majority. An absolute assignee cannot affect nomination under the policy because policy is not on his life.

(ii) The proposer may appoint a nominee while submitting the proposal on his own life by giving suitable reply to the appropriate question in the proposal form.

(iii) After issue of the policy, nomination can be made only by an endorsement on the back of the policy itself and such a nomination is required to be notified through notice to the insurer who will register it in its books.

(iv) The nomination should either be incorporated in the text of the policy at the time of its issue or it should be made by an endorsement on the back of the policy. The nomination on a separate sheet of paper would be invalid.

(v) Where no blank space is available on the policy to make an endorsement of the nomination, the same may be done on a slip of paper pasted to the policy.

(vi) Nomination merely gives the nominee the right to receive the policy money in the event of death of the life assured.

In the even of the death of the nominee, the nomination becomes ineffective and the nominees or heirs do not have any right to the policy moneys. The assured has the right to make a fresh nomination in favour of another person during the currency of the policy.

(vii) When a nominee is a minor, an appointee may be appointed to receive the policy moneys in the event of death of the life assured during the minority of the nominee. The appointee should be a major person.

(viii) Where there are more nominees than one, the policy moneys will be available to them jointly or to the survivors or survivor of them.

(ix) An assignment automatically cancels a nomination.

A notice of nomination is required in:

(a) all nominations subsequent to first, or

(b) change of nomination, or

(c) cancellation of nomination.

Notice should be signed by the policyholder and witnessed at least by one person.

Differences between Assignment and Nomination

1. Method. Assignment may be made by an endorsement on the policy itself or by a separate instrument. Nomination may be made by mentioning the name of the nominee in the policy or endorsement thereon.

2. Ownership. On assignment, the property is transferred to the assignee. In case of nomination, the policy continues to be at the disposal of the assured during his lifetime.

3. Revocation. Once an assignment is made, it cannot be revoked. Nomination can always be revoked before the policy matures.

4. Rights. An assignee gets the rights of the owner of the policy. A nominee gets only beneficial interest in the policy.

5. Cancellation. An assignment automatically cancels the nomination. A nomination does not cancel the assignment.

6. Dealing. On assignment, the assignee can deal with the policy in any manner he likes. The nominee gets a right in the policy on the death of the assured.

7. Payment. In case of assignment, money is paid to the assignee. In case of nomination, money is to be paid to the nominee, if he survives the assured.

8. Consideration. For a valid assignment some consideration is essential unless it is made by way of gift. Nomination does not require any consideration.

9. Purpose. An assignment is made for the purpose of transferring the rights, etc. under the policy, to the assignee. A nomination is made so that the beneficiary may recover the amount when the policy matures after the death of the assured.

Days of Grace

It is that period during which the policy does not lapse on the ground of non-payment of premium on the due date. The insurance cover continues as it is during this period even without payment of premium for the current period. The following are the days of grace:

(a) Not less than 30 days...for payment of yearly, half-yearly or quarterly premiums, and

(b) 15 days...for monthly premiums.

If death occurs within that period and before payment of the premium then due, the policy will still be valid and the sum assured will be paid after deduction of the said premium, and also the unpaid premiums falling due before the next date.

Premium

"Premium" is the amount which is paid by the assured to the insurance company which has accepted the risk under the policy. Thus, premium is:

1. The monetary value of the risk, contingent upon the duration of human life, and accepted by the insurer, or
2. The 'consideration' against the payment of which the insurer has undertaken the risk.

The premium can be a single lump sum amount or a smaller amount spread over a period, i.e., specified number of years or months. This smaller amount, payable for a specified period, is also called the 'Level Premium', as against 'stepped premium' i.e., lump sum. The former is better.

The IRDA have named the premium as "Office yearly Premium" which is defined as:

(i) Regular premium payable in a policy year by the policyholder to secure the basic benefits under the policy.

(ii) Extra premium where chargeable shall be down separately.

The table shows the yearly premium for ₹ 1,000 sum assured for every age and every term of the policy. There is a separate table for each type of policy, i.e., endowment, whole life, money-back and children deferred, etc.

Tabular premium/Tabular office yearly premium—Risk Premium = Amount according to mortality rate. Net Premium = Risk premium plus income from with investment of insurance funds. Gross premium = Net premium plus administrative expenses. The gross premium shown in the table form is called the tabular premium for sum assured of ₹ One thousand. Let us assume an Endowment Policy's premium table reads like this:

Yearly Premium Rate for Sum Assured ₹ 1000

	Term of Policy		
Age	5 yrs.	6 yrs.	7 yrs.
25	201	170	150
26	201.25	170	150
27	201.25	170	150.40
28	201.50	170.30	150.40
29	201.50	170.30	150.40
30	201.70	170.30	150.50

The tabular premium for a policy of ₹ 1000 for duration of six years for a policyholder aged 26 years is ₹ 170 yearly. Similarly for a person of 30 years, it will be ₹ 170.30 for the same duration of six years.

Rebates. From the above example, premium for a policy of ₹ 1 lakh (aged 26 years) would normally be:

$$\frac{₹170 \times 1{,}00{,}000}{1000} = ₹17{,}000 \text{ yearly.}$$

However, in practice, the insurers are always fair in their approach and ensure that economies gained in their operations are passed on to the policyholders. Therefore, some concessions or rebates are given in the table premiums. Usually, following types of rebates are allowed:

For large sum-assured. The rebate in table premium increases with the increase in sum assured and is either a percentage of tabular premium or at a flat rate, for example:

(i) For sum assured above ₹ 50 thousand to 1 lakh	Rebate @ ₹ 1 per thousand
(ii) Over 1 lakh to ₹ 1.5 lakh	₹ 2 per thousand

For mode of payment of premium. If the life assured pays his premium quarterly, it means that the insurer is required to deal it four times a year instead of one time, if the mode were yearly. As such generally yearly and half-yearly modes of payments are allowed rebate or concessions. These can be:

Yearly ₹ 2 per thousand or 3% of the table premium.

Half-yearly ₹ 1 per thousand or 1.5% of the table premium.

Extra premium. IRDA have defined extra premium to mean a charge for any risk not provided for in the minimum contract premium. It is obvious that extra premium is charged for extra mortality. From insurer's viewpoint the extra premium means the compensation for the risk being higher than the average.

Extra premium may arise due to:

(i) hazardous occupation

(ii) adverse health of the life assured

(iii) adverse family history

(iv) temporary health risk such as pregnancy.

Rider premium. Sometimes, insurers give an option to the policyholder to opt for extra benefits under the policy. These add-on benefits are called Policy Rider or rider benefits. The additional premium charged for these rider benefits are called "Rider Premium".

Example:

(i) Premium Waiver Benefits

(ii) Family Benefits

(iii) Disability Benefits.

Calculation of Age

(a) The importance of the recording of accurate age of the policyholder is very important. Calculation of age for determination of premium rates is referred to as follows:

(i) Age nearer birthday, or

(ii) Age last birthday, or

(iii) Age next birthday.

(b) For example, suppose the birth date of the proposer is 27-10-1970, the age as on 1-10-2003 (the date of proposal) will be:

(i) Age nearer birthday—

Date of calculation	1-10-2003
Date of birth	27-10-1970
Difference	4-11-31 yrs.

32 years, 11 months, and 4 days are nearer to next birthday, i.e., 27-10-2003, than last birthday which is 11 months 4 days old. Therefore, the age nearer birthday is 33 years.

(ii) If we calculate it on 25-4-2003, the difference is:

25-4-2003
27-10-1970
28-5-32 years.

It shows last birthday is past 5 months and 28 days, whereas next birthday is still away 6 months 2 days. Therefore, nearer birthday age is 32 years.

How to calculate age? Thus, the rule for finding the age near birthday is:

If the difference between the date of calculation and date of birth is:

(i) 6 months or more, add one to the difference in years to arrive at the age.

(ii) less than 6 months, the exact number of years as shown by the difference is the age of the life assured.

The other two methods of calculating ages need no clarification as they are self-evident.

Calculation of Premium: Example*

The following information is available:

(i) Age of life assured	26 years
(ii) Table endowment	For 7 years
(iii) Sum assured	₹ 2 lakh
(iv) DAB Extra	₹ 1 per thousand
(v) Health Extra	₹ 1.50 per thousand
(vi) Mode	Yearly
(vii) Rebate for yearly mode	3% of premium
(viii) Rebate for large amount	₹ 2 per thousand S.A.

Solution

(a) Table premium for 7 years	₹ 150.00
(b) Less for large Sum assured	(–) 2.00
	₹ 148.00
(c) Less for Mode (3% of ₹ 150)	(–) 4.50
(d) Add DAB Extra	(+) 1.00
(e) Health Extra	(+) 1.50
Net premium	₹ 146.00
Total premium for 2 lakhs	₹ 29,200

* P.R. Khanna 'LIC Agents' (Taxman).

Rider Premium. If there is rider premium for premium waiver benefit, the same should also be added after (e) above.

Depending upon the fact that extra risk, to which a life assured is exposed, is likely to be nil after a particular period, the extra premium imposed is removed after the expiry of that stipulated period.

Example:

(a) First Pregnancy Extra	It is removed after the first delivery.
(b) Aviation Extra	If life assured is put on ground duties or changes his job.
(c) Premium waiver Extra	The policy vest in the child on his attaining majority.

Benefits

1. Surrender value or cash value. A policy reserve is the amount set aside to pay future claims as well as cash/surrender value. This reserve is created out of excess amount of premiums received over cost of insurance.

The surrender value of a life policy is the amount which the insurers are prepared to pay in total discharge of the contract, in case the assured wishes to surrender his policy and extinguish his claim upon it. The surrender values are based on the actual premiums paid, and usually the policy is required to have run for two or three years before the surrender value will be allowed. Surrender values increase with each payment of premium. Some companies guarantee a minimum surrender value of 40% of the total premium.

Life Insurance Corporation of India provides the following rule to know the period when policy acquires surrender value:

(a) Policies taken before 1-4-1973

(i) after two years' premiums when the term is 20 years or more, or

(ii) after 1/10 of the total premiums due have been paid when the term is 11 to 9 years, or

(iii) after more than one year's premium is paid where the term is 5 to 10 years.

(b) Policies taken on or after 1-4-1973 after payment of three full years' premiums.

(c) Policies completed on and after 1-1-1976, five full years' premiums or for at least four years of the total term of the policy (but in no case less than three years' premium whichever is less).

(d) Policies completed on after 1-1-1979, three full years' premiums.

2. Loan value. Where the policy has acquired a 'surrender value', it also acquires a 'loan value'. The loan value is calculated at 90% of the surrender value in case of policies which are in force for full sum assured and 85% of the surrender value in case of policies which are in paid-up condition. However, housing loans are given to the extent of 95% of the policy money. The rate of interest charged at present in 9% per annum and it is payable half-yearly. Loans are not granted for a shorter period than six months. If the loan is repaid, it is cancelled, otherwise it is adjusted together with interest against the sum payable at the time of maturity.

(a) Section 113(1) of the Insurance Act, 1938 lays down that a policy acquires surrender value after premiums have been paid for three consecutive years. To this surrender value will also be added the surrender value of all bonuses that have vested in the policy upto the date of surrender.

(b) It is also the responsibility of the insurer to show on the back of the policy either:

(i) surrender value guaranteed under the policy by a formula, or

(ii) surrender value at the close of each year or at the close of every three years till maturity.

3. Paid-up value. Section 113(2) states that a policy which has acquired surrender value shall not lapse by non-payment of further premiums and it shall be kept alive to the extent of paid-up sum-assured which will also include all the bonuses vested in the policy.

The paid up value of a policy is the amount to which the sum assured would be reduced at any time if the assured requested a rearrangement of his contract so that no further premium should be payable. The amount on the paid up policy is payable on the happening of the event assured against.

Formula for calculation of paid-up value. A provision has also been shown for calculation of paid-up value. It is like this:

(i) *Paid-up value*

$$= \frac{\text{Sum assured } \times \text{No. of years premium paid}}{\text{No. of years for which premium is required to be paid}}$$

(ii) *Bonus*. A policy issued under Profits Plan does not participate in the profits disclosed in valuation for the period in which it was made a paid-up and in subsequent valuations, i.e. the existing vested bonus additions will also be added to the paid-up value.

Treatment of bonus. The paid-up value together with attached bonus, if any, is payable in the same manner as the original sum assured, i.e., on death of the life assured or on maturity as the case may be.

Paid-up policy not eligible for additional benefits. A paid-up policy loses all the additional benefits attached to the policy, viz.:

(i) Accident Benefit, Double Accident Benefit and Extended Permanent Disability Benefits.

(ii) Survival benefit installments payable under Money Back Policy.

Future premiums and paid-up policies. The paid-up policy is free from payment of further premiums, but is subject to the loan, interest and other charges, if any. Interest on any such loan is required to be paid regularly.

Calculation of Paid-up Value

Example 1

Sum assured	₹ 20,000
Mode	Yearly
Type of Policy	Endowment for 20 years
Date of commencement	1-10-2000
Due date of last premium paid	1-10-2005
Premiums paid	6 years

Premium payable period 20 years

Paid-up value $\frac{6 \times 20{,}000}{20} = 6000$

In case of with profits policy the vested bonus is added to ₹ 6000.

The rate of bonus per thousand sum-assured for valuation as on 31-3-2001, 31-3-2003 and 31-3-2005 being ₹ 20, ₹ 25 and ₹ 26 the total bonus accrued comes to:

(20 × 2) + (25 × 2) + (26 × 2) = ₹ 142 × 20 = ₹ 2840.

Thus, the paid-up value will be:

₹ 6000 + ₹ 2840 = ₹ 8840.

Paid-up value under anticipated endowment assurance. The proportionate paid-up value arrived at as in the case of Endowment Assurance is to be reduced by any Survival Benefit payments made already.

Term Assurance. No paid-up value is allowed under this plan.

Calculation of Surrender Value

Example 1

Information

(i)	Sum assured	₹ 25,00,000
(ii)	Plan and Term of the policy	Endowment for 50 years
(iii)	Type of Policy	Endowment
(iv)	Date of commencement	5-11-2000
(v)	Mode of payment	Quarterly
(vi)	Due date of last premium paid	5-8-2004
(vii)	Vested bonus	Nil
(viii)	Date of calculation of surrender value	10-8-2004

1. Number of years' premium paid

(a) Due date of last premium paid 5-8-2004

(b) Minus-date of commencement of the policy (3 years 9 months) 5-11-2000

Add: Duration corresponding to modes of premium 3 months

(c) One month for monthly mode

3 months for quarterly mode

6 months for half-yearly mode

12 months for yearly mode

(d) Total number of years' premium paid: 4 years.

2. Paid-up value

Paid-up value:

$$= \frac{\text{Number of years' premium paid} \times \text{sum assured}}{\text{Number of years' premium payable}}$$

$$= \frac{4}{50} \times ₹\ 25{,}00{,}000 = ₹\ 2{,}00{,}000.$$

3. Vested Bonus

Assume there is not vested bonus so far.

4. Duration

	Day-Month-Year
(a) Date of calculation of surrender value	10-8-2004
(b) Minus—date of commencement of policy	5-11-2000
	5-9-3
(c) Nearest to half-year	4 years.

5. Surrender Value Factor

(a) For term 50 and duration 4 years

Surrender value factor is: 14.8% under endowment policy

(b) Surrender value:

$$= \frac{\text{Paid-up value (inclusive of vested bonus, if any)} \times \text{S.V. Factor}}{100}$$

$$= \frac{₹2{,}00{,}000 \times 14.8}{100}$$

Surrender value will be = ₹ 29,600.

Example 2

Information

(i) Sum assured ₹ 10 lakh	
(ii) Plan and Term of the policy endowment for 20 years	
(iii) Date of commencement of the policy	10-8-2000
(iv) Mode of payment	Half-yearly
(v) Due date of the last premium paid	10-8-2008
(vi) Vested Bonus	To be calculated
(vii) Date of calculation of surrender value	1-9-2008

1. Number of years' premium paid

	Day-Month-Year
(a) Due date of the last premium paid	10-8-2008
(b) Minus—date of commencement of policy	10-8-2000
	0-0-8
(c) Add: Duration corresponding to half-yearly mode of payment of premium	0-6-0
	0-6-8
(d) Total number of years' premium paid	8½ years

2. Paid-up value

$$\text{Paid-up value} = \frac{\text{Number of years premium paid} \times \text{ sum assured}}{\text{Number of years' premium payable}}$$

$$\text{i.e., } \frac{17}{2} \times \frac{1}{20} \times ₹10{,}00{,}000 = ₹4{,}25{,}000.$$

3. Vested bonuses

(i) Premiums have been paid for 8½ years.

(ii) Therefore bonuses will be added for not more than 8½ years.

Let us assume that bonuses came to ₹ 1,13,200

Vested bonus	₹ 1,13,200
Add: Paid up value of sum assured	4,25,000
Total paid-up value	₹ 5,38,200

4. Duration

Date of calculation of surrender value	1-9-2008
Date of commencement of the policy	10-8-2000
	21-0-8

i.e., 8 years (nearest half-year duration)

5. Surrender value factor

For plan endowment assurance and term 20 years with duration 8 years,

Surrender value factor is 50.8%

$$\text{S.V.} = \frac{5{,}38{,}200 \times 50.8}{100} = ₹2{,}73{,}405.60$$

(Surrender value is rounded up to next higher rupee)

For factor of surrender value, every insurer prepares Surrender Value Booklets from where with reference to "duration" against "Term of Policy", factors can be easily noted down. Duration in the context of surrender value is always nearest to "half-year".

Difference between date of calculation of S.V. and date of commencement of policy	*Duration nearest "half-year"*
(a) 5 years, 2 months and 29 days	5 years
(b) 5 years and 3 months	5½ years
(c) 5 years and 6 months	5½ years
(d) 5 years, 8 months and 29 days	5½ years
(e) 5 years and 9 months	6 years
(f) 6 years, 2 months and 29 days	6 years

Claims. Two types of claims arise in life insurance:

(a) Maturity claims

(b) Death claims

Maturity claims are already known as their maturity date is known. The insurer sends a letter to the policyholder, with a copy to agent, to the insured, called claim intimation letter. The insured has to submit original policy, age proof (if formerly not given), any assignment deed and discharge form sent by insurer duly filled.

If insured is alive on date of maturity, the nominee has no claim. But, if insured died after the date of maturity, but before receiving the amount of claim, the nominee shall receive the claim.

The claim in case of joint life policy on the lives of the response, claim by way of maturity arise in ways:

(a) When both lives survive, maturity claim will be paid to both.

(b) If one of the insured dies within the period of insurance, death claim is paid for the deceased. The second insured who has survived will be paid maturity claim if he survives till the date of maturity.

(c) Under money-back plans, survival benefits are treated as maturity claims because they become due after a particular date.

(d) Under fixed term educational or marriage annuity plan, benefits are payable on maturity date EVEN if the policyholder dies before that date.

In case of death claims, either the nominee or assignee or any nearest relative has to inform the insurer first. A claim form will be filled by the claimant, along with following documents, giving the date, place, and cause of death, policy number and address on which correspondence will be done:

(a) *Certificate of death*. It is issued by municipal committee or corporation or village panchayat or cremation or burial ground authorities. If any of these does not exist, particularly in remote rural areas, then certificate from employer or medical/post mortem report can be submitted. In case of unnatural death copy of F.I.R. and post mortem report will be submitted.

(b) Insurance Policy.

(c) Assignment deed.

(d) Proof of age (if not already given).

(e) Claim form.

(f) Form of discharge of claim.

(g) Proof of title like court order in case there are many claimants or copy of probate or letters of administration in case of a will issued by court or if no will was made by the insured (i.e., he died INTESTATE), then succession certificate issued by court or if the insured was missing for seven years, he is presumed to have died, then order of the court under sections 107 and 108 of India Evidence Act.

In case policy is missing or lost, the insurance company may make payment on the basis of "INDEMNITY BOND" executed by insurer or claimant.

Note that if any installment of premium is due in case of monthly/half-yearly or quarterly premium payment, the amount due will be deducted from the amount of claim. This is because premium is to be paid yearly e.g. if an insured dies after he paid half-yearly premium and half yearly premium is due, then half-year premium due shall be dedicated from the claim (see chapter on 'Protection of Policyholders' Interest deducted).

Types of Life Insurance Contracts

Under Section 2(11) of the Insurance Act, 1938, the following types of life assurance contracts can be made:

(i) Payment of money is assured on death or the happening of any contingency on human life;

(ii) The granting of disability and double or triple indemnity accident benefit;

(iii) Granting of annuities upon human life; and

(iv) Granting of superannuation and annuities.

Types of Life Insurance Contracts:

1. Own life insurance contract.
2. Joint life contract.
3. Other life insurance contract.
4. Immediate/Deferred Annuity contract.
5. Superannuation contract.
6. Annuity with/without life cover contract.
7. Keyman Insurance contract.
8. Employer-employee Insurance.

Basic Policies. There are two types of Basic Policies:

1. Pure assurance
2. Term assurance

1. Pure Assurance. The sum assured is payable if the life assured survives the selected term. On death nothing is payable.

This policy is given to those who do not have any dependants and need money only for old age. It is also given to some substandard lives who because of medical reasons are not acceptable for ordinary plans.

2. Term Assurance. The sum assured is payable only if death occurs during the selected period. On survival nothing is payable.

Combination of two basic policies. All other plans of life assurance are combination of the above two plans with certain variations as warranted by the benefits envisaged under a particular policy. They can be divided into:

1. Individual Plans
2. Group Plans.

Types of Life Insurance Policies

Based on the definition of life insurance contract under Section 2(13B) of the Insurance Act 1938 and classification of life insurance business under IRDA regulations. Following are various types of life insurance policies:

(1) Traditional Policy and unit linked plan policy.

(2) (a) Individual policies: (i) Whole life assurance, (ii) Term Assurance, (iii) Endowment Assurance—Limited payment, Anticipated, Double or Triple cover endowment, (iv) Joint life assurance.

(b) Group policies: (i) Superannuation plan, (ii) Term plan, (iii) Gratuity plan, (iv) Savings or employees linked Insurance scheme.

(3) With profit (Par) or without profit (Non-Participating) policies.

(4) Annuities: (i) Immediate, (ii) Deferred, and (iii) Guaranteed.

Policies for special category of people:

(a) Policies for children.

(b) Policies for elderly persons.

(c) Policies for women.

(d) Policies for Physically/Mentally handicapped persons.

Traditional Policy

Traditional policy is that in which all benefits including sum-assured and premium are expressed in rupees. It does not take care of inflation, which, by the time policy matures, has already reduced the monetary worth of the benefits as compared to the greater worth of the premium paid under the policy.

The policyholder has no control or choice over where investments will be made by insurer. There are six types of such policies—endowment plan, money-back plan, whole life plan, pension plan, children's plan and term plan.

Unit Linked Policy. In Unit Linked Policy, the sum assured is expressed in units whose price is linked to an inflation related index. So, the price of units keep on fluctuating with the rise or fall of the index.

The benefits are also paid in units which when expressed in its prevailing price on the date of payment of claim, protect the life assured against inflation. The policyholder has many choices based on different combinations of equity debt and cash. The regulation relating to ULIP by IRDA and different types of ULIPS are given in next chapter.

Individual and Group Policies

Individual policy. Individual policy means granting life assurance cover/protection to one individual or joint lives, i.e., two individuals such as husband and wife. Under such policies risk is assessed on individual basis who is in fact the subject-matter of the contract of assurance. Every policy forms a separate contract.

These are also called "conventional policies".

Individual Plans

(A) Whole Life Assurance. Under this plan, the sum assured is payable only on the death of the life assured. The premium under this policy is the lowest of all the other plans and is payable till death. IRDA has fixed minimum death cover at 10 times of annualized premium. It is an ideal policy for a young man with meagre income whose family and growing children need maximum financial security. There are no survival benefits and the final payment to the nominee on death of the insured. It may be of two types.

(a) Limited payment whole life assurance. Under this plan premiums are payable for a limited number of years, chosen by the life assured. However, sum assured is payable on death only. This plan is suitable for persons in whose case the need for money would arise only on death and whose do not want to extend the premium paying period beyond their earning years, or just want to be free from the worry of paying premium within shortest possible time because they feel that perhaps financial going may not remain so good beyond a certain period.

(b) Convertible whole life. The policy begins as a whole life but the life assured has the option to convert it into an Endowment Plan, after a lapse of say five or six years. This plan is suitable for young men whose present income may not justify an Endowment Policy but has the chances of earning more after some years.

(B) Endowment Assurances. This is taken for a specified period whereunder sum assured is payable on expiry of the specified period (maturity) or earlier death. Premiums are normally payable throughout the term of the policy or till the prior death of the life assured.

This policy provides security to family in case of death and accumulated savings as succour for old age.

(i) Limited payment endowment assurance. It differs from the endowment in one respect that premiums are payable for a shorter duration than the maturity period.

(ii) Anticipated endowment or money-back plans. It is a modified endowment assurance plan under which sum assured is paid in three or four periodic installments on the survival of the life assured till the end of each term of four or five years. The periodic installment is fixed at 15% or 20% of the sum assured and balance with bonuses is paid at maturity. The added advantage is that in the event of death of the life assured at any time during the term full sum assured is payable irrespective of the periodical payment or payments if made earlier.

(iii) Double endowment. It may take two forms:

(i) Basic sum assured if assured dies during the term of the policy, and

(ii) Double the sum assured on maturity of policy.

In the plans savings component is more than the risk element and premia are payable for the full term or earlier death of the life assured.

(iv) Triple cover endowment plan. It is an endowment plan which provides:

(i) Thrice of the basic sum assured in the event of death before maturity.

(ii) Sum assured on maturity.

These are generally without Profits Plans and ideal for collateral security housing loans.

(C) Pure Term or Temporary Assurance Plan. These policies are taken for short period such as six months to five or six years. Sum assured is payable ONLY in the event of death occurring during the term of the plan.

Insurance element is very high whereas savings component is nil because money is not returned if no death occurs. These are always without Profits Plan.

These policies are popular for foreign travel for a short period of three-six months or so.

Term plan can be combined with accidental death and disability, hospital and surgical care by paying extra premium.

Decreasing temporary assurance. It is a policy in which:

(i) Usually premium is payable in a lump sum or limited to one-half of the term of the policy.

(ii) Sum assured payable at death within the term of policy decreases every year.

(iii) Suitable to secure housing loan which gets also reduced every year.

Mortgage redemption assurance policy plan is a policy which ensures that all his outstanding loans and debts are automatically paid-up in the event of his death. Such policies are issued to persons of less than 50 years of age, but will not cover beyond 65 years. The policy has no surrender value. It is a type of term assurance usually to cover home loan payment. The home is mortgaged with any bank and it is redeemed over a number of years. This policy help in mortgage redemption.

Joint life plan. This is usually an endowment plan whereunder a single policy is issued on two lives, such as:

(a) Husband and wife.

(b) Business partners.

(c) Two children.

In all respects, it is an endowment assurance plan under which premium is payable for the full term or till the earlier death of one of the life assured.

Partnerships contain a clause whereby a partner has the option to pay off the amount to the heirs of another partner on his death and take his share. This policy is very suitable for partnership firms.

Interest sensitive plans. Sometimes an insurer would float plans of assurance which: (i) provides for guaranteed "additions" to the sum assured every year, say, ₹ "X" per thousand sum assured every year, or (ii) Guarantees a certain fixed rate of interest in determining the amount of annuity.

In giving such type of guaranteed benefits, the insurer takes a calculated risk because financial market may not enable the insurer to sustain high returns on its investments. In such situations old plans are withdrawn and replaced by new ones.

Group policies. Group policies are the plans of insurance which are offered to groups of individuals. These differ from individual assurance in the following way:

Group is considered as a unit for assessing the risk. Therefore, the group should be:

(a) Homogeneous belonging to an organisation or a profession.

(b) There is regular inflow of new members in the group.

(c) Group is not formed merely to take insurance rather group insurance is incidental to the group.

(d) A fairly representative group is formed when over 75% of the existing members join the scheme with the condition that all future incoming members must join the scheme.

Guidelines on Group Insurance Policies

Group Insurance constitutes an important activity of insurance business and the schemes offered by the insurance companies provide certain classes of individuals, the advantage of a beneficial coverage at a moderate cost. The tremendous growth of the economy and the consequential growth of the organised sector lead the insurers to play a decisive role in designing various group insurance schemes. Most of the Group Insurance Schemes pertain to employer-employee groups, but Group Insurance is also being sold to organisations where there is some commonality of interest. There are various aspects that are connected with group insurance, e.g., what shall constitute a "group" in the context of group insurance, the market conduct that is supposed to be adopted by the insurers in canvassing group insurance schemes and setting up administration standards for group schemes. With a view to rationalize the approach to be adopted by insurers in dealing with various groups the following guidelines are being issued under Section 34 of Insurance Act, 1938 to be adhered to by all the insurers.

A: Definition of a Group

1. A group should consist of persons who assemble together with a commonality of purpose or engaging in a common economic activity like employees of a company. Non-employer-employee groups, like employee welfare associations, holders of credit cards issued by a specific company, customers of a particular business where insurance is offered as an add on benefit, borrowers of a bank, professional associations or societies may also be treated as a group provided the president/secretary/manager/group organizer in his capacity as organizer of the group has an authority from majority of the members of the group to arrange insurance on their behalf or is doing so as part of a necessary security for other matters such as a bank on the life of borrowers. For employer-employee groups the scheme may be either contributory or non-contributory and there will be no limit to employer contribution. Where an insurer is not clear whether a particular group insurance proposal can qualify as per these guidelines, the insurer may refer the matter to IRDA with facts of the case for clarification.
2. No group should be formed with the main purpose of availing insurance. There should be a clearly evident relationship between the member and the group manager for services

other than insurance. While a homogeneous group of persons may decide to buy a group insurance policy to achieve saving in cost, a person negotiating "group" rates and then going round finding members to insure will not be considered as a legitimate group.

3. While it is not proposed to prescribe the minimum size of a group through these guidelines, it is expected that insurers will exercise prudence in requiring a minimum group size. However, different criteria may apply to micro-insurance groups.
4. Though entry into or exit from the group may go on continuously, entry into the group insurance policy for individual members will be either from a well-defined date such as the next anniversary of the policy or from the first of the following month or from a clearly identifiable even other than merely joining the group, such as date of commencement of employment or date of sanction of a loan, etc. subject to payment of premium in time. Insurance will, however cease as soon as a member leaves the group except where it is agreed in advance to continue the benefit even after the member leaves the group, such as in case of an employee who retires. In case of travel-created insurance, insurance may attach from the date of the travel subsequent to acceptance of risk and receipt of the premium.

B: Marketing of Group Insurance

1. An insurer may sell group insurance policies either directly or through an insurance agent or insurance intermediary.
2. An insurer shall not enter into any memorandum of understanding or marketing arrangement, or referral arrangement or any similar arrangement, howsoever described, for sale of insurance products with any person or entity not licensed under the Insurance Act. Any existing arrangement that is not in compliance with these guidelines should be terminated forthwith. However, this should not prejudice transactions up to the effective date of termination so long as it is not in violation of the provisions of the Insurance Act or Regulations. The IRDA may relax this condition in case of sale of micro-insurance products either on a case to case basis or through a regulation on micro-insurance. This does not affect any arrangement made by the insurer with the group organizer or manager with regard to administration of the group insurance so long as there is no payment or reimbursement of expenses other than the commission that is legally payable.
3. An insurer who is using corporate agents for sale of its products shall require the corporate agent to file certificates at least once a year, from an independent auditor at the expense of the corporate agent, confirming compliance by that corporate agent with Section 64VB relating to collection and credit of premium, IRDA (Insurance Advertisements and Disclosures) Regulations, 2000, IRDA (Protection of Policyholders' Interests) Regulations, 2002 and Sections 40A and 40G of the Insurance Act, 1938.

C: Group Insurance Administration

1. The premium charged and benefits admissible to each member of the group shall be clearly specified in the group policy and the administrator group manager shall not have the liberty to vary the premium or benefits with regard to the individual members unless the same is a part of the change in the policy benefits and conditions by the insurance company or is made in accordance with a predetermined basis of determining the sum

insured such as the outstanding loan amount. In any case, such changes should be agreed to by the insurer.

2. Group discounts on premium are given for the benefit of the insured members of the group and should not be appropriated as additional remuneration by the agent or corporate agent or broker or group organiser or manager. Such discounts should be based on valid underwriting considerations such as the group size and shall be passed on to the members. Where a part or whole of the premium is paid by the group organiser, for example, the employer in respect of insurance of his employees, the discounts may be shared by those who paid the premium in proportion to the premium paid by them.
3. The commission paid to the agent or corporate agent in respect of a group insurance policy shall not exceed the percentage approved by IRDA or as specified in the Insurance Act, 1938 read with the IRDA Act, 1999 and Regulations framed thereunder. Insurer will pay commission at a predetermined and published rate and should not indulge in determination of commission rate on a case-to-case basis.
4. There shall be no other payment whether as management expenses or documentation expenses or profit commission or bulk discount or payment of any other description, to the agent or corporate agent or group organizer or group manager. The group manager should be specifically prohibited from collecting by way of premium from the members of a group, any amount higher than the amount charged by or paid to the insurer for such insurance. If the group manager wishes to collect a service charge from the members to cover his costs, he should clearly disclose it as an additional cost and not as premium, in his communications to his members.
5. There shall attach to each group insurance policy, a complete list of the persons insured thereunder. Where this is not feasible, in view of the large size of the group, a clear reference shall be made to a list maintained in the books of the group organiser or manager that cannot be subsequently manipulated, as being the list of persons insured.
6. Where an employer buys a group insurance policy as a service benefit for its employees and pays the premium in full or in part, the employer may be treated as the policyholder with the employees being treated as the beneficiaries. In such cases, the employer may issue confirmation of insurance protection to individual employees with clear reference to the group insurance policy and the benefits secured thereby. In respect of such group policies, the claims of individual persons insured thereunder may be processed through the employer.
7. In non-employer-employee cases, the individual group member would be treated as the insured beneficiary and the group organiser will be only the holder of the group policy. In such cases, every care should be taken by the insurer in the matter of issue of certificate of insurance to the members of the group, who are truly the insured. It is necessary that such certificate contains information on the schedule of benefits, the premium charged and important terms and conditions of the insurance contract. The certificate shall also state the procedure to be followed to register a claim with the insurer including the full address of the office of the insurer where the claim should be registered. While the group organiser or manager may play a role in facilitating the registering and settlement

of a claim, the insurer is totally responsible to ensure that the claim payment is made in the name of the insured member even if the cheque is sent to the group manager for administrative convenience.

8. For operational convenience, in respect of non-employer-employee groups the insurer may provide the facility to the group organiser or manager to issue certificates of insurance to persons insured under the group, provided the underwriting guidelines for acceptance or rejection of such a risk do not require use of subjective judgement and can be easily programmed into a computer that will review acceptance and print the certificate of insurance. In such cases, the certificate forms shall be supplied by the insurer with in-built security features and in pre-numbered lots to the group organiser or manager. Utilisation and full accounting of the certificate forms should be independently checked by the staff of the insurer every time before furnishing a fresh lot of forms, either by personal verification or based on a certificate by the auditor of the agent.
9. Under any circumstances the insurer will be responsible for the certificate of insurance issued by a group organiser or administrator, in certificate forms provided by the insurer.
10. The insurer shall remain responsible to ensure that all sales material and prospectus of the insurance planned are properly drawn up and comply with the Regulations on Insurance Advertisements and Disclosures and on Protection of Policyholders Interests.
11. The insurer shall conduct a surprise inspection of the books and records of the group organiser or manager at least once a year to ensure total compliance with these guidelines or require a certificate of such compliance from the auditors of the group organiser or manager, at least once a year.
12. The insurer shall be held responsible to the persons insured, in respect of the group policy in case of failure of the group organiser or manager to account for the business to the insurer, if the person insured can prove that.

Group Schemes

Group insurance schemes offer life insurance shield to employees of a corporate sector and partnership firms or professionals and people from economically weaker section.

1. Group superannuation plan. This plan allows employer and an employee to make a certain fixed regular contribution to a fund. The accumulated amount is utilised to provide various benefits on employee's retirement, death or on withdrawal.

ICICI Prudential's superannuation scheme offers retirement benefits for each member of the group. The employees also have an option of choosing from various annuity options or opting for a partial commutation of the annuity at the time of retirement.

2. Group term plan. This plan provides for life cover to members of a group. The benefit is paid to the beneficiary nominated by the member on death.

This Term Plan which gives employers the option of providing in insurance cover for their employees at a very affordable cost. It has got riders like accidental death, dismemberment, critical illness along options to cover spouse and also an option to convert plan to an individual policy. The premium may be deducted from the salary or from the contribution of Provident Fund of the employee. Former is called "Savings linked" and latter "employees deposit linked" Scheme.

3. Group gratuity plan. This plan helps the employers to fund their statutory obligation under payment of Gratuity Act. Each member is under an obligation to pay half month salary for every completed year of service to each of his employees on their exist. At the end of the accumulation period, the policyholder has an option to choose pension for self only or pension for self and spouse.

Most of the private sector companies are offering customized gratuity plans to employers to structure schemes, which would provide benefits beyond the statutory obligations.

With Profit Policies or Participating Policies

These are the policies which participate in the profits (surplus) of the insurer and are entitled for bonus allocation (additions) after every valuation. The IRDA has renamed these policies as "Par Policies" or "Policies with participation in profits".

Non-participating/without profits/non-par/policies without participation in profits. These policies are not entitled for any share in the surplus (profits) during the term of the policy.

The premium under the "Par policies" are higher than that under the "Non-par policies" since extra is charged while making the premium structure.

Sources of surplus. There are four sources of surplus:

(i) **Interest.** Excess of interest earned by the insurer over the assumed rate in calculation of premium contributes towards surplus. It shows sound investment policy.

(ii) **Mortality.** If the mortality actually experienced is less than that assumed at the time of calculation of premium, there is addition to surplus.

(iii) **Loading of office expenses.** Better management results in lesser office expenses than those assumed.

(iv) **Other sources.** Surrender, lapses, alterations, etc., also contribute towards surplus.

Bonus system. Divisible profit is allotted to the various types of policies in proportion to individuals' contribution to the surplus. The distribution is made in cash to be applied to reduce the premiums.

Simple and compound reversionary bonus. The bonus is allotted as a uniform percentage addition to the sum assured or sum assured plus existing bonus addition, and is payable along with the sum assured in terms of the policies conditions. If the bonus is allotted on the sum assured alone, it is termed as a "Simple Reversionary Bonus"; if on the sum assured and existing bonus, as "Compound Reversionary Bonus". In India, we apply, at present, the "Simple Reversionary Bonus" system. Bonus paid on maturity of a policy is called "Terminal Bonus".

Interim bonus. This is not a method of distribution of surplus in the usual sense. Bonuses are allotted only after a valuation made and if it discloses a surplus available for distribution.

A valuation has to made every year under law. Policies which result into claims by death or maturity between two valuation dates also contribute to the surplus, although it is disclosed only in the valuation made after their exit. As these policies have gone out of the books before the valuation date, they will not participate in the valuation. However, insurance companies pay as "interim bonus" to such policies at the rates as per the last valuation. In India, the payment of interim bonus is made mandatory under Section 112 of the Insurance Act, 1938.

Under non-reversionary method, an insurance company may pay bonus in cash or allow to adjust in future payment of premium or to buy term insurance or to buy paid up additional insurance or leave it as a deposit with the company for a particular period or till-attainment of a fixed age. The last option is called 'TONTINE' method.

Annuities

Annuities provide regular periodic payments for a period which is contingent upon the duration of human life. The considerations for this type of plans are either:

(i) lump sum or

(ii) regular payments spread over a specified number of years.

Annuities, under law, are treated at par with subscription to the National Pension Scheme.

These are, broadly, three types of Annuity Plans:

(a) Immediate annuity. It provides a fixed annual income so long as the annuitant (purchaser) is alive in consideration of a lump sum premium amount. This is a good investment for a retiring employee who gets a safer avenue for conversation of his capital and also gets regular income.

The total of the annuity instalment receivable in a year is subject to income-tax.

(b) Deferred annuities

(i) Annuity payment starts after some fixed period called deferment period and continues till the death of the annuitant.

(ii) Consideration is paid in lump sum or in regular premium installments during the deferment period.

(iii) If the purchaser dies during the deferment period, purchase price is returned.

(iv) It is often opted by the annuitant to make the annuity payments certain for a fixed number of years so that even payments if the annuitant were to die earlier, the annuity for the balance period shall continue to be paid.

(v) It is often opted by the annuitant to make the annuity payments certain for a fixed number of years so that even if the annuitant were to die earlier, the annuity for the balance period shall continue to be paid.

They are most popular in insurance market.

(c) Guaranteed or certain annuities. Some persons do not like to risk the whole of the purchase price and would like that a portion thereof be returned in case of early death. This can be secured by purchasing an annuity, guaranteed for a certain number of years, and payable thereafter for life.

It is an improvement upon deferred annuity.

Every instalment of annuity is composed of the return of capital and partly of interest premium for annuity may be paid in lump sum or periodically.

Interest portion of the annuity is therefore liable to income-tax payment.

Monthly Income Plans

Most monthly or regular income plans with a limited premium paying period after which the payment begins. Premium is based on monthly income wanted. If the insured dies before the premium paying period ends, dependants receive monthly income from the anniversary following the date of death till the end of payout term. If death occurs after the premium paying term, payouts will be as per schedule. This policy secures one's future financial needs. The entry age varies from 18 to 25 years to 55 or 65 years. The usual monthly income ranges from ₹ 1000 to 2000. Premium payment term varies from 15 years to 25 years and monthly income payout periods 8 to 15 years. Met Life, Bharti AXA and Max New York Life Insurance monthly income plans are popular. It is a type of endowment plan.

Pension Scheme: Regular Income after Retirement

In fact, the entry of private sector insurance companies have not only increased the awareness for saving for retirement, but also flooded the market with innovative products.

A pension provides a regular income for a life after a specified period. The amount of pension varies depending upon the contribution made by a person every year or a single premium.

Pension Fund Regulatory and Development Authority has launched national pension scheme. Besides tax benefit under Section 80CCD(2), one can withdraw for marriage up to 60% of the fund. It has a fund called 'Life cycle fund'. The asset allocation i.e. equity debt ratio is as follows:

Age	Equity	debt	Age	Equity	debt
up to 35 years	50%	50%	up to 50 years	20%	80%
up to 40 years	40%	60%	up to 60 years	10%	90%
up to 45 years	30%	70%			

Under National Pension Scheme the accumulated savings are invested when employee retires. IRDA has laid down that employee has to purchase an annuity with 60% of accumulated savings. Annuity policies are treated at par with subscriptions to NPS.

The **unit linked pension plan** works like a mutual fund in the manner of investment in equity and debt in the market, while under the participating model, the premium is deposited in the personal accumulation account from where the head office expenses, mortality contribution, etc. are deducted and the balance is invested in various financial instruments. IRDA has laid down 4.5% minimum return compulsory on all pension products. Stringent conditions by IRDA have been put on ULIP pension plans as they were sold under pension plans whereas they were mutual fund schemes.

Benefits

There is a death benefit attached to almost every pension policy. In case the policyholder dies before reaching retirement date, the nominee gets the life cover sum assured.

Some pension schemes also have an option to cover critical illness and accidental death and dismemberment along with life cover.

Cash surrender benefit in between the plan period, but no minimum guaranteed returns.

On retirement, the policyholder becomes entitled to the sum assured along with bonus. The policyholder also has an option to take out a part of his accumulated amount in cash, while the balance gets converted to an annuity, which provides pension to him for the rest of his life.

Risk Factors

Like mutual fund schemes, the value of a pension scheme is unit linked and could go up or down depending upon the market condition especially the equity as well as debt market.

Tax Benefits

The pension schemes are eligible for exemption under Section 80CCC of the Income Tax Act up to a maximum of ₹ 1,00,000 per annum.

The lump sum money at the time of the maturity of death is also exempt from income tax under Section 10 (10D).

Policies for Children

These policies are meant for various needs of children such as education, marriage, start in life and security of life assurance at an early age. These policies are of two types:

(i) On the life of child, or

(ii) On the life of the parent of the child and for the benefits of the child.

Many variations of such policies are available e.g. AEGON Religare Life insurance offers "Rising Star Plan" which allows to invest premium in a mutual fund. AVIVA offers 'young scholar advantage' covering parents death, funds investment and any eventuality.

Some of these policies are discussed below:

Children's Deferred Assurances

(i) This policy is taken on the life of child and father is the proposer and financier.

(ii) Risk on the life of child commences from the age 18 to 22 years. It is called the vesting age.

(iii) The period from commencement of policy to the vesting date is called deferment period. If child dies during the deferment period, premiums paid are refunded.

(iv) A premium waiver benefit is also allowed against payment of an additional premium whereby future premiums are waived if the proposer present dies during the deferment period.

(v) On commencement of risk on the life of child, policy continues as Endowment Assurance whereunder all benefits have vested in the child.

This plan is more comprehensive as it is not specific to one purpose of marriage or education. The child begins his life with security of life assurance at the comparatively cheap rates.

Children Anticipated (Money-back) Plan. Nowadays, these policies are also issued whereunder after vesting in the child, the policy operates as a Money-back Policy.

Fixed Term (Marriage) Endowment and Educational Annuity Plans

(i) Policy is on the life of father who pays the premium till maturity or earlier death.

(ii) Child is named as a beneficiary.

(iii) In the event of death of the father or maturity of the policy, benefits remain intact.

(a) In marriage endowment sum assured is paid in lump sum at the maturity date of the policy.

(b) Under educational annuity plan, the sum assured is paid in 10 half-yearly installments which is usually the period for receiving higher education.

"ChildGain" Plan

Common features of "ChildGain" Plan:

1. Limited Premium Payment Term which means that the premiums are payable till the child attains 18 years of age.
2. The contributions grow by the way of compounded annual bonuses, which will be paid with the first guaranteed payout (policy anniversary following age 18 of the child), for in-force policies, in addition to the annual bonuses, a terminal bonus may also be paid.
3. One are also eligible for Tax Benefits under Section 88 and Section 10 (10D) of the Income Tax Act.

In-Built Benefits

(a) **Premium waiver benefit.** In case of death or Accidental Total Permanent Disability of the policyholder during the premium payment term, all future premium payments are waived. This benefit will not be available in the event of accidental permanent total disability after age 65 of the policyholder.

(b) **Family income benefit.** In case of death or accidental total permanent disability of the policyholder during the term of the policy, a monthly income benefit of 1% of the sum assured (12% per annum) subject to a maximum of ₹ 10,000 p.m. becomes payable till the end of the policy term. This benefit will not be available in the event of accidental permanent total disability after age 65 of the policyholder.

4. **Option to purchase further insurance at maturity.** For ensuring continuity of the valuable insurance protection that the child was enjoying, the offer is to the child an option to purchase a with-profits endowment or an equivalent plan from the insurance company for twice the amount of face value of this policy, without any medical examination, on the premium rates prevailing at that time (the application must be made at least six months prior to maturity of this policy).

Payout Structures

Under one option the minimum guaranteed payouts are as follows:

Policy Anniversary following completion of Age	18	19	20	21
Payment as % of Sum Assured	20% + Accrued Bonuses	25%	25%	35%

Under second option the minimum guaranteed payouts are as follows:

Policy Anniversary following completion of Age	18	20	22	24
Payment as % of Sum Assured	25% + Accrued Bonuses	25%	25%	40%

Start of Life Benefit

Unique Feature of "ChildGain". These packages offer the choice of providing a unique Start of Life Benefit for child. For a nominal amount, an additional Sum Assured subject to a maximum limit of ₹ 10 lakhs will become payable to enable the child start his/her professional life smoothly, in case of an unfortunate death or Accidental Permanent Total Disability of the policyholder during the term of the policy. This benefit will not be available in the event of accidental permanent total disability after age 65 of the policyholder.

Death Payout. In the event of unfortunate death of the child during the policy term, the payouts shall be as under:

Age	Payout
Below 7 years	Premiums paid will be refunded without interest and the policy will terminate.
Above 7 and below 18 years	Sum assured with accrued bonuses will be paid and the policy will terminate.
Above 18 and below 24 years	Outstanding payouts will be paid as one lump sum and the policy will terminate.

Important Details of "ChildGain" Solutions

Eligibility Conditions	ChildGain 21 and ChildGain 21 Plus	ChildGain 24 and ChildGain 24 plus
Minimum age of policyholder	20	20
Maximum age of policyholder	50	50
Minimum age of child	0	0
Maximum age of child	13	13
Minimum Premium Payment Term	5	5
Maximum Premium Payment Term	18	18
Maximum Policy Term	21 less age at entry of Child	24 less age at entry of Child
Maximum age of child at maturity	21	24
Minimum Sum Assured	₹ 1,00,000	₹ 1,00,000
Maximum Sum Assured	₹ 50,00,000	₹ 50,00,000

Minimum Premium — Minimum Premium ₹ 5000 for yearly mode, ₹ 2500 for half-year mode, ₹ 2000 for quarterly mode and ₹ 700 for monthly mode.

(Monthly mode available under salary deduction scheme only and minimum proposal should be ₹ 2100 i.e., three months payment in advance.)

Age = Age on last birthday. The Policy Term + Age of policyholder should not exceed 70 years for all plans.

Loans

Loans are not available with "ChildGain" Plan.

Exclusions

The Death Cover is subject to the following exclusion:

Suicide within one year from commencement of risk, whether sane or not.

Note 1:

Prohibition of Rebate. Section 41 of the Insurance Act, 1938 states:

1. No person shall allow or offer to allow, either directly or indirectly, as an inducement to any person to take out or renew or continue an insurance in respect of any kind of risk relating to lives or property in India, any rebate of the whole or part of the commission payable or any rebate of the premium shown on the policy, nor shall any person taking out or renewing or continuing a policy accept any rebate, except such rebate as may be allowed in accordance with the published prospectuses or table of the insurer.
2. Any person making default in complying with the provision of this section shall be punishable with a fine that may extend to five hundred rupees.

Note 2:

Section 45. No policy of life insurance effected after the coming into force of this Act shall, after the expiry of two years from the date on which it was effected, be called in question by an insurer on the ground that a statement made in the proposal for insurance or in any report of a medical officer, or referee, or friend of the insured, or in any other document leading to the issue of the policy, was inaccurate or false, unless the insurer shows that such statement was on a material matter or suppressed facts which it was material to disclose and that it was fraudulently made by the policyholder and that the policyholder knew at the time of making it that the statement was false or that it suppressed facts which it was material to disclose.

Policies for Women

LIC has offered following policies for women:

"Jeevan Saathi" (Life-Partners Plan)—Joint Life Plan:

(i) Both husband and wife are covered under this endowment type policy.

(ii) Benefits:

(a) on maturity if both are alive, full sum assured with bonus is paid,

(b) on the death of one of lives assured during the term of the policy, basic sum assured is paid to the surviving partner who is not required to pay the future premium,

(c) the surviving partner remains covered for full sum assured. If he also dies before the maturity date, against sum assured is paid to the nominee,

(d) the surviving partner will be paid sum assured with bonuses if he survives on the maturity date.

"*Jeevan Sukanya*":

(i) Only female children between age 1 and 12 years are given this plan.

(ii) Risk on the life of child starts not before the age of seven or two years after taking the policy, whichever is later.

(iii) Husband is automatically covered under the policy after marriage.

(iv) Premium paying period is 20 years minus age at entry.

(a) On surviving the age of 20, the (life) assured receives sum assured as survival benefit, and

(b) Policy continues to cover the (life) assured till maturity date when vested bonuses will be paid only. If life assured dies before maturity, sum assured with bonuses will be paid.

(v) If husband dies before maturity date, pre-deceasing wife (life assured) sum assessed alone is payable to the wife. The risk on husband's life ceases on the death of the life assured.

"Jeevan Sneha"

This policy is exclusively issued to women and includes the features of money-back policy, annuity options and flexibility in premium payment. The summary of the plan is as under:

(i) Eligibility—All females' lives between the ages 18 years (completed) and 50 years are covered under the policy.

(ii) Benefits-Survival Benefits:

20% of sum assured at the end of 5 years

20% of sum assured at the end of 10 years

20% of sum assured at the end of 15 years

40% of sum assured together with accrued guaranteed additions and loyalty additions, if any, at the end of 20 years.

(iii) Special Benefits:

(a) Encashment of survival benefit as and when needed, corpus earns interest @ 11%.

(b) Free insurance cover for full sum assured will continue for three years from the due date of first unpaid premium, provided at least two years' premiums have been paid.

(c) Accident benefit of the period of extended cover of three years also without any extra premium.

(d) *Flexibility in Premium Payment*—The policyholder will have the flexibility to pay the next yearly premiums in advance and will be eligible for a premium rebate of 10% per annum.

(e) Pregnancy and child birth risk covered.

(f) Option for annuity in lieu of maturity proceeds.

(iv) *Term*—The policy is for a fixed term of 20 years.

(v) *Miscellaneous*:

1. Sum assured ₹ 25,000

₹ 50,000, thereafter in multiple of ₹ 50,000 subject to a maximum of ₹ 5,00,000.

2. Minimum age at entry 18 years (completed)
3. Maximum age at entry 50 years
4. Maximum age at maturity 70 years
5. Mode of payment Yearly only

Under Sections 5 and 6 of Married Women's Property Act, 1874 (MWPA), any married woman may effect a policy of insurance on her own behalf and independently of her husband (Section 5). A policy of life insurance effected by any married man on his own life for the benefit of his wife and/or children stall be deemed to be a trust or policy bond. Note that two or more persons named as beneficences jointly or to the survivor or survivors of them and wife and children as a class not allowed to be proposed by a Muslim. Named as a class means not named in the policy. In case of non-Muslims wife and children as beneficences as a class is allowed. Under the Act, the policy is a simple method to make a settlement for dependents, no need of settlement is needed and even creditors of the policy have no claim against the policy. Under the Act, joint life and children deferred plans are not allowed. The life assured is authorised to appoint trustees to manage the trust money secured by the policy.

Policies for Physically/Mentally Handicapped Persons

There is now greater awareness about the welfare of this class of handicapped lives who are generally dependent on their parents. Therefore, a need has been felt to provide for these handicapped lives after the parent dies or becomes old enough to support them.

There are at present two policies introduced by LIC of India. These are discussed below:

"Jeevan Aadhar"

Under the plan an individual or a member of HUF, can take an assurance on his/her own life to provide for payment of a lump sum and an annuity to the handicapped dependent or a trust created for the benefit of the child:

(i) *Term of Assurance and Premium Paying Term*—This is whole life plan, premiums under which are payable for chosen premium term or till death of the life assured.

(ii) *Notional Sum Assured*—The notional sum assured will comprise three components viz.: (i) Basic sum assured, (ii) Guaranteed additions, and (iii) Terminal addition.

(iii) *Manner of Payment of Benefits*—Twenty per cent of the notional sum assured [as defined in (ii) above] will be paid in lump sum and the balance eighty per cent will be utilised to provide an annuity certain for 15 years and life thereafter on the life of the handicapped dependant.

(iv) *Special Provisions*—In the event of handicapped dependant predeceasing the life assured during the term of the policy, the contract, ceases and the life assured will receive refund of premiums paid.

(v) *Other Conditions*:

(a) Minimum sum assured: ₹ 50,000

(b) Mode of Payment of Premium: Yearly, half-yearly, quarterly, monthly, and monthly (SSS).

(c) Minimum age at entry: 22 years

(d) Maximum age at entry: 60 years

(e) Maximum Premium Ceasing Age: 70 years

(f) No surrender value or loan will be allowed under this plan.

(g) Contributions under this plan are eligible for income-tax relief under section 80DD of the Income-tax Act.

"Jeevan Vishwas"

This plan is an endowment securing cover for the parent and annuity for the dependent handicapped child.

Benefits:

(a) *Maturity Benefit*. Basic sum assured together with accrued guaranteed additions and loyalty addition, are payable on the life assured (parent) surviving the date of maturity of the policy.

(b) *Payment on Death*. On death of the life assured during the term of the policy, basic sum assured together with accrued guaranteed additions and loyalty additions, will be payable.

Manner of Benefit Payment. Twenty per cent of the total of the basic sum assured with accrued guaranteed additions and loyalty addition, if any, will be paid in a lump sum. The remaining eighty per cent will compulsorily be utilized to provide an immediate regular income to the handicapped dependant payable as per the chosen mode. The regular income will be at the rates prevailing at the time of claim. The following are the regular income options under the plan:

(i) Regular income for life.

(ii) Regular income for 5, 10 or 15 years and life thereafter.

(iii) Other features:

Eligibility	Age limit of proposer 20-65 years
Term	10 to 40 years
Premium paying term	10 to 25 years
Sum assured	Minimum of ₹ 50,000 and in multiples of ₹ 25,000 thereafter
Frequency of premium payment	Yearly, Half-yearly, Single Premium

Jan Suraksha (Social Security Schemes)

On 9 May 2015, three social security schemes were announced by Central Government. They are:

(1) PRADHAN MANTRI SURAKSHA YOJNA

(2) PRADHAN MANTRI JEEVAN JYOTI BIMA YOJNA

(3) ATAL PENSION YOJNA

The two are relating to insurance and pension and the third is to widen the process of the financial inclusion.

(1) *Pradhan Mantri Suraksha Bima Yojna*

(a) Type of Insurance: Accident Insurance.

(b) Insured amount: ₹ 2 lakhs.

(c) Premium: ₹ 12 per annum.

(d) Coverage: Insurance covers death and permanent disability due to accident.

(e) Eligibility: Age between 18 to 70 years for all bank account holders.

(2) *Pradhan Mantri Jeevan Jyoti Bima Yojna*

(a) Type of Insurance: Life Insurance

(b) Insured Amount: ₹ 2 Lakhs.

(c) Premium: ₹ 330 per annum.

(d) Coverage: Life Insurance amount for insured's family after him.

(e) Eligibility: Age between 18 to 50 years for all bank account holders.

To be shared by ICICI, and Prudential Life Insurance Co.

(3) *Atal Pension Yojna*

(a) Type of Insurance: Pension after 60 years of age.

(b) Insured amount: ₹ 1000 to ₹ 5000 per month.

(c) Premium: ₹ 42 to ₹ 210 per month for entry at 18 years.

(d) Coverage: Monthly pension after 60 years of age.

(e) Eligibility: Age between 18 to 40 years for all bank account holders.

Note: The period of Insurance, annual: 1st June to 31st May. The premium will be deducted from account holder's saving bank account through 'auto debit' facility. The person would be eligible to join these schemes through one saving bank account only. All banks, bank mitra and micro insurance agents are authorised to insure as well as insurance companies.

Pradhan Mantri Vaya Vandana Yojna

Exclusively for Senior Citizens

For the welfare of senior citizens of the country, the Government of India has announced a subsidised and attractive pension scheme, with LIC as the exclusive administrator. The features are:

(1) Eligibility: 60 years of age and above.

(2) Single lump sum premium: Minimum ₹ 1,50,000 (for monthly pension) maximum ₹ 7,50,000.

(3) Minimum pension: ₹ 1,000 per month, maximum ₹ 5000 per month.

(4) Assured return of 8% p.a., payable monthly (equivalent to 8.30% p.a.)

(5) Mode of pension payment; monthly, quarterly half yearly, or yearly.

(6) On death of pensioner during policy term of 10 years, beneficiary receive the purchase price.

(7) On Survival: The pensioner at the end of 10 years purchase price along with final pension, pension installment will be paid.

Postal Life Insurance

This policy is issued to those who are (a) between 19 and 50 years as on next birth date of the proponent and (b) are employees of central and state governments and defence services or government, aided educational institutions, universities established by government or all nationalized bank or state and central undertakings or corporations.

It has the advantages of 100% security by G.O.I., easy transfer to any place in India free of cost, rebate of 1% to 2% on payment of 6 to 12 months premier in advance, payment of policy money through any post office in India and centralised accounting for quick and easy settlement of claims. Like other insurance companies offering life insurance, postal life insurance given option of repayment of loan, pass book facility and nomination facility.

Riders, Options and Guarantees

IRDA has brought out Actuarial Report and Abstract Regulations 2000. In its Regulation (2), it defines these terms as under:

(a) Regulation 2(e)—"Guarantees" means the terms in regard to:

(i) benefits, or

(ii) premiums, or

(iii) charges.

Which may not be altered during the currency of the policy.

(b) Regulation 2(k)—"Options" means right available to a policyholder under a policy.

(c) Regulation 2(o)—"Rider" or "Rider benefits" means add-on benefits, which are, in addition to basic benefits under a policy, e.g., accident cover, disability cover, dreaded disease cover.

'*Proviso*'. Clause in the policy bond states that privileges and conditions printed on the back of the policy shall form the part of the policy contract. The privileges can be grouped under three heads:

(1) Policy guarantees,

(2) Policy option,

(3) Policy riders.

These privileges enhance the benefits. But they are subject to some conditions because unchecked or uncontrolled privileges in life insurance contract can work against the insurer. Moreover, the absence of them will make the contract very harsh. Life insurance is a long-time contract and assured may face some genuine difficulties in complying with some conditions such as payment of premium time. Therefore, some relaxations are needed without jeopardizing the interest of the insurer and strict compliance is not imposed.

Guarantees

(i) Day of grace. To show consideration for the unintentional delay in payment of premium on the due date, a grace time is allowed for paying the premium, which is 30 days for yearly, half-yearly and quarterly premiums and 15 days for monthly premiums.

The days of grace means that if premium is paid during the period of grace, no interest or fine is charged, it being presumed that premium has been paid when due. The rule for computation has been that the day upon which the premium becomes due and payable is not to be counted and the following day is the first day of grace.

(ii) Example. Premium due on 3-7-2006—days of grace: 30 days.

1st day of grace will be 4-7-2006.

Last day of grace will be 2-8-2006 (28 + 2 days).

Premium should be paid on before 2-8-2006.

(iii) The practice of granting 'days of grace' has the effect of legality which goes in favour of the life assured.

Residence, travel or occupation. Nowadays, life assurance policies are free from restrictions of travel, occupation or residence. It means that insurer will not question the legality of the policy if assured travels anywhere or follows any profession or resides anywhere after the issue of the policy.

The insurer assesses the risk on the date of acceptance and puts no major restrictions except in some extreme cases where risk increases such as assured joining aviation duties. But here again the approach is very humane and considerate.

War and aviation risks. At present it is a normal practice to grant full cover against war and aviation risk to:

(a) Civilians and army and navy personnel (who are not likely to engage in aviation duties).

(b) Aviation personnel (civilians and service aviators), ground staff having non-technical duties and technical ground staff who are not likely to fly in the course of their duties. Normally, no extra is charged in both the above cases.

(c) Those engaged in aviation duties [other than those in (b) above]:

  (i) are charged extra premium depending upon rank or number of flying hours.

  (ii) in the alternative no extra is charged but cover for war and aviation is excluded.

Guarantees of surrender value and paid-up value. Granting of surrender and paid-up values have been made mandatory as per Section 113 of the Insurance Act and even the method of fixing paid-up value is laid down.

The additional clause in the Act, making it obligatory on the insurer to show the guaranteed surrender value on the policy bond, goes to further safeguard the interest of policyholder.

The guarantees provided with regard to paid-up value and surrender value prevent the insurer from adopting unethical means of frittering away policyholder's money.

Policy Options

As a rule all policies should have regular payment options. But to enhance the benefits for policyholder without in any way harming the interest of the insurer options are:

1. Revival. If the assured is able to tide over his financial problems, he can revive the policy by paying arrears of premium subject to satisfactory health proof. The insurer may give him the option to revive the policy by:

(i) Easy instalment payments, or

(ii) Special scheme where arrears are reduced considerably.

2. Loan. If the difficulty is temporary, he can raise loan under the policy which is 90% of the surrender value. Why one should surrender the policy when for every ₹ 100 surrender value he is able to get ₹ 90 as loan and also keep the death cover intact.

3. Non-forfeiture clause. This clause allows the insured to receive all or a portion of the benefits or a partial refund on the premiums paid, if the insured misses premium payment, causing policy of lapse. Section 50 of Insurance Act lays down that a policyholder must be informed by the insurer within three months of the first un-paid premium of the options available to him unless these are already laid down in the policy.

4. Settlement options. Most of the policies provide for payment of maturity proceeds in a lump sum. It often happens that the claimant desires to conserve the amount in a safe way and also avails of the benefits of the funds. So a good number of options are given by the insurer:

(i) to receive annuity for lifetime, or

(ii) to receive annuity certain for 5, 10, 15 or 25 years and for life thereafter.

(iii) to receive some amount by way of interest or annuity till the funds are exhausted.

In U.S.A., some brokers or life insurance settlement companies purchase the policy from the insured before maturity. An insured may make a settlement either to avoid financial burden like in case of medical treatment or to invest money in a security or real estate e.g., a senior citizen may need money. The former is called "VIATICAL" settlement and second is called "Senior life insurance" settlement.

Policy Riders

These are additional benefits which supplement the basic benefit of sum-assumed. In fact, policy riders enhance the policy benefits and assured is required to pay a specific additional premium for these additional benefits. This additional premium is called Rider Premium. Following are some examples:

Children's policies. Policies taken for the educational/marriage needs of children usually fall under two categories:

(i) Those taken on the lives of children and financed by parents.

(ii) Those taken on the lives of parents and financed by children. If a parent financing the policy dies before the policy vests in the child, the family may not be able to continue the policy, thus, defeating the purpose of assurance. This eventuality is overcome by granting:

Premium waiver benefits. It means that in the event of the death of a parent further premiums, till the vesting date, are waived and policy is kept alive for full benefits.

Family benefits. It provides for additional payment linked to the basic-sum-assured (say 20% of S.A.) in the event of death of the parent, as family benefits, so that the family is able to sustain itself. Here again additional premium is charged with the condition that family benefit is allowed in conjunction with premium waiver benefit so that the main purpose of policy, i.e., child welfare, remains intact.

It may be noted here that rider premium in both the above cases is based on the life of the parent.

Double accident and extended disability benefits. Accident is defined on the back of each policy. Accident should be caused by external, violent, and visible means. A snake bite is an accident. Double accident provides for payment of an amount double the sum assured in the event of life assured's death due to an accident before a specific age (say 65 years) of the life assured.

The extended disability benefits "include waiver of future premium, grant of some periodic payments, etc." in the event of permanent disability. Disability benefits are disallowed in certain occupations and in case of deafness.

Note: An Indian resident cannot take a policy from a foreign insurer under FEMA, without the permission of RBI.

Settlement of Claims

An insurer has to settle claims either on maturity of the policy or on death of the insured sickness/accident of the insured.

In case of endowment policy, the date of maturity of policy is known. In case of joint life policy, one insured dies and other is alive, the death claim is paid for the date and surviving insured is covered up to the date of maturity. In case of fixed term plan like for marriage or education the benefits are paid as maturity claim even if policyholder dies at an earlier date. No tax paid on claims money.

Documents Required

In case of maturity claims, following documents are required to be given, along with claim form prescribed by the insurance company:

(1) Original Policy Band
(2) Assignment deed, if any
(3) Discharge form
(4) Age proof, if not given earlier.

In case of death, the following documents are attached along with prescribed claim form.

(a) Certificate of death—given by municipal committee or cremation ground or medical authorities or employer
(b) Assignment deed, if any
(c) Original policy bond
(d) Proof of age—if not given earlier
(e) Copy of FIR/Post Mortem report—in case of accident/murder.

Following points be noted in case of claims:

(1) The claimant shall produce either succession certificate or probate or letters of administration in case of will, from a court, if there is no nominee or assignee.
(2) If policy is missing, the insurer can make a payment on indemnity bond executed by the claimant.
(3) In case of other claimant (other than nominee or assignee) the insurer will make the payment to nominee or assignee unless injunction order is received from the court within specified legal period.

(4) No insurer can dispute the policy after the expiring of two years from the date of the policy on the ground of inaccurate or false statement unless insurer proves that there was a fraud or suppressed information was material.

(5) An insured convicted of murder is not entitled to claim.

(6) The claim money shall invest in official receiver or assignee in case of insolvency of the insured.

(7) In case of a minor nominee, a major person as guardian shall be appointed by the holder of the policy, till minor attains majority.

(8) In case of trust, the trustee shall receive the payment, A nominee holds the policy money in trust on behalf of heirs of the deceased insured. If heirs bring an order from the court, they have a right to receive the claim.

Note: See chapter 10 for claims procedure.

Setting the Right Price on a Policy—Insurance Products Costing

In India, competitive pressure drive down the premium rates of term insurance policies. The premium rates of other products haven't seen a similar decline. There's reason for it. In case of term products and without-profit endowment policies (where no bonuses are declared), the sum of the premiums is the price of the policy. But in the case of a with-profit policy, where the company may declare a bonus each year (thereby effectively returning part of the price paid), what the policy will finally cost can only be known at the time of maturity after taking into account all the bonuses paid to insured.

Actuaries take into consideration four factors for setting the price of a policy—investment return, mortality, lapses/withdrawals and expenses.

1. Investment return. If the investment return is poorer than expected, then bonuses will also be poor, and a with-profit endowment policy will prove costlier to the buyer. In case of an annuity (where the insurer takes a sum of money from you and pays you a monthly amount to you post-retirement), if the investment return is lower than expected, then it is the insurer who takes a hit. He has to continue paying the guaranteed sum despite poor investment performance.

For the last 50 years, interest rates had mostly been rising. Hence, estimating long-term interest rate trend was easy. Take the current rate, reduce it by two per cent, and one has a conservative estimate of long-term rates. One could not go wrong because interest rates only rise, thereby bringing higher returns. Over the last three years, rates have been falling. Moreover, economists are divided over their future course. Some believe that they will fall further and stabilize only at 2-3 per cent. Others believe they will bounce back to 7-8 per cent soon. Actuaries have the uphill task of deciding the price of insurance policies after taking a call on future rate movements (in the case of annuities, for as long as 30-40 years).

2. Demography and mortality. If the mortality rate among the insured is higher than expected, then the insurer has to pay more claims. Hence, he will have to set a higher price on his policy. But if fewer people die, then the insurer makes a profit. In the case of annuities, the case is just the opposite. If the mortality rate is lower than expected, then the insurer has to pay annuity for longer time, and hence incurs losses.

Some companies use "Numerical Rating Method". Under this method, each factor of insurability is compared with standard chart prepared by an actuary. Deviations are measured.

More debit deviations give extra mortality of a particular life (risk). For them extra premium is charged.

In most developing countries, mortality rates have been improving steadily in line with economic progress. By extrapolating past trends, you could get a good idea of future mortality rates. In recent times, among senior citizens and the 0-10 age group mortality rates have been improving in line with expectations. But in the 30-50 age group, mortality rates have not been improving as much as expected (due to higher incidence of lifestyle-related diseases).

In India, all insurers use LIC's mortality rates as the base, and then adjust it a little. Given the paucity of data and the fact that nobody knows what will be actual mortality experience, insurers may be taking a risk by pegging term insurance premiums at today's low levels. But some among the private insurers argue and their mortality experience will be significantly better than that of LIC because they sell to a primarily urban and richer clientele, which enjoys better nutrition, has greater access to healthcare, etc. Having pegged prices so low, private insurers will have to exercise extreme caution in underwriting so that high-risk customers don't get insured by them.

As for annuities, the world over senior citizens are living longer, making annuities a loss-making product. The dilemma before actuaries is that if they assume too low a mortality rate and set the price of annuities too high, these products won't sell. On the other hand, if they price them too aggressively, and people live longer, then their company will make a loss. Given all these difficulties, suggests Sampad Bhattacharya, chief actuary with Watson Wyatt India Pvt. Ltd., the very concept of guaranteeing a fixed annuity till death may have to be done away with.

3. Persistency. Another factor that affects pricing is whether customers stay with the policy throughout its life or drop out mid-course. If lapse rate is high, it leads to lower profitability. This is because the upfront costs borne by an insurer in selling a policy are quite high. These are recovered only if the policyholder stays with the policy for a few years.

Insurance companies monitor their lapse rate closely and are sometimes forced to re-price their policy if the actual lapse experience differs significantly from the assumed rate. If an insurer offer guarantees on surrender rates, then it needs to ensure that these are not keep too high.

4. Management expenses. The expenses of the insurance company need to be monitored closely. For new companies specially, cost of advertising, agent recruitment, claims cost, business acquisition cost, management expenses, margin for fluctuations due to inflation rate, etc. can push expenses up significantly.

In addition to the four criteria mentioned above, there is also the profit criteria, the price set by competitors, inter-class and inter-generation equity, etc. Product prices are constantly fine-tuned based on actual experience and feedback from the market.

In case of general insurance, whose delivery is only contingent in nature, its products has some unique features. The uniqueness arises from the fact that the actual claims cost, the major element of the cost becomes known only later unlike any other product pricing where the main cost elements are generally known in advance.

While fixing the premium rates, the insurers make estimates of the claims cost based on past experience. Obviously, these have to be reviewed from time to time. The factors considered when pricing general insurance products are claims costs, business acquisition cost, management expenses, and margin for fluctuations in claims experience and reasonable profit.

Products pricing requires external regulation for ensuring inter-class and inter-generation equity to the insured, solidity of the insurers so that they deliver. The promised service when eventualities arise and stability of the insurance market. Inter-class and inter-generation means that different segments of the population will be dealt with (to the extent they are relevant) differently, e.g., males and females, mother and non-mothers, standard and non-standard lives, limitations on entry ages, rural and urban population. It also includes considerations like individual or group insurance, linked and non-linked insurance, par or no par insurance. IRDA has prescribed different application forms for different types of insurance to be filled in by insurance companies.

Price regulation also extends to the terms and conditions of insurance contracts. In many countries, actual price regulation takes the form of premium schedules drawn up by trade associations, rating bureau or associations of insurers based on estimates of all loses across all insurance companies, average administrative costs, and average expected profit. This rate, calculate on the above basis, becomes the minimum for each insurer and often the maximum price as well.

Adverse Selection

Insurers have to deal with the problem of adverse selection (also called **anti selection**), which can never be completely eliminated, only can be controlled by careful underwriting. Those who do not fulfill under writing standards have to be insured for high premium rates. It is the tendency of persons with a higher than average chance of loss to seek insurance at standard rates, which if not controlled by underwriting, results in higher than expected loss levels e.g. high risk truck drivers or persons with serious health problem, or a business that is repeatedly robbed or burglarised.

Adverse selection arises because it is too costly to classify insureds perfectly. If each customer's expected claim costs could be observed costlessly then insurance premiums (barring government restrictions) would vary exactly with expected claims costs and there would be no adverse selection. But classification is costly.

The net result of adverse selection is that customer's with low expected losses purchase less coverage than they would if classification were costless. Thus, adverse selection limits insurability of risk for customers with low expected losses. Therefore, an insurer should design policies to help sort-out the high expected loss customers from the low expected customers.

"Deductibles" is one method that can be used to induce high expected loss customers to choose a policy that is priced to reflect their expected loss claims and low expected loss consumers to choose a policy with larger deductible that is priced to reflect their lower expected claim costs. 'Deductible' means that the insured shall bear the loss up to a particular amount and rest the insurer will pay subject to the amount of policy. If A insures his car for ₹ 5000 and deductible amount is ₹ 800. If loss is ₹ 3000, then insurer will pay ₹ 2200, insured will bear loss of ₹ 800 himself.

Tariff Rates and Detariff

When all the insurance companies operating in a market, follow the practice of pricing, the market is considered as tariffed market. Tariffs may be feasible for certain class or classes of business or certain products. Some companies in the market may opt to tariffs while other may opt to remain non-tariff insurers if such an option is available under the insurance law of the land.

Another variant in pricing insurance products is a firm-specific cost-plus pricing in which a particular firm's cost plus an allowance for profit is used as the basis for price in a non-tariff market. Price regulation is frequently used to bring about equity and fairness between different risk categories and classes of insured.

The price of an insurance product is linked to the scope of the cover. In some markets like India, it is common to find specific legal provisions governing the way in which the insurance policy is worded. These provisions also govern the terms and conditions elaborating the scope of the cover incorporated in the policy. Standardization of the policy or a plain vanilla product offering makes the price a clearly identifiable variable. This facilitates comparison of insurance products by consumers. One argument against this arrangement is that such standardization inhibits innovation and restricts the choice of customers who are on the hunt for non-typical insurance products.

In underdeveloped markets, however, alternative arrangements may provide opportunities to competing insurance companies to offer the same contract with only cosmetic changes and to charge inequitable rates of premium. In many markets, prior approval of insurance products by the regulatory authority is mandatory. Even in more mature and developed markets a system of 'file and use' is followed.

In Germany, deviation from approved tariff is not allowed. In Japan, the rating association formed under law sets rates for insurance against fire, personal accident, and vehicle insurance, which constitutes 92% of the non-life market in Japan. These rates are reviewed periodically. This system has provided stability to the Japanese insurance market for decidees. In India, general insurance has been put is NON-TARIFF category w.e.f. January 2007 and marine (hull) insurance w.e.f. 1-4-2005 and gradually dispense with it for life insurance as well.

The marine cargo policies were de-tarrified from 1-4-1994. The de-tariff was done because insurance sector is expanding and to attract foreign joint.

The nature and extent of price regulation reflect the attitude and philosophy of a state towards insurance operations in its territory. The tariff mechanism provides floor rates for various products. This was brought in to prevent uneconomic competition, which could lead to bankruptcy and loss of credibility for the sector. The tariff mechanism facilitates classification of risks according to their special characteristics.

The main argument against tariff is that it greatly reduces the scope for competition. Also tariffs introduce rigidity in the market and once framed are in practice seldom appropriately revised in response to change in the market.

General insurance, after de-tariff has been plagued by menace of de-tarrifying woes. There is a mad rush by insurance companies to offer too much discount up to 80%.

The Insurance (Amendment) Act, 1968 which introduce social control on general insurance, provided for a Tariff Advisory Committee replacing of the general insurance council and its regional council at four metropolises. The primary objective was to make rate setting more scientific and base it on proper analysis of statistical data.

Fire rates had been reduced twice after nationalization, in 1979 and 1987. In motor insurance however the rates were revised upwards once in 1982 and then in 1990 as the high cost of repairs coupled with high third party claims had adversely affected the incurred loss ratio. The claims cost of all classes of business taken together are high, essentially due to the claims experience of motor business.

Since the Insurance Regulator has granted full freedom in pricing General Insurance products in view of maturity of the General Insurance Sector and the efficiency of the market players. In turn the market players are also prepared themselves to enjoy the freedom in pricing products. They are also convinced that this freedom may be utilized by going for individual risk-based underwriting. Now the underwriters need to acquire complete knowledge about the profile, process and dynamics of all risks they assume to underwrite in general insurance.

Non-life market is totally risk bearing business that deals with only pure risks both probabilistic and catastrophic with average claim ratio of 70% (as expected but no way more than 100% as in the case of liability and health insurance areas)—unlike life insurance business where the death claims are only 5% and maturity claims are 30% of total premium income. In our journey of professional business, surveyors have been rendering their services to all the major corporate, multinational, banking and almost all the major insurance companies to assist and support them for carrying out the valuation for their respective purposes. They are handling the valuation assignments for the purpose of insurance on the reinstatement/market value basis and also advising the clients on insurance for their safety, considering the best option available in todays de-tariff market.

The per-acceptance inspection in this de-tariff market is principally carried out by the professional and highly qualified surveyors considering the various individual risk exposures and features involved in a particular risk situation and location. This also includes Risk Management Inspections with particular reference to selection of equipments for Machinery Breakdown Policy and associated L.O.P. thereof. This may help insured in optimizing the premium too. Reputed surveyors also provide services including property and asset valuation along with associated Techno Economic Viability study for new projects applying for loan.

The surveyors are providing their professional support to all their esteem clients for the purpose of insurance. Assessment of claims by the surveyors in time will enhance the image of the insurance industry having protected the interest of the clients. It is a strong hope in the insurance market that the surveyors will provide the requisite resources for the purpose of catering the growing insurance market needs. As a result of de-tarrif gross premium written by Indian General Insurance reported compound annual growth of 18% in F.Y. 15-16.

Computation of Premiums/Bonuses

The premium is the amount paid by the insured as value of risk. It is consideration of the contract and dependents upon the duration of the risk. In case of life of life insurance the amount of premium may be paid as a lump sum or in a smaller amount spread over a period of time and is called 'Level Premium'.

Premium in life insurance is based on mortality rate. The premium worked out is called 'basic premium'. A premium table shows the premium for every age and every term of policy according to the sum assured. For example, for a policy of ₹ 1000 for a period of six years of an insured age 26 is the ₹ 170 yearly. So for a policy of ₹ 1 lakh the premium will be 170 × 1,00,000/1000 = ₹ 17,000. Following rebates are allowed in this premium.

(a) *For large sum assured*, e.g. for sum assured of ₹ 50,000 to 1 lakh rebate @ ₹ 1 per thousand.

(b) *For mode of payment of premium.* Premium paid yearly is allowed rebate as compared to premium paid quarterly.

(c) *Age.* This may be age near birthday or last birthday or next birthday. For example, if birth date of the proposer is 27-10-1967, the proposal is made on 1-10-2000, the age near birthday will be (1-10-2000) minus (27-10-1967) 4-11-32 years, which is near to next birthday. Then age will be taken as 33 years.

If date of proposal is 25-4-2000, then nearer birthday age will be 32 years. It means if the difference is six months or more, add one to the difference in years to arrive at the age and if the less than six months, the exact number of years is taken.

Surrender Value and Paid-up Value

According to Section 113(1) of the Insurance Act, 1938, a policy acquires surrender value after premium have been paid for three consecutive years. To this is added surrender value of all bonuses. The insurer should show on the back of the policy (A) formula by which surrender value is guaranteed or (B) surrender value at the close of each year or at the close of every three years till maturity.

A policy which has acquired surrender value shall not lapse by nonpayment of further premiums and it shall be kept alive to the extent of paid-up sum assured which will also include all the bonuses vested in the policy [Section 133(2)]. The formula for calculation of paid-up value is:

$$\text{Paid up value:} \frac{\text{Sum Assured } \times \text{No. of years' premium paid}}{\text{No. of years for which premium is required to be paid}}$$

Suppose sum assured is ₹ 1,00,000 for 20 years on yearly payment basis on 1-1-2000 and the due date of last premium paid is 1-1-2005. So premium paid is for six years. Paid-up value will be

$$= \frac{6 \times 1{,}00{,}000}{20} = ₹30{,}000.$$

In case of with-profits policy the vested bonus will be added.

The paid-up value, along with bonuses, if any, will be paid on the death of the assured or on maturity as the case may be. The PAID-UP VALUE WILL BE REDUCED BY THE AMOUNT paid already as survival benefits, a paid up policy loses all other additional benefits e.g., accident benefits, disability benefit or survival benefit. No paid-up value is allowed for "Term Insurance".

Example: Suppose the number of years of premium paid is 5 years, sum assured ₹ 50,000 and number of years of premium payable, i.e., endowment policy period 50 years. Then paid-up value is $\frac{5}{50} \times 50{,}000 = ₹5{,}000$.

After that the surrender value is calculated by formula:

$$\text{Surrender Value} = \frac{\text{Paid up value (inclusive of bonus)} \times \text{S.V. factor}}{100}$$

$$= \frac{₹5000 \times 14.8}{100}$$

$$= ₹\ 740.00$$

Note: For factor of surrender value, every insurance prepares a surrender value table, where with reference to time and terms of policy, factor can be easily noted down.

Consumer Grievance Redressal—Ombudsman, Lokayukta, and Consumer Court

The word 'ombudsman' is of Swedish origin. It means an official appointed to check political corruption. In 1998, the institution of insurance ombudsman was created. Lok Ayukts have been appointed in twelve states at present on these lines. The basic function of insurance ombudsman is to remove the grievances of the policyholders of any type of insurance. An Insurance Council was set up in 1999. It has a governing body consisting of seven members, are of them shall be the chairman. Chairman of LIC, Chairman of GIC and immerging directors of four subsidiaries of GIC are members of this council. The council has set up Insurance Ombudsman offices at major cities. It has the authority to point them. The management expenses of ombudsman are shared equally by life and other insurance companies. These companies further share it on their "gross premium income".

An insured person or his legal heirs can make a complaint. Firms and companies cannot make a complaint. It should be in writing and within one year after the insurer has rejected his representation or sent his final reply to the complaint. If an insured has not received the reply over one month period can make a written complaint. Individual policyholders can make complaint either of life or non-life insurance, but not if a matter is already before Consumer Forum or Arbitrator. Ombudsman can play a role as a mediator or can give an 'award' within three months from the date of complaint. An appeal against award lies either in consumer court or a civil court.

An insurer can also file a suit in consumer court under Consumer Protection Act, 1986 for deficiency in service against insurer, IRDA has also set up a central grievance redressal mechanism. Under it each company will lay down a consumer grievance policy and will set up a grievance cell under a CEO or compliance officer.

How to File a Complaint?

Following steps may be taken to file and follow a complaint by insurer against insurer:

(1) Approach the grievance cell of the insurer with the complaint.
(2) The company has to acknowledge within three days and resolve it within 15 days.
(3) If not satisfied, file complaint with the IRDA.
(4) The insured can also approach the ombudsman or a consumer forum.
(5) If the insured is not satisfied be can take the matter to a civil court.

Rights of an Insurer

(1) **Right to cancel the policy:** An insured can cancel within 15 days the policy after receiving it. The 15-day period starts after the buyer receives the policy. The premium paid shall be refunded and the company can deduct the expenses incurred on medical rests, stamp duty and cover. The agent may use some trick on the buyer so that 15 days may expire e.g. he may say plans are being sent.
(2) **Detailed information:** All information about the cover must be provided to the buyer e.g. a comprehensive policy by shopkeeper was taken. Rainwater damaged the goods in the godown. IRDA ruled that insurer's plea that godowns were not covered was rejected.
(3) **Time limit for complete procedure:** Insurer must respond complete procedures within a time frame e.g. to settle claim not more than six months from the date of claim should be taken. Death claims and medical claim should be settled within 30 days.

(a) **Proposal.** It must be processed within 15 days and in case of cancellation, it must be conveyed within 15 days.

(b) **Service requests** e.g. mistakes or charges in the policy should be done within 10 days.

(c) **Payment of benefits.** Surrender value payments, annuity payment and pension processing within 10 days. Maturity sum to be paid within 15 days.

(d) **Surveyor report.** In case of damage report should be given within 30 days.

(e) **Claims settlement.** 30 days of receiving all required documents.

(f) **Grievances.** Must be acknowledged within three days and resolved within 15 days.

(4) **Renewal of policy:** Insurer cannot refuse to renew medical insurance unless there is fraud, moral hazard or misrepresentation. However, on renewal premium can be increased as per assessment of the risk. Supreme Court ruled that refusal to renew a medi-claim policy is "unfair practice".

(5) **Change of frequency of premium:** An insurer can change the frequency of premium payment at the beginning of a policy year but before 15-20 days before policy anniversary. Nomination can be changed.

Note: See Chapter 10 on grievance redressal procedure.

Insurance Agents

"One who can sell insurance can sell everything." So the work of an insurance agent is not so easy. The general law of agency given in Indian Contract Act applies to insurance agents as well. The insurance company is the "Principal" under Section 2(10) of Insurance Act. An insurance agent means an insurance agent licensed under Section 42 of the Act who receives or agrees to receive payment by way of commission or other remuneration in consideration of his soliciting or procuring insurance business including business relating to continuance, renewal or revival of policies of insurance.

Insurers are liable for acts of Agents to curb misspelling. He can procure only that business as defined under Section 2(11), e.g., no life insurer can insure a person for accidental death in insulation. He can only forward the proposal form, along with other documents, to the insurance company who can make an insurance contract with the insured. Sections 42A to 42D of the Act lay down the rules laid down by "Insurance Regulatory and Development Authority". IRDA has laid down eleven regulations about their issue and renewal of license, qualifications, practical training, pre-recruitment examination, code of conduct, cancellation of license, issue of duplicate license, etc. An agent is not salaried employee and get commission as specified under Section 40A of the Insurance Act, 1938.

An individual, firm or a body corporate can be appointed as insurance agent. In case of a company the director or person in charge should hold a valid license.

All insurance agents must have passed an examination conducted by Insurance Institute of India. Further he should have gone for a practical training as required by IRDA. The remuneration of an agent is specified under Section 40A of the Act. It may be first commission as sales, bonus commission and renewal commission.

Insurance intermediaries can be divided into two classes:

1. Agency building distribution. It includes:
   (a) career agency either as branch agency,
   (b) multiple line exclusive agency,
   (c) home service agents,
   (d) salaried employees of insurance company.
2. Non-agency building distribution. It includes brokers, personal producing general agent, independent property and casualty agents and producers group, i.e., independent and self-supporting group specialise in high-end market.

Procedure for Becoming an Agent

1. Licensing of agents. Every insurer (insurance company) is required to nominate an official, duly approved by the IRDA, who will issue or renew licences. This officer will be known as "Designated person". Licensing system for insurance agents ends w.e.f. 01-04-2015.

Section 42(4) and agents. The other main consideration in selection of the candidates is the licensing requirements as specified in Section 42(4) of the Insurance Act, 1938. These are:

A person shall be appointed as an agent if he:

(a) is a citizen of India;
(b) is at least 18 years of age as on the date of application;
(c) has not been found to be person of unsound mind by court of competent jurisdiction;
(d) has not been found guilty of criminal misappropriation or criminal breach of trust or of cheating of or forgery or of an abetment of or attempt to commit any such offence by a court of competent jurisdiction;
(e) has not been guilty of or has not knowingly participated in or connived at any fraud, dishonesty or misrepresentation against an insurer or an insured;
(f) possess the minimum educational qualification of a pass in 12th or equivalent examination conducted by any recognised Board/Institute of Education, if the applicant resides in a place with population of five thousand or more as per last census and a 10th pass if the applicant resides in any other place;
(g) has passed the pre-recruitment examination in life or general insurance business to be conducted by the Insurance Institute of India;
(h) has not violated the "Code of Conduct" of agents.

Company sponsorship. Once the company has shortlisted the probable candidates, they shall be sent for practical training to company's own training centre or some approved institute. The training orientation is going to be company specific who sponsored the candidates. Those who are fellow/associated of Insurance Institute of India or I.C.A.I. or I.C.W.A. or Actuarial society or an M.B.A. require 50 hours training and others 100 hours training.

2. Disqualification of agent. Section 42(4) of the Insurance Act, 1938 states that an agent is to be disqualified, if he is:

(a) a minor;
(b) found to be of unsound mind by a court of competent jurisdiction;

(c) found guilty of criminal misappropriation or criminal breach of trust or cheating or forgery or an abetment of or attempt to commit such offence by a court of competent jurisdiction;
(d) found guilty of having knowingly participated in or connived at any fraud, dishonesty or misrepresentation against as insurer or an insured;
(e) not a pass in 12th standard (reduced to 10th standard for rural area);
(f) not in receipt of practical training for the prescribed period;
(g) not qualified in the pre-recruitment test.

3. Suspension or revocation

(a) If an agent has been adjudged insolvent by a court, the insurance company may immediately suspend the agent who will thereafter no procure any business.
(b) If the agent is fully discharged by the court by grant of absolute discharge, the agent will be reinstated.
(c) If an agent fails to obtain an absolute order of discharge up to the end of two agency years following the agency year in which the order adjudicating him insolvent was passed, his appointment shall be liable to be terminated.
(d) If the agent applied to the court for being adjudged insolvent, he will be treated as above in option (a).

4. Termination of appointment. The insurer shall forthwith terminate the appointment of an agent, without notice, if he:

(a) is found to be of unsound mind by a court of competent jurisdiction.
(b) is found to be guilty of criminal misappropriation or criminal breach of trust or cheating or forgery or an abetment of or attempt to commit any such offence by a court of competent jurisdiction.
(c) in any judicial proceeding, has been found to have knowingly participated in or connived at any fraud, dishonesty or misrepresentation against the insurer.

5. Termination for lapses. The appointment of an agent may be terminated:

(a) if he has failed to discharge his function as an agent;
(b) if he acts in manner prejudicial to the interests of the insurer or to the interests of its policyholders;
(c) if evidence comes to its knowledge to show that he has been allowing or offering to allow rebate of the whole or any part of the commission payable to him;
(d) if it is found that any averment contained in his agency application or in any report furnished by him as an agent in respect of any proposal is not true;
(e) if he becomes physically or mentally incapacitated for carrying out his functions as an agent.

Code of Conduct for Agents

Selling of life assurance involves selling of an idea. It is an intangible goods that an agent sells. Therefore, an agent is required to observe a set of norms in his professional conduct which make him worthy of trust and faith.

The IRDA have formulated under Regulation 8 of Agent Regulations, 2000 a Code of Conduct for agents which broadly can be grouped under two heads "Does and Don'ts".

Code of Conduct

Every person holding a licence, shall adhere to the code of conduct specified below:

(i) Every insurance agent shall:

(a) Identify himself and the insurance company of whom he is an insurance agent;

(b) Disclose his licence to the prospect on demand;

(c) Disseminate the requisite information in respect of insurance products offered for sale by his insurer and take into account the needs of the prospect while recommending a specific insurance plan; i.e., should not be MISSPELLING.

(d) Disclose the scales of commission in respect of the insurance product offered for sale, if asked by the prospect;

(e) Indicate the premium to be charged by the insurer for the insurance product offered or sale;

(f) Explain to the prospect the nature of information required in the proposal form by the insurer, and also the importance of disclosure of material information in the purchase of an insurance contract;

(g) Bring to the notice of the insurer any adverse habits or income inconsistency of the prospect, in the form of a report (called "Insurance Agent's Confidential Report") along with every proposal submitted to the insurer, and any material fact that any adversely affect the underwriting decision of the insurer as regards acceptance of the proposal, by making all reasonable enquiries about the prospect;

(h) Inform promptly the prospect about the acceptance or rejection of the proposal by the insurer;

(i) Obtain the requisite documents at the time of filing the proposal form with the insurer; and other documents subsequently asked for by the insurer for completion of the proposal;

(j) Render necessary assistance to the policyholders or claimants or beneficiaries in complying with the requirements for settlement of claims by the insurer;

(k) Advise every individual policyholder to effect nomination or assignment or change of address or exercise of options, as the case may be, and offer necessary assistance in this behalf, wherever necessary;

(ii) No insurance agent shall:

(a) Solicit or procure insurance business without holding a valid licence;

(b) Induce the prospect to omit any material information in the proposal form;

(c) Induce the prospect to submit wrong information in the proposal form or documents submitted to the insurer for acceptance of the proposal;

(d) Behave in a discourteous manner with the prospect;

(e) Interface with any proposal introduced by any other insurance agent;

(f) Offer different rates, advantages, terms and conditions other than those offered by his insurer;

(g) Demand or receive a share of proceeds from the beneficiary under an insurance contract;

(h) Force a policyholder to terminate the existing policy and to effect a new proposal from him within three years from the date of such termination;

(i) Have, in case of a corporate agent, a portfolio of insurance business under which the premium is in excess of fifty per cent of total premium procured, in any year, from one person (who is not an individual) or one organisation or one group of organisations;

(j) Apply for fresh licence to act an insurance agent, if his licence was earlier cancelled by the designated person, and a period of five years has not elapsed from the date of such cancellation;

(k) Become or remain a director of any insurance company or is not close relative of an insurer;

(iii) Every insurance agent shall, with a view to conserve the insurance business already procured through him, make every attempt to ensure remittance of the premiums by the policyholders within the stipulated time, by giving notice to the policyholder orally and in writing.

Termination of Agency

An agency can be terminated in the following eventualities:

(i) Failure to bring in minimum guaranteed quota. If an agent fails to fulfil the minimum guaranteed quota of new business required for an agency year, his agency shall stand terminated at the end of such agency year. Insurance agents benchmark for annual business minimum is ₹ 1 lakh.

(ii) Termination of agency on cancellation of or failure to renew licence. If the licence of an agent is cancelled or is not renewed in accordance with the provisions of Section 42 of the Insurance Act, his appointment as agent shall stand terminated from the date the licence is cancelled or as the case may be, from the date the licence ceased to be valid.

Insurance Brokers

Scales of Remuneration/Commission Payable to Insurance Brokers

RBI has allowed banks to act as brokers.

Insurance Amendment Act, 2002 amended the provisions of Section 40 of the Insurance Act, 1938 to permit the payment of a portion of the premium received by an insurer for purposes of intermediation. An agency other than an insurance agent has also been recognized for this purpose. Arising out of this, this Authority had received, considered and granted licenses to various organizations to permit them to carry on insurance broking business either as direct brokers or as reinsurance brokers or as composite brokers in the country.

The persons who have been licensed to act as brokers have necessarily to be members of the Insurance Brokers Association of India. The brokers association has taken steps to convert itself into a self-regulatory body with a Disciplinary Committee being put in place. The association has also accepted to include one of the members of the Authority as a permanent member of the Disciplinary Committee.

The insurance company shall have a Principal Officer as a full time post and not on part time basis to it. He is responsible for conducting the affairs of the broking company in a professional manner and as per the rules and regulations laid down/prescribed by the Authority. He is the interface between the customers and the insurers, he also acts as a link between the Regulator and the Broking Company. The Principal Officer of a broking company is not permitted to look after any other assignment or position long as he is the Principal Officer of a broking company.

Documentation and Procedural Requirements for Obtaining Broker License

A. *Submission of Completed Application*

1. Submission of relevant information as required in the FORM A format available on the IRDA website [www.irdaindia.org].
2. The declaration forming part of the application format should be signed by two directors.

B. *Documents/Requirements*

1. Remittance of requisite fee as per category of insurance broker applied by demand draft.
2. Printed copy of Memorandum and Articles of Association issued by Registrar of Companies.
3. Steps should be undertaken by the applicant to ensure compliance of the training requirements as specified.
4. One Principal Officer has to be there in a broking company fulfilling the requirements.
5. Information on whether any person associated with the applicant company in his capacity as Directors/shareholder/promoter/key management personnel or employees is holding any insurance agency or insurance surveyor's licence. If yes, then complete details thereof. As per the regulations, no agent survey or can work as a broker. The applicant should take steps to cancel the agencies and submit documentary proof of the same to the Authority.
6. Detailed CV of all the directors highlighting their past and present activities.
7. Detailed CVs and attested copies of testimonials of the educational qualifications of the Principal Officer and key management personnel.
8. Principal Officer to submit an affidavit, duly notarized certifying to the effect that the application (directors, principal officer, key management personnel and employees of the company) are not suffering from any of the disqualifications specified under sub-section 42D of the Insurance Act, 1938.
9. List of all shareholders (current as well as proposed) of the applicant company.
10. Photocopy of the asset register of the firm, duly certified by CA.
11. List of employees who will be responsible for soliciting and procuring insurance business along with their qualifications.
12. Details of statutory auditors and Principal Bankers along with the Bank Account Number of applicant.
13. If shareholder is firm/firms, confirm whether it/they is/are Non-Banking Finance Companies. If yes, submit a No Objection Certificate from Reserve Bank of India regarding

their promoting and investing in Applicant Company. If not, submit a certificate to that effect from the statutory auditors.

14. If shareholder is firm/firms, furnish the Board Resolution passed by it/them in promoting and investing in Applicant Company.
15. If shareholder is firm/firms, submit the audited annual report, balance sheet for the last three years along with certified copies of income-tax returns.
16. In case of individual promoters, submit certified copies of income-tax returns along with copies of balance sheet filed duly certified by the auditors for the last three years along with net worth certificates certified by CA.
17. Balance sheet of the applicant company.
18. Explain in detail the existing activities undertaken by the applicant company.
19. Clarification on how the applicant company proposes to deal with its existing customers/ business/liabilities once it enters the field of insurance broking.
20. The company must have the words 'Insurance Broker' or 'Insurance Broking' in its name so as to reflect its line of activity i.e., insurance broking.
21. Details of infrastructure along with supporting evidence thereof like ownership/lease agreement papers with regard to office space/equipment/trained manpower, etc. for the registered office and the future planning for opening branch offices at various locations in the country and the estimated timeframe with photographs of premises.
22. Projections of administrative expenses, salaries and wages and other expenses, draw the revenue account, the profit and loss account and the balance sheet for the projected three years.
23. Organisation chart giving a complete picture of the company's activities like IT, underwriting, risk assessment, claims settlement, marketing, accounts, back office, etc.
24. List of experienced personnel inducted from general and life insurance background with good knowledge and experience of working in the areas of risk assessment, underwriting and claims management, etc. Submit detailed CV, copies of educational qualifications along with their appointment/joining letters of the people, so selected, to the Authority.
25. Bring on record any other information which is relevant to the nature or services rendered by the applicant for the growth and promotion of insurance business.

C. *Personal Presentation*

The application after fulfilling the given requirements is required to appear before the Authority for a presentation of business plans in connection with the application.

The above list of documents/requirements is indicative only and not exhaustive. The additional documents will be advised based on the category of license applied, pattern of shareholding, any other compliance matter required as per IRDA (Insurance Brokers) Regulations, 2002 and views of the Authority.

Keeping in view the international experience and practice corporate houses can have both insurance companies and broking activity subject to certain safeguards. It was felt that organisations with high standard of corporate governance alone may be permitted to establish/ continue insurance broking companies subject to the conditions set out in the circular. These conditions shall be in addition to the conditions already specified in the Act/Regulations.

(A) *Obligations of the Promoter*

The promoter company should give an undertaking that none of the clients within the promoter group will be compelled to use the broker for their insurance requirements.

(B) *Obligations of the Insurer*

The insurer within the group should give an undertaking that—

(i) it will not pay higher remuneration to the broker within the group compared to what is payable to other brokers for the same class of insurance or insurance product; an audit certificate on compliance with this undertaking should be filed annually with the audited accounts of the insurer;

(ii) it will not quote terms to the broker within the group, that are more favourable than the terms quoted of other brokers on the same proposal for insurance; and

(iii) it will not design special insurance products for sale exclusively through the broker.

(C) *Obligations of the Broker*

(i) The broker shall make an explicit disclosure of its being a sister company of the insurer within the same promoter group, in all its stationery used for communication with clients and in all publicity materials and at the offices of the broker.

(ii) The broker shall make an explicit declaration in all communications relating to terms and conditions of insurance if a client requires disclosure of the remuneration receivable by the broker on the insurance effected for the client.

(iii) Where the broker recommends a product and quotes rates and terms offered by an insurer within the same promoter group, the broker shall inform the client about the logic in support of its recommendation and also inform the client about the next best product, rates and terms offered by an insurer not part of the promoter group.

(iv) The broker shall ensure that not more than 25 per cent of the insurances handled by it in any financial year is placed with the insurance company within the promoter group separately for life and for general insurance business. The broker shall establish internal machinery to monitor this on an on-going basis.

(v) It shall be mandatory for the broking company to disclose Related Party transactions with the insurance company belonging to the promoter group in its audited accounts and balance sheet as described in the Accounting Standard 18 of ICAI.

(D) *Obligations of both the Insurer and Broker*

(i) The insurance company and broking company shall maintain arm's length distance between themselves. More explicitly, no employee or director of the broking company shall be a director, employee, or agent of the insurance company.

(ii) The broking company shall not offer loans or other facilities or incentives to officers or employees of the insurer within the group and vice versa.

[For this purpose, "Group shall be as defined in the IRDA Investment Regulation, 2000 and Guidelines issued thereunder.]

The above prudential requirements are in addition to the requirements stipulated under Regulation 20 of the IRDA (Brokers Regulations) which reads as under:

The business of the insurance broker shall be carried in such a manner that, not more than 50 per cent of the premium (quantum, receipts, etc., as the case may be) in the first year of business, 40 per cent of the premium in the second year of business, and 30 per cent of the premium from the third year of business onwards shall emanate from any one client.

Note: For the purposes of this regulation, the term "client" shall include, in the case of a firm or a company, an associate or a subsidiary or a group concern under the same management.

Corporate Agents

Corporate Agent means a firm, company, a corresponding new bank, regional rural bank, a cooperative society or bank, a panchayat or a local authority, non-governmental organisation or a micro lending finance organisation. A corporate agent should hold a license to act as an insurance agent for a life or general insurers. A corporate agent or a corporate insurance executive i.e., a director or a partner or officer of the organisation should be atleast an education of 12th standard and should have completed training in insurance from an approved institution for a specified period. They shall be abide by code of conduct laid down by IRDA.

Licensing of Corporate Agents

Introduction

In order to spread awareness about insurance and to increase the coverage of a large section of population who have remained outside the pale of insurance coverage all these years, the Insurance Regulatory and Development Authority introduced a variety of intermediaries as "distribution" is key to insurance penetration. The Corporate Agent is a concept introduced with a view to taking advantage of the presence of a large number of firms, corporations, banks, NGOs, co-operative societies and panchayats who are in contact with people in the normal discharge of their activities and utilize their presence and services for canvassing the sale of insurance contracts. Since insurance contracts are highly technical in nature, the Regulations issued by the Authority stipulated that the canvassing should be done only by "Specified Persons" engaged by the Corporate Agents and such specified persons should have the qualification prescribed by the Authority. In the case of corporate executives also, the Authority prescribed certain qualifications in order for the Corporate Agent to obtain a license. It can have tie up with more than are insurer.

Authority Competent to Grant License

The decision to engage any 'Person' as a Corporate Agent will be taken only in the Corporate Office of the Insurance Company and proceedings appointing the 'Person' as Corporate Agent will be issued by an officer who will specially be designated by the Chief Executive Officer to issue such orders. The officer so designated shall maintain a list of Corporate Agent appointed by the company and will be responsible for ensuring that the Corporate Agents comply with the Regulations and the circulars and instructions issued by the Authority from time to time. The officer will also communicate to the Authority the up-to-date list of Corporate Agents engaged by the insurer on a half-yearly basis. In this communication the officer should specially highlight the cancellation of licenses, if any, and give brief reasons leading to the cancellation.

Constitution of Corporate Agency/Insurance Marketing Firm

1. The applicant for Corporate Agency should normally be a company or firm whose principal business should be other than distribution of insurance products. Insurance distribution should be a subsidiary activity. While selecting the Agent, stress should be placed on the availability of client base or access to data which would facilitate identification of prospects. A corporate agent should be registered under IRDA (Registration of Corporate Agents) Regulations 2015. Every corporate agent, where revenues from their insurance intermediation activities is more than 50% of their total income from all activities shall takeout a "Professional indemnity insurance cover."
2. The Corporate Agent should canvass insurance products with the help of insurance professional who satisfy the qualifications laid-down in the Regulations. They should not use any other modes like introducers, finders or sub-agents by whatever name they are called for procuring business.
3. In exceptional cases, grant of Corporate Agency for exclusively doing insurance intermediation can be considered by an insurer. In respect of such cases the Corporate Agent should be a Public Limited Company with a minimum share capital of ₹ 15 lakhs. The capital should be kept in the form of a deposit in a bank account to be utilized for setting up the office, or be invested in assets, subject to approval by the insurer. A Corporate Agent should have minimum equity capital or contribution and net worth of ₹ 50 lakhs at all times.
4. Such companies or firm created exclusively to canvass insurance business shall be set-up and owned by insurance professionals or its employees should be insurance professionals. Business will be transacted by only full time employees having required qualification as per regulations based on properly documented needs analysis process. The record of sales process should be available. These records should available for inspection by the insurer and/or the IRDA, if required. Such an Agent can make use of the client data base from any organisation for which they can pay a fee not related to success or otherwise of the prospects becoming clients. The payment for client data plus Corporate Agency commission should be within the overall commission limit as per the Insurance Act.
5. As indicated in the second provision to Regulation 3(2) of the Licensing of Corporate Agents Regulations, ordinarily, one license can be granted to one group provided the group does not have any other insurance activity such as broker, insurer, etc. Hence, any application from a company for a Corporate Agency licence there any member of the group is already engaged in insurance agency or brokerage or similar insurance activity.
6. It should have minimum equity share capital or contribution and net worth of ₹ 50 lakhs at all times.

Underwriting

Underwriting is the process by which an insurance company decides whether to issue requested insurance. If it agrees to insure what will be the terms and conditions and the premium (price). From this definition two points emerge (a) selection i.e., evaluation of prospective customer and (b) classification i.e., assigning. The insured to a particular group of insured. Underwriting deals with probabilities and thus rely on statistical figures. It is needed because of following reasons:

(i) *Risk pooling and fair prices.* Every insured contributes to a common pool out of which insurer pays in case of loss or happening of an event. The contribution by the insured is based on expected loss potential. Therefore, he should pay a fair price. Insurer determines the expected loss and determines the price.

(ii) *Group versus individual insurance.* In group insurance, the whole group is an insured unit. So each group must contribute an amount sufficient to cover the expected loss. The insurer also makes a distinction between group and individual insurance. He studies the characteristics of the group as a whole. No individual underwriting is conducted.

(iii) *Mandatory and voluntary insurance.* Social insurance is essential for a country. The government makes insurance compulsory e.g. in India 'Employees State Insurance Act, 1948' makes obligatory for employees and employers to contribute towards insurance fund. The contribution is also fixed by law. The underwriting is unnecessary and irrelevant in such cases of social insurance.

(iv) *Fair price.* If any insured pays premium that is not sufficient to cover the expected loss, then those who do not suffer any loss are in a way subsidize the deficit of the pool of course, insureds who do not suffer losses always subsidize these who do. Thus, premiums should vary from insured to insured. The insurer has to resort to adverse selection. The insurer should have knowledge of mortality or morbidity or probability of loss i.e. information should be adequate about the insured.

(v) *Competition.* Insurers also have to underwrite because of competition in private insurance market. One insurer will try to seek advantage over the other. One way of getting such advantage is through latest and correct information through underwriting. IRDA regulates tariff in India for life insurance and these are indications that there may detarrified, already for general insurance rates have been detarrified.

Underwriting in insurance is a technical function. It requires expertise and multi-disciplinary approach. It refers to the process of selecting and classifying applicants for insurance.

Insurance underwriting means the process of making assessment and accepting risk. Underwriting or selection of risks is the process of evaluating each proposed subject-matter of insurance in terms of the degree of risk it represents and then deciding whether to grant insurance and on what terms. A standard is laid down in the form of tabular for rates of premium e.g. mortality tables in life insurance for this purpose. If any insured's life does not correspond or come close to the table, then the role of underwriting comes. The purposes of under-written or selection are two. First, to avoid ANTI SELECTION i.e., not to select a wrong customer. Secondly to differentiate, classify and promote similarity among risks.

The underwriter is an expert who does these work of underwriting. But he has to follow certain guidelines and policy. The underwriter will consider the following factors:

1. The type of customers i.e. their health status, age, occupation, etc.
2. The type of policy that is to the customer.
3. Development of agent and intermediaries.
4. Competition among insurance.
5. The extent of risk involved.
6. The cost of providing insurance. Underwriters follow two approaches (a) the Judgement method, (b) Numerical method. The underwriter may either accept the proposed with

an extra premium or accept with a restrictive clause or change in the product category and term of insurance or postpone the risk cover or reject it.

Insurance underwriting is entirely different from securities underwriting and bank underwriting.

1. Selecting the insureds according to the company's under standards.
2. The frequency and probability of risk is assured.
3. The terms and condition and scope of the case is assured.
4. These should be proper balance with each rate classification i.e., these should be equity among policy owners.
5. The appropriate premium is to be considered. The rating exercise is done by Tariff Advisory committee under IRDA Act.
6. Risk adequacy for each class and reinsurance availability.

For example in property insurance underwriting should be based on COPE analysis i.e. construction, occupation, protection, external factors relating to property.

From above it is evident that insurance company should select for underwriting purposes a large standard group. It should balance between the size of substandard group as well as within each class. The insured should be rated on the principle of actuarial equity. Lastly, the classification factors used should be socially acceptable.

Ideally, the selection and classification system in underwriting should (a) measure accurately the effect of each factor affecting the risk, (b) assess the combined impact of interrelated factors, (c) produce equitable results, and (d) be relatively simple and in expensive to operate. Some companies may use judgement method or rating method.

"Appointed Actuary"

An actuary is a highly skilled mathematician who is involved in all phases of insurance including planning, pricing and research. Actuary is an expert who fixes the premium for various plans of assurance, maintains solvency margins for the insure, and analyses the causes of deaths among assured persons. He keeps the underwriting standards. Every life insurance company must appoint an actuary and should not be more than 70 years and should be a member of actuarial society of India. He should be a graduate in science, mathematician statistics or actuarial. According to IRDA regulations, his main duties are:

1. To maintain solvency margin of the company.
2. To advise in matters of (a) product design and pricing and claims, (b) policy bond wordings, (c) investments, (d) reinsurances, and (e) loss rating schedules and of discounts.
3. Keeps record of adverse trend in insurance and suggest remedial measures.
4. Responsible for valuation and determination of surplus.
5. Gives certificates or actuarial matters required by law.

An actuary should possess a certificate of practice issued by Actuarial Society of India. This appointment is to be approved by IRDA.

There is a great scope for actuaries in general insurance and health insurance. For report of appointed actuary on estimation of IBNR claims.

Assessors and Surveyors

They are different from actuary. They assess the extent of loss of the subject matter of insurance in case of non-life insurance. They are divided in India in three categories: (1) Licentiate, (2) Associate and (3) Fellow. He can be allotted upto three departments. A surveyor should be a member of Indian Institute of Insurance Surveyors and Loss Assessors (IIISLA). He should be a graduate in Engineering or member of I.C.A.I. or I.C.W.A. or degree or diploma in actuarial science or insurance. He should follow the rules of conduct laid down by IRDA. To sum up, the loss surveyor and assessor inspects, investigates, estimates the loss, takes measure to protect damaged property, surveys and assesses the loss, check the ownership of the subject-matter and suggest measures to minimize and control loss and recommends quantum of depreciation on property.

Code of Conduct for Surveyors and Loss Assessors

1. To exhibit the identity card and/or the license issued by the Authority while carrying out the job of survey and loss assessment and be physically fit to undertake the rigorous of the job.
2. To conduct the survey job in a manner and behaviour which is transparent, honest, sincere, fair, objective and free from personal interest and ensure that the professional, technical standards of competence are upheld.
3. To endeavor to keep abreast with professional standards and advancements by attending professional courses, trainings, seminars, and workshops meant for upgrading the required skills.
4. To uphold not only ethical behaviour but professional reputation and credibility while refraining from making remarks, comments or grievances in the public or to the press without exhausting internal professional and legal avenues.
5. No Surveyor and Loss Assessor shall agree or take the work of survey and loss assessment where he or his family members are interested through shareholding or employment or business dealings.
6. No Surveyor and Loss Assessor shall act as an insurer or an insurance agent or an insurance broker or an insurance consultant, owner or partner or otherwise connected with motor garage or workshop taking accidental jobs and be an employee or Director of any of these.
7. Not to advertise or solicit directly or indirectly or through middlemen for work or receive remuneration from both insured and insurer simultaneously for the same work or seek any discount or trade commission or favour in connection with the discharge of professional work.
8. Not to share and exchange with others the confidentiality of the information of the insured and insurer or other parties connected with the job, which as gained by him during the course of discharge of duties.
9. Not to render professional services as a second surveyor for resurvey/reassessment unless and until it is called by the instructions of the Authority or its Designated Officer or by an insurer with specific written terms of reference to do so. The intimation and information of such jobs rendered must be furnished to the Surveyors and Loss Assessors' Committee.
10. To issue survey and loss assessment report including the annexures duly signed and stamped after due verification and satisfaction.

11. Every licensed surveyor and loss assessor shall provide practical training to any aspiring applicant for the period not less applicant. The certificate issued on completion of training shall be in the form and manner specified by the Authority. The refusal to do so shall be deemed as misconduct unless and until the refusal is with valid and cogent reasons to the satisfaction of the Authority.
12. To maintain a register of survey work containing the relevant information as specified in the prescribed form and keep important records of the survey reports, photographs and other important documents for a period of six years and furnish the same and such other specified returns as and when called for by the Authority or by any investigating authority or the insurer.
13. Not to allow the use of his name, license number to any other person or lend his survey reports and other documents for direct or indirect use by the said person or to any other licensed surveyors whether for consideration or reward or for any other purpose.
14. Not to suppress any material fact known to him in his capacity as a surveyor and assessor.

Corporate Surveyors and Loss Assessors

According to S and L Assessors (licensing, professional requirements and Code of Conduct) (amendment) Regulations 2013 of IRDA, following are the requirements:

1. There shall be at least two directors/partners in the company/firm at any point of time who are members of the institute and are licensed. They shall undertake survey jobs and issue a survey report.
2. If SLAs are employees of any company/firm shall undertake survey jobs only of that company where they are employed.
3. None of directors/partners of one corporate surveyor shall be appointed as director/partner in another corporate surveyor.
4. The main object of company/firm shall be to carry out insurance survey and loss assessment. The last words of the company shall include "insurance surveyors and loss assessors".
5. A foreign company can hold up to 26% of paid up equity of SLs firms/companies.

The surveyors profession is not progressing in India. This is because of surveyors can work only on fire marine, motor and engineering departments. The fee has not been revised since 2007. Moreover, Indian Institute of Insurance, Surveyors and Loss Assessors has not come up to the mark. IRDA released Surveyor's Regulations (amendments), 2013. The regulation lays down that a surveyor has been registered with IIISLA as members. These members are divided into three categories as (a) Licentiate, (b) Associate, and (c) Fellow.

Mortality and Morbidity Tables

Edmund Halley, the astronomer and Mathematician in 18th century developed mortality tables. In 1757, Equitable insurance company introduced premium payment according to age duration of life sum insured.

Morbidity tables show yearly probability of death. Morbidity tables show yearly probabilities or other information on loss of health. Actuaries and underwriters make use of item profitability and loss of large numbers play great role in their construction. Morbidity and mortality tables are of following types:

(i) Valuation tables and basic tables.
(ii) Select, ultimate and aggregate tables.
(iii) Static tables and projected values.
(iv) Morbidity table for annuities.

Sometimes companies may develop tables for a special group e.g., smokers and non-smokers. A mortality table is constructed by using arbitrary number of persons, called RADIX assumed to be a alive at a given age. A valuation morbidity table contains margins, used as the basis for calculating minimum reserves and cash surrender values. They may also be used for gross premium calculate. A basic morbidity table reflects actual experience of the population from which it was drawn. No margin is added to such table. They may be used for calculation of gross premium rates and development of current mortality charges. A select mortality table is based on data of newly insured lives only. An ultimate mortality table excludes early data—usually 5 to 15 years following entry and is based on ultimate mortality among insured lives in later policy years. An aggregate mortality table includes all mortality, the early years following entry as well as later years.

A mortality table based on experience is not suitable for annuities as it will overstate expected mortality rates. Annuity mortality table shows the lower rates of mortality anticipated in future rather than the rates that have been experienced in the past.

Static tables do not provide for changes in rates depending upon the calendar year to which they are applied. Tables with projection show a secular trend towards mortality improvement. Due to increase in average age of the mortality has led to small margins. People have to make additional annuity payments. To avoid this different bases are applied to static table.

The sources of mortality may be either population statistics or records of lives insured with the company. The former is taken after 10 years and is usually doubtful as proof of age is not accurate. The insurance company's records give a correct figure. A mortality table contains the age, number of lining, number of deaths, mortality rate and survival rate.

Legal Cases—Life

(1) Death Claim: Death claim lodged by the complainant on the death of his wife take Chandrikaben K. Tailyani was repudiated by the respondent alleging incorrect statement and with holdment of material information with regard to health of DLA at the time of filling up the proposal and before commencement of the insurance.

The respondent produced various reports like Endoscopies, Histopathology from cancer hospitals which confirm that DLA was diagnosed and suffering from squamous cell carcinoma Grade III during the period between completion of proposal on 19-02-2008 and insurance of first premium, receipt on 24-03-2008. However, repudiation of claim by the is upheld without any relief to the complainant (*Chandural K. Purwani* vs. *LIC of India Ahmedabad*, Case No. 21-001-0222-10).

(2) Settling Maturity Claim: Inordinate delay occurred in settling maturity claim, since computer records were not available for the policies. The insurance has paid penal interest for delayed settlement @8%, the rate prevailing at the time of settlement of claim. But the complainant demanded 12.5% as interest.

It was held that rate of interest applicable should be the rate of interest prevailing at the time of maturity and not at the time of settlement of the claim. The rate of interest at the time of maturity date was higher i.e. 9%. Hence, the complainant will get interest @ 9% and difference of 1% interest, inclusive of income tax, if any ₹ 12090.63. (*A. Thampi* vs. *LIC of India Kochi*, Case No. 10/KCH/21/21-001-018/2010-11).

(3) Non-payment of Premium Claim: The complainant has taken the policy with term of 10 years with a sum assured of ₹ 4,99,95 and annual premium ₹ 99,999. The policy bond was received by the complainant and renewal premium was also paid for ₹ 10,000, the respondent has refunded the premium due to short premium. At the request of the complainant the premium was reduced to ₹ 10,000, but the respondent has reduced sum assured to ₹ 50,000 as per regulatory limits and policy provisions.

It get established that the respondent has not produced the sum assured as per the regulatory provisions and request of the complainant. Hence, respondent has been directed to provide cover as per policy in the result the complaint fails to succeed (*Mrs. Rajul N. Shah*, Ahmedabad, Case No. 22-005-0334-11).

(4) Non-receipt of Policy Bond: The complainant has submitted that premium was paid and policy number was given, but the policy document was not issued to her. The respondent submitted that document was sent on specified address by courier and was also delivered. The respondent pleaded that she had sent a letter for alteration and a legal notice in which confirmation for receipt of document was given. It was established that document of policy was received. Complaint failed (*Mrs. Rina M. Parmar* vs. *Kohak Mohindra*, Case No. 25-008-099-11, Ahmedabad).

But in *Deepa Kumar H. Rao* vs. *Birla Sun Life*, the complainant submitted a letter for cancellation of policy as policy bond was not received. The respondent refused to cancel the policy and to refund the premium, the respondent informed that policy bond was received. The company sent a duplicate policy bond without complainant request and returned the policy bond. The respondent failed to show for receipt of policy and the respondent's decision to refuse to cancel the policy under free look in period is not justified and directed to refund the premium.

(5) The following cases were referred to Ombudsman of different states for decision:

(a) The insurer could not prove suppression of facts about pre-existing illnesses was directed to settle the claim.

(b) An insured gave I.D. card as proof of age, whereas his actual age by X class certificate deposited in his postal department. Claim dismissed as he deliberately under stated his age. Had he declared his correct age, proposal would not have been accepted. His plea that proposal form was filled by agent had no relevance.

(c) Insurer alleged that it was a case of suicide and nothing is payable as per suicide clause. No suicide note was found and no poison was found in body by past mortem. The report of panel of doctors also confirmed it. Held sum assured be paid to the nominee/complainant.

(d) A man, his wife and brother were travelling in a two wheeler. They met with an accident. Wife and brother died. Nothing was paid as under MV Act only two persons are permitted to travel. There was a breach of law.

(e) The life assured did not disclose that he had suffered from pulmonary T.B. with Hemoptysis and now suffering from acute Lymphoblastic Leukemia. The insured's claim was rejected for nondisclosure of material fact.

4

Insurance in India

In India, British insurers introduced general insurance in its modern form. The first known company was Sun Insurance in Calcutta in the year 1710.

Bombay Insurance Company Ltd. was the first insurance doing life insurance business in 1793. This company failed in 1834 and was transformed into 'New Oriental Company'. Royal Insurance company in 1845 was the first company insuring Indian lives. The first Indian company was formed in 1870, called Bombay Mutual Life Insurance Society Ltd. By 1871, there were all 15 companies working in India, out of which seven were Indians. Later between 1870 to 1900 many insurance companies were formed and registered under Indian Companies Act, 1856. In 1912, the government passed the 'Insurance Act and the Provident Fund Insurance Societies Act' was passed. Indian Life Assurance offices association was formed in 1927. In 1938, Insurance Act was passed.

Insurance Act, 1938

The Act contains 120 sections and eight schedules. Brief summary of the Act is given below. The following sections have been incorporated in the book at appropriate places.

Who can transact insurance business—Only an Indian Insurance Company is permitted. It includes:

> a company registered under the Companies Act, 1956 in which the total equity shares holding by a foreign company (including subsidiaries and nominees) do not exceed 26% of the paid-up equity capital of Indian company. [*Section* 2(7A)]

Registration

(a) An insurer carrying on business in India must obtain from the IRDA a certificate of registration for the particular class of insurance business. [*Section* (3(1)]

(b) An insurer shall have the registration renewed annually for each year. [*Section* 3(A)]

Capital requirements

(a) Paid-up equity capital of ₹ 100 crores for Life and General Insurance business, and

(b) Minimum paid-up equity capital of ₹ 200 crores for re-insurance business. [*Section* 6]

Voting Rights: The capital of a life insurer shall consist only of ordinary shares each of which has a single face value. The voting rights of every shareholder shall in all cases be strictly proportionate to the paid-up amount of the shares held by him. If the paid-up holding of any person exceeds 2½ per cent of the paid-up capital in case of banking company or investment company, or 5 per cent in any other case, he shall not be entitled to any vote as a shareholder in respect of such excess holding of shares. [*Section* 6A]

Dilution of Excess shareholding by promoters: The promoters of Indian insurance companies shall divest their shareholding in excess of 26% in a phased manner after 10 years.

[*Section* 6AA]

Deposits with RBI: Every insurer is required to keep deposited the amount of:

(i) Life insurance business	1% of the gross premium income in a year not exceeding ₹ 10 crores.
(ii) General business	3% of the gross premium income in a year not exceeding ₹ 10 crores.
(iii) Re-insurance business	₹ 20 crores.

[*Section* 7(1)]

Separation of Funds: Where the insurer carries on the business of life insurance, all receipts due to respect of such business shall be carried to and shall form a separate fund to be called a life insurance fund the assets of which shall be kept distinct and separate from all other assets of the insurer. [*Section* 10(2)]

Accountant, Balance Sheet: Every insurer shall at the end of each financial year prepare in accordance with the regulations made by IRDA:

(1) a balance sheet,
(2) a profit and loss account,
(3) a revenue account, and
(4) a separate account of receipts and payments.

[*Section* 11(1A)]

Audit: The balance sheet, profit and loss account, revenue account and profit and loss appropriation account of every insurer shall be audited annually by an auditor. [*Section* 12]

Valuation: Every insurer carrying on life insurance business shall in respect of his life insurance business every year cause an investigation to be made by an actuary into the financial condition of the life insurance business carried on by him, including a valuation of his liabilities in respect thereto. [*Section* 13]

Submission of returns: The Audited accounts and the valuation report and/or abstract thereof shall be furnished as returns to the IRDA within six months in case of the accounts and within nine months in case of actuarial report and/or abstract thereof, from the end of the period to which they refer. [*Section* 15(1)]

Powers of IRDA regarding returns and order of re-valuation: The IRDA has powers to decline to accept any such returns unless the inaccuracy, if any, has been corrected or deficiency supplied. It has also power to order re-valuation if it appears that the valuation report or abstract thereof does not properly indicate the condition of the affairs of the insurer by reason of the faulty basis adopted in the valuation. [*Sections* 21 and 22]

Investment: Every insurer carrying on the business of life insurance shall invest and at all times keep invested his controlled fund.

Pension and General Annuity Business: Every insurer shall invest and at all times keep invested assets of Pension business, General Annuity Business and Group business.

[*Section* (27C)]

Prohibition for investment of funds outside India: No insurer shall invest the funds of policyholder outside India. [*Section* (27C)]

Prohibition of Loan or Advances

(i) No grant of loans or advances on personal security or hypothecation or property is allowed (housing loan is exception);

(ii) Temporary advances are granted to insurance agent to facilitate the carrying out of his functions as such where such advances do not exceed in the aggregate his earning of renewal commission in the year immediately preceding temporary advances.

[*Section* 29]

Restriction on payment of excessive remuneration: The IRDA reserves its right to restrict remuneration to any person whether by way of commission or otherwise, if it is considered disproportionate according to the normal standards prevailing in insurance business, to the resources of the insurer. [*Section* 31B(1)]

Power of investigation: IRDA has the powers to order an investigation into the affairs of an insurer and report thereon. [*Section* 33]

Assignment of insurance policies. [*Section* 38]

Nomination by policyholder. [*Section* 39]

Cap on commission payable to agents. [*Section* 40A(i)]

Prohibition of rebate: To allow or offer to allow any rebate, as an inducement, to prospects is prohibited. [*Section* 41]

Licensing of insurance agents. [*Section* 42]

Licensing of insurance intermediaries. [*Section* 42D]

Hereditary Commission to agents. [*Section* 44]

Wrong statement, policy can't be rejected after two years. [*Section* 45)

Insurance business in rural or social sector and backward class: Every insurer must ensure a specified percentage of its total business from these areas/classes. [*Section* 32(B)/(C)]

Insurance Association of India. [*Sections* 64A to 64T]

Solvency Margins to be kept by the insurer. [*Sections* 64V and 64(VA)]

No risk on policy to be assumed unless premium is received in advance. [*Section* 64(VB)]

Interim bonus: It is payable on policies that result into claim within the inter-valuation period. [*Section* 112]

Acquisition of surrender value by policy

(i) A guaranteed surrender value is payable after three years premiums have been paid under a policy issued by the insurer.

(ii) Policies issued by Co-operative Societies acquire S.V. after five years premiums have been paid.

(iii) The S.V. also includes the surrender value of any bonus, if acquired. [*Section* 113]

In 1956, life insurance business was nationalised and a single "Life Insurance Corporation" was formed, taking over 245 insurance companies. The Insurance Act, 1938 was amended in 1950, 1968, and 1999. The exclusive privilege of LIC has ceased in 1999 and as a result many privately owned, foreign as well as Indian, life insurance companies have come in the market.

Britishers also introduced general insurance in India, including marine insurance, around 1700. These companies were member of Lloyd's Association (1692) England. The government nationalized general insurance business in 1973. Only four companies were allowed to carry on general insurance business including marine insurance, which were subsidiaries of "General Insurance Corporation". They were National Insurance Company Calcutta, New India Assurance Company, Bombay, Oriental Fire and General Insurance Company, New Delhi and United India Fire and General Insurance Company Madras. These four state-owned insurers have formed "General Insurers (Public Sector) Association".

The GIC is the biggest **Reinsurer** in India. Export Credit Guarantee Corporation setup in 1983 (renamed twice) insures shipments of exports as well as against POLITICAL risks Deposit Insurance and Credit Guarantee (renamed) Corporation 1978, guarantees credit facilities given by credit institutions.

Fire Insurance in India in 1870 entered the field of insurance. The different companies, owned mostly by foreigners, were Sun Insurance (1710), London Assurance and Royal Exchange Assurance (1720), Phoenix Assurance Co. (1782), Insurance Co. of North America (1792), Norwich Union Fire Insurance Society (1797) and Law Union and Rock Insurance Society (1806). In the field of miscellaneous insurance Workmen's Compensation Act (1923) and Motor Vehicles Act (1939) were introduced to cover accident insurance in the country. A Bill called "Road Transport and Safety Bill 2014" is pending before the Parliament.

Malhotra Committee—Liberalisation Step

The committee appointed in 1993, under chairmanship of R.N. Malhotra, former Governor, RBI submitted its report in January 1994 recommending that private insurers be allowed to coexist along with government companies like LIC and GIC companies. Major recommendations were:

(a) *Capital Base*: Raising the capital base of LIC and GIC upto ₹ 200 crores, half retained by the government and rest sold to the public at large with suitable reservations for employees.

(b) *Private Sector Entry*: Private sector be granted permission to enter insurance industry with a minimum paid up capital of ₹ 100 crores.

(c) *Foreign Companies Entry*: Foreign insurance companies be allowed to enter by floating an Indian company preferably joint venture with Indian partners.

(d) *Regulatory Authority*: Steps to be initiated to set-up a strong and effective insurance regulatory in the form of statutory autonomous board on the lines of SEBI.

(e) Tariff Advisory Committee (TAC) is delinked from GIC to function as a separate statutory body under necessary supervision by the insurance regulatory authority.

(f) Limited number of private companies to be allowed in the sector. But no firm be allowed to operate in both lines of insurance (life or non-life).

(g) All insurance companies be treated on equal footing and governed by the provisions of the insurance act. No special dispensation is given to government companies.

The committee found that (i) choice available in price, service and product inadequate to customers, (ii) little use of information technology, (iii) integration with world's insurance services/market lacking. IRDA was set up in 1999 and private sector/companies was allowed to enter insurance sector.

Recent Position

At the beginning of 21st century a lot of initiatives have taken place in Indian Insurance Industry. The insurance industry has undergone profound changes as a result of:

(a) Globalisation

(b) Deregulation

(c) Technology.

The industry is moving from a product-oriented industry to customer-oriented service provider.

Deregulation allowed non-insurance companies such as banks, even retailers, to enter the insurance market and compete against the established firms. At the same time, deregulation also allowed insurance companies to enter different financial markets requiring the development and marketing of new products and identification of potential customer groups.

Globalisation accentuated this change, insurance companies are now facing competitors from many parts of the world, many of which move aggressively into new markets trying to attract customers with low rates and improved services. Challenging market conditions, led by accelerating price competition, are causing insurers to look more closely at streamlining their underwriting procedures to improve their profitability. This is creating a new focus by senior executives on data, technology and process management.

Technology further added to the momentum of change, due to computerization, Internet and software to support business operations. Computers allowed a decentralisation of computer resources within a company. As a result emphasis shifted from the traditional product portfolio to innovative products targeting selected customer segments. Technology has brought consistency, accuracy, efficiency and time saving in industry. The following chart shows emerging market scenario in Indian insurance industry.

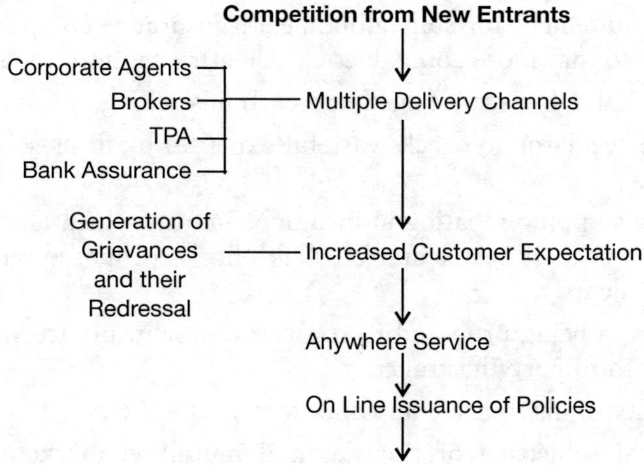

Status view of policy, claim and grievance unfortunately the growth developments in Indian market are geographically uneven. The unprofitability of the industry is rising faster.

Since denationalization of insurance sector in 1999, private players have entered the market. In 2009, out of 25 life insurance companies famous private sector companies are:

AVIVA, Bajaj Allianz, AMP-Sanmar; Birla Sun Life (Canada); Dabur CGNU; HDFC-Sunlife; Iffco Tokio; Max India-NY Life (USA); Met Life; ICICI-Prudential (U.K.); KOTAK Mohindra; OM (old mutual); Reliance Life; Tata-AIG; SBI Life; Sahara Life; Shri Ram Life; Vysya-ING; Bharti Axo Life and Future General. In 2008, DLF Pramerica, Aegon Religare and Canara HSBC-OBC. Royal Sundaram, Chola Appollo, CGC Universal and Royal were started. The highest equity share capital is of ICICI, Prudential, followed by Birla Sun Life and HDFC Std. Except AMP Sanmar, Sun Life, New York Life Vysya Bank, who were already in insurance field, others were in different business. Since 1999 to 2009, it has been observed that LIC still leads in terms of premium amount, number of policies, and number of lives covered, group schemes compared to all other private sector insurance companies. Among other companies Bajaj Allianz tops the list in terms of individual single/non-single premium. These companies have not done well in case of group single premium as well as group non-single premium policies both in terms of number of policies or number of lives covered or in terms of premium amount. The government has increased FDI limit upto 49% in insurance sector.

The Insurance Act, 1938, Life Insurance Act, 1956, General Insurance Business Act, 1972, Marine Insurance Act, 1963, Employees State Insurance Act, 1948, Civil Aviation Act, 1982, Public Liability Insurance Act, 1991, Export Credit and Guarantee Corporation Act, 1983, Motor Vehicles Act, 1988 and Insurance Regulatory and Development Authority Act, 1999 and regulations by I.R.D.A. contain the relevant laws relating to insurance. Law relating to Fire Insurance is given in Insurance Act, 1938. Insurance has been amended in 2012.

Some major highlights of the Insurance Amendment are as below:

1. FDI has been hiked to 74% which will allow foreign companies to increase their stake in Indian joint venture. It will also help the Indian partner to raise money to beef up operations.

2. The capital requirement for standalone health insurance companies has been lowered to ₹ 50 crores so that more companies can be attracted into the sector.
3. Insurers to be liable for acts of agents to curb mis-selling.
4. The insurance regulator to check wasteful expenses by firms so that policyholders get better returns.
5. Norms for the stopping rebating in insurance industry. Insurers to be held responsible for the conduct of their agents and ₹ 10 lakh fine is proposed on agents trying to offer money to the clients.
6. A separate law is being proposed to regulate motor insurance which shall address the concerns over third party insurance.
7. Lesser flexibility to insurance companies to cancel policies.
8. Stopping illegal subletting of agencies and multilevel marketing set-ups which has continued despite a ban since long.
9. Safeguards to be introduced for frauds by way of assignment of policies. The bill shall recognise partial assignment of insurance policies. Further the bill also proposes to empower insurers to reject requests for assignment if it is against the interest of policyholders. This has been done to prevent trading in insurance policies.
10. The public sector general insurance companies shall be able to raise money from the market with the overall cap of 51% government's stake.
11. Foreign reinsurers to be permitted to open branches.
12. Lloyds of London allowed to set up operations in India.
13. Period for repudiating insurance policy capped at three years.
14. Insurance companies allowed to appoint insurance agents who passed IRDA exam.
15. As per an estimate by IRDA the capital requirement of the insurance industry shall be ₹ 61,200 crores over the next five years and the Indian investors have already pumped ₹ 21,000 crores in this sector.
16. India which has an insurance penetration of 4.61% on life insurance business and 0.61% in general insurance business is likely to see an increase in the penetration level.
17. Liberalisation of restrictions on sanctions of loan and advances by insurers to vendors, employees and agents.
18. These amendments are aimed at removing archaic and redundant provisions in the legislations and incorporating certain provisions to provide the Insurance Regulatory Development Authority (IRDA) with flexibility to discharge its functions effectively and efficiently.
19. To improve the functioning of surveyors and bring in greater transparency, certain modifications are made to provide for regulations on qualifications regarding appointment of surveyors and to strengthen the Institute of Indian Insurance Surveyors and Loss Assessors (IIISLA). The amendments proposed in the Bill seek to do away with the existing statutory prescriptions pertaining to licensing insurance surveyors and loss assessors, etc. and leave these issues to be addressed by way of regulations.

Registration

Each insurance company has to register with IRDA, giving following particulars in a prescribed form.

An insurance company should have paid-up capital of ₹ 50 crores in case of life and general insurance, and of ₹ 100 crores in case it carries on reinsurance business.

1. Geographic spread. Give the addresses of the administrative offices in each State and Union Territory in India and overseas, also in Rural Areas with the name of person in charge of the office [if the applicant has not decided, he might give the proposed number and locations of administrative offices in each State and Union Territory in India, and overseas, also in Rural Areas].

2. Market research and analysis. The company may have undertaken some form of market analysis to ascertain the market potential, consumer needs, target market, product research, along with the conclusions reached.

3. Products to be sold. Based on the market research and analysis undertaken, the partners would have decided upon the products to be marketed—individual or group insurance. The description should include the following:

- Description of the product features.
- The target markets where the products will be sold.
- Specification of the names of the products in life/general insurance, linked/non-linked, health insurance.

4. Distribution. This section should describe how the products will be or are proposed to be distributed. This should cover the following:

- The channels of distribution to be used, with an indication on the relative degrees of importance placed on each of the channels.
- The distribution network that will be set up in the marketplace.
- Any limitations on the products to be sold by any of the channels.
- Remuneration to be paid to each channel of distribution.

5. Sales promotion. The approach to be used for advertisement and sales promotion, e.g., the media to be used, frequency, etc. Copies of sales material, literature advertising the product, if any, should be provided.

6. Underwriting. This section should describe the approach used for underwriting of proposals; the arrangements made for medical and other reports, etc.

The nature of support to be provided in underwriting and in training of underwriters by the foreign promoters should also be stated.

7. Investments. Each company will have established its investment philosophy that will the appropriate for the products intends to market. This should be described. Other information should include the investment personnel, investment adviser (if outsourced), location of the investment operations, investment brokers to be used, etc. Regulations regarding Investment, Valuation, Exposure—Prudential-Provisioning Norms—Life and Non-Life issued by the Authority may be taken into account.

8. Information technology. Insurance industry is very much dependent on computer technology. Full description should be provided for the following:

- The different areas where computer systems will be employed.
- Whether the systems will be bought off the shelf (with some customization), developed locally or imported into India by the foreign promoter (with some customization).
- The degree to which the systems will be used for policyholder servicing.
- The degree of inter-connectivity of the systems.
- A description of how the IT systems will be used to develop the required Management Information Systems.
- Extent of procedures and operations which will remain manual.

9. Customer service. Customer service could be provided either centrally through the head office or decentralised to the branch offices/operational units. The degree to which customer service is planned to be decentralised to the branch offices should be described. The service standards planned to be introduced for the various aspects of customer service should be described. Any plan to introduce "call-centres" or customized grievance settlement machinery may be indicated.

Mention the time schedule for various types of service offered by the company.

10. Retention limits and reinsurance. The nature of reinsurance arrangements should be described fully, giving the following details:

- The name(s) reinsurer(s).
- The basis of reinsurance.
- Terms of reinsurance.

The manner in which the retention limit(s) have been established should be discussed.

11. Recruitment and training. Different areas of the company require personnel with different skill sets. These personnel will include agents, sales supervisors, branch managers, administrative staff for various departments, etc. Some of the departments will require special technical skills (e.g., underwriting, actuarial, accounting, sales, information technology, etc.). This section should set out the following information for each of the categories:

- Desirable skill sets.
- Sources for recruitment.
- Approach to be used for training—in house/outsource.

12. Internal controls. The company will need to establish a set of procedures and norms for various activities. The manner in which these will be monitored should be described. These activities will relate to underwriting and policy issue, customer and Required Solvency Margins, regulatory compliance, claim processing and settlement procedures, etc.

13. Expenses of administration

Life. In arriving at the premium rates, the appointed actuary will need to build the estimated expense levels into the premium calculations. The manner in which the expenses of administration have been estimated and converted into average factors should be described. These expenses will have to be distinguished between first year and renewal, fixed and variable. All overhead expenses will also have to be covered.

General. The proposed expenses as a per cent of premium at levels of operational offices and each level of supervisory offices and head office.

14. New product pricing

Life. The financing projections will incorporate the sale of planned products. A description of these products to the extent possible should be provided. This should include the following:

- The product features, such as coverage periods, premium levels, non-forfeiture values, loan provisions, etc.
- Distribution channels to be used.
- Commission scales.
- Average policy size.
- Reserving method used.
- The levels of the various parameters built into the computations. These will relate to mortality, policy terminations, expenses, interest and any other parameters that may be relevant for the products. The values of these parameters will have to be specified at two levels at the expected level and at a level inclusive of the Margins for Adverse Deviations. The justifications for both levels should be provided.
- Profitability criteria used in product pricing.

General. In respect of products not governed by market tariff indicate how the products will be priced, the database which will be used to determine premium bases and the terms and conditions, the statistical system which will be established to review adequacy of rates.

15. Information policy. Mention the company's policy regarding insurance awareness in the public.

16. Premium rates. Enclose the company's Premium Tables for the products along with rebates, if any, offered.

Certification. The undesigned, solemnly declare that the facts given in this application form on behalf of the Applicant Company, are true and that the projections and estimations are based on reasonable assumptions.

Place:

Date: Signature of the Authorised Person (with Seal)

Form IRDA/R3

Insurance Regulatory and Development Authority

(Seal of the Authority)

Certificate of Registration

Registration Number:

This is to certify that (Name of Insurer and his address) has this day been registered in accordance with the provisions of sub-section (2A) of section 3 of the Insurance Act, 1938 (IV of 1938) to transact the classes of business specified in the Schedule below:

Given under the seal of the Authority at New Delhi

this _________ day of _________

two thousand and _____________.

Corporate Governance

Insurance regulator IRDA has framed guidelines on corporate governance for the sector focusing on key areas such as lock-in period for promoters, whistle blowing policy, governance structure and disclosures.

On lock-in period, the IRDA guidelines said promoters of insurance companies would have a lock-in period of five years, which the insurers have to report compliance by the next fiscal year. "No transfer of shares of the promoters would be permitted within this period."

On 'whistle blowing', it said the insurers are to put in place a whistle blowing policy that would allow employees to raise concerns about possible irregularities, governance weaknesses, financial reporting issues, among others.

The appointed actuary and the statutory or internal auditors have the duty to 'whistle blow'. The auditors have to report in a timely manner to IRDA if the insurer has failed to take appropriate steps to rectify a matter, which has a material adverse effect on its financial condition. NOT A SINGLE INSURANCE COMPANY IS A LISTED COMPANY IN INDIA. Therefore, SEBI mandatory disclosures relating to corporate governance are applicable to them. In USA, Insurance Market Place Standards Association has laid down two standards (i) Principles of Ethical market conduct, and (ii) code of Life Insurance ethical market conduct. They are voluntary.

Special Provisions Relating to External Companies

Power of Central Government to impose reciprocal disabilities on non-Indian companies. Where, by the law or practice of any country outside India in which an insurer carrying on insurance business in India is constituted, incorporated or domiciled, insurance-companies incorporated in India are required as a condition of carrying on insurance business in that country to comply with any special requirement whether as to the keeping of deposits or assets in that country or otherwise which is not imposed upon insurers of that country under this Act. The Central Government shall, if satisfied of the existence of such special requirement, by notification in the Official Gazette, direct the same requirement, or requirements as similar thereto as may be, shall be imposed upon insurers of that country as a conditions of carrying on the business of insurance in India.

Particulars to be filled by insurers established outside India. Every insurer, having his principal place of business or domicile outside India, who establishes a place of business within India, or appoints a representative in India with the object of obtaining insurance business shall, within three months from the establishment of such place of business or the appointment of such representative, file with the Authority:

(a) A certified copy of the charter, statutes, deed of settlement or memorandum and articles or other instrument constituting or defining the constitution of the insurer, and, if the instrument is not written in the English language, a certified translation thereof,

(b) a list of the directors, if the insurer is a company,

(c) the name and address of someone or more persons resident in India authorised to accept on behalf of the insurer service of process and any notice required to be served on the insurer, together with a copy of the power-of-attorney granted to him,

(d) the full address of the principal office of the insurer in India,

(e) a statement of the classes of insurance business to be carried on by the insurer, and

(f) a statement verified by an affidavit setting forth special requirements, if any, of the nature specified in Section 62 imposed in the country of origin of the insurer on Indian nationals.

and, in the event of any alteration being made in the address of the principal office or in the classes of business to be carried on, or in any instrument here referred to, or in the name of any of the persons here referred to, or in the matters specified in clause (f) above, the company shall forthwith furnish to the Authority particulars of such alteration.

Books to be kept by insurers established outside India. Every insurer having his principal place of business or domicile outside India shall keep at his principal office in India such books of account, registers and documents as will enable the accounts, statements and abstracts which he is required under this Act to furnish to the Authority in respect of the insurance business transacted by him, in India to be compiled and, if necessary, checked by the Authority and shall furnish to the Authority on or before the last day of January in every calendar year a certificate from an auditor to the effect that the said books of account, register and documents are being kept as required at the principal office of the insurer in India.

Performance Review

Private insurance companies gave Life Insurance Corporation a sum for its business, since their entry in the market in the year 2001. One of the reasons for their success was crisis in UTI, where government was forced to dole out nearly ₹ 14,000 crores to meet its requirement. Moreover, some more financial institutions which had government backing were on the varge of default. The private companies were doing business only in the beginning in the start. The LIC had a huge network and government backing. But increased insurance market size gave the private companies to grow.

At the end of 2011, there was a sharp drop in sales of unit limited products, especially individual pension products led to the lackluster performance by life insurance industry. The LIC (Amendment) Bill, 2009 was passed aiming to raise the equity base upto ₹ 100 crores. Mckinsey report in January 2012 found that Indian Life Insurance market is least profitable in Asia. Health, home and motor insurance getting costlier. The 56-year-old LIC already holds significant stakes in many Indian companies. Private companies only hold 10%. For them it is good because they started from zero. Nearly 80% of Indian population is without life insurance.

The life insurance industry has declined marginally in 2011-12. The first year premium had declined by 14%. The private insurance business suffered a decline of 17.7% and LIC posted a 11.3% fall in first year premium. This is attributed to low paying capacity of the consumers or poor cash flow in the market or collection of taxes by State and Central Governments. Inflation was another major reason. The Central Government has announced to infuse a sum of ₹ 8000 crores in 2012-13 and 2013-14 to improve the functioning of PSU insurers.

The 44000 crores domestic general industry is in a huge setback due to heavy losses. The main cause was that general insurance players face difficulty getting intermediaries to distribute their products. Moreover further cause was excessive claims in third party motor portfolio. The underwriting losses of non-life insurance companies increased 68% to ₹ 9969 crores in 2010-11, compared with ₹ 5944 crores in 2009-10. Insurance sector in India may see a de-growth of 13-14% in future. Recently, IRDA has relaxed solvency norms for general insurers.

To sum up "Deterred due to the regulatory changes, low margins and lack of a policy road map, the life insurance industry is reeling under effect of negative growth. The unabated inflation, recessionary trends and fall in industrial production have all had their impact on the economy. During the year stock markets witnessed violent swings, coupled with reduction in margins on account of new guidelines, which dented the performance of ULIPs. The industry is currently going through a period of adjustment. Insurers are trying to cut down cost through rationalisation of infrastructure. They are trying to sell products on the basis of customer needs, encouraging transparency and timely renewal payments to retain customers. Insurance is a 'push' rather than a 'pull' product."

Alternative Distribution Channels

For marketing insurance products now becoming popular are banks, post offices, partner agents like Micro Finance institutions, mutual insurance agents through cooperative credit union, besides TPA and corporate agents. A corporate agent is a company, mostly trust companies, that are empowered to act as agents through outsourcing. Internet, on line selling call centres, kiosks are other distribution channels.

Insurance through Bank

BANCASSURANCE, also known as Referral business originated in France and is popular in European countries. IRDA gave permission for it in 2000. The tie up of banks with insurance is beneficial for banks, insurers and ultimate customer. Bank may follow any of the three models: (a) Referral model: It is simple arrangement with banks, while controlling access to clients database, parts with only the business leads with agents/sales staff of insurance company for a referral fee or commission for every business deed that was passed on. (b) Corporate model, i.e. by obtaining corporate agency from one or more insurer: Under this the banks are distributing the entire range of products of the insurer starting from elementary term assurance plans to complex insurance on an "as is where is" basis after training and licensing the employees. (c) Wrapper products: Distribution of insurance product wrapped around the banks saving and loan products, i.e. bank sets up its own insurance company. The first is not so popular.

Prospect of Bancassurance has been achieved very effectively. Currently, the Bancassurance is related to around 28 Public Sector Banks, 29 Private Banks and 31 Foreign Banks. These banks have their combined network of over 53,000 branches which is also involving the co-operative banks whose number of branches will be around 70,000. There is an estimate that on an average each office is serving 16,000 people. Hence, it is a win-win situation for banks, insurers and customers.

Advantage of Bancassurance

Following are the advantages to the banks:

- Productivity of employees increases.
- Diversification of risk.
- Incomes out of insurance operation through cross sales.
- Banks can cover a large chunk of operating expenses through this route. They get their share of commission from bancassurance product sales.
- Lower cost per sales lead over traditional insurance distributors.

Following are the advantages to insurers:

1. Insurers can exploit the banks network for distribution of products.
2. Customer database like financial standing, spending habits can be used to customize the product and volume of personal-line insurance business can be increased.
3. Since banks have already established relationship with customers, conversion ratio of leads to sales is likely to be high.

Following are the advantage to consumers:

1. Comprehensive financial service under one roof i.e. banking, insurance, mutual funds, etc.
2. Competitive rates.
3. Easy access for claims.

Strategic Challenges are being Faced by Current Bancassurance Market

- Possible disruptions to client relations arising from more frequent non-life insurance claims.
- Cost of servicing non-life policies is high.
- Bankers require strong motivation of both monetary and non-monetary, since there were no occasions in the past to deal in insurance products.
- Resistance from the bank employees.
- Lack of involvement of some sections.

Regulations Relating to Bancassurance

- Banks can sell their insurance product by taking Corporate Agency or through Referral arrangement. A corporate agent (life, health, general) can have arrangement with not more than three insurers.

- Since insurance contracts are highly technical, it is stipulated that the canvassing should be done only by "Specified Persons".
- Specified person should have the qualification prescribed by the Authority.
- The Authority also prescribed certain qualifications for Corporate Executives to obtain license.
- The Corporate Agent should canvass insurance products with the help of insurance professionals who satisfy the qualifications laid-down in the Regulations.
- They should not use any other modes like introducers, finders or sub-agents.
- If a Corporate Agent terminates its representation for an insurer, it should secure the specific written approval of IRDA before it can enter into an agreement with another insurer.
- A Corporate Agent shall not charge an administration fee or service charge to the policyholder.
- The insurer shall not pay any amount other than the permitted agency commission.
- Sharing expenses of co-branded sales literature is permitted.
- Such expenses should be reasonable and should not in any way be linked with the success in sale or premium earned.

Quite large number of people are in future expected to buy insurance from their banks rather than the time-tested insurance agents. There are several "pull" (demand) and "push" (supply) factors for why this will happen.

Pull Factors

Trust. The bank is one financial institution with which almost every earning adult has a relationship (in fact, 50 per cent of all household savings are kept with banks). This long-standing relationship gradually leads to trust. So when somebody at the bank tries selling a life insurance policy, the customer is often more receptive to buying it.

One-stop service. It is also becoming evident that customers want to be able to meet all their financial needs, including insurance need, banks are increasingly transforming themselves into financial supermarkets, offering bonds, mutual funds, and now insurance, in addition to savings account and fixed deposits.

Push Factors

Quick penetration. Banks and insurers have already formed alliances in a bid to exploit the potential of the bancassurance channel (bancassurance refers to the selling of insurance through banks). While LIC has its agents in every nook and cranny of the country, the same can't be said of private insurance companies. It would take the latter a lot of time (given the 100 hours training requirement for agents) and money to set up branch offices in all parts of the country. On the other hand, there are about 65,000 bank branches in the country (one bank for every 15,000 people). If insurance companies want to penetrate the vast hinterlands fast, tying up with banks offers the quickest way. Bancassurance alliances with large nationalised banks have enabled many insurers to acquire a nationwide footprint—a fear that would in the normal course have taken them ten years or so to accomplish.

Information. The bank has a lot of information on the financial status and life stage of customers, which it could leverage to sell insurance. For instance, it knows that a certain fixed deposit is maturing on a given date. Why not put the money into a retirement plan, the banker or financial planner at the bank advises you. Many banks now offer personal banking or wealth management service to select clients, where they offer detailed financial planning. Having insurance products in their basket enables them to meet their clients' protection needs.

Convenience. Banks already have multiple channels in place—branch network, ATMs, telebanking, Internet banking, etc. All these could be used to sell and service the insurance buyer too. For instance, electronic clearance mechanism could be used to deduct premium payment automatically from the customer's savings account. Using Internet banking, the customer could see a statement of his insurance policy (whether premium has been paid, how much cash has accumulated in his policy, the NAV of a unit-linked policy, etc.). E-mails, SMS, etc. could be used a alert customers as the date for premium payment approaches.

Wrapping Insurance on to Banking Products

Several insurance products sell very well in banking-related situations. Look at credit insurance products. Suppose you are taking a home loan, then for a small addition to your EMI you can get an insurance cover added to the loan. In the event of the demise of the breadwinner of the family, the insurance company takes on the liability of paying off the rest of the loan. The family is protected for losing possession of its home. Birla Sun Life's Credit Shield (term insurance wrapped on to a home loan) is one such product. Commercial banks act as a corporate agents.

Who Has Tied Up With Whom

Insurer	Bank	Paid-up Capital (₹ in Crores)
Allianz Bajaj	Standard Chartered, ABN AMRO	(250)
Aviva	American Express, Canara Bank Laxmi Vilas	(283)
ICICI Prudential	ICICI Bank, Bank of India, Federal Bank of India, South India Bank, Allahabad Bank, Punjab & Maharashtra Co-operative	(675)
HDFC Standard	HDFC Bank, Union Bank of India, Indian Bank, Lord Krishna Bank	
Tata AIG	HSBC Corporation Bank	(255)
LIC	Central Bank of India, Bank of Punjab, Indian Overseas Bank	(251)
SBI Life	SBI and Subsidiaries	(245)
ING Vysya	Vysya Bank	(16)
Met Life	J&K Bank, Dhanlaxmi Bank, Karnataka Bank	(175)
Birla Sun Life	Citi bank, Deutsche Bank, Bank of Rajasthan, Development Credit Bank, Bank Muscat, Andhra Bank, Catholic Syrian, IDBI	(290)
OMKOTAK	N.A.	
Max New York Life	N.A.	(340)
SBI Cardiff	SBI	(175)
AMP San Mar.	(AMP)	(160)

Over-the-counter Products

They offer over-the-counter insurance products. With these products, you may not have too many options. For instance, you may have to pay only three or four premium. But they offer convenience. Often, no medical checkup is required. Just hand over the money and walk away with the insurance certificate. These days when everyone is short of time, such products do have an appeal.

Treasure Plus (Aviva Life's Easy Life, a simple endowment added on to ABN AMRO Bank's child saving account called (Treasure), Birla Sun Life's Family Protector (pure term) and Young Scholar (money-back policy or children) are examples of such packaged products.

Insurance companies are hopeful about the prospects of bancassurance. Aviva Life claims to have registered more than 50 per cent sales from this channel since starting its operations.

Guidelines for Entry of Banks into Insurance

Banks are allowed tie up only with one life as well as one non-life and act stone-alone health insurance company for distributing insurance products. They can act as brothers as well.

Reserve Bank of India has laid-down the following **guidelines** in this regard:

1. Banks which satisfy the following eligibility criteria as on March 31, 2000, will be permitted to set up a joint venture company for undertaking insurance business with risk participation:
   (i) The net worth of the bank should not be less than ₹ 200 crores.
   (ii) The capital to risk asset ratio of the bank should not be less than 10%.
   (iii) The level of non-performing assets should be reasonable.
   (iv) The bank should have net profit for five continuous years.
   (v) The track record of the performance of the subsidiaries if any, of the concerned ban should be satisfactory.
2. The maximum equity contribution of the abovementioned eligible bank in the Joint Venture will normally be 50% of the paid up capital of the insurance company. Reserve Bank of India may permit higher contribution by a promoter bank initially pending disinvestment of equity within the prescribed period.
3. In cases where a foreign partner contributes 26 per cent of the equity with the approval of the Insurance Regulatory and Development Authority/Foreign Investment Promotion Board, more than one public sector bank or private sector bank may be allowed to participate in the equity of the insurance joint ventures. These banks should also satisfy the criteria stated in (1) above, as they will also assume insurance risk.
4. A subsidiary of a bank or of another bank will not normally be allowed to join the insurance company on risk participation basis.
5. Banks which are not eligible as joint venture participants as above, can make investments up to 10% of the net worth of the bank or ₹ 50 crores whichever is lower, in the insurance company for providing infrastructure and services support. Such participation shall be treated as an investment and should be without any contingent liability for the bank.

The banks permitted to invest in the insurance company must satisfy conditions (ii) to (iv) stated in para (1) above.

6. Any scheduled commercial bank would be permitted to undertake insurance business as agent of insurance companies on fee basis, without any risk participation.
7. The subsidiaries of banks would also be allowed to undertake distribution of Insurance products on agency basis.
8. All banks entering into insurance business will be required to obtain prior approval of the Reserve Bank of India.
9. There should be an 'arms length' relationship between the bank and the insurance company. It should be ensured that the risks involved in the insurance business do not get transferred to the bank.

Regional Rural Banks (RRB) can also enter into insurance business. For them the conditions are:

1. The RRB should have positive net worth.
2. The bank should have complied with the prudential norms on income recognition, asset classification, provisioning, investment norms, exposure norms.
3. The bank should not have violated any directive in last two years.
4. The Gross NPAs of the RRB should not be more than 10%.
5. The bank should be in net profit during last three years and should not have any accumulated losses.
6. The bank should comply with IRDA Regulations for acting as a corporate agent.
7. The bank should not adopt any restrictive practices of forcing its customers to go in only for a particular insurance company in respect of assets financed by the bank. The customers should be allowed to excuse their own choice.
8. The risk, if any, involved in insurance agency should not get transferred to the business of the bank.
9. The RRB should obtain prior permission from the concerned regional office of RBI before taking up the insurance agency business. The application should be recommended by sponsor bank and ranked through NABARD for their recommendation. The permission is valid for two years and is to be renewed.

Urban Cooperative Banks (UCB) are also allowed to enter insurance business provided their minimum net worth in ₹ 50 crores. They also have to seek permission from R.B.I. and I.R.D.A.

Referral Arrangements

1. The referral fee shall be for access to bank's customer database.
2. The referral fee should not exceed the ceilings on agency commission prescribed under the Insurance Act, 1938 and the IRDA Regulations.
3. The participation by bank's customers shall be purely on voluntary basis.
4. It should be stated prominently in all publicity materials distributed by the bank insurance company.

5. It should also clearly mention that the contract of insurance is between insurance company and the insured, and not between bank and the insured.
6. There should not be any linkage either direct or indirect between the provision of banking services by the banks to its customers and use of the insurance products.
7. No interest surcharge, concession dependent upon non-use/use of the insurance service by the customer.
8. Any administrative/management expenses to be incurred for distributing literature other information should be brought out in the agreement.
9. Information exchanged should be exclusively for the promotion of the business only and not for any other purposes.
10. The bank will not be paid for any referral fee for promotional campaigns.
11. The insurance company will not provide any details of its customers to the bank on account of confidentiality obligations.
12. The insurance company and the bank shall enter into a referral fee arrangement based on Memorandum of Understanding which needs to be filed with the Authority.
13. Banks are not permitted to enter into any agreement with more than one LIFE and one GENERAL INSURANCE company.
14. This is to ensure that a bank does not act *de facto* as an insurance agent or broker without any license.
15. For use of premises and existing infrastructure of bank insurance company should enter into a separate agreement.
16. A copy of the agreement should be filed with the Authority.
17. Reimbursement of infrastructure expenses should not be linked to premium. It should be on flat basis.
18. All agreements should be for fixed period and should be with the prior approval of the boards of both the insurance company and the bank.
19. The bank should comply IRDA Regulations and IRDA shall have the discretion to apply its own criteria to reject or discontinue such arrangements.

A SWOT analysis of banks and pure insurance companies is given below:

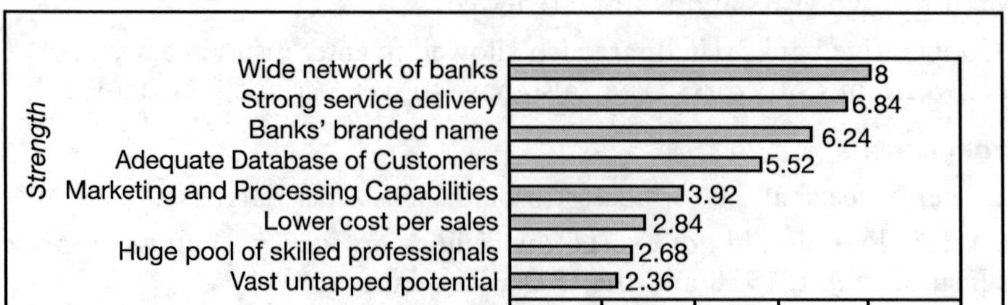

Fig. 1: Strengths of Banks in Bancassurance

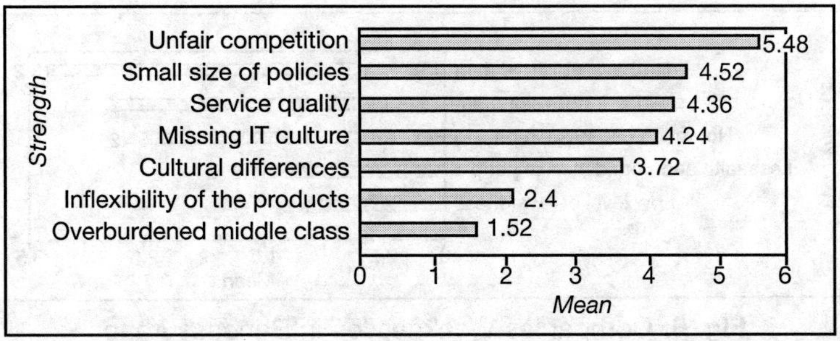

Fig. 2: Weaknesses of Banks in Bancassurance

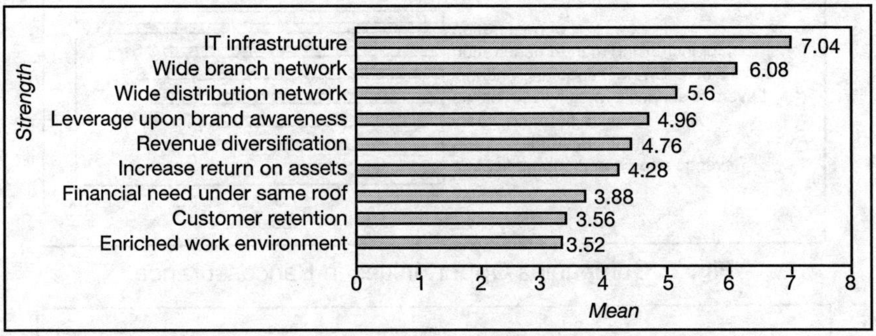

Fig. 3: Opportunities of Banks in Bancassurance

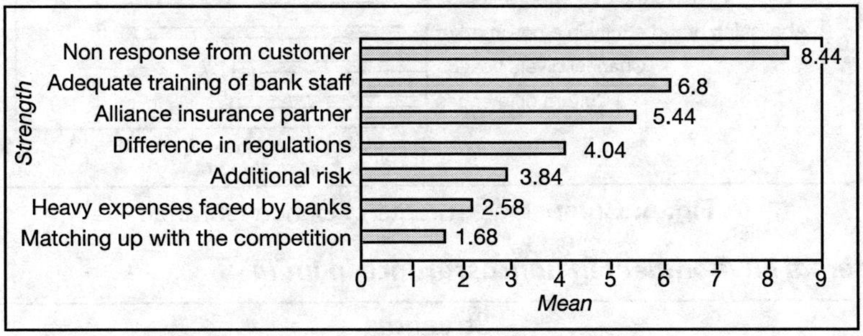

Fig. 4: Threats of Banks in Bancassurance

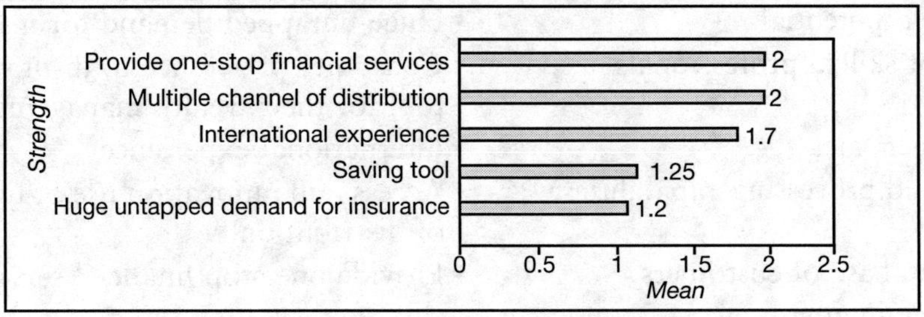

Fig. 5: Strengths of Companies in Bancassurance

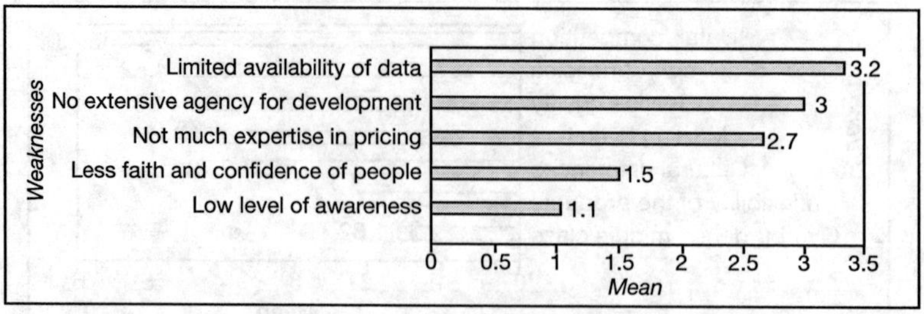

Fig. 6: Companies Weaknesses in Bancassurance

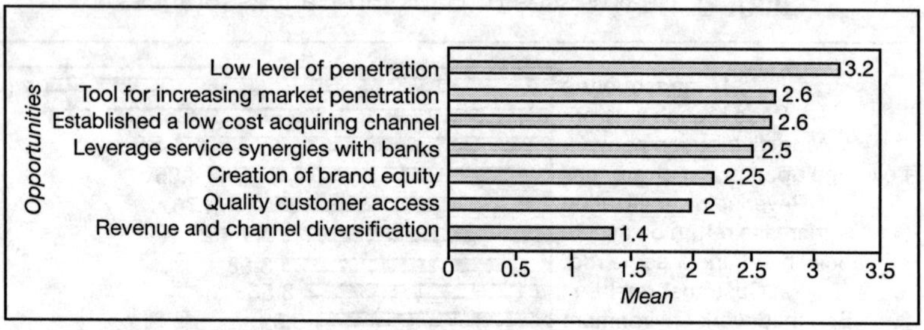

Fig. 7: Companies Opportunities in Bancassurance

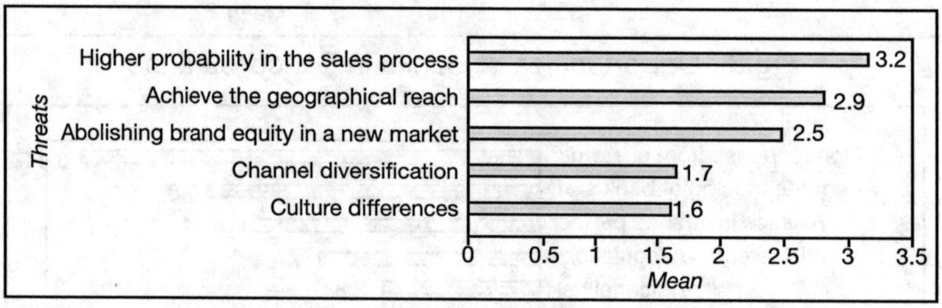

Fig. 8: Companies Threats in Bancassurance

Internal and External Environment in Bancassurance in India

Strengths	
Banks	**Insurance Companies**
• Vast untapped potential	• Huge untapped demand for insurance
• Huge pool of skilled professionals	• Consumer preference to insurance as a saving tool for their wealth management
• Lower cost per sales	• International experience
• Marketing and processing capabilities	• Access and innovation use of multiple channel of distribution
• Adequate database of customers	• Provide one stop financial services
• Banks' branded name	
• Strong service delivery	
• Wide network of banks branches	

Weaknesses	
Banks	**Insurance Companies**
• Overburdened middle class • Inflexibility of the products • Cultural differences between insurers and banks • Missing IT culture • Service quality • Small size of policies • Unfair competition	• Low level of awareness • Less faith and confidence of people • Not much expertise in pricing products for the Indian market • No extensive agency for development • Limited availability of data
Opportunities	
Banks	**Insurance Companies**
• Enriched work environment • Customer retention • Satisfaction of more financial need under same roof • Increased return on assets • Revenue diversification • Leverage upon brand awareness • Leveraging the wide distribution • Wide branch network • IT infrastructure	• Revenue and channel diversification • Quality customer access • Creation of brand equity • Leverage service synergies with banks • Establish a low cost acquisition channel • Tool for increasing market penetration • Low level of insurance penetration network
Threats	
Banks	**Insurance Companies**
• Caching up and matching up with competition • Heavy expenses faced by banks • Additional risk • Difference in regulations • Alliance insurance partner • Adequate training of bank staff • Non response from customer	• Cultural differences • Channel diversification • Abolishing brand equity in a new market • Achieve the geographical reach • Higher probability in the sales process

Insurance through Post Offices

Post office circles are allowed by IRDA as corporate agents. Each circle has to obtain a license for doing insurance. Each circle has to tie up with two non-life, two life, one agriculture and one stand-alone health insurance company.

Oriental Insurance and Department of Posts have taken a giant leap to come closer to insured. India post would now offer Oriental's range of insurance products through over 1.5 lakh post offices all over the country. For the first time ever, insurance policies for hospitalisation, personal accident, household goods, shops, etc. are now available at Post Offices. This revolutionary move will have far-reaching benefits. Rural India will get a new impetus through specialised products being made accessible with ease now. Oriental's wide range of rural insurance products viz., Kissan Package Policy, Agricultural Pump-Set Insurance, Raj Rajeshwari Mahila Kalyan Bima and Universal Health Insurance will be available at the post offices in interior rural areas. Initially, the scheme has been launched only in seven states: Karnataka, Maharashtra, West Bengal, Gujarat, Kerala, Tamil Nadu and Rajasthan, which will be expanded in a phased manner in the future to cover the entire country.

Postal Life Insurance

This policy is issued to those who are (a) between 19 and 50 years as on next birth date of the proponent and (b) are employees of Central and State Governments and defence services or government-aided educational institutions, universities established by government or all nationalized bank or state and central undertakings or corporations.

It has the advantages of 100% security by G.O.I., easy transfer to any place in India free of cost, rebate of 1% to 2% on payment of 6 to 12 months premier in advance, payment of policy money through any post office in India and centralised accounting for quick and easy settlement of claims. Like other insurance companies offering life insurance, postal life insurance given option of repayment of loan, pass book facility and nomination facility. Maximum limit 50 lakhs. Rebate in tax age 19 to 55 years. Payment by cash/cheque or on line. It has also started Rural Postal life Insurance.

Unit Linked Insurance Plans (ULIP)

A dispute between IRDA and SEBI about the jurisdiction relating to ULIPs reached the Supreme Court. The government passed the Securities and Insurance Laws (Amendment and Validation) Act, 2010. Under the Act IRDA has been given jurisdiction over ULIPs. The Act has amended the RBI Act, Insurance Act, SEBI Act and Securities Regulation Act (for IRDA regulations about ULIPs). The new regulations apply prospectively and existing ULIP customers need not worry. Most of the old ULIPs will be off the market and new products are introduced adhering to new guidelines under ULIP, the insured decides where to invest his premium, i.e. the unit fund.

Many alternative unit linked insurance plans are being offered in insurance market. These plans differ on the basis of their features, working, benefits available, flexibility, mode, age of entry, tax benefits, nominations, loan facility charges, free look period and risks.

They are explained below:

(1) *Benefits*: The various benefits offered are death benefit, survival benefit, maturity benefit, accident benefit, disability benefit, illness benefit, hospitalisation benefit and cash benefit.

(2) *Investment options*: The various types of funds like equity funds, debt fund, balanced fund, equity index fund, debt or equity plus fund, cash plus or balanced plus fund are available for investment.

(3) *Withdrawal*: Allowed both partial full.

(4) *Age of entry*: 0 to 60 years.

(5) *Unit value or bid price*: The formula to calculate it is:

$$\text{Unit value} = \frac{\text{Market/fair value of investments of the fund plus working capital and provisions/transaction charges}}{\text{Number of outstanding units in the fund}}$$

(6) *Premium payment mode*: Monthly/quarterly/half-yearly/yearly.

(7) *Free look period*: 15 days.

(8) *Days of grace*: 30 days.

(9) *Paid value/Surrender value*: (It is the fund value on the date of surrender based on NAV of that date minus surrender charges) Nomination, revival, loans—same as other life insurance policies.

(10) *Termination*: By surrender of units, if account value becomes less than required and on death of insured.

(11) *Tax liability*: Death benefit is tax free. Withdrawals are tax free under 10(D) of Income Tax. Premiums on critical illness benefit and hospital cash benefit are tax exempted under Section 88(D) of Income Tax Act.

(12) *Charges*: Fund management charges, transaction charges, switching charges, mortality charges according to age, allocation charges, bid/offer spread, and additional benefit charges.

(13) *Risk of investment*: Each ULIP has to mention the risks involved in investment, e.g. name of policy does not in any way indicate the quality of the policy, its future prospects or returns. Past performance of other funds of the company is not necessarily indicative of the future performance of the fund.

(14) *Exclusion*: Suicide.

Some of the ULIPs available in the market are given below:

Name of the Company	Name of the Policy
(1) SBI Life Insurance Co.	Saral Maha Anand
(2) AIVA Life Insurance Co.	Life saver/advantage
(3) ING Vysya Life Insurance Co.	Market Shield
(4) Met Life	Smart Platinum
(5) Aegon Religare	Rising Star plan
(6) LIC with UTI	Group Superannuation plus

Caution: These days insurance companies are using fancy names for their products. They may be misleading, e.g. annuities are sold as retirement plans. One should know whether it is insurance plan or a mutual fund. A child education product should disclose that it bifurcates the premium into insurance and investment and offers a portfolio return along with insurance.

IRDA has laid down that sale of highest NAV guaranteed products is not allowed. It is a dangerous product and has been banned in many countries.

The unit linked plans are "**linked Business**" (see p. 28).

The advantages of ULIP are that insured can benefit from the returns in the capital market without direct investment. He decides where his money is to be invested, whereas in traditional policies, the insurer decides where to invest.

But the disadvantage of ULIPs is that there are heavy chances of dying in an index down turn. The trust of people is lost and it effects future sales for insurance companies. Life insurance is a contingent claim contract, whereas ULIP is based on market return and a contingent claim. Market risk is transferred to insured in ULIP, but in traditional policy insured gets timely help. It is better to buy an ULIP after providing adequate life insurance cover.

W.e.f. 24 Oct. 2010, IRDA has banned ULP (Universal life insurance policy). Under ULP one part of the insurance goes to buy life insurance, the other goes to be invested in bonds and equities. Now these policies are called "VARIABLE INSURANCE POLICY". It has a lock in period of three years. The rate of commission is fixed. There is no group insurance and only it is for mortality.

Note: IRDA has capped the amount insurance companies can charge under Unit Linked Plans from the funds offered.

Keyman Insurance

Insurance Prioritization

People insure their factories, machinery, company vehicles, etc. to mitigate the risk of loss to business in case of loss/damage to them. However, we often forget to insure some of our key human resources. Loss of these key human resources can sometimes prove to be potentially more damaging than the loss of machinery or goods. When one thinks of risks associated with the loss of a key person—Loss of Business, Delay/Cancellation of a project, etc. would it not be wonderful to find a solution that protects one from these risks while providing with attractive tax benefits?

Keyman Insurance provides with the unique opportunity to protect business against the unfortunate loss of key people, while giving valuable tax advantage and a lovely tool to help employee loyalty too.

What is Keyman Insurance?

Keyman Insurance is a Life Insurance cover under a suitable plan and assurance affected by the company to compensate for the financial loss suffered following the death of a Key Member or Staff of the organization. Keyman Assurance does not provide for indemnification of loss incurred but only for the benefits as per the plan of assurance selected.

Purpose of Keyman Cover

It provides a financial cushion to the company for:

- The loss of customers or sales affected by the keyman's ability and personality.
- The loss of day-to-day specialised skills.
- The cost of recruiting and training a suitable replacement.
- Delay or cancellation of any business project that the keyman is working in.
- The loss of opportunity to expand in the future.

- The loss of stable management and good labour relations.
- Reduction of credit worthiness—recall of loans guaranteed by the keyman.

Who can be a Keyman?

Key person includes chief executive officer, chief marketing officer, appointed actuary, chief investment officer, chief internal auditor, chief finance officer, chief risk officer and chief compliance officer.

Benefits to the Company

1. Insulate the risk of financial loss against loss of a keyman.
2. Premiums paid under keyman insurance may be fully allowed as Business Expenses under Section 37(1) of the Income Tax Act, 1961, subject to satisfaction of the assessing authority.
3. Interest on loans taken against a keyman insurance policy may also be allowed as business expenses.
4. Premiums paid by the company on the life of a keyman would not be treated as perquisites in the hands of such a keyman when the company's request is accepted by the assessing authority.
5. Keyman Insurance policy is a positive measure to improve the retention of the keyman in the company.

Note: That partnership insurances through endowment or unit linked plans are not 'keyman insurance'. An employer buying Keyman insurance for his own benefit cannot prove insurable interest beyond a certain cover protecting against death of key employee and similar is the position of a partner it is a term insurance, buying insurance on the life of another partner.

Treatment of Payments—for the Company

- All claims—maturity, surrender or death benefit received by company are taxable.
- In case of the keyman retiring, the company may surrender policy for its cash value, or assign the policy absolutely in favour of the keyman.
- In case of an assignment, the surrender value of the policy at the time of assignment may be treated as perquisite in the hands of the employee, and taxed accordingly by the assessing authority.

Insurance Worth of a Keyman

The insurance worth of a keyman is the lower of:

- five times the average net profit of the company for the past three years.
- two times the average gross profit of the company for the past three years.
- ten times of the keyman's annual compensation package.

Note: If number of shareholders or number of employees are less than or equal to 10 but greater than or equal to 5, the maximum sum assured will be two times of average of three years' net profit. For new companies where three years Profit and Loss Account is not available, the maximum cover will be equal to net profit if accounts are available for one year, and two times average net profit if accounts are available for two years.

Limits in Keyman Insurance

Keyman cover is permissible if:

- Key person shareholding is less than or equal to 51%.
- Family shareholding is less than or equal to 70%.

  Family includes spouse and minor child.

Requirements for Keyman Insurance

- A resolution from the Board of Directors stating that they desire to have a policy on the life of the keyman named, with the amount for which the policy is desired.
- Copies of Memorandum and Articles of Association.
- Keyman questionnaire duly signed by persons authorised by the company.
- Copy of audited accounts, P&L Account, Balance sheet for the last three years duly certified.
- Proposal form signed by a person authorised by the company.

What Kind of Plans are Ideal for Keyman Insurance?

- Typically, a limited premium payment endowment policy is a preferred form of keyman cover.
- It combines the benefit of risk cover for company, while giving the company an option to have the policy assigned to the keyman.
- Loans are also available against endowment policies.

Products Available for Keyman Insurance

Endowment Plan:

- It is participating (with profits) endowment plan.
- Limited premium payment options available, making it an attractive proposition.
- Loans available against the policy.
- Various packages with differing levels of additional protection also available.
- Attractive additional benefits available.
- Best value for money.

Other Products Available for Keyman Insurance

- CashGain—Money-back Plan.
- Risk Care—Pure Term Insurance Plan.
- Term Care—Term Insurance plan that returns premiums paid at maturity.
- With all these plans, attractive additional benefits like Comprehensive Accident Protection and Critical Illness Benefit are also available for Keyman Insurance.

Free Look Period

Within 15 days from the date of receipt of the policy, one has the option to review the terms and conditions and return the policy, if one disagrees to any of the terms and conditions, stating the reasons for objections. One will be entitled to a refund of the premium paid, subject only to a deduction of a proportionate risk premium for the period on cover and the expenses incurs on medical examination and stamp duty charges.

IRDA Guidelines on Unit Linked Insurance Products

Part-I Product Design

Approved terminology stated under various items under these guidelines should be used as per Annexure-1 at all times and shall not be changed and other terminology/definitions shall not be used.

1. *Benefit payable on death*

1.1 Table 1.2 below specifies the minimum sum assured in respect of death benefit under unit linked life insurance contracts where:

1.1.1 T is Policy Term (PT) chosen by the policyholder (T shall be taken as 70 minus age 4 at entry in case of Whole Life Products).

1.1.2 AP is Annualized Premium selected by the policyholder at the inception of the policy.

1.1.3 SP is Single Premium chosen by the policyholder at the inception of the policy.

1.2 The minimum sum assured shall be at least equal to:

Table 1.2

Type of Products	Minimum Sum Assured
Single Premium Products	123% of the SP
Non-Single Premium Product	0.5 × T × AP or 5 × AP, whichever is higher

1.2.1 In respect of products under pension and annuity business it should be like single premium products.

1.3 *Other Conditions*

1.3.1 The sum assured payable on death shall not be reduced at any point of time during the term of the policy except to the extent of the partial withdrawals made during the two-year period immediately preceding the death of the life assured. However, on attainment of 60 years of the life assured, all the partial withdrawals may be set off against the sum assured payable on death.

1.3.2 No cover should be extended after the expiry of the policy term and only settlement options (which are clearly outlined at the commencement of the contract) may be allowed.

2. *Minimum policy term*

The minimum policy term shall be ten years.

3. *Guarantees on policy benefits*

A linked product must have a guaranteed sum assured payable on death and may have a guaranteed maturity value:

3.1 General aspect on guarantees: Guarantees provided on death and/or on maturity shall be reasonable and consistent in relation to the current and long-term interest rate scenario. In this regard demonstration of proper pricing, including the appropriateness through sensitivity and scenario testing shall be required under the File and Use Procedure for all the guarantees provided for.

4. *Surrender value (SV)*

4.1 Where a Unit Linked Life Insurance Policy acquires a surrender value, it shall become payable only after the completion of the third policy anniversary.

4.2 The "Surrender value" or the "surrender value formula" must be published in the policy document and all other promotional materials of the life insurance contract.

5. *Options available on discontinuance of premium*

5. (i) Discontinuance of due premiums after paying at least three consecutive years and subsequent premiums.

5.1 If all the due premiums have been paid for at least three consecutive years and subsequent premiums are unpaid, life insurers shall give an opportunity to the policyholders to revive the contract within the limited period allowed for revival as per policy conditions.

5.2 During this limited period for revival, the insurance cover under the Unit Linked Life Insurance contracts shall be continued levying appropriate charges.

5.3 At the end of the allowed period for revival, if the contract is not revived, the contract shall be terminated by paying the surrender value. However, the life insurers can offer to continue the insurance cover under such contracts, if so opted to by the policyholder, levying appropriate charges until the fund value does not fall below an amount equivalent to one full year's premium.

5.4 When the fund value reaches an amount equivalent to one full year's premium, the contract shall be terminated by paying the fund value. It is clarified that the intention is to ensure payment of a minimum of one full year's premium to the policyholder.

5. (ii) Discontinuance of due premiums within three years of inception of the policy.

5.5 If all the due premiums have not been paid for at least three consecutive years from inception, the insurance cover under the Unit Linked Life Insurance contracts shall cease immediately.

5.6 Insurer shall give an opportunity to the policyholders to revive within the period allowed for revival as per policy conditions.

5.7 In case the contract is not revived during this period, the contract shall be terminated and the surrender value, if any, shall be paid at the end of third policy anniversary or at the end of the period allowed for revival whichever is later.

6. *Loans*

No loans shall be granted under linked insurance products.

7. *Top-up premium*

7.1 A top-up premium is an amount of premium that is paid by the policyholders at irregular intervals besides basic regular premium payments specified in the contract and is treated as single premium.

7.2 Top-up premiums can be remitted to the insurer during the period of contract only, where due basic regular premiums are paid up to date and if expressly stated in the terms and conditions of contract. Top-up premium shall have a lock-in period of three years from the payment date of much premium.

7.3 At any point of time during the term of the contract, so long as the total amount of top-up premiums remain within the 25% of the total amount of the basic regular premiums paid up to that date, the top-up premium will not be required to have any insurance cover (as required in Table 1.2 above) and the balance amount of such top-up premium shall have an insurance cover as specified in Table 1.2 (for single premium contracts) above and shall remain constant during the period of the contract. The provisions in this para shall not apply in respect of pensions and annuity business.

No top-ups will be allowed during last three years of policy's existence. Death benefit will be given on the top-up amounts.

8. *Partial withdrawal*

8.1 The first partial withdrawal is allowed only after five policy anniversary for all regular premium contracts and single premium contracts. Partial withdrawal is not allowed for ULIP person and annuity products.

8.2 Where partial withdrawals have been granted in case of death during the term of the policy, the sum assured may be reduced to the extent of the amount of partial withdrawals made during the two-year period immediately preceding the death of the life assured. However, on attainment of 60 years of age of the life assured, all the partial withdrawals can be set off against the sum assured payable on death. The provision in this para shall not apply in respect of pensions and annuity business.

8.3 For the purpose of partial withdrawals, all top-up premiums—whether or not associated with insurance cover—shall be treated as single premium, for a top-up premium made during the period of the contract, a look-in period of three years shall apply from the date of payment of that top-up premium (this condition will not apply if the top-up premiums are paid during the last three years of the contract).

9. *Settlement option*

9.1 There is no objection for an insurer providing to the policyholder settlement options, providing only periodical payments in the contract so as to avoid the possibility of fluctuations affecting the maturity value. Settlement options should clearly indicate the inherent risk being borne by the policyholder during the period and should be explicitly understood by the policyholder. The period of settlement should not, in any case, be extended beyond a period of five years from the date of maturity. The provision in this para shall not apply in respect of pensions and annuity business.

10. *Unit pricing*

10.1 The basic equity principle of unit pricing for any unit linked fund offered by the life insurer shall be:

"The interests of policyholders who have purchased units in that fund and not involved in a unit transaction should be unaffected by that transaction."

10.2 The unit pricing shall be computed based on whether the company is purchasing (appropriation price) or selling (expropriation price) the assets in order to meet the day-to-day transactions of unit allocation and unit redemptions i.e., the life insurer shall be required to sell/purchase the assets if unit redemption/allocation exceed unit allocation/redemption at the valuation date.

10.3 The appropriation price shall apply in a situation when the company is required to purchase the assets to allocate the units at the valuation date as stated in 10.2. This shall be the amount of money that company should put into the fund in respect of each unit it allocates in order to preserve the interest of the existing policyholders.

10.4 The expropriation price shall apply in a situation when the company is required to sell assets to redeem the units at the valuation date as stated in 10.2. This shall be the amount of money that the company should take out of the fund in respect of each unit it cancels in order to preserve the interests of the continuing policyholders.

10.5 *Computation of NAV*

10.5.1 When appropriation price is applied: The NAV of a Unit Linked Life Insurance Product shall be computed as market value of investment held by the fund plus the expenses incurred in the purchase of the assets plus the value of any current assets plus any accrued income net of fund management charges less the value of any current liabilities less provisions, if any. This gives net asset value of the fund. Dividing by the number of units existing at the valuation date (before any new units are allocated), gives the units price of the fund under consideration.

10.5.2 When expropriation price is applied: The NAV of a Unit Linked Life Insurance Product shall be computed as a market value of investment held by the fund less the expense; incurred in the sale of the assets plus the value of any current assets plus any accrued income net of fund management charges less the value of any current liabilities less provision; if any. This gives the net asset value of the fund. Dividing by the numbers of units existing at the valuation date (before any units are redeemed), gives the unit price of the fund under consideration.

10.6 *Uniform cut-off timings for applicability of net asset value*: The allotment of units to the policyholder should be done only after the receipt of premium proceeds as stated below:

10.6.1 Allocations (premium allocations, switch in)

10.6.1.1 In respect of premiums/funds switched received after 4.15 p.m. by the insurer along with a local cheque or a demand draft payable at par at the place where the premium is received, the closing NAV of the day on which premium is received be applicable.

10.6.1.2 In respect of premiums/funds switched received after 4.15 p.m. by the insurer along with a local cheque or a demand draft payable at par at the place where the premium is received, the closing NAV of the next business day shall be applicable.

10.6.1.3 In respect of premiums received with outstation cheques/demand drafts at the place where the premium is received, the closing NAV of the day on which cheques/demand draft is realized shall be applicable.

10.6.1.4 Having regard to the above, insurer shall ensure that each and every payment instrument is banked with utmost expedition at the first opportunity, given the constrains of banking hours, prudently utilizing every available banking facility (e.g. high value clearing account transfer, etc.). Any loss in NAV incurred on account of delays, shall be made good by the insurer.

10.6.2 *Redemption*

10.6.2.1 In respect of valid applications received (e.g. surrender, maturity claim, switch out, etc.) up to 4.15 p.m. by the insurer, the same day's closing NAV shall be applicable.

10.6.2.2 In respect of valid application received (e.g. surrender, maturity claim, switch, etc.) after 4.15 p.m. to the insurer, the closing NAV of the next business day shall be applicable.

10.7 *NAV*: NAV for each segregated fund provided under unit linked life insurance contracts shall be made available to the public in the print media on a daily basis. Also the NAV shall be displayed in the respective web portals of the life insurer.

11. *Charges*

ULIP charges by insurers allowed upto 4% of annual premium for first five years and thereafter charges will be reduced. For plans of 15 years and above charges will be 2.25% of the annual premium.

Surrender charges will be maximum ₹ 3000 if premium is less than ₹ 25,000 and ₹ 6000 if its is more than ₹ 25,000.

12. *Other conditions*

12.1 Riders

12.1.1 All the riders to be attached to a unit linked life insurance contracts shall be filed separately with the Authority. The rider premium shall be exclusive of expense loadings. The expenses shall be explicitly stated and levied separately in a transparent manner to the fund.

12.1.2 However, insurers have the option to continue the existing practice of appropriating the cost of rider by cancellation of units, provided, the rider cost including all the other charges on the fund, relating to the rider premium (like allocation charge, fund management charge, etc.), shall not exceed the actual rider premium filed with the Authority.

12.2 Exposure to money market instruments under all linked products and to equities in respect of group gratuity and group superannuation shall be as per existing investment guidelines prescribed for other products.

12.3 Lock in period for all ULIPs raised to five years including top-up premium.

12.4 The concept of compulsory annuitisation to pension policies. All pension products should have a guaranteed return of 4.5% per annum. On surrender of such policies 1/3rd of the fund as lump sum and 2/3rd in annuity shall be paid.

Note: Insurance companies have launched a product scheme. These finds, launched under ULIPs, replicate the portfolio of a particular Index such as BSE sensitive Index, NIFTY, etc. The schemes invest in securities in same weight age comprising on index NAV of such schemes would rise or fall in accordance with the rise or fall in the index, though exactly not same percentage. So index funds are available for investment.

ANNEXURE-1

Terminology

1. Approved Terminology

1. *Sum assured*: Sum assured is the guaranteed amount, net of permissible partial withdrawals (as per paras 13.1 and 8.2) of the benefit that is payable on death of the life assured.
2. *Guaranteed surrender value*: As defined in the provision of Section 113 of Insurance Act, 1938.
3. *Top-up premium*: A top-up premium is an amount(s) paid at irregular intervals during the period of contract. This is an additional amount of premium over and above the contractual; basic premiums charged at the commencement of the contract.
4. *Fund value*: Fund value at any point of time represents the value of units at that point of time, i.e. number of units multiplied by the price of the units.
5. *Partial withdrawals*: Any part of fund that is encashed/withdrawn by the policyholder during the period of contract is referred to as partial withdrawal.
6. *Switches*: This is the facility allowing the policyholder to change the investment pattern by moving from one fund to other fund(s) amongst the funds offered under the underlying product of the insurer.
7. *Premium redirection*: This is the facility allowing the policyholder to modify the allocation of amount of renewal premium into a different investment pattern from the option (investment pattern) exercised at the inception of the contract.
8. *Surrender*: Surrender means terminating the contract once for all. On surrender a surrender value is payable which is usually expressed as fund value less the surrender charge (the surrender charge could be zero at latter part of the contract).
9. *Regular premium contracts*: ULIPs where the premium payment is level and paid in regular intervals like yearly, half-yearly, etc.
10. *Single premium contracts*: ULIP where the premium payment is made by a single contribution (a one time payment) at the inception.

11. *Limited premium payment contracts*: ULIPs where the premium payment period is limited compared to the policy term. The premium is payable at regular intervals like yearly, half-yearly, etc. premium contracts.
12. *Whole life contracts*: ULIPs which do not have a definite policy term and the contract terminates on death of the life assured. This can be issued with item 9 or 10 or 1 stated above.
13. *Sales illustrates*: This is a document furnished in accordance with life insurance council circular number LC/SP/Ver 1.0 dated 3 February 2004, conceals the effect of charges on the value of benefits at various stages of a unit linked contract. The illustrations furnished for these contracts shall inter alia furnish the yield, net of charges, corresponding to both the higher and lower interest rate scenario.
14. *Death benefit*: The amount of benefit which is payable on maturity i.e., at the end of the term, as specified in the policy document. This is stated at the inception of the contract.
15. *Maturity benefit*: The amount of benefit which is payable on maturity, i.e. at the end of the term, as specified in the policy document. This is stated at the inception of the contract.
16. *Survival benefit*: The amount of benefit which is payable at specific intervals.
17. *Units*: This is a portion or a part of the underlying segregated unit linked unit fund ₹ 1. This is stated in the unit linked policy documents.
18. *Rider benefits*: The amounts of benefit payable on a specified event (for instance, accident), and is allowed as add on to main benefit.
19. *Settlement options*: A facility made available to the policyholder to receive the maturity proceeds in defined manner (the terms and conditions are specified in advance at the inception of the contract).
20. *Unit linked fund*: Unit-linked fund pools together the premiums paid by policyholders and invest in a portfolio of assets to achieve the fund(s) objective. The price of each unit in a fund depends on how the investments in that fund perform. The fund will be managed by the insurer.

*Issues, Challenges and Opportunities**

Before Insurance Regulatory and Development Authority Act, 1999, Malhotra Committee (1993) and Mukerjee Committee (1995) were appointed to review the insurance sector and regulations. Mukerjee Committee report was not made public. In 2000 report of the advisory group on insurance regulations, in 2004 Law Commission report on the revision of Insurance Act, 1938 and IRDA Act, 1999 and in 2005 report of KPN Committee on provisions of investment (Sections 27A, 27B, 27C, and 27D) of the Insurance Act, 1938 were steps to regulate insurance sector.

In 2012, the Indian insurance market ranked 16th globally and was the fifth largest in Asia. Although it accounts for only 2.5% of premiums in Asia, it has the potential to become one of the biggest insurance markets in the region. A combination of factors underpins further strong

* *Source*: *The Insurance Times*, May 2013.

growth in the market, including sound economic fundamentals, rising household wealth and a further improvement in the regulatory framework.

Current Scenario in Insurance Industry

- As at end-September 2012, there are fifty-two insurance companies operating in India; of which twenty-four are in the life insurance business and twenty-seven are in non-life insurance business. In addition, General Insurance Corporation (GIC) is the sole national reinsurer. The life insurance industry recorded a premium income of 2,87,072 crores during 2011-12 as against 2,91,639 crores in the previous financial year, registering a negative growth of 1.57 per cent. While private sector insurers posted 4.52 per cent decline (11.08 per cent growth in previous year) in their premium income, Life Insurance Corporation (LIC), the fully state-owned insurance company, recorded 0.29 per cent decline (9.35 per cent growth in previous year), in its total premium underwritten. While the renewal premium accounted for 60.31 per cent (56.66 per cent in 2010-11) of the total premium received by the life insurers, first year premium contributed the remaining 39.69 per cent (43.34 per cent in 2010-11). During 2011-12, the growth in renewal premium was 4.77 per cent (6.23 per cent in 2011-11). First year premium registered a decline of 9.85 per cent in comparison to growth of 15.02 per cent during 2010.
- In the non-life segment, the insurers underwrote gross direct premium of 52.876 crores in India for the year 2011-12 as against 42,576 crores in 2010-11, registering a growth of 24.19 per cent as against an increase of 22.98 per cent recorded in the previous year. The public sector insurers exhibited growth in 2011-12 at 21.50 per cent; as against the previous year's growth rate of 21.84 per cent. The private sector general insurers registered a growth of 28.06 per cent, which was higher than 24.67 per cent achieved during the previous year.

Insurance Penetration and Density in India

Year	Life		Non-Life		Industry	
	Density (USD)	Penetration %	Density (USD)	Penetration %	Density (USD)	Penetration %
2001	9.1	2.15	2.4	0.56	11.5	2.71
2002	11.7	2.59	3.0	0.67	14.7	3.26
2003	12.9	2.26	3.5	0.62	16.4	2.88
2004	15.7	2.53	4.0	0.64	19.7	3.17
2005	18.3	2.53	4.4	0.61	22.7	3.14
2006	33.2	4.10	5.2	0.60	38.4	4.80
2007	40.4	4.00	6.2	0.60	46.6	4.70
2008	41.2	4.00	6.2	0.60	47.4	4.60
2009	47.7	4.60	6.7	0.71	54.3	5.20
2010	55.7	4.40	8.7	0.71	64.4	5.10
2011	49.0	3.40	10.0	0.70	59.0	4.10

A. Insurance density is measured as ratio of premium (in US Dollar) to total population.

B. Insurance penetration is measured as ratio of premium (in US Dollar) to GDP (in US Dollar).

- The potential and performance of the insurance sector is universally assessed with reference to two parameters, viz., insurance penetration and insurance density. These two are often used to determine the level of development of the insurance sector in a country. Insurance penetration is defined as the ratio of premium underwritten in a given year to the Gross Domestic Product (GDP). The insurance penetration in India, which surged consistently till 2009-10, has slipped since 2010-11 on account of slowdown in life insurance premium as compared to the growth rate of the Indian economy. Life insurance penetration had consistently gone up from 2.15 per cent in 2001 to 4.60 per cent in 2009, before slipping to 4.40 per cent in 2010 and further slipping to 3.40 per cent in 2011. However, penetration of the non-life insurance sector in the country has remained near constant in the range of 0.55-0.75 per cent over the last 10 years (0.71 per cent in 2010 and 0.70 per cent in 2011).
- *Insurance density* is defined as the ratio of premium underwritten is a given year to the total population (measured in USD for convenience of comparison). India has reported consistent increase in insurance density every year since the sector was opened up for private competition in the year 2000. However, for the first time in 2011, there was a fall in insurance density. The life insurance density in India has gone up from USD 9.1 in 2001 to USD 49.0 in 2011, though it reached the peak of USD 55.7 in 2010. The insurance density of non-life sector reached the peak of USD 10.0 in 2011 from its level of USD 2.4 in 2001.

Problems

While the macro-economic backdrop remains favourable to growth, there are still major hurdles to overcome in order for India to realize this growth potential.

- On the regulatory side there are outstanding issues concerning solvency regulations, further liberalizing of investment rules, caps on foreign equity shareholdings as well as the enforcement of price tariffs in the non-life insurance sector.
- The proliferation of bancassurance is rapidly changing the way insurance products are distributed in India. This will also have strong implications on the process of financial convergence and capital market development in India.
- Health insurance is still underdeveloped in India but offers huge potential, as there will be increasing needs to purchase private health cover to supplement public programmes. Likewise, the deficiencies in current pension schemes should offer significant opportunities to private providers.
- With the majority of the population still residing in rural areas, the development of rural insurance will be critical in driving overall insurance market development over the longer term.

Opportunities

- *Mass marketing*: India is a highly populated country and would continue to be so in the near future. New players may tend to favour the "creamy" layer of the urban population. But, in doing so, they may well miss a large chunk of the insurable population. The rural sector is a perfect case for mass marketing.

- *Job opportunities*: Job opportunities are likely to increase manifold. The liberalization of the insurance sector promises several new job opportunities for those who are equipped with degrees in finance. Apart from this, there will be high demand for professionals in streams like underwriting and claims management, and actuarial sciences.
- *Inflow of funds*: There is a huge inflow of funds into the country. Given the industry's huge requirement of start-up capital, the initial years after opening up we can see a strong inflow of foreign capital. A rise in the equity share of foreign partners to 49 per cent will act as a boost to them.
- *Reinsurance*: Huge capacity is likely to be created in the area of reinsurance. Apart from pure reinsurance activities, which involves providing insurance protection, there will be a revolution in service-related fields like training, seminars, workshops, know how transfer regarding risk assessment and rating, risk inspections, risk management and devising new policy covers, etc.
- *Marketing strategies*: Also, with more players in the market, there will be significant increase in advertising, brand building, and this will benefit whole lot of ancillary industries. A substantial shift is likely to take place in the distribution of insurance in India.
- *Bancassurance*: In India too, banks hope to maximize expensive existing networks by selling a range of products. Many bankers have boosted insurance marked by leveraging their strengths in the areas of brand image, distribution network, and face to face contact with the clients and telemarketing coupled with advanced information technology systems. Insurers in India should also explore distribution through non-financial organization.
- *Information technology*: Worldwide interest in E-commerce and India's predominant position in Information Technology and software development are also likely to be major factors in the marketing of insurance.

Challenges

In many industries opening of the sector to private participation has weakened the market position of the incumbent making it easier for the new entrants to grow and prosper. However, in Indian insurance sector, the incumbent continues to dominate even 10 years after the opening-up of the sector. This puts the onus on the private sector players to differentiate themselves in terms of product innovation and customer servicing, so that they could grab a bigger share of the Indian insurance pie.

As insurance is a 'push' rather than a 'pull' product, it is a big challenge for the companies to make their products meaningful to prospective customers. As a first step, companies should simplify and de-jargonise insurance products and design the benefits so as to suit the specific needs of policyholders, suggested the panel. A higher degree of transparency on policy terms will ensure that the customer understands the product and its benefits, minimizing fears of being cheated. It is, therefore, important for the industry to invest not just in expansion and distribution but also in client servicing and processing, the panel pointed out.

In general insurance, for instance, many customers are discouraged from buying insurance due to the anticipated complexity involved in settlement of claims. Insurance companies do assert that the competition in the industry is forcing them to speed up their claim processes, but the fact remains that a lot more needs to be done to make general insurance a hassle-free experience for the customers, noted the panel.

There are certain factors that need to be considered by the Indian insurance industry to ensure a seamless growth in business. These factors are:

- *Distribution channels*: The ineffectiveness and cost of diverse distribution strategies of different players is crucial in ensuring the success of players in the insurance business, particularly in the retail lines of business.
- *Focus on financial inclusion*: The approach to insurance must be in sync with the evolving times. The mission of the insurance sector in Indian should be to extend the insurance coverage over a larger section of the population and a wider segment of activities.
- *Consumer needs and preferences*: The growth in insurance industry has been spurred by product innovation, vibrant distribution channels, coupled with targeted publicity and promotional campaigns by the insurers. Innovation has come not only in the form of benefits attached to the products, but also in the delivery mechanism through various marketing tie-ups. All these efforts have brought insurance closer to the customer as well as made it more relevant.
- *Premiums to keep increasing*: One of the most common expectations was that premiums would continue to rise.
- *Underwriting market opens up*: One emerging trend is in regard to underwriting agencies. This shift has really opened up the market space and is allowing small agencies, normally backed by Lloyds of London, to show off their underwriting skills and knowledge for their particular niche.
- *Climate change will have major impact*: The changing environment scenario around the world is a challenge for general insurance providers.
- *Mixed views on technology*: There are definitely pros and cons to emerging technologies and brokers have mixed feelings about the trends in this area. Grant of Affinity says a lot of insurers are trying to drive the distribution path by making online products easier to use for brokers.
- *Effect of rising interest rates and inflation*: The rising interest rates are keeping the insurance buyers deterrent from buying insurance. Due increase interest rates and inflation, insurance has become beyond the reach of common man.

Changing Scenario in Insurance Business in India

- Insurance was strictly dominated by agents and development officers till 2000. But IRDA has opened up new distribution channels such as Corporate Agent, Insurance Broker, Bancassurance, Mall Assurance, Online Sale of Insurance, Direct Sale, etc. These new channels are growth engines of the insurance industry. One interesting aspect of this growth is that Insurance Sector is heading towards SERVICING from merely Selling. The mantra of "Sell it and Forget it" is now converting as "Service and Retain Client". This requires core insurance knowledge and not merely Selling Expertise.
- The commission rates of insurance agents are slowly getting downward trend. The servicing of client is now taken care by customer servicing department.

- The technology has now key role in policyholders servicing and provides better knowledge and expertise than agents. Companies are now offering new gateway awareness about insurance products and services through advertisement, seminars, workshops, comics, e-literature, animated films, etc.
- As insurance need is vertical as well as horizontal, the insurance business is spreading across the country. Insurance companies are focusing and spreading network in rural markets as it has huge potential. Technological development is helping this drive of rural expansion.
- Health Insurance and Bancassurance sectors will grow drastically. General Insurance Sector will also develop. In Life Insurance Sector, Term Insurance Business will dominate.
- In future, Online Insurance will have a key role in new business. It will be difficult to get insurance claims in future. There will be huge scope for claim consultants who will help people to get insurance claims.
- Insurance sector will slowly dominate the economy and there will be overall developments in insurance sector. There will huge revenue generation form insurance business in India as well as outsourced insurance business from outside India.

Regulatory Challenges in Insurance

IRDA has to focus attention on two aspects of insurance sector. There is a need for rigorous corporate governance and global compliance norms. These two areas are:

(1) *Money laundering*: The antimoney laundering and Know Your Customer (KYC) framework in insurance companies have been under the spotlight vulnerable area. For example, a single customer is prohibited for mailing premium payment in cash above ₹ 50,000 for transaction. The rule is evaded by individual policyholder taking multiple policies and making premium payment in cash. The cash so received in invested by insurance companies in financial products. Thus, it becomes a clear case of money laundering.

(2) *Fake documentation*: While issuing new policies there is a fraud in forged documentation e.g. PAN cards, proof of residence or date of birth, etc. Insurance companies need to put measures to verifying the documents.

5

Insurance Companies Types, Insurance Councils, Insurance Intermediaries

Insurer

Under Section 2(9) of Insurance Act, 1938, insurer means (a) any individual or unincorporated body of individuals or body corporate under the law of any county other than India, carrying on insurance business not being a person specified in subclause (c) of this clause which (i) carries on that business in India, or (ii) has his or its principal place of business or is demiciled in India, or (iii) with the object of obtaining insurance business or employs a representative or maintains a place of business in India; (b) any body corporate, not being a person specified in subclause (a) of this clause, carrying on business of insurance which is body corporate incorporated under any law for the time being in force in India or stands to any such body corporate in the relation of a subsidiary company; and (c) any person who in India has a standing contract with underwriters who are members of the society of Lloyd's whereby such person is authorised within terms of such contract to issue protection notes, cover notes, or other documents granting insurance cover to others on behalf of the underwriters, but does not include a principal or chief or special agents of an insurance agent or provident society.

Note: (1) *Listing*: IRDA has set a time frame for insurance companies to go for listing in stock exchanges. It has also laid down IPO norms for life insurance companies which have been exempted from three-year profit track record to help them to go public earlier. Disclosure requirements have been laid down for companies that are listed on stock exchange. An insurance depository has been created.

(2) *Demat or 'e insurance' accounts*: Insurance buyers can have demat account which allows them to hold policies in electronic form. It reduces hassles for buyers as it does away with need to provide age and address proof every time. It will save insurers crores in printing and dispatching policies. IRDA has created an insurance repository on lines of National Securities Depository.

(3) *Stock transfer*: Companies will require IRDA approval when (a) total shareholding of transferee exceeds paid up capital, (b) in case of a bank or investment company, the limit is 2.5%, and (c) shares transferred by any individual, firm, group exceed 1% of paid up equity capital of the insurer. Under Section 6A of the Insurance Act, insurance companies can transfer to other insurers are subject to IRDA approval.

Insurance Company means any insurer being a company, association or partnership under Companies Act, 1956 or Partnership Act, 1932: Section 2(8).

Types of Insurance Companies

(1) **Proprietary companies.** Registered under Indian Companies Act, 1956 and Insurance Act, 1938.

(2) **Cooperative insurance companies.** Registered under Cooperation Societies Act, 1912.

(3) **Provident society companies.** Registered under Sections 65 to 94 under Insurance Act, 1938.

(4) **Captive insurance company.** A Subsidiary of another Insurance Company.

(5) **Govt. insurance companies.** Like DGIC, GIC, LIC.

Composite Insurance Companies (i.e. who do both life and non-life business) and mutual insurance companies (i.e. policyholders own such company) are not allowed in India.

Indian Insurance Company means any insurer being a company (a) which is formed and registered under Companies Act, 1956; (b) in which the aggregate holdings of equity shares by a foreign company, either by itself or through its subsidiary companies or its nominees, do not exceed 26% paid up equity capital of such Indian insurance company; (c) whose sole purpose is to carry on life insurance business or general insurance business or re-insurance business—Section 2(7A).

Insurance Cooperative Society means any insurer being a cooperative society: (a) which is registered on or after the commencement of Insurance (Amendment) Act, 2002, as a cooperative society under Cooperative Societies Act, 1912 or under any other law or under the Multi State Cooperative Societies Act, 1984; (b) having a minimum paid up capital (excluding deposits required to be made under Section 7) of ₹ 100 crores; (c) in which no body corporate, whether incorporated or not, formed or registered outside India either by itself or through its subsidiaries or nominees, at any time, holds more than 26% of the capital of such cooperative society; (d) where sole purpose is to carry on life insurance business or general insurance business in India [Section 2(8A)].

Organisation. Departmentalisation

The operation of insurance companies involve three basic functions to sell, to service and to invest. Consequently, most insurers operate within seven major functional departments; actuarial, marketing, accounting and auditing, investment, legal, underwriting and administration. The end ministration includes policy owners service, claims administration, information systems and human resources.

The organisation structure of insurance need for profitability and increased demand for better customer services. The new organisational concept is not hierarchical but reflect network. There are fewer layers of management, wider open of control, small work groups and teams and reliance on joint venture and strategic alliances. These are now alliances with banks, foreign insurers, health care organisations and technological firms.

Provident society. Provident society means a person or body of persons (whether incorporated or not) which, not being an insurer registered under Insurance Act, 1938, carries on the business of insuring the payment, of an annuity of or equivalent to one hundred rupees or less payable for an uncertain period or a gross sum or in two or more instalments over a certain period in happening of following contingencies:

(a) The birth, marriage or death of any person or the survival by a person of a stated or implied age or contingency.
(b) Failure of issue.
(c) The occurrence of a social, religious or other ceremonial occasions.
(d) Loss of or retirement from employment.
(e) Disablement in consequence of sickness or accident.
(f) The necessity of providing for education of a dependent.

A provident society must either be a public company or a cooperative society or a body incorporated or not in a foreign country but not as a private company such society must use the words 'Provident' and 'life'. It has to get a certificate of registration from IRDA. It has to make a deposit with RBI in cash or approved securities of ₹ 5000 and then every year at least 1/5th of the premium income till it is ₹ 50,000.

A provident society shall cause any scheme which it proposes to put into operation for the first time, after such commencement to be examined by an actuary, and shall not receive any premium or contribution in connection with the scheme until the actuary has certified that the rates, advantages, terms and conditions of the scheme are workable and sound, and such certificate has been forwarded to the Authority.

The provisions of sub-section (1) shall apply to any alteration of a scheme already in operation, but the Authority may, if he is of opinion that the alteration unfairly affects the interests of existing policyholders, prohibit the alteration and, if he does so, the society shall not put the altered scheme into operation unless it first discharges to the satisfaction of the Authority all its liabilities to those of the existing policyholders who dissent from the alteration.

Every provident society registered before the commencement of this Act under the provisions of the Provident Insurance Society Act, 1912 (5 of 1912), shall, as soon as may be and in any event before the expiry of six months from the commencement of this Act, submit all schemes of insurance which the society has in operational at the commencement of this Act to examination by an actuary and shall, before the expiration of six months from the commencement of the Insurance (Amendment) Act, 1941 (13 of 1941) send the report of the actuary thereon to the Authority.

The report of the actuary shall state in respect of each scheme whether the rates, advantages, terms and conditions are workable and sound, and where no actuarial report such as is referred to in Section 81 has been made within the two years preceding the examination, the report shall also state whether the assets of the society are sufficient to meet its liabilities under the existing scheme, and if not, how in the opinion of the actuary the existing contracts should be modified.

If the rates, advantages, terms and conditions of any scheme are not reported by the actuary to be workable and sound the Authority shall give notice to the society prohibiting the scheme and the society shall not after its receipt of such notice enter into any new contract of insurance under the scheme, but all rights and liabilities in respect of contracts of insurance entered into by the society before receipt of the notice shall, subject to the provisions of sub-section (6), continue as if the notice had not been given.

Where a scheme is prohibited under the provisions of sub-section (5) the society shall, where its assets are sufficient to meet all existing liabilities, set apart out of its assets the sum sufficient in the opinion of the actuary to meet the liabilities incurred under the scheme so prohibited, and where its assets are not so sufficient, within three months from the date of the prohibition, apply to the court for a modification of its existing contracts or failing such modification for the winding up of the society.

Separation of Accounts and Funds

Where a provident society effects policies of insurance in connection with more than one of the classes of contingency separately specified in sub-section (2) of Section 65, the receipts and payments in respect of each such class shall be recorded in a separate account in the cash-book kept in accordance with Section 79.

Investment of Funds

No funds or investments of a provident society except a deposit made under Section 73 or under the law of any state or country relating to insurance shall be kept otherwise than in the name of the society or in the name of a public officer approved by the Central Government.

No loan shall be made out of the assets of a provident society to any director, manager, managing agent, auditor, actuary, officer or partner of the society, except on the security of a policy of insurance held in the society and within its surrender value and no such loans shall be made to any concern of which a director, manager, managing agent, actuary, officer or partner of the society is a director, manager, managing agent, actuary, officer or partner:

Nothing shall apply to loans made by a provident society to a banking company:

Where any event occurs giving rise to circumstances, the existence of which at the time of the grant of any subsisting loan would have made such grant a contravention of this sub-section, such loan shall, notwithstanding any contract to the contrary, be repaid within three months from the occurrence of such event or from the commencement of the Insurance (Amendment) Act, 1946 (6 of 1946) whichever is later; and in case of default, the director, manager, auditor, actuary or partner concerned shall, without prejudice to any other penalty which he may incur, cease to hold office in the society on the expiry of the said three months.

Any loan prohibited under sub-section (3) made before and outstanding at the commencement of the Insurance (Amendment) Act, 1940 (20 of 1940) shall be repaid before the 1st day of January, 1941, and in case of default the director, manager, managing agent, auditor, actuary, officer or partner who has received the loan or is connected with the concern which has received the loan, as the case may be, shall cease to hold office in or be a partner of the society and shall be ineligible to hold office in or to be a partner of the society until the loan is repaid.

Any director, manager, managing agent, auditor, actuary, officer or partner, of a society which contravenes the provisions of sub-section (3), who is knowingly a party to the contravention, shall without prejudice to any other penalty which he may incur by jointly and severally liable to the society for the amount of the loan, and such amount, together with interest from the date of the loan at such rate not exceeding twelve per cent per annum as the Authority may fix, shall on application by the Authority to any Civil Court of competent jurisdiction be recoverable by execution as if a decree for such amount had been passed by that court.

The provisions of Section 86D of the Indian Companies Act, 1913 (7 of 1913), shall not apply to a loan granted to a director of a provident society being a company if the loan is one granted on the security of a policy on which the society bears the risk and the policy was issued to the director on his own life and the loan is within the surrender value of the policy.

Captive Insurance: It refers to a subsidiary corporation established to provide insurance to parent company and its affiliates. It represents can option to many corporations and groups that want to take financial control and manage risks by underwriting their own insurance rather than paying premiering to third party insurers. It insures risks of its parent company and affiliated groups. Day-to-day operating is controlled by owners, who will be principal insured. These operations include underwriting and claims decisions as well as investment policy of the captive. Captive is a wholly owned subsidiary. It collects premium, setting aside reserves sufficient to pay claims, issue divided to insureds and owners and manage the investment policy of the capture. They may be single percent captive or group captive (owned by a group of companies which are not related).

1. LIC—New Jeevan Anand—Death and disability benefits is a participating non linked plan.
2. New India Assurance Co.—Machinery breakdown policy.
3. Aviva Life Insurance—Heart care.
4. Cigna TTK—Pro health care.
5. Exide Life Insurance Com—Smart term plan-protection with return of premium.
6. Universal Sampo General—Domestic travel insurance.

Insurance Companies

7. Max Life Insurance—Future genius education plan.
8. Oriental Insurance—Nagarik Suraksha product.
9. HDFC Life Insurance—Cancer case.
10. L&T General Insurance—Standard Fire & Special Perilis Insurance.
11. Bajaj Allianz—My home insurance cover.
12. Aviva Life—Health secure plan.
13. L&T General Insurance—My asset Insta Home Insurance.
14. ICICI Lombard General—Assess Individual Student Travel Insurance.
15. HDFC Life—Click protect plus-on line terms insurance.
16. Bajaj Alianz Life—Life Principal plan.
17. TATA AIG General Insurance—Well insurance women policy.
18. Bajaj Alianz General—Cash Assure-participating policy pegs investment returns to the part a filing fund.
19. PNB Met Life Insurance—Mera Term Plan.
20. IFFCO Tokio private car policy.
21. Edelweiss Tokio Life Insurance—My life.
22. Reliance Life Insurance—Education plan.

23. Religare Health 2—Care Health.
24. New India Assurance—Griha Suvida Policy.
25. SBI Life—Smart Humsafar—Smart Plan—A Joint Life, non-linked participating endowment plan.
26. HDFC—Health Medisure Plus.
27. Liberty Videocon General Insurance Co. Ltd.—Private care insurance.

Mutual Insurance Company and Cooperative Life Insurance Society

Mutual insurance company means an insurer, which was incorporated under Companies Act, 1866 or 1882 or 1913 (now repealed), which has no share capital and of which by its constitution only and all policyholders are members. They are not allowed in India. Cooperative Life Insurance Society means an insurer being a society registered under central or state cooperative society Act, which carries on the business of life insurance and which has no share capital on which dividend or bonus is payable and of which by its constitution only original members on whose application the society is registered and all policyholders are members. Both such companies must have working capital of ₹ 15,000. They also have to deposit with RBI a sum of ₹ 2,00,000 in cash or securities either lump sum or in instalment of ₹ 25,000 each or at least one-third of the premium income. Transferors and assignees can't become members of such insurers.

Insurance Intermediary

Insurance intermediary or intermediary includes brokers, reinsurance brokers, insurance consultants, surveyors and loss assessors, or any other person representing or assisting an insurer in one or more of the following:

(i) Soliciting, negotiating, processing or effectuating an insurance contract or a renewal of an insurance contract.

(ii) Disseminating information relating to coverage or rates.

(iii) Forwarding an insurance application.

(iv) Servicing and delivering an insurance policy or contract.

(v) Inspecting a risk.

(vi) Setting a rate.

(vii) Investigating or assessing a claim or loss.

(viii) Transacting a matter after the effectuation of a contract.

(ix) Representing or assisting an insurer or other person, in any other manner in the transaction of insurance with respect to a subject of insurance resident, located or to be performed in India.

(x) Servicing a policy or a contract.

Intermediaries are required to take a license under Section 42(a) of the Insurance Act, 1938 from IRDA. A broker has also to take a license and he acts as agent of assured. An agent is appointed by insurance sponsor and acts on his behalf.

Insurance Association of India, Councils of the Association and Committees

Insurance Association of India

All insurers carrying on insurance business in India at the commencement of the Insurance (Amendment) Act, 1950, all insurers who may after such commencement being to carry on insurance business in India, and, if the Central Government, by notification in the Official Gazette, so declares all provident societies carrying on insurance business in India on the date of such notification and all provident societies which may begin to carry on insurance business in India after such date are hereby constituted a body corporate by the name of the Insurance Association of India.

All insurers and provident societies incorporated or domiciled in India shall be known as members of the Insurance Association of India, and all insurers and provident societies incorporated or domiciled elsewhere than in India shall be known as associate members of that Association.

The Insurance Association of India shall have perpetual succession and a common seal and shall have power to acquire, hold and dispose of all property, both movable and immovable, and shall by the said name sue and be sued.

Councils of the Insurance Association of India

There shall be two councils of the Insurance Association of India, namely:

(a) the Life Insurance Council consisting of all the members and associate members of the Association who carry on life insurance business in India, and

(b) the General Insurance Council consisting of all the members and associate members of the Association who carry on general insurance business in India.

It shall be lawful for any member of the Life Insurance Council or the General Insurance Council to authorise any individual, whether an office of the insurer or not, to act as the representative of such member at any meeting of the council concerned or to stand as a candidate for any election held by that council.

The authorities of the Life Insurance Council and the General Insurance Council shall be the Executive Committees constituted.

Executive Committees of the Life Insurance Council and the General Insurance Council

(1) The Executive Committee of the Life Insurance Council shall consist of the following persons, namely:

(a) Two officials nominated by the Authority, one as the chairman and the other as a member;

(b) Eight representatives of members of the Insurance Association of India carrying on life insurance business elected in their individual capacity by the said members in such manner, from such groups of members and from such areas as may be specified by the Authority;

(c) One non-official and connected with any insurance business, nominated by the Authority; and

(d) Five persons connected with life insurance business, nominated by the Authority for the purpose of representing such groups of insurers carrying on life insurance business or such areas as have not been able to secure adequate representation on the Executive Committee of the Life Insurance Council or for any other purpose.

(2) The Executive Committee of the General Insurance Council shall consist of the following persons, namely:

(a) Two officials nominated by the Authority, one as the chairman and the other as a member;
(b) Eight representatives of members of the Insurance Association of India carrying on general insurance business elected in their individual capacity by the said members in such a manner, from such group of members and from such areas as may be specified by the Authority;
(c) One non-official not connected with any insurance business, nominated by the Authority; and
(d) Five persons connected with general insurance business nominated by the authority for the purpose of representing such groups of insurers carrying on general insurance business or such areas as have not been able to secure adequate representation on the executive committee or for any other purpose.

(3) The Authority may nominate any person to fill the vacancy, and any person so nominated shall be deemed to be a member of the Executive Committee of the Life Insurance Council or the General Insurance Council, as the case may be, as if he had been duly elected thereto.

The secretary of the Executive Committee of the Life Insurance Council and of the Executive Committee of the General Insurance Council shall in each case be an official nominated by the Authority.

Power of Executive Committee of Life Insurance Council to Hold Examinations for Insurance Agents

The Life Insurance Council may, with the approval of the [Authority] authorise its Executive Committee to hold examinations for individual wishing to qualify themselves as insurance agents for the purpose of procuring life insurance business, and if the [Authority], by notification in the Official. Gazette, so declares then, notwithstanding anything contained in Section 42, only individuals who have passed any such examination shall be eligible to apply for a licence.

Functions of Executive Committee of Life Insurance Council

(1) The functions of the Executive Committee of the Life Insurance Council shall be:

(a) To aid, advise and assist insurers carrying on life insurance business in the matter of setting up standards of conduct and sound practice and in the matter of rendering efficient service to holders of life insurance policies;
(b) To render advice to the Authority in the matter of controlling the expenses of insurers in respect to their life insurance business in India;
(c) To bring to the notice of the Authority the case of any insurer acting in a manner prejudicial to the interests of holders of the life insurance policies;
(d) To act in any matter incidental or ancillary to any of the matters specified in clauses (a) to (c) as, with the approval of the [Authority], may be notified by the Life Insurance Council in the Gazette of India.

(2) For the purpose of enabling it effectively to discharge its functions, the Executive Committee of the Life Insurance Council may collect such sums of money, whether by way of fees or otherwise, as may be prescribed from all members and associate members of the Insurance Association of India who carry on life insurance business.

Functions of the Executive Committee of General Insurance Council

(1) The functions of the Executive Committee of the General Insurance Council shall be:

(a) To aid and advise insurers, carrying on general insurance business, in the matter of setting up standards of conduct and sound practice and in the matter of rendering efficient service to holders of policies of general insurance;

(b) To render advise to the Authority in the matter of controlling the expenses of such insurers carrying on business in India in the matter of commission and other expenses;

(c) To bring to the notice of the Authority the case of any such insurer acting in a manner prejudicial to the interests of holders of general insurance policies;

(d) To act in any matter incidental or ancillary to any of the matters specified in clauses (a) to (c) as with the approval of the Authority may be notified by the General Insurance Council in the Gazette of India.

For the purpose of enabling it effectively to discharge its functions, the Executive Committee of the General Insurance Council may collect such fees as may be prescribed from all insurers carrying on general insurance business:

If the General Insurance Council thinks fit, it may by a resolution passed by it, waive the collection of the prescribed fees for any year and where any such resolution has been approved by the Authority, the Executive Committee of the General Insurance Council shall not collect any fees in relation to that year.

General Powers of Life Insurance Council and General Insurance Council

(1) For the efficient performance of its duties, the Life Insurance Council of the General Insurance Council, as the case may be, may:

(a) Appoint such officers and servants as may be necessary and fix the conditions of their service;

(b) Determine the manner in which any prescribed fee may be collected;

(c) Keep and maintain up-to-date a copy of the list of all insurer who are members or associate members of the Insurance Association of India;

(d) With the previous approval of the Authority make regulations for:

  (i) The holding of elections other than the first elections;

  (ii) The summoning and holding of meetings, the conduct of business threat and the number of persons necessary to form a quorum;

  (iii) The submission by insurers to the Executive Committee of the Life Insurance Council, or the General Insurance Council, of such statements or information as may be required of them and the submission of copies thereof by the insurers to the Authority;

  (iv) The levy and collection of any fees;

  (v) The regulation of any other matter which may be necessary for the purpose of enabling it to carry out its duties under this Act.

(2) The Life Insurance Council or the General Insurance Council may authorise the Executive Committee concerned to exercise any of the powers conferred on the Life Insurance Council

or the General Insurance Council, as the case may be, under clause (a), clause (b), clause (c) of sub-section (1).

Tariff Advisory Committee and Control of Tariff Rates

With effect from the commencement of the Insurance (Amendment) Act, 1968, there shall be established a committee, to be called the Tariff Advisory Committee (hereafter in this Part referred to as the Advisory Committee) to control and regulate the rates, advantages, terms and conditions that may be offered by insurers in respect of general insurance business.

The Advisory Committee shall be a body corporate having perpetual succession and a common seal, with power, subject to the provisions of this Act, to acquire, hold and dispose of property, both movable and immovable, and to contract, and may, by the said name, sue and be sued.

Composition of the Advisory Committee

(1) The Advisory Committee shall consist of the following members, namely:

(a) The Chairperson of the Authority *ex officio*, who shall be the Chairman;

(b) A senior officer of the office of the Authority nominated by the Authority, who shall be the Vice-Chairman;

(c) Not more than ten representatives of Indian insurers, elected (in their individual capacities) by such insurers in such manner, from such areas and from among such insurers or groups of insurers as may be prescribed;

(d) Not more than four representatives of insurers incorporated or domiciled elsewhere than in India but registered in India, elected (in their individual capacities) by such insurers in such manner, and from among such insurers or groups of insurers as may be prescribed.

(2) The Secretary to the Advisory Committee shall be an officer of the office of the Authority, nominated by the Authority.

Note: The Regulatory bodies for insurance are:

1. Insurance regulatory and development authority of India (see p. 384).
2. Insurance Councils—General and for life (given above).
3. Insurance Ombudsman at state loads for setting disputes between insurers and insureds.
4. Tariff advisory committee (given above).

Professional Bodies:

1. Chartered Insurance Institute—London
2. Insurance Institute of India—Mumbai
3. Indian Institute of Surveyors and Loss Assessors—Hyderabad
4. Institute of Actuaries—Mumbai.

6

Health Insurance: Rural or Social Sector Insurance and Micro Insurance

Health Insurance in India began with issue of mediclaim policy by four public sector companies in 1986. This policy was revised in 1991 where sum insured was raised, group mediclaim policies were allowed and persons above 60 years were insured. The year 2001 saw the advent of TPAs.

Ministry of Health and Family Welfare, GOI came out with National Health Policy 2017. This will help government in shaping health systems and reinforce trust in public health care system.

"Health Insurance business or health cover" means "effecting of contracts which provide sickness benefits or medical, surgical or hospital expense benefits" whether in-patient or out-patient, on an indemnity, reimbursement, service, prepaid, hospital or other plan basis, including assured benefits and long-term care. Health insurance is subject to principle of indemnity. But the principal of indemnity is not applicable to defined health insurance plan, i.e. the plan under which insured gets a fixed amount to care hospital expenses.

Health services means all services rendered by a **Third Party Administrators (TPA)** under an agreement with an insurance company in connection with health insurance business or health cover, but does not include an insurance company or soliciting, directly or through an insurance intermediary including insurance agent, of insurance business.

TPA means a TPA who, for the time being, is licensed and registered by IRDA and is engaged for a fee or remuneration, by whatever name called as may be specified in the agreement with an insurance company, for the provision of health services. TPA should have net worth of ₹ 1 crore. No promoter can hold two TPA licenses.

From above definitions, we find that health insurance or health cover is insurance that provide:

(a) Sickness benefits—It covers sickness during international and domestic travel.

(b) Medical, surgical or hospital expense benefits.

(c) Reimbursement of expenses of any type of disease treatment.

(d) Health care through TPA. (At present are 27 TPA registered with IRDA.) TPA has no direct touch with the customer.

Health insurance is an adjunct of life insurance. Health insurance helps in regular check-up, financial security through reimbursement or meeting hospital expenses and psychological satisfaction, IRDA has allowed to cover life and health insurance in one policy. Ayurveda, unani and homeopathic treatment are also eligible for mediclaim reimbursement.

Health insurance or cover may be of an individual or a group (family, workers, etc.). Both life and non-life insurers provide health insurance in India, offering about 30 health products. There is a huge potential for growth in the segment as currently health insurance is 2% of India population. Tata AIG introduced 'Hospi cash back' and Met Life 'Met health care' as new products. Customers can avail health insurance without undergoing any medical test. Some hospitals and insurance companies are giving claim for private home treatment.

IRDA has allowed portability of health insurance, i.e. insured can change insurance company. Policyholders can switch to another company and forward for the waiting period for pre-existing diseases cover. For those who have no claim bonus or elderly people, it is allowed and only policies aimed by non-life insurance companies. Portability is not a right of insured.

Managed Health Care

This type of insurance has two characteristics. It finances health care and provides health care through TPA service providers. Thus, there is insurer, insured and TPA (hospitals, nursing homes, clinics). The IRDA has laid down the conditions and procedures for licensing of TPA, its revocation and cancellation. There is prescribed code of conduct for them by IRDA. From June 2009, non-life insurance companies can neither reject the renewal of existing health insurance policies on ground that claim has been made in previous years, non-arbitrarily increase promises while renewing the cover. A TPA shall maintain records of health care patients and the information shall be kept confidential about them except when it is required by government or a court or IRDA.

In case of individual health insurance, the insurance may be against illness or injury or medical/surgical treatment. The policy may be either (a) disability insurance—partial or total and (b) medical expense insurances—indemnity health insurance plan or managed health care. In case of former the expenses of hospitalisation or medical treatment are reimbursed. In case of group health insurance a group (e.g. office personal) is insured by employer against disability, illness, accident, etc.

Usually, health insurance is for one year. The insurance company may charge extra premium for critical or dreaded illness like cancer, by pass surgery, kidney failure, coma, heart valve repair or paralysis or major surgical operation. The company may exclude disease due to self-inflicted injury or HIV/AIDS, use of drugs or radioactive or nuclear fuel materials.

For settlement of claim the insured has to produce report from hospital doctor or specialist. Insurer cannot reject claim on ground of delayed intimation or submission of documents.

The IRDA has allowed TPA to tie up with more than one insurer or with a foreign partner having not more than 26% stake. The insured will approach to TPA who will refer him to a hospital. All TPA have been notified and listed by the government.

Only a registered company with minimum paid up capital of ₹ one crore of equity shares can be given licence to act as TPA. One of the directors should be a qualified medical doctor. It should keep all information confidential on behalf of insurance company. IRDA has laid down a code of conduct for them. Health insurance companies can no longer hold an individual policy claim. The entry age of at least up to 65 years of age. Discount on premium shall be disclosed on policy.

Suggestions for Health Insurance Development

1. Awareness: This will be the key to success. IRDA should plan extensive media campaign to popularize the benefits of health insurance to attract common man. Ministry of Welfare should plan publicity campaigns through government channels to popularise health insurance. Similarly, insurance companies too must create awareness about the products in the market.

2. Health insurance pool: A health insurance pool should be created in line of motor insurance pool to offset the losses in health insurance. The government must also contribute in this pool up to a certain percentage from its health budget so that this portfolio remain profitable for insurers and they do not shy away from health insurance. A portion of claims for senior citizen may be contributed by this pool so that cover is not denied to senior citizens.

3. Health insurance cess: In order to boost up the health expenditure, government may think of imposing additional cess like Health Cess. This cess will help to create a reservoir which will help the government to expand health care facilities and also contribute a portion to the health insurance pool.

4. Health insurance regulator: Looking to the size of the health insurance industry a separate regulator may be instituted or a separate wing may be created within IRDA to work exclusively on this sector. This regulator services are available to all persons at reasonable cost.

5. Grading of hospitals: Government must initiate steps for grading of hospitals according to the facilities available, charges, quality of treatment provided so that before approaching the hospital people can have idea of charges and they are not put in a tight spot once a patient is admitted.

6. Categorisation of policies: Insurance companies should launch different version of policy for different category of people by charging premium according to the policy opted. For example, economy, premium policies or gold/silver category, in these policies the premium will be higher for premium policies and people opting for it will be eligible for higher sublimates of expenses.

7. Sponsoring of hospitals by insurance companies: Looking to the huge health care market the insurance companies may jointly think of promoting hospitals initially in all major metro cities in public/private partnership. Thereafter facilities may be extended in smaller cities in form of health care centers for treatment of poor people. This will have many advantages:

(a) Insurance companies can save huge cost in treatment of policyholders.

(b) People may be attracted to take insurance policies. If they know that quality treatment will be available at a cheaper cost.

(c) Government may support the venture of insurance companies as it will help to expand health care facilities and fulfill the duty of government.

(d) The losses in health portfolio can be reduced to great extent.

(e) The insurers can very well provide treatment to BPL population in order to achieve social objective.

Rajiv Gandhi Rashtriya Swastya Bima Yojna (RSBY)

The RSBY was launched in April 2008 by Ministry of Labour, Government of India. The purpose is to provide financial protection from health care expenses to the poor and improve access to quality health care. It covers:

(a) Cover for hospitalisation expenses of ₹ 30,000 per family per annum on a floater basis.

(b) Family can be of maximum five—husband, wife and three children.

(c) 727 pre-defined surgical packages including maternity and networking care and cover for day care surgeries.

(d) Pre/post hospitalization and limited transport cost.

Both public and private providers can be empanelled. Enrolment is done at village level and smart card-based cashless health insurance cover of ₹ 30,000 per family per annum is provided. Up to February 2010, cards issued were 8.9 million and people enrolled 35 million.

It is a social security measure for those who are below poverty line. The financing cost of this insurance is shared in the ratio of 3 : 1 by Central and State Government. It is implemented in 22 states. TPA will settle the claims by payment to hospitals on receiving the health report of the patients. OPD services are not covered.

A beneficiary gets cashless benefit and paperless transactions. He has to only carry his smart card. He can use this card in any RGRSBY empanelled hospital in India. Thus, this scheme has a feature of portability. The scheme has been extended to unorganized workers like MNREGA beneficiaries, street vendors, domestic helps, beedi workers and building workers.

Drawbacks

(1) Enrolment conversion ratio is not very high.

(2) Hospitalization awareness is less.

(3) Few hospitals are willing to join the scheme.

(4) To build the capacities of the State Government insurance companies and TPAs to handle.

Health insurance is a product easy to sell but difficult to manage. A key process control chart is presented to manage health insurance efficiently.

Key process/Control cycle

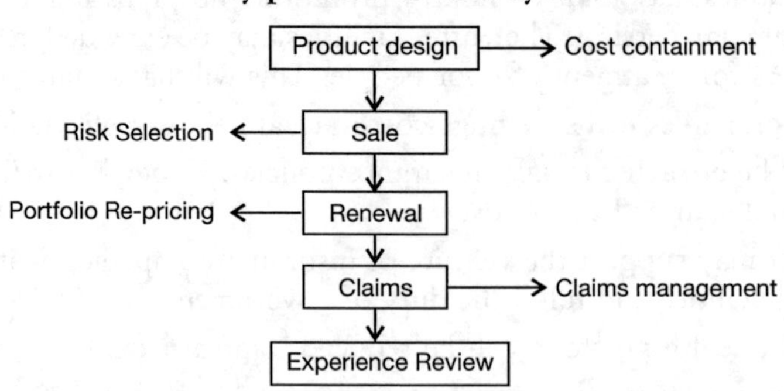

Experience may be effected by medical inflation, length of stay in hospital, incidence rates of disease and interesting cause of claim.

Note: PSU non-life corporations are now allowed to cover mediclaim insurance. w.e.f. 1-7-2011 health insurance can be changed to another insurer without looking any benefits and extra changes portability. Funeral expenses are covered under accident and health insurance. The principle of contribution applies in health insurance if two policies are taken that are similar in principle e.g., if both policies are reimbursement policies. But if one is reimbursement policy and other is fixed benefit policy (combo), then this principle will not apply or if rules of company so state.

Health insurance for companies is a loss making portfolio because it is not reaching the masses.

LIC Health Policies

Cancer Cover: The policy cover both early stage and major stage cancer

	Early Stage	Major Stage Cancer
1. Lump-sum benefit	25% of sum insured shall be payable	100% of sum insured, less any previously paid claims in respect of early stage cancer shall be payable
2. Premium waiver benefit	Premium for next three policy years or balance policy term whichever is lower shall be waived	All future premiums shall be waived

(a) Early state: Minimum 20 years; maximum 65 years

(b) Policy term: 10-30 years

(c) Sum assured: ₹ 10 lakhs to ₹ 50 lakhs

Jeevan Arogya: A non-linked, non-participation individual, health insurance plan.

1. It cover extended family i.e. self + spouse + kids + parents/in-laws.
2. Hospital cash benefit.
3. Day care procedure benefit.
4. Major surgical benefit for 140 more listed surgeries and all other surgical procedures.
5. Full entitlement paid respective actual expenses.
6. 50% advance HSB available under quick cash facility.
7. No claim benefit increasing health cover.
8. Term/accident insurance riders for principal insured and spouse.

Money-Back Health Insurance Plan

Indian First Life has launched the unit linked plan with this plan like LIC Health Plus. It is an indemnity-based plan—the insurer will reimburse the expenses incurred on hospitalization. The insurer has to choose any specified fund. It is available to individual and family floater plan (spouse, two children and two parents). The policyholder is called "primary life assured" and others as "other life assured". Sum assured ranges from 1.5 lakh to 5 lakhs. The maximum age of parents should be 65-75 years. The plan is costlier than pure health plans.

Hospitalisation cash policy offers a fixed daily benefit to the individual upon hospitalisation. Critical illness cover is of two types: (a) initial diagnosis stage and (b) accelerated critical illness. The premium for both critical illness rider is different.

Many companies give bonus for no claim (5%) on premium each year. The bonus paid for past years will be withdrawn and adjusted from mediclaim if in later year insured falls sick.

Different Health Insurance Schemes

Companies have issued many health insurance schemes. Their differences are only about eligibility of insured, sum assured, term of insurance and coverage note that tax benefits are available under Section 80D of Income Tax Act for health insurance. Some health insurance policies are given below:

Name of Company	Name of Policy	Main Feature
1. LIC	(a) Jeevan Arogya	for self, spouse, children and parents
	(b) Bhavishya Arogya	after retirement hospitalisation
2. Max New York	(a) Life Line Healthy Plan	0 day to 75 years, hospitalisation surgical cash, critical illness
	(b) Life line safety net plan	18 years to 60 years. Minimum amount 2 lakhs. Maximum amount 40 lakhs
3. Star Health and Allied Insurance	(a) Unique Insurance Policy (b) Shri individual care	5 years to 80 years. Day care Individual mediclaim. HIV/AIDS war and nuclear perils excluded
4. AVIVA Life Insurance	Health Plus	18 to 55 years, only self-sum assured 3 lakhs
5. Reliance General Insurance	Individual Mediclaim	5 years to 8 years Children-Day care
6. HDFC	Hospital Cash	No Medical check-up
7. Cholamandalam HS General Insurance	Individual health line	Maximum age 55 years can be extended up to 69 years

Below are given comparison of health insurance plans of three companies:

Comparison of Health Insurance Plans

Sum Assured ₹ 3 lakhs

Comparison Attributes	Apollo Munich Optima Restore	Max Bupa Heartbeat Silver	L&T Insurance Medisure Classic
Hospitalisation	Covered up to the Sum Insured	Covered up to Sum Insured Limit for room: ₹ 3,000 or expenses for shared room	Covered up to Sum Insured Room Rent limit 1%, Restores cover amount for accidental claims
Domiciliary Hospitalisation	Covered up to the Sum Insured	Covered up to ₹ 15,000	Covered
Pre Hospitalisation	Provided for 60 days	Provided for 30 days (Pre + Post up to max 20% of S.I.)	Provided for 30 days
Post Hospitalisation	Provided for 180 days post discharge	Provided for 60 days post discharge (Pre + Post up to max 20% of S.I.)	Provided for 60 days post discharge

Comparison Attributes	Apollo Munich Optima Restore	Max Bupa Heartbeat Silver	L&T Insurance Medisure Classic
Pre-Existing Diseases Coverage	Covered after 3 years of continuous coverage	Covered after 4 years of continuous coverage	Covered after 3 years of continuous coverage
Critical illness	Covered on indemnity basis	Covered on indemnity basis	Covered on indemnity basis for double Sum Insured
Daily Hospitalisation	Not provided	Not provided	Provided @ ₹ 500 (max 7 days) per day (after first 3 days)
Nursing Allowance (per day amount)	Not provided	Not provided	Not provided
Ambulance Service	Covered up to ₹ 2000 per hospitalisation	Covered at actual costs in Network Hospitals or ₹ 2000 per hospitalisation	Covered up to ₹ 1500 per hospitalisation
Free Health Checkup (No. of claim free years)	Not provided	Provided biennially for tests mentioned in the company list	Provided up to 1% of Sum Insured after every four claim free years
Organ Donor	Covered up to the Sum Insured	Covered up to the Sum Insured	Covered up to the Sum Insured
Cumulative Bonus	Increment of 50% (max. 100%) of Sum Insured on claim free renewal	Discount on renewal premium of 10% every renewal	Increment of 5% (max. 50%) of Sum Insured on claim free renewal
Day Care Treatment	Covered (140 listed day care procedures)	Covered for all day care procedures	Covered for all day care procedures
Indicative Premium	₹ 12,270	₹ 9090	₹ 4990

Source: *The Insurance Times*, March 2014.

Preferred Provider Network System: This system was introduced by public sector insurers collectively **hospital whereby** companies through TPAs entered into an agreement with hospital/nursing homes in some major cities for providing CASHLESS benefits to their respective policy holders. Under it a **fixed packaged** rates for various specified procedures are agreed upon by hospitals/NH to be charged from insured in exchange of cashless benefit to be provided to the insured. Such packaged rates various based on sum insured.

IRDA had proposed creating a "Pandemic Risk Pool", a practice of insurance companies together and committing funds to meet claims in proportionate to business they do, i.e. claim payout on a shared basis. IRDA has directed life and non-life insurance companies to introduce for any sum, a short-term covid-19 health cover. They will also cover for pre-existing co-morbidities. This will make policies affordable and increasing insurance penetration. It is called "AROGYA SANJEEVANI".

The governments covid-19 insurance policy covering health providers for ₹ 20 lakhs each issued by New India Assurance Company. The scheme was funded through health ministry's NATIONAL DISASTER RESPONSE FORCE (NDRF). The government went for a group personal accident cover, linked to death due to covid-19. The health workers, health care providers who are in direct contact with covid-19 patients and private health care staff roped in by government. The claim procedure is straight forward—a death certificate and a certificate from nodal office. The beneficiary has been defined as one named by claimant in their gratuity application.

Health Insurance Regulations 2013

Definitions

- *Break in policy* occurs at the end of the existing policy term, when the premium due for renewal on a given policy is not paid on or before the premium renewal date or within 30 days thereof.
- *Cashless facility* means a facility extended by the insurer to the insured where the payments, of the costs of treatment undergone by the insured in accordance with the policy terms and conditions, are directly made to the network provider by the insurer to the extent pre-authorization approved.
- *File and use procedure* means a procedure to be followed for health insurance product approval by the insurers in accordance with guidelines/circular issued by the Authority.
- *Health insurance business* or *health cover* means the effecting of insurance contracts which provide for sickness benefits or medical, surgical or hospital expense benefits, including assured benefits and long-term care, travel insurance and personal accident cover.
- *Health services by TPA* means the service rendered by a TPA to an insurer under an agreement in connection with health insurance business but does not include the business of an insurance company or the soliciting either directly or indirectly, of health insurance business or deciding on the admissibility of a claim or its rejection.
- *Health plus Life Combi Products* mean products which offer the combination of a Pure Term Life Insurance cover of a life insurance companies and a health insurance cover offered by non-life and/or stand-alone health insurance companies. IRD has banned indemnity-based health products.
- *Network provider* means hospitals or health care providers enlisted by an insurer or by a TPA and insurer together to provide medical services to an insured on payment by a cashless facility.
- *Portability* means the right accorded to an individual health insurance policyholder (including family cover), to transfer the credit gained for pre-existing conditions and time bound exclusions, from one insurer to another insurer or from one plan to another plan of the same insurer, provided the previous policy has been maintained without any break.

Loading: When an extra risk is undertaken for an extra premium it is called loading in underwriting.

Registrations and Scope of Health Business

(a) Health insurance products may be offered only by entries with a valid registration under the Insurance Regulatory and Development Authority (Registration of Indian Insurance Companies) Regulations, 2001.

(b) Life Insurance Companies may offer long-term health products but the premium for such products shall remain unchanged for at least a period of every block of three years, thereafter that the premium may be reviewed and modified as necessary.

(c) Non-Life and Stand-alone Health Insurance companies may offer individual health products with a minimum tenure of one year and a maximum tenure of three years, provided that the premium shall remain unchanged for the tenure.

(d) Group Health Insurance Policies may be offered by any insurance company, provided that all such products shall only be one year renewable contracts. However, the non-life and stand-alone health insurers may offer group personal accident products with term less than one year also to provide coverage to any specific events.

(e) Overseas or Domestic Travel Insurance policies may only be offered by non-life and stand-alone health insurance companies, either as a stand-alone product or as an add-on cover to an existing health policy. Provided that the premium for the add-on cover is approved by the Authority under File and Use Procedure.

Withdrawal of Health Insurance Product

(i) To withdraw a health insurance product, the insurer shall take prior approval of the Authority by giving reasons for withdrawal and complete details of the treatment to the existing policyholders.

(ii) The policy document shall clearly indicate the possibility of withdrawal of the products in the future and the options that would be available to the policyholder on withdrawal of the products.

(iii) If the existing customer does not respond to the insurer's intimation, the policy shall be withdrawn on the renewal date and the insured shall have to take a new policy available with the insurer, subject to portability conditions.

(iv) The withdrawn product shall not be offered to the prospective customers.

(a) All particulars of any product shall after introduction be reviewed by the Appointed Actuary at least once a year. If the product is found to be financial unviable, or is deficient in any particular the Appointed Actuary may revise the product appropriately and apply for revision under File and Use Procedure.

(b) Five years after a product has been accorded File and Use approval, the Appointed Actuary shall review the performance of the product in terms of morbidity, lapse, interest rates, inflation, expenses and other relevant particular as compared to the original assumptions made while designing such product and seek fresh approval with suitable justifications or modifications of the earlier assumptions made.

General Provisions Relating to Health Policies

(a) Health insurance product may be designed to offer various covers:
   (i) To specified age or gender groups.
   (ii) To different age groups.
   (iii) To treatment in all hospitals throughout the country, provided the definition of hospital is met.
   (iv) To treatment in specified hospitals only, provided the morbidity rates used are representative.
   (v) To treatment in specified geographies only. Provided the morbidity rates used are representative, etc.

Provided, such specifications are disclosed up front and clearly in the product prospectus, documents and sale process.

(b) Insurer shall not compel the insured to migrate to other health insurance products, if it is to the disadvantage of insured.

(c) Insurers shall ensure adequate dissemination of product information on all their health insurance products on their websites. This information shall include a description of the product, copies of the prospectus as approved under the File and Use Procedure, proposal form, policy document wordings and premium rates inclusive and exclusive of service as applicable.

(d) Nomination and Assignment:

(i) All health insurance policies shall provide for a nomination registered at the time of the proposal in accordance with Section 39 of the Insurance Act, 1938.

(ii) No assignment of health insurance policies shall be allowed irrespective of whether the coverage provided under such policies are indemnity based or benefit based. Provided that, in Life-Health Combi products, assignment may be allowed only for the life insurance component of the product in accordance with component of the product in accordance with Section 38 of the Insurance Act, 1938.

(e) Entry and exit age:

(i) Except as provided for in regulation, all health insurance policies shall ordinarily provide for an entry age of at least up to 65 years.

(ii) Except travel insurance products and for products in accordance with Regulation, once a proposal is accepted and a policy is issued which is thereafter renewed periodically without any break, further renewal shall not be denied on grounds of the age of the insured.

(f) Renewal of policies:

(i) A health insurance policy shall ordinarily be renewable except on ground of fraud, moral hazard or misrepresentation or non-cooperation by the insured.

(ii) The renewal of a health insurance policy sought by the insured shall not be denied arbitrarily, if denied, the insurer shall provide the policyholder with cogent reasons for such denial of renewal.

(iii) A insurer shall not deny the renewal of a health insurance policy on the ground that the insured had made as claim or claims in the previous or earlier years, except for benefit-based policies where the policy terminates following payment of the benefit covered under the policy like critical illness policy following payment of the critical illness benefit, the policy terminates.

(iv) The insurer shall provide for mechanism to condone a delay in renewal up to 30 days from the due date of renewal without deeming such condonation as a break in policy. However, coverage need not be available for such period.

(v) The promotion material and the policy document shall explicitly state the conditions under which a policy terminates, such as on the payment of the benefit in case of critical illness benefits policies.

(g) Free Look Period:

All health insurance policies shall have a free look period. The free look period shall be applicable at the inception of the policy.

1. The insured will be allowed a period of at least 15 days from the date of receipt of the policy to review the terms and conditions of the policy and to return the same if not acceptable.
2. If the insured has not made any claim during the free look period, the insured shall be entitled to:
   (a) A refund of the premium paid less any expenses incurred by the insurer on medical examination of the insured persons and the stamp duty charges, or
   (b) Where the risk has already commenced and the option of return of the policy is exercised by the policyholder, a deduction towards the proportionate risk premium for period on cover, or
   (c) Where only a part of the risk has commenced, such proportionate risk premium commensurate with the risk covered during such period.
   (d) In respect of unit linked policy, in addition to the above deductions, the insurer shall also be entitled to repurchase the unit at the price of the units as on the date of the return of the policy.

(h) Cost of pre-insurance health check-up:

(i) The cost of any pre-insurance medical examination shall generally form part of the expenses allowed in arriving at the premium. However in case of products with term of one year and less if such cost is to be insured by the insured, not less than 50% of such cost shall be borne by the insurer once the proposal is accepted, except in travel insurance policies where such costs need not be reimbursed.

(ii) Insurers shall maintain a list of, and the fees chargeable by, institutions where such pre-insurance medical examination may be conducted, the reports from which will be accepted by them. Such list shall be furnished to the prospective policyholder at the time of pre-insurance medical examination.

(i) Cumulative Bonus:

(i) Insurers may offer cumulative bonuses on indemnity-based health insurance policies, which shall be stated explicitly in the prospectus and the policy document.

(ii) If a claim is made in any particular year, the cumulative bonus accrued may be reduced at the same rate at which it is accrued.

(iii) Cumulative bonus shall not be allowed on benefit-based policies.

(j) Option to migrate to suitable health insurance policy:

(i) Insurers offering health covers specific to age groups such as maternity covers, children under family floater policies, students, etc. shall offer an option to migrate to a suitable health insurance policy at the end of the specified exit age or at the renewal of the policy by providing suitable credits for all the previous policy years, provided the policy has been maintain without a break.

(k) All health insurance policies shall allow the portability of any policy in accordance with Schedule 1.

(l) AYUSH coverage:

(i) Insurers may provide coverage to non-allopathic treatments provided the treatment has been undergone in a government hospital or in any institute in a government hospital or in any institute recognised by government and or accredited to Quality Control of India National Acceleration Board on Health or any other suitable institutions.

(ii) For benefit-based products above shall not be applicable.

(m) Disclosures/Declarations:

(i) Subject to the provisions of these regulations, prospectus of health insurance policy shall mandatorily contain all the information regarding:

1. Disclosures about the terms of its renewal.
2. Overage and premium applicable as per the age progression.
3. Disclosure of the maximum age up to when the renewal would be available, if product is offered to specified age groups and the option available to migrate to other policies in all such cases.
4. Any changes in the scope of the cover after certain duration of the policy or after a certain age such as including but not limited to coverage for pre-existing diseases.
5. Whether renewal premium would be guaranteed or subject to revision.
6. Details of specific circumstances, if any, where premium could be loaded (or discount withdrawal) by the insurer and also to the extent to which it could be done.
7. Procedure and terms for enhancing the sum insured or scope and cover if any.
8. All the exclusions cancellation conditions.
9. Other aspects in accordance with the extent regulations, guidelines, circulars, etc. on advertisements and disclosure requirements.

(ii) Declaration shall only form part of the proposal form and shall not be included in the policy document. The standard declarations in the proposal form shall be:

1. "I/we hereby declare on my behalf and on behalf of all persons proposed to be insured that the above statements, answers and/or particulars given by me are true and complete in all respects to the best of my knowledge and that I/we am/are authorized to propose on behalf of these other persons.
2. I understand that the information provided by me will form the basis of the insurance policy, is subject to the Board approved underwriting policy of the insurance company and that the policy will come into force only after full receipt of the premium chargeable.
3. I/We further declare that I/we will notify in writing any change occurring in the occupation or general health of the life to be insured/proposer after the proposal has been submitted but before communication of the risk acceptance by the company.
4. I/We declare and consent to the company seeking medical information from any doctor or from a hospital who at any time has attended on the life to be insured proposer or from any past or present employer concerning anything which affects the physical or mental health of the life to be assured proposer and seeking information

from any insurance company to which an application for insurance on the life to be assured proposer has been made for the purpose of underwriting the proposal and/or claim settlement.

5. I/We authorize the company to share information pertaining to my proposal including the medical records for the sole purpose of proposal underwriting and or claims settlement and with any governmental and/or Regulatory authority."

- Standard Nomenclature and Procedures for Critical Illnesses:
  (i) The nomenclature and procedures incorporated into policies offering 'critical illness cover' shall be as defined by the Authority from time to time.
  (ii) However, insurers may offer to cover as part of hospitalization expenses, items in the standard excluded list or exclude items not in the list provided that such modification is clearly stated and such modified list as annexed to the policy document.
- Special Provisions for Insured Persons who are Senior Citizens:
  (i) The premium charged for health insurance products offered to senior citizens shall be fair, justified, transparent and duly disclosed up front. The insured shall be informed in writing of any underwriting loading charged over and above the premium and the specific consent of the policyholder for such loadings shall be obtained before issuance of a policy.
  (ii) All health insurers and TPAs as the case may be, shall establish a separate channel to address the health insurance-related claims and grievances of senior citizens.
- Multiple Policies:
  (i) If two or more policies are taken by an insured during a period from one or more insurers, the contribution clause shall not be applicable where the cover benefit offered.
    1. Is fixed in nature.
    2. Does not have any relation to the treatment costs.
  (ii) In cost of multiple policies which provide fixed benefits, on the occurrence of the insured event in accordance with the terms and conditions of the policies, the insurer shall make the claim payments independent of payments received under other similar policies.
  (iii) If two or more policies are taken by an insured during a period from one or more insurers to indemnify treatment costs, the insurer shall not apply the contribution clause, but the policyholder shall have the right to require a settlement of his claim in terms of any of his policies.
    1. In all such cases the insurer who has issued the chosen policy shall be obliged to settle the claim without insisting on the contribution clause as long as the claim is within the limits of and according to the terms of the chosen policy.
    2. If the amount to be claimed exceeds the sum insured under a single policy after considering the deductibles or co-pay, the policyholder shall have the right to choose insurers by whom the claim to be settled. In such cases, the insurer may settle the claim with contribution clause.
    3. Except in benefit policies, in cases where an insured has policies from more than one insurer to cover the same risk on indemnity basis, the insured shall only be

indemnified the hospitalization costs in accordance with the terms and conditions of the policy.

Note: Matters to be stated in a health insurance policy—see Chapter 10.

Underwriting

(a) All insurance companies shall evolve a Health Insurance Underwriting Policy which shall be approved by the Board of the company. The policy should among other matters prescribe the proposed form which prospects may apply for purchasing a health policy. Such form should capture all the information necessary to underwrite a proposal in accordance with the stated policy of the company.

(b) The underwriting policy shall be filled with the Authority. The company retains the right to modify the policy as it deems necessary, but every modification shall also be filed with the Authority.

(c) Any proposal for health insurance may be accepted or denied wholly based on the Board approved underwriting policy. A denial of a proposal shall be communicated to the prospect in writing, recording the reasons for denial.

(d) The insured shall be informed of any underwriting loading charged over and above the premium and the specific consent of the policyholder for such loading shall be obtained before issuance of a policy.

(e) If an insurance company requires any further information, such as charge of occupation, at any subsequent stage of a policy or at the time of its renewal, it shall.

 (i) Prescribe standard from to be filled up by the insured and shall make these forms part of the policy document.

 (ii) Clearly state the events which will require the submission of such information.

 (iii) Clearly state the conditions applicable in such event.

(f) Insurers may devise mechanisms or incentives to reward policyholders for early entry, continued renewals, favourable claims experience, etc. with the same insurer and disclose upfront such mechanism or incentives in the prospectus and the policy document, as approved under file and use.

Principles of Pricing of Health Insurance Products

The premium for a health insurance policy shall be based on:

(i) for individual policies, the completed age of the prospect on the date of inception of the policy or on the date of its renewal.

(ii) for provision of cover under family floater, the impact of the multiple incidence rates of all family members proposed to be covered.

The policy premiums shall be unchanged:

(i) for all group products and travel insurance products, for the entire period of cover.

(ii) for all individual and family floater products, other than travel insurance products, format least:

 1. period of one year in case of one year renewable policies and

2. for the period of the tenure as stipulated in Regulations 3(b) and 3(c) herein in the case of multi-year policies.

For a period of three years after a product has been cleared under File and Use Procedure the premiums filed shall ordinarily not be changed. Thereafter, the insurer may vary the premium rates depending on the experience, such rate shall not be changed for a period of at least one year from the date of clearance from the Authority.

Changes in rates will be applicable from the date of approval by the Authority and shall be applied only prospectively thereafter for new policies and at the date of renewal for renewals.

The reasonableness of the pricing as arrived at by the insurer will be assessed having regard to the financial sustainability and viability of the product with respect to the rates, loadings, guarantees and discounts, and the accuracy of the assumptions underlying the pricing model adopted.

At the time of filing the product under the File and Use Procedure, the insurer shall provide:

(i) complete pricing details including the methodology adopted to arrive at the premium, together with the data sources utilized;

(ii) assumptions made shall include the expected claim frequency and claim severities across age bands, expected expenses, lapse rates, etc.;

(iii) specific loading, if any, allowed;

(iv) the profit margin at various model points or the expected loss ratios and the expected combined ratios across various model points across the entire portfolio;

(v) the underwriting capacity required for the product and the actual capacity available with the insurer;

(vi) the retention capacity to manage the business;

(vii) internal capacity building measures if any required to offer the proposed product; and

(viii) any other relevant metric for the product proposed.

Applications for revision of premium rate product be filed before the Authority for approval under the File and Use Procedure and shall encompass:

(i) the justification for the revision in price;

(ii) the claims experience of the three immediately preceding years compared to the expected experience duly explaining the variations, the experience of any similar product;

(iii) the expected claims experience, the assumptions underlying the proposed pricing along with an analysis of how the proposed pricing would address the adversities experienced sustainably.

Loading on Renewals:

(i) The loadings on renewals shall be in terms of increase or decrease in premiums offered for the entire portfolio and shall not be based on any individual policy claim experience.

(ii) The discounts and loadings offered shall:

1. not be at the discretion of the insurer;

2. be based on an objective criteria;

3. be disclosed upfront in the prospectus and policy document along with the objective, criteria, and shall be as approved under the File and Use.

Upper Limit/Maximum Cover offered under a contract:

(i) If in a benefit-based health insurance policy the insurer has prescribed any upper limit for any specified benefit or cover, the insurer shall not accept any proposal for a cover beyond such upper limit, unless the premium for such cover is separately charged.

(ii) Complete pricing details on how such inbuilt limits are considered in arriving at the total premium shall be provided under the File and Use.

(iii) If any proposal is accepted beyond such upper limit, the insurer shall not deny a claim on the ground that the policy exceeds the upper limit prescribed for that policy.

(iv) However, the insurer may cancel the cover beyond such upper limit and shall return the proportionate premium, provided that:

1. The policyholder, at the time of proposal, has not disclosed the existing and simultaneous policy details in the proposal form.
2. The existence of such policy is revealed only subsequently resulting in the cover accepted beyond the upper limit.
3. Such other policy has been underwritten by another insurance company.

Administration of Health Policies

(a) Subject to the terms of a policy, insurers shall extend to all policyholders a cashless facility for treatment of specified establishments or the reimbursement of the costs of medical and health treatments or services availed at any medical establishment.

(b) Cashless facility shall be offered only at establishments which have entered into an agreement with the insurer to extend such services. Such establishments will be termed as Network Providers. Reimbursement shall be allowed at any medical establishment. All such establishments must be licensed or registered as may be required by any local, state or national law as applicable.

Agreement between Insurers, Network Providers and TPAs

(a) Insurance companies may offer policies providing cashless services to the policyholders provided:

(i) The services are offered in network providers who have been enlisted to provide medical services either directly under an agreement with the insurer or by an agreement between health services provider, the TPA and the insurer.

(ii) The Authority may, from time to time, prescribe clauses to be included in such agreements as stipulated in (b).

(iii) the Agreements which shall be entered into between insurers, network providers/ TPAs shall cover the following amongst others:

1. the tariff applicable with respect to various kinds of healthcare services being provided by the network provider.
2. a clause empowering the insurer to cancel or otherwise modify the agreement in case of any fraud, misrepresentation, inadequacy of service or other non-compliance

or default on the part of TPAs or network provider; provided no such cancellation or modification shall be done by the insurer unless the concerned TPA's network provider is given an opportunity of being heard.

3. a standard clause providing for continuance of services by a network provider to the insurance company if the TPA is changed or the agreement with TPA is terminated.
4. a clause providing for opting out of network provider from a given TPA for reasons of inadequacy of service rendered by the TPA to the network provider.
5. a clause specifying the fees and other charges leviable by an insurance company to the TPA for services rendered.
6. a clause specifically requiring only the insurance companying the power to deny a claim.
7. a clause enabling insurer to inspect the premises of the network provider at any time without prior intimation.

(b) The Authority may from time to time prescribe standard clauses to be included in such agreements.

(c) The insurance company shall endeavour to enter into Agreements with adequate number of both public and private sector providers with adequate geographical spread.

Payments to Network Providers and Settlement of Claims of Policyholders

For the purpose of claim settlement, insurer shall make direct payments to the network provider and to the policyholders by integrating their banking system platform with the network providers or the insured, as the case may be. Provided that, if a claimant opts for payment through a cheque or Demand Draft, the insurer shall not deny such request.

Note: See claims procedure is respect of health insurance—Chapter 10.

Services Offered by TPA in Relation to Health Insurance Policies

(a) The insurer may enter into an Agreement for the provision of defined services with a TPA holding a valid license issued in accordance with the IRDA (Third Party Administrators) Regulations, 2001 as may be amended from time to time.

(b) The services offered by a TPA shall not include:

(i) Claim settlements and rejections with respect to the health insurance policies; however, TPA may handle claims admissions and recommend to the insurer for the payment of the claim settlement, provided a detailed guideline is prescribed by the insurer to the TPA for claims assessments and admissions in terms of capacity requirements, internal control requirements, claim assessment and admissions procedure requirements, etc. under the agreement.

(ii) Any services directly to the policyholder or insured or to any other person unless such service is in accordance with the terms and conditions of the Agreement entered into with the insurer.

(c) The TPA shall have in place the infrastructure necessary to extend the health services as required to the policyholders at all times.

(d) Settlement and denial of claims:

(i) All documents submitted to TPA shall be electronically collected and shall be forwarded to the insurers for taking a decision on the claim settlements or claim rejections.

(ii) TPA shall, in the correspondence to the policyholder with respect to settlement/denial of the claims, state clearly the following:

"As per the instructions of the insurer (Name of the Insurer) the claim is being settled/ denied for ₹ (amount) on account of (specifics of treatment/grounds of denial). For any further clarifications, you may directly contract the insurer."

(iii) The above statement shall form the mandatory part of the communication to be sent to the policyholder in every case of settlement or denial of the claims.

(iv) The insurer and the TPA shall be responsible for the proper and prompt service to the policyholders at all times.

(e) Bar on non-insurance healthcare schemes:

(i) The TPA shall offer health services only in accordance with the IRDA (Third Party Administrators) Regulations, 2001 and shall not provide any service:

1. directly or indirectly to non-insurance healthcare schemes, or
2. directly to health insurance schemes promoted, sponsored or approved by entities not being insurance companies, such as governments, PSUs, etc.
3. directly or indirectly to the policyholder or insured, except the health services as per the agreement with the insurer.

Change of TPAs for Servicing of Health Insurance Policies

(a) A change in the TPA by the insurer shall be communicated to the policyholders 30 days before giving effect to the change.

(b) The contact details like helpline numbers, addresses, etc. of the new TPA shall be made immediately available to all the policyholders in case of change of TPA.

(c) The insurers shall take over all the data in respect of the policies serviced by the earlier TPA and make sure that the same is transferred seamlessly to the newly assigned TPA, if any. It shall be ensured that no inconvenience or hardship is caused to the policyholders as a result of the change. In this regard, the following aspects shall receive special attention:

(i) Status of cases where pre-authorization has already been issued by existing TPA.

(ii) Status of cases where claim documents have been submitted to the existing TPA for processing.

(iii) Status of claims where processing has been completed by the TPA and payment is pending with the insurer/TPA.

SCHEDULE I

Portability of Health Insurance Policies Offered by Life and General Insurers

1. A policyholder desirous of porting his policy to another insurance company shall apply to such insurance company, to port the entire policy along with all the members of the family, if any, at least 45 days before the premium renewal date of his/her existing policy.

2. Insurer may not be liable to offer portability if policyholder fails to approach the new insurer at least 45 days before the premium renewal date.

3. Portability shall be opted by the policyholder only as stated in (1) above and not during the currency of the policy.

4. In case insurer is willing to consider the proposal for portability even if the policyholder fails to approach insurer at least 45 days before the renewal date, it may be free to do so.

5. Where the outcome of acceptance of portability is still waiting from the new insurer on the date of renewal.

(a) the existing policy shall be allowed to extend, if requested by the policyholder, for the short period by accepting a pro-rata premium for such short period, which shall be of at least one month.

(b) shall not cancel existing policy until such time a confirmed policy from new insurer is received or at the specific written request of the insured.

(c) the new insurer, in all such cases, shall reckon the date of the commencement of risk to match with date of expiry of the short period, wherever relevant.

(d) if for any reason the insured intends to continue the policy further with the existing insurer, it shall be allowed to continue by charging a regular premium and without imposing any new condition.

6. In case the policyholder has opted as in 5(a), and there is a claim, then existing insurer may charge the balance premium for remaining part of the policy year provided the claims is accepted by the existing insurer. In such cases, policyholder shall be liable to pay the premium for the balance period and continue with existing insurer for the policy year.

7. On receipt of such intimation, the insurance company shall furnish the applicant, the Portability Form as set out in Annexure T to these guidelines together with a proposal form and relevant product literature on the various health insurance products which could be offered.

8. The policyholder shall fill in the portability form along with proposal form and submit the same to the insurance company.

9. On receipt of the Portability Form, the insurance company shall address the existing insurance company seeking necessary details of medical history and claim history of the concerned policyholder. This shall be done through the web portal of the IRDA.

10. The insurance company receiving such a request on portability shall furnish the requisite data in the data format for porting insurance policies prescribed in the web portal of IRDA within seven working days of the receipt of the request.

11. In case the existing insurer fails to provide the requisite data in the data format to the new insurance company within the specified time frame, it shall be viewed as violation of directions issued by the IRDA and the insurer shall be subject to penal provisions under the Insurance Act, 1938.

12. On receipt of the data from the existing insurance company, the new insurance company may underwrite the proposal and convey its decision to the policyholder in accordance with the Regulation 4(6) of the IRDA (Protection of Policyholders' Interest) Regulations, 2002.

13. If on receipt of data within the above time frame, the insurance company does not communicate its decision to the requesting policyholder within 15 days in accordance with its

underwriting policy as filed by the company with the Authority, then the insurance company shall not retain the right to reject such proposal and shall have to accept the proposal.

14. In order to accept a policy which is porting-in, insurer shall not levy any additional loading or charge exclusively for the purpose of porting.

15. No commission shall be payable to any intermediary on the acceptance of a ported policy.

16. Portability shall be allowed in the following cases:

(a) All individual health insurance policies issued by non-life insurance companies including family floater policies.

(b) Individual members, including the family members covered under any group health insurance policy of a non-life insurance company shall have the right to migrate from such a group policy to an individual health insurance policy or a family floater policy with the same insurer. Thereafter, he/she shall be accorded the right mentioned in 1 above.

17. The portability shall be applicable to the sum insured under the previous policy and also to an enhanced sum insured, if requested by the insured, to the extent of cumulative bonus acquired from the previous insurer(s) under the previous policies.

For example: If a person had a SI of ₹ 2 lakhs and accrued bonus of ₹ 50,000 with insurer A; when he shifts to insurer B and the proposal is accepted, insurer B has to offer him SI of ₹ 2.50 lakhs by charging the premium applicable for ₹ 2.50 lakhs by charging the premium applicable for ₹ 2.50 lakhs. If insurer B has no product for ₹ 2.50 lakhs, insurer B would offer the nearest highest slab say ₹ 3 lakhs to insured by charging premium applicable for ₹ 3 lakhs SI. However, portability would be available only up to ₹ 2.50 lakhs.

18. Insurers shall clearly draw the attention of the policyholder in the policy contract and the promotional material like prospectus, sales literature or any other documents in any form whatsoever, that:

(a) all health insurance policies are portable;

(b) policyholder should initiate action to approach another insurer, to take advantage of portability, well before the renewal date to avoid any break in the policy coverage due to delays in acceptance of the proposal by the other insurer.

ANNEXURE – I

Portability Form

PART-I

(1)	Name of Policyholder/insured(s)	

PART-II

1. Whether the PED exclusion/time bound exclusion have longer exclusion period than the existing policy.

(Please indicate Yes/No)

"I _____ am aware that the waiting period of the following disease(s)/treatment(s) is day/years more than the previous policy terms. I hereby agree to observe the additional waiting period for the following disease(s)/treatment(s):
Signature of the Policyholder

SCHEDULE II

Administration of Health Plus Life Combi Products

1. The product of this class shall be named as 'Health Plus Life Combi Products' referred as 'Combi Products' hereinafter in this schedule.

2. This schedule does not apply to Micro Insurance Products which are governed by IRDA (Micro Insurance) Regulations, 2005.

3. All insurance companies that promote 'Health plus Life Combi products' shall adhere to the following:

(a) Scope of Combi Product Class:

(i) The 'Combi Products' may be promoted by all Life Insurance and non-Life Insurance Companies.

(ii) The 'Combi Product' shall be the combination of Pure Term Life Insurance cover offered by life insurance companies and Health Insurance cover offered by non-life insurance/stand-alone health insurance companies.

(iii) The Products offered under the combi product shall be individually cleared under the File and Use Procedure.

(iv) Rider/Add-on covers may be offered subject to File and Use clearance.

(v) The premium components of both risks are to be separately identifiable and disclosed to the policyholders at both pre-sale stage and post-sale stage and in all documents like policy document, sales literature.

(vi) The product may be offered both as individual insurance policy and on group insurance basis. However in respect of health insurance floater policies, the pure term life insurance coverage is allowed on the life of one of the earning members of the family who is also the proposer on health insurance policy subject to insurable interest and other applicable underwriting norms of respective insurers.

(vii) The integrated premium amount of the 'Combi Product' shall be basis for reckoning the threshold limit/applicability of extent Regulations, guidelines and circulars, etc. issued by the Authority or any other statutory body.

(viii) Commission and Claim payouts in respect of 'Combi Products' shall be by respective insurers only.

(ix) 'Combi product' shall have a free look option as outlined in IRDA (Health Insurance Regulations), 2010. Free Look option is to be applied to the 'Combi Product' as a whole.

(x) The health portion of the 'Combi Product' shall entitle its renewability at the option of policyholder from the respective non-life/stand-alone health insurance company.

(b) Tie-up between insurers:

(i) It is mandatory that insurance companies offering the 'Combi Product' shall have in place a Memorandum of Understanding covering the *modus operandi* of marketing, policy service and sharing of common expenses.

(ii) Insurers forming the tie-up shall obtain prior approval of IRDA by duly filing the copy of the agreement entered in this regard. Approval may be obtained by any one of insurers.

(iii) A tie up is permitted between one life insurer and one non-life insurer only. Thus, a life insurer is permitted to tie-up with only one non-life insurer and vice versa.

(iv) Between these two insurers any number of 'Combi Products' may be promoted.

(v) Insurance companies shall carry out an appropriate due diligence before establishing the business relationship for the purpose of promoting 'Combi Products'—Insurers are also expected to have a long-term understanding for effective policy service of the proposed 'Combi Products'.

(vi) Withdrawal from the tie-up is generally not desirable. However, in exceptional cases where insurers desire to withdraw from MOU they shall obtain prior permission of the Authority.

(vii) There shall be specific time frames/Turn around Times (TAT) to be agreed between the insurance companies as part of MOU for effective policy service, transmission of premiums received, etc. at various stages of policy i.e., at pre-sale stage and post-sale stage.

(viii) Filing the advertisements in accordance with IRDA (Insurance Advertisements and Disclosures) Regulations, 2000 within 30 days from the date of issuing the advertisement with Authority.

(ix) Proposed procedures for obtaining the prior approval of IRDA for issuing Joint Sale Advertisements along with the common corporate agents.

(x) The *modus operandi* of proposed policy service at various stages of the policy viz., proposal stage, policy servicing, premium collection arrangements and claims service, etc.

(xi) The Information Technology systems put in place for supporting the sale and policy service of the 'Combi Products'.

(xii) Agreement on reimbursement of expenses in consideration of common services rendered by each other of insurance companies.

(xiii) Distribution channel-wise maximum commission allowed under the 'Combi Products'.

(xiv) The manner in which premium is proposed to be collected subject to provisions of Section 64 VB of Insurance Act, 1938.

(xv) The procedures put in place for expeditious transfer of the portion of premium that pertains to the other insurer of the product.

(xvi) Operational procedures put in place for updating premium on policy data base on a real-time basis.

(xvii) Options available to policyholders of 'Combi Products' to discontinue either portion of risk coverage while continuing with the other portion, subject to the extant law, regulations, guidelines, etc.

(xviii) Copy of proposed common Sales Literature/Sales Illustrations, proposal form to be issued by both the insurers in respect of 'Combi Products', subject to the conditions that these documents cleared under File and Use Procedure are not modified.

(xix) Common Advertisements of 'Combi Products', subject to the condition that this shall be restricted to the features, terms and conditions of the 'Combi Products'.

(c) Lead Insurer:

(i) As two insurance companies are involved in offering the 'Combi Product' one of the insurance companies may be mutually agreed to act as a lead insurer in respect of each 'Combi Product' marketed with agreed terms, conditions and considerations.

(ii) The Lead Insurer for this purpose is the insurance company mutually agreed by both the insurers to play a critical role in facilitating the policy service as a contact point for rendering various services as required for combi products. The lead insurer may play a major role in facilitating underwriting and policy service.

(iii) The role of lead insurer shall not deter in relying upon the existing operational infrastructure of the partner-insurance company for effective policy servicing of 'Combi Products'.

(iv) Either of the insurers shall not be absolved of their responsibility proactive settlement of claims and other obligations in accordance with the terms and conditions of their respective policies.

4. Underwriting: Under the 'Combi Product', underwriting of respective portion of risk shall be carried out by respective insurance companies, that is: Life insurance risk shall be underwritten by Life Insurance Company and the Health Insurance portion of risk shall be underwritten by Non-Life/Standalone Health Insurance Company.

5. File and Use:

(a) The life insurance product and the health insurance product to be offered as a combi product shall have prior approval under File and Use Procedure.

(b) Both the independent approved products shall be integrated as a single product and shall be filed with a common brand name.

(c) The single product shall be offered without making any modifications to the cleared products.

(d) 'Combi Product' is to be filed at the stage of integrating for getting File and Use approval irrespective of the earlier approval to either of products.

(e) 'Combi Product' filing shall follow the File and Use guidelines in vogue and all such guidelines that would be issued from time to time.

(f) 'Combi Product' is to be filed with Actuarial Department of Authority in File and Use formats that are in vogue.

(g) The 'Combi Product' shall be approved by the Authority at File and Use.

(h) The File and Use application of the 'Combi Product' shall also specify the following:

(i) Lead insurer for the 'Combi Product' and demarcation of functions between insurers for carrying out activities.

(ii) Procedures proposed for issuance of the premium notices, where applicable and final lapse notices in terms of Section 50 of the Insurance Act, 1938.

(iii) Where the servicing is to be necessarily attended by the original insurer, the lead insurer shall facilitate the policy servicing. As far as the policyholder is concerned lead insurer shall be made as the single nodal point for receiving the servicing requests, fulfilling the services and issuing acknowledgements.

(iv) Results of feasibility study, if any, in giving a limited access to the policy data base of policies for effecting over-the-counter-policy service requests to the lead insurer.

(v) The results of the cost benefit analysis carried out by both the insurers and the possibility of offering any discounts on the premium in the 'Combi Product'.

6. Lead insurer's duty in settlement of claims:

(a) Based on the type of claim, the other insurer shall also take proactive measures for settlement of claims. In no case, the lead insurer shall guarantee the settlement of claim on behalf of the other insurer.

(b) The risks accepted by one insurer under 'Combi Product' shall not affect the business of other insurance company.

(c) As far as health portion of 'Combi Policies' are concerned, the extent regulations and guidelines shall apply.

(d) Where the policies are serviceable directly, the lead insurer shall play a facilitative role.

(e) The operational procedures proposed to be put in place for timely dispatch of the policy bond of 'Combi Products'.

7. Distribution Channel:

(a) The sale of 'Combi Product' shall be solicited through:

(i) Direct marketing channels,

(ii) Brokers, and

(iii) Composite Individual and Corporate Agents, Common to both insurers.

(b) 'Combi Products' shall not be marketed through 'Bank Referral' arrangements.

(c) Insurers shall ensure that the 'Combi Product' is not marketed by those insurance intermediaries who are not authorized to market either of the products of either of the insurers.

8. Mandatory Minimum Disclosures:

(a) The mandatory minimum disclosures for a 'Combi Product' shall be:

(i) The product is jointly offered by "abc insurance company" (specify non-life/stand-alone health insurer name) and "xyz insurance company" (specify life insurer name).

(ii) The risks of this 'Combi Products' are distinct and are assumed/accepted by respective insurance companies.

(iii) The liability to settle the claim vests with respective insurers that is for health insurance benefits "abc insurance company" (specify non-life/stand-alone health insurer name) and for life insurance benefits "xyz insurance company" (specify life insurer name).

(b) Policy documents of 'Combi Products' shall contain the above referred points (iii) to (xi) as minimum disclosures.

(c) Declaration from the prospect shall be obtained and attached to proposal form that he/she has understood the disclosures mentioned above.

9. In respect of 'Combi Products' both the insurers shall comply with the provisions Insurance Act, 1938 and Regulations notified thereunder and other guidelines, circulars that are applicable to health insurance business and life insurance business respectively.

10. For the purpose of these guidelines non-life insurance company includes stand-alone health insurance company also.

11. In order to monitor the progress of the penetration of the product class before enlarging the scope of the same all insurance companies that are marketing 'Combi Products' shall submit the information that is required by the Authority from time to time.

Legal Cashes—Health

(1) In *Jayanth C. Shah* vs. *LIC* (Chennai) case, the plaintiff complained regarding non-settlement of claim for medical treatment under "Asha Deep Policy" on 6-8-1999. He under went a coronary Angiogram on 5-4-2004 and Pericardial Patch closure on ASD on 5-5-2004. The insurer denied the claim on ground that the said surgery was not covered by the policy. The policy covered only by pass surgeries. The medical opinion was that he did not have by pass surgery. Hence, complaint was dismissed.

(2) In *P.P. Justin* vs. *LIC* (Kochi), the complainant claimed under the rules claim for permanent and total disability. He lost his vision and impaired hearing. On doctor's certificate that only 30% disability and injuries in medical records convincing on personal hearing if was found that distant vision was a problem the answered all questions orally. The complaint was dismissed.

(3) The insured was operated for right side Ureteric Colic. The company refused to pay on ground that the said disease existed prior to insurance. The insured was operated from left side seven years ago. No relief to insured for suppression of material fact (*Shri Pankaj N. Patel* vs. *United India Insurance Co.* Ahmedabad).

(4) The mediclaim was repudiated on the ground that the hospitalisation was for observation only. A claim of ₹ 3,629 for ankle injury was made. The doctor certified that he was admitted for observation and reassessment. As per policy condition mediclaim benefit was to be allowed when hospitalisation takes place upon the advice of a qualified surgeon. Doctor's certificate stated that hospitalisation was as per advice of qualified doctor. The insurer was directed to pay. (*Mr. Paresh H. Desai* vs. *Oriental Insurance Co. Ltd.* Ahmedabad).

(5) A universal health insurance policy was issued to win centre, a social and charitable organisation for the period 1-7-2007 to 30-6-2008. Covering 2,144 BPL families including that of complainant on 28-11-2007, the complainants' son S. Raron was admitted in hospital. The

claim was repudiated on ground that treating doctor did not mention about history of illness. The matter was referred to an expert by complainant who gave a certificate that illness occurred for first time. However, a panel of doctors of insurance company did not give a definite opinion. The opinion of the defecating doctor, who was M.D. and Neuro was accepted. The Ombudsman of Kochi awarded claim of ₹ 3905 with interest @8% and cost of ₹ 5006 (*Shri T.X. Schastian* vs. *United India Insurance* Co. Kochi).

(6) The complainant was issued Health Plus unit linked policy, which provides hospital cash benefit and major surgical benefit. He was hospitalised for treatment of ligament tear sustained in an accident for hospital cash benefit was settled, but not for surgery as it was not among those specified surgeries. 39 surgical procedures were specified and only two related to muscular skeletal system. Those two were (1) total replacement of hip or knee (b) amputation of arm or hand or foot or leg, both in case of accident. The complaint was dismissed as the surgery was not in the list.

(7) In *G.S. Venkataraman* vs. *The Royal Sundaram Alliance Ins. Co. Ltd.* Chennai case, the health shield policy was taken. He was hospitalised and filed a claim. The claim was repudiated on ground of pre-existing disease. Held the claim be paid because the definition of disease means that for a disease to exist there should be a manifestation by way of set of symptoms and signs. The insurer failed to prove it.

(8) Insured was hit by cracker on his ear on Deepawali day. He contacted hospitals and ENT experts, who held that he had a chronic "Suppurative Otitis Media" and it was a long-standing condition. The claim was rejected by insurer. But court held that pre-existing condition means a condition for which insured was under treatment or advice received from a physician before the take of contract. Hence, he got the claim.

Rural or Social Sectors Insurance

"Rural Sector" means the places or areas classified as "rural" while conducting the latest decennial population census (Census of India):

"Social sector" includes unorganised sector, informal sector, economically vulnerable or backward classes and other categories of persons, both in rural and urban areas.

"Unorganised sector" includes self-employed workers such as agricultural labourers, bidi workers, brick kiln workers, carpenters, cobblers, construction workers, fishermen, hamals, handicraft artisans, handloom and khadi workers, lady tailors, leather and tannery workers, papad makers, powerloom workers, physically handicapped self-employed persons, primary milk producers, rickshaw pullers, safai karamcharis, salt growers, sericulture workers, sugarcane cutters, tendu leaf collectors, toddy tappers, vegetable vendors, washermen, working women in hills, or such other categories of persons.

"Economically vulnerable or backward classes" means persons who live below the poverty line.

"Other categories of persons" includes persons with disability as defined in the Persons with Disabilities (Equal Opportunities, Protection of Rights, and Full Participation) Act, 1995 and who may not be gainfully employed; and also includes guardians who need insurance to protect spastic persons or persons with disability.

"Informal sector" includes small scale, self-employed workers typically at a low level of organisation and technology, with the primary objective of generating employment and income, with heterogeneous activities like retail trade, transport, repair and maintenance, construction, personal and domestic services and manufacturing, with the work mostly labour intensive, having often unwritten and informal employer-employee relationship.

Types of Rural Insurances

1. Life Insurance: It is an agreement between the insurance company and the policyholder to pay a certain sum of money on the occurrence of any unforeseen event like death of an individual, critical illness, etc.

2. Health Insurance: This policy is usually taken to cover the medical expenses incurred by an individual in case critical illness. It may be purchased either individually or in groups. This kind of policy is more important in rural areas because of lack of access to lump sum amount of money required during emergencies.

3. Credit Insurance: This kind of policy is particularly beneficial to small and marginal farmers and also small and medium scale entrepreneurs. It is particularly useful during the time of occurrence of any natural disasters like flood, drought, cyclone, etc.

4. Property Insurance: This kind of policy safeguards the property of an individual or an organization from the losses arising on account of theft, floods, fire, earthquakes, etc. It includes policies like fire insurance, income insurance, earthquake insurance and flood insurance.

5. Crop Insurance: These kinds of policies are usually purchased by small and marginal farmers and others who operate on a small scale. This covers losses arising on account of disasters like hailstorms, floods, drought or any other revenue loss, like fall in the value of agricultural products, etc. (See no. 8 below)

6. Weather Insurance: This kind of policy is designed to protect against adverse weather conditions. It covers losses arising on account of rains, extreme temperature conditions snow, fog, wind, etc.

7. Livestock Insurance: This type of insurance safeguards the income from livestock production. It covers animals like cows, buffaloes, etc. In India, this scheme is sponsored by General Insurance Corporation of India (GIC).

For better understanding the prospects of insurance companies in rural areas, one should have a clear idea about the prevailing conditions, requirements of villagers, their specific needs and occupational structure. This is because people from different occupations like farmers, craftsman, weavers, and laborers engaged in casual and construction activities, shopkeepers, artisans, etc. live in villages. Each one will have a diverse need in terms of insurance. Therefore, it is very much essential for these companies not only to create awareness and confidence to tap the market but also design and develop products that may match this need. They should also devise a viable and cost effective distribution channel to market their policies.

8. Pradhan Mantri Fasal Bima Yojna: The following are the salient features of PMFBY:

(1) **Objective:** (a) Coverage of all risks

(b) Financial support to farmers in event of natural calamities, pests, plants disease, etc. giving rise to loss.

(c) To provide strength and stability to farmer.

(d) to promote use of latest technologies in farming.

(2) **Implementation:** A multi agency framework of selected insurance companies under-over all control of various government departments—financial institution, banks, etc.

(3) **Empanelled Insurers to Handle Scheme:** The agriculture insurance of India and 10 private general insurance companies including ICICI, Lombard, HDFC Ergo, IFFO Tikio, Cholamandalam, Bajay, Allianz, Reliance General, Future Generali, Tata AIG, SBI and universal sampo.

(4) **Management:** State level coordination committee direct, direct level monitoring committee for existing NIAS, WBCIS, MNAIS and CPIS schemes implementing agency—IA will manage PMFBY schemes implementation.

(5) **Unit of Insurance:** (a) Area approach basis at village panchayats—talukas, districts.
(b) Unit of insurance can be Geo-fanced and Geo-mapped.

(6) **Crop-N-Notified Area:** All the crops gain in the area during specific seasons yield, estimations, crop cutting, etc.

(7) **Formers covered by PMSBY:** (a) All farmers who have insurable interests are eligible.
(b) Who are given crop loan are compulsorily covered and others whom government decides to cover.
(c) Voluntary coverage for farmers who are non-loan 'y'.

(8) **Risk Covered:** (a) Yield losses due to Act of God peril including draughts, floods, storms, cyclones, five/lightning.
(b) Yield damaged by plant diseases, pests, etc.
(c) Protections from adverse weather conditions ccausing loss of expenditure incurred.
(d) Post harvest losses of expenditure against AOG Perils.
(e) Localised calamities.

Exclusions-war-civil war—SRCC, MD—theft of energy crop, crop destroyed by grazing cattles.

(9) **Sums insured are fixed on coverage.**

(10) Premium rates will be fixed by IA considering bases of loss—cost.

(11) **Sharing of Risks:** The liability of insurance company will be 35% of TSI of all the insurance companies combined whichever is higher.

(12) **Indemnity level:** (a) Three level: 70%, 80%, 90% of corresponding crop risk.
(b) Thresh-hold yield as bench mark yield level at which insurance protection is given this is based on last seven years average.

(13) **Claim Procedure:** Assuring effective speedy disposal of claims assessment on prevented sowing, localized calamity, post harvest losses, on account payment of claims due to mid season adversities.

(14) **Management of PMFBY scheme:** (a) GOI issue operational guide lines and modalities which are to be part of scheme review redesign-

renew are continuous process to make the scheme practically effective. Due publicity is to be given in the media.

(b) PMSEY is exempt from service tax and PMFBY is replacement of NAIS-MNAIS.

(c) Innovative technologies.

(15) High lights of the scheme:

(a) A uniform premium of 2% to be paid by farmers for all KHARIF crops and 1.5% RABI crops. In case of annual commercial and horticulture crops the only 5% premium is to be paid by the formers.

(b) The premium rates for farmers are very low. Balance premium will be paid by the government to provide full sums insured against crop loss on account of natural calamities.

(c) There is no upper limit on government subsidy, it will be borne by the government.

(d) Capping of premium rates is abolished and farmers will get full indemnity limit for claim.

(e) Latest technology will been couraged to minimize delay in claims settle to farmers. Remote seeming techniques will reduce the number of crop in forms experts.

Flaws: The states do not release their part of subsidy on time. Secondly the insurance company has no direct connection with formers.

Source: *The Insurance Times*, May 2016, p. 21.

Obligations

Every insurer, who begins to carry on insurance business after the commencement of the Insurance Regulatory and Development Authority Act, 1999 (41 of 1999), shall, for the purposes of Sections 32B and 32C of the Act, ensure that he undertake the following obligations, during the first five financial years, pertaining to the persons in:

(a) Rural sector,

(i) In respect of a *life insurer*:

(I) seven per cent in the first financial year;

(II) nine per cent in the second financial year;

(III) twelve per cent in the third financial year;

(IV) fourteen per cent in the fourth financial year;

(V) sixteen per cent in the fifth year; of total policies written direct in that year.

(ii) In respect of a *general insurer*:

(I) two per cent in the first financial year;

(II) three per cent in the second financial year;

(III) five per cent thereafter, of total premium income written direct in that year.

(b) Social sector, in respect of all insurers:

(I) five thousand lives in the first financial year;

(II) seven thousand five hundred lives in the second financial year;

(III) ten thousand lives in the third financial year;

(IV) fifteen thousand lives in the fourth financial year;

(V) twenty thousand lives in the fifth year.

In the first financial year, where the period of operation is less than twelve months, proportionate percentage or number of lives, as the case may be, shall be undertaken.

In case of a general insurer, the obligations specified shall include insurance for corps.

The Authority may normally, once in every five years, prescribe or revise the obligations as specified in this Regulation.

Obligations of Existing Insurers

1. The obligations of existing insurers as on the date of commencement of IRDA Act shall be decided by the Authority after consultation with them and the quantum of insurance business to be done shall not be less than what has been recorded by them for the accounting year ended 31 March 2002.
2. The Authority shall review such quantum of insurance business periodically and give directions to the insurers for achieving the specified targets.

Note: w.e.f. 1-4-2013, IRDA permission is not needed to open branches of insurance companies in small towns.

Challenges

Though rural markets are a lucrative option for capturing market share and increasing penetration levels, it still requires heavy investments to educate the people. Special kinds of awareness programmes have to be undertaken for this purpose, because of the low literacy levels and suspecting nature among the villagers.

One major hurdle is lack of motivation on the part of the people for purchasing policies. They need to be highly motivated and educated about the benefits of purchasing insurance for future requirements.

Another major challenge is in terms of product innovation. Traditionally, rural Indians are averse to purchasing an insurance policy and also different people require different kinds of policies. What may be suitable to one may not be suitable for the other.

Another important challenge is distribution and servicing in rural areas.

The future lies with those companies who see the poor as their customer. This has become true with the insurance companies offering policies in rural areas. This is because these areas have a lot of potential consumers for various kinds of goods and services. In fact, these are the most happening and most untapped parts in India. In the past, these areas have been ignored by insurers but with the increase in educational opportunities, and development of communication, transportation and employment opportunities there is a lot of awareness even among the people from rural areas about insurance and many of them have the capability to buy them to meet their future needs.

Due to immense competition and saturation of urban markets for insurance policies, rural markets have become a haven for insurers. With the substantial growth of the Indian economy, the purchasing capacity of rural communities has increased. This has led to the development of rural insurance. In fact, some of the insurers have introduced special products exclusively for rural people.

Rural insurance protects the interest of rural people against probable financial risks and can be used as a preventive measure against future losses. The rural initiative started in 1999 with the opening of first private insurance company in November 2000. Much development has not been witnessed in this sectors as rural areas are still looked down as commercially not viable. There is a huge potential for insurance products in the rural areas, which needs to be rightly tapped by insurers. Some companies though offering products for rural people are restricting themselves to the mandatory requirements as specified by IRDA.

Cases Rural Insurance

(1) The national consumer commission has directed ICICI Lombard General insurance Co. to settle the claims of 73 farmers of Durg district of Chhattisgarh who had suffered wheat crop damage due to reliance on wrong whether data. They were covered by pilot weather-based crop insurance scheme. The insurance premium was paid in equal proportion by the Central and State Government. The farmers complained that the user gave then a 'manipulated chart' relating to temperature and they suffered losses. Basis of calculation was also not explained.

Micro Insurance

Micro insurance refers to the insurance of the low-income people. It is very different from the other types of the insurance available in the urban areas and is a low value product. It requires different design, different distribution strategies and it also requires active involvement of an intermediate agency, health providers, and third a party administrator representing the target community.

Insurance is emerging as the necessity for the low-income people also. 90% of Indian population and 80% of Indian working, remain uninsured. Recent developments in India, as elsewhere, have shown that not only can the poor make small periodic contributions that can go towards insuring them against their health risks but also that the risks they face (such as those of illness, accident and injury, life, etc.) are eminently insurable as those risks are mostly independent or idiosyncratic. Thus, insurance is fast emerging as a prepaid financing option for the various risks facing the poor. Micro insurance is of two types:

(a) "General micro-insurance product" means any health insurance contract, any contract covering the belongings, such as, hut, livestock or tools or instruments or any personal accident contract, either on individual or group basis, as per terms stated in (see Schedule I) the regulations;

(b) "Life micro-insurance product" means any term insurance contract with or without return of premium, any endowment insurance contract or health insurance contract, with or without an accident benefit rider, either on individual or group basis, as per terms stated in (see Schedule II) the regulations.

Micro schemes like Ratriya Swasthya Bima Yojna (RSBY, Vajpayee Arogya—Shree (VAS), National crop insurance scheme (NAIS), Pradhan Mantri Suraksha Bima Yojana are examples.

"Micro-insurance agent" means:

(i) a Non-Government Organisation (NGO); or

(ii) a Self-Help Group (SHG); or

(iii) a Micro-Finance Institution (MFI), who is appointed by an insurer to act as a micro-insurance agent for distribution of micro-insurance products.

(iv) Farmer producers company.

Explanation:

(a) **Non-Government Organisation (NGO)** means a non-profit organisation registered as a society under any law, and has been working at least for three years with marginalized groups, with proven track record, clearly stated aims and objectives, transparency, and accountability as outlined in its memorandum, rules, by-laws or regulations, as the case may be, and demonstrates involvement of committed people;

(b) **Self-Help Group (SHG)** means any informal group consisting of ten to twenty or more person and has been working at least for three years with marginalized groups, with proven track record, clearly stated aims and objectives, transparency and accountability as outlined in its memorandum, rules, by-laws or regulations, as the case may be, and demonstrates involvement of committed people;

(c) **Micro-Finance Institution** means any institution or entity of association registered under any law for the registration of societies or co-operative societies, as the case may be, inter alia, for sanctioning loan/finance to its members;

(d) Farmers' producers company has been defined in the Companies Act, 2013.

"Micro-insurance policy" means an insurance policy sold under a plain which has been specifically approved by the Authority as a micro-insurance product. They are exempted from tax;

"Micro-insurance product" includes a general micro-insurance product or life insurance product, proposal form and all marketing materials in respect thereof.

Tie-up between Life Insurance and Non-Life Insurer

An insurer carrying on life insurance business may offer life micro-insurance products as also general micro-insurance products, as provided.

Where an insurer carrying on life insurance business offers any general micro-insurance product, he shall have a tie-up with an insurer carrying on general insurance business for this purpose, and subject to the provisions of the Act, the premium attributable to the general micro-insurance product may be collected from the prospect (proposer) by the insurer carrying on life insurance business, either directly on through any of the distributing entities of micro-insurance products as specified in Regulation 4, and made over to the insurer carrying on general insurance business:

In the event of any claim in regard to general micro-insurance products, the insurer carrying on life insurance business or the distributing entities of micro-insurance products, as the case may be, as may be specified in the tie-up referred to in the first proviso, shall forward the claim to the insurer carrying on general insurance business and offer all assistance for the expeditious disposal of the claim.

An insurer carrying on general insurance business may offer general micro-insurance products as also life micro-insurance products, as provided herein:

Where an insurer carrying on general insurance business offer any life micro-insurance product, he shall have a tie-up with an insurer carrying on life insurance business for this purpose, and subject to provisions of the Act, the premium attributable to the life micro-insurance product may be collected from the prospect (proposer) by the insurer carrying on general insurance business, either directly or through any of the distributing entities of micro-insurance products as specified in Regulation 4, and made over to the insurer carrying on life insurance business.

In the event of any claim in regard to life micro-insurance products, the insurer carrying on general insurance business or the distributing entities of micro-insurance products, as the case may be, as may be specified in the tie-up referred to in the first proviso, shall forward the claim to the insurer carrying on life insurance business and offer all assistance for the expeditious disposal of the claim.

Distribution of Micro-Insurance Products

In addition to an insurance agent or corporate agent or broker licensed under the Act, read with the regulations concerned made by the Authority for licensing of individual or corporate agents, or insurance brokers, as the case may be, micro-insurance products may be distributed through the micro-insurance agents:

A micro-insurance agent shall not distribute any product other than a micro-insurance product.

Appointment of Micro-Insurance Agents

A micro-insurance agent shall be appointed by an insurer by entering into a deed of agreement, which shall clearly specify the terms and conditions of such appointment, including the duties and responsibilities of both the micro-insurance agent and the insurer:

Before entering into every such agreement, the same shall be got approved by the head office of the insurer.

A micro-insurance agent shall not work for more than one insurer carrying on life insurance business and one insurer carrying on general insurance business.

The deed of agreement shall specifically authorize the micro-insurance agent to perform one or more of the following additional functions, namely:

(a) collection of proposal forms;
(b) collection of self-declaration from the proposer that he/she is in good health;
(c) collection and remittance of premium;
(d) distribution of policy documents;
(e) maintenance of register of all those insured and their dependants covered under the micro-insurance scheme, together with details of name, sex, age, address, nominees and thumb impression/signature of the policyholder;
(f) assistance in the settlement of claims;
(g) ensuring nomination to be made by the insured;
(h) any policy administration service.

The micro-insurance agent or the insurer shall have the option to terminate the agreement, after giving a notice of three months by the party intending to terminate the agreement:

No such notice shall be necessary, where the termination is on account of any misconduct or indiscipline or fraud committed by the micro-insurance agent.

Employment of Specified Persons by Micro-Insurance Agents

A micro-insurance agent shall employ specified persons with the prior approval of the insurer for the purpose of discharging all or any of the functions stated in above.

Corporate agents and insurance brokers procuring micro-insurance business shall continue to be governed by the Insurance Regulatory and Development Authority (Licencing of Corporate Agents) Regulations, 2002, and Insurance Regulatory and Development Authority (Insurance Brokers Regulations, 2002, as the case may be.

Code of Conduct of Micro-Insurance Agents

Every micro-insurance agent and specified person employed by him shall abide by the Code of Conduct as laid down in Regulation 8 of the Insurance Regulatory and Development Authority (Licensing of Insurance Agents) Regulations, 2000, and the relevant provisions of Insurance Regulatory and Development Authority (Insurance Advertisements and Disclosure) Regulations, 2000:

The insurer shall ensure compliance of the Code of Conduct, advertisements and disclosure norms by every micro-insurance agent.

Any violation by a micro-insurance agent of the Code of Conduct and/or advertisement or disclosure norms as aforesaid shall lead to termination of his appointment, in addition to penal consequences for breach of Code of Conduct and/or advertisement or disclosure norms pursuant to the provisions of sub-regulation (1).

Filling of Micro-Insurance Product Design

1. Every insurer shall be subject to the "file and use" procedure with respect to filling of micro-insurance products with the Authority.
2. Every micro-insurance product which is cleared by the Authority for the purpose of micro-insurance shall prominently carry the caption "Micro-Insurance Product".

Issuance of Micro-Insurance Policy Contracts

Every insurer shall issue insurance contracts to the individual micro-insurance policyholder in the vernacular language which is simple and easily understood by the policyholders.

Where insurance of policy contracts in the vernacular language is not possible, the insurer shall as far as possible issue a detailed write-up about the policy details in the vernacular language.

Every insurer shall issue insurance contracts to the group micro-insurance policyholder in an unalterable form along with a schedule showing the details of individuals covered under the group, and also issue a separate certificate, to each such individual evidencing proof of insurance, containing details of validity period of cover, name of the nominee, and address of the underwriting office and the servicing office, where both offices are not the same.

Underwriting

No insurer shall authorize any micro-insurance agent or any other outsider to underwrite any insurance proposal for the purpose of granting insurance cover.

Capacity Building

Every insurer shall impart at least twenty-five hours of training at its expense and through its designated officer(s) in the local vernacular language to all micro-insurance agents and their specified persons in the areas of insurance selling, policyholder servicing and claims administration.

Remuneration/Commission

A micro-insurance agent may be paid, remuneration for all the functions rendered as outlined in Regulation 5 and including commission, by an insurer, and that the same shall not exceed the limits as stated below:

(a) For Life Insurance Business:

Single premium policies	:	Ten per cent of the single premium.
Non-single premium policies	:	Twenty per cent of the premium for all the years of the premium paying term.

(b) For non-Life Insurance Business : Fifteen per cent of the premium.

Where the agreement between the micro-insurance agent and insurer is terminated for any reason whatsoever, no future commission/remuneration shall be payable.

For group insurance products, the insurer may decide the commission subject to the overall limit as specified.

Overall Compliance

Every insurer shall ensure that all transactions in connection with micro-insurance business are in accordance with the provisions of the Act, the Insurance Regulatory and Development Act, 1999 (41 of 1999), and Micro Insurance Regulations Act, 2005.

Submission of Information

Every insurer shall furnish information in respect of micro-insurance business in such form and manner and containing such particulars, as may be required by the Authority from time to time.

Obligations to Rural and Social Sectors

All micro-insurance policies may be reckoned for the purposes of fulfillment of social obligations by an insurer pursuant to the provisions of the Act and the regulations made thereunder.

Where a micro-insurance policy is issued in a rural area and falls under the definition of social sector, such policy may be reckoned for both under rural and social obligations separately.

Handling of Complaints/Grievances

It shall be the responsibility of the insurer to handle and dispose of complaints against a micro-insurance agent with speed and promptitude.

Every insurer shall send a quarterly report to the Authority regarding the handling of complaints/grievances against the micro-insurance agents and wherein a particular quarter, there are not complaints/grievances, a "Nil" report shall be sent.

Schedule 1

Item	Type of Cover	Min. Amount of Cover	Max. Amount of Cover	Term of Cover Min.	Term of Cover Max.	Min. Age at entry	Max. Age at entry
1.	Dwelling and contents, or livestock or tools or named assets/or corp insurance against all perils	₹ 5000 per assets/ cover	₹ 30000 per asset/cover	1 year	1 year	NA	NA
2.	Health Insurance Contract (Ind.)	₹ 5000	₹ 30000	1 year	1 year	Insurers' discretion	
3.	Health Insurance Contract (family) (Option to avail limit for Individual/Float on family)	₹ 10000	₹ 30,000	1 year	1 year	Insurers' discretion	
4.	Personal Accident (per life/earning member of family)	₹ 10,000	₹ 50,000	1 year	1 year	5	70

Note: The minimum number of members comprising a group shall be at least twenty.

Schedule 2

Type of Cover	Min. Amount of Cover	Max. Amount of Cover	Term of Cover Min.	Term of Cover Max.	Min. Age at entry	Max. Age at entry
Term Insurance with or without return of premium	₹ 5000	₹ 50,000	5 years	15 years	18	60
Endowment Insurance	₹ 5000	₹ 30,000	5 years	15 years	18	60
Health Insurance Contract (Individual)	₹ 5000	₹ 30,000	1 year	7 years	Insurer's discretion	Insurer's discretion
Health Insurance Contract (Family)	₹ 10,000	₹ 30,000	1 year	7 years	Insurer's discretion	Insurer's discretion
Accident Benefit	₹ 10,000	₹ 50,000	5 years	15 years	18	60

Notes: 1. Group insurance products may be renewable on a yearly basis.
2. The minimum number of members comprising a group shall be at least twenty.

The State of Micro-Insurance in India

According to a UNDP study, 90% of our population is not getting any form of social protection, though they are poor and economically vulnerable. For nation to grow, the government has to take care of this economically weaker section as part of consolidating its efforts for financial inclusion.

In India, it is often assumed that a micro-insurance policy is simply a low-premium insurance policy. This is not so. There are a number of other important factors. Low income clients live in remote areas and are illiterate and unfamiliar with the concept of insurance. They also have little experience of dealing with formal financial institutions with the exception of the National Bank of Agriculture and Rural Development (NABARD).

For the policyholder, the transaction costs are high. Thus, middle-class, urban, policyholder can send a completed claims form to an insurance company with relative ease: a quick call to the insurance company, receipt of the claims form by post, and then return of the form by post. For a low-income policyholder, submitting a claims form may require an expensive trip lasting a day to the nearest insurance office (thereby losing a day of work), obtaining a form and paying a typist to type up the claim, sending in the claim following by a long trip back home.

Aside from the real costs of doing this, the low-income policyholder may be uncomfortable with the process; clerks and the other officials are often haughty with such low-income clients and can make clients feel ill at ease. Designing micro-insurance policies requires intensive work and is not simply a question of reducing the price of existing insurance policies.

Step to be Taken by Government

In India, people generally consider non-life insurance as unnecessary expenditure. The government has to strengthen the financial infrastructure, develop capacity for potential insurance providers and build knowledge of micro-insurance mechanism and products among potential policyholders. Micro-insurance is a low-price, high volume business. Transaction costs have to be kept low. There is a need for public and private sector to work together. The government has to create and enabling environment for the micro-insurance sector to flourish.

Many clients do not understand the concept of insurance and do not trust insurance companies. The level of trust is very important which is why the Tata-AIG policies had much greater credibility. Some of the actions that can be taken as part of marketing strategy could be:

- Public reimbursement of claims at village meetings. This can be used as a marketing opportunity.
- Exposure tours/Roadshows/Melas.
- Meetings.
- Careful, well-managed rejection of claims.
- Feedback, use it to improve your processes.

As of now, there are three models, namely Partnership Model, Agency Model and Micro Agent Model. One has to look at other models of distribution besides partnership and agency. Insurers should differentiate from competitors, on some basis other than price. Satisfactory relations with agents like MFIs and NGOs definitely helps.

Co-variant risk is a risk or a combination of risks, which affects a large number of the insured items/people at the same time. Example—tsunami, earthquake, flood. It is better to reconsider whether co-variant risks have to be excluded. It is worthwhile to conduct a workshop for agent and partners, and obtain a reinsurance for co-variant risks.

Since 2002, when providing micro-insurance became a legal requirement, there has been a surge in product innovation and experimentation with new distribution channels. The total market for micro-insurance in India is estimated to be between 140 and 300 million policies. As per Marsh, the trends that will shape the future of micro-insurance will include economic growth, urbanization, financial sector development, climate change including extreme weather events and structural adaptation, the rapid pace of product and logistics innovation and innovative use of communication and information technology. One needs to understand the simple world of low income groups to tailor path-breaking solutions.

There are 130 micro-insurance products in the market. Some amount of consolidation is needed as regional dynamics won't change much. Having said that, one has to remember that there are regional dissimilarities as far as demographics are concerned. Look at the neo rural rich in Haryana and Gurgaon. You can't sell them the same insurance policies that you would sell to a poor farmer in Satara, Maharashtra.

The Southern part of India is more prominent in micro-insurance purchase than Northern/Western/Eastern parts. This is because in the Southern states, penetration of micro-finance has increased and this has resulted in increase in micro-insurance.

Challenges Faced by Micro-Insurance Companies

Micro Save's India Focus Note 88 examines the challenges faced by players in the Indian micro-insurance sector, including insurance companies and their distributors. These challenges are more systemic than institution specific.

1. Access to clients is difficult.
2. Operating costs are huge.
3. Greater need for innovative, simple and flexible products considering the lifestyle of rural population.
4. Enhance role of self-help groups.
5. Enhanced insurance awareness among the bottom-of-the-pyramid population.
6. It is difficult to decide whether standardized underwriting procedures are needed for micro-insurance.
7. There is a need for innovative strategies for sustainability.
8. Administrative costs, fraud, adverse selection, moral hazard.

Senior Citizen Mediclaim Plans from the Public Sector Companies

Product Attributes	New India Assurance Company Ltd.	National Insurance Company Ltd.	Oriental Insurance Company Ltd.	United Insurance Company Ltd.
Plan name	Senior Citizen Mediclaim Policy	Varishta Mediclaim Policy	Hope Insurance	Senior Citizen Health Insurance
Minimum entry Age	60	60	60	61
Maximum entry Age	80	80	Nil	80
Sum Assured	₹ 1 lakh-₹ 1.5 lakh	Under hospitalization & Domiciliary hospitalization cover sum insured is ₹ 1,00,000/- and under critical illness cover sum insured is ₹ 2,00,000/-	₹ 100,000/- and higher sum insured can be selected in multiplies of ₹ 100,000/- upto a maximum sum insured of ₹ 5,00,000/-	Sum insured: ₹ 50,000/- to ₹ 3,00,000/-
Coverage	1. Hospitalization expenses incurred for the treatment of illness/injury	1. Hospitalization expenses incurred for the treatment of illness/injury	1. Hospitalization expenses incurred for the treatment of illness/injury	1. Hospitalization expenses incurred for the treatment of illness/injury

Product Attributes	New India Assurance Company Ltd.	National Insurance Company Ltd.	Oriental Insurance Company Ltd.	United Insurance Company Ltd.
Coverage	2. Ambulance charges. 3. Limited cover for hospitalizations in government and/or registered Ayurvedic/ Homeopathic and Unani hospitals	2. Ambulance charges	2. Ambulance Charges 3. Only reasonable and necessary expenses based on the severity will be payable under the policy but not exceeding the maximum limit	2. Ambulance charges
Pre- and post-Hospitalization	Pre- and post-hospitalization expenses up to 30 and 60 days respectively	Pre- and post-hospitalization expenses up to 30 and 60 days respectively	Pre- and post-hospitalization expenses up to 30 and 60 days respectively	Pre- and post-hospitalization expenses up to 30 and 60 days respectively
Premium (60-65 yrs)	For ₹ 1 lakh SA – ₹ 3850 For ₹ 1.5 lakh SA–₹ 5720	For Mediclaim ₹ 4180 and for critical illness ₹ 2007	₹ 4500, ₹ 8700, ₹ 12400, ₹ 16100, ₹ 19700 for SA ₹ 1 lakh to 5 lakh	₹ 1918 for ₹ 50000 SA and ₹ 10221 for ₹ 3 lakh
Discounts	10% for voluntary excess of ₹ 10,000/-, 10% Family Discount in case spouse is also covered	5% discount in respect of each claim-free year subject to the maximum of 10 claim free years of insurance	The insured shall be entitled for No Claim Discount at the rate of 5% of the renewal premium payable after every claim-free policy year, subject to a maximum of 20%. Premium discount available on voluntary co-payment	A family discount of 5% of the total premium will be allowed comprising the insured, spouse, dependant children. The insured shall be entitled for No Claim Discount at the rate of 5% of the renewal premium payable after every claim-free policy year, subject to a maximum of 20%
Income tax benefit	Under Section 80D of IT Act	Under Section 80D of IT Act	Under Section 80D of IT Act	Under Section 80D of IT Act
Reimbursement	Reimbursement of Cost of Health Check once in block of 4 claims-free years	Reimbursement of cost of Health Check once in block of 3 claims-free years	Reimbursement of Cost of health check-up after a block of 4 claim-free years	Reimbursement of Cost of health chick-up after a block of 3 claim-free years
Bonus	The cumulative bonus is allowed when a policy is renewed after a claim-free year at the rate of 5% of the expiring sum insured. Cumulative Bonus will be limited to a maximum of 30%	The SA is increased by 5% in respect of each claim free year subject to the maximum accumulation of 10 claim free years	No Bonus allowed	No Bonus allowed
CD payment	Insured has to bear 10% of all the admissible claims (Compulsory Excess)	Insured has to bear 10% of all the admissible claims (Compulsory Excess)	Co-payment of 20% on admissible claim amount claim amount	Co-payment in the ratio of 80:20 is allowed in respect of hospitalization of all major illness
Pre-Existing Diseases	Covered only after 18 months of continuous insurance with the company	Covered after one year of claim free renewal	Covered after 2 yrs of policy inforce	Covered after 4 yrs of policy inforce

7

Financial and Marketing Management

In evaluating insurers' financial management, following five measures are discussed:

(1) Ratio Analysis
(2) Cash Flow and Funds Flow
(3) Budgeting
(4) Risk Management
(5) Valuation of Assets and Liabilities—Solvency Margin.

Ratio Analysis

The traditional elements of financial analysis of an insurance company are (a) Surplus adequacy, (b) Assets quality, (c) Profitability, and (d) Leverage. Ratios are commonly used as a tool of financial analysis. But the problem with ratio analysis is that it fails to reveal interrelationships among the variables. It may omit important information. However, multivariable approaches are better.

IRDA has prescribed w.e.f. 28-01-2010 that every insurer has to make public disclosures. Those disclosures in prescribed format include preparation of Revenue accounts, Profit and Loss account, Balance Sheet (in the form of sources and uses of funds) and Key Analytical ratios.

These ratios are given below, separately for life insurance companies and other insurance companies.

Key Analytical Ratios (for Life Insurance Companies)

1. Gross Premium Growth Rate.
2. Gross Premium to Shareholders' Funds.
3. Gross Rate of Shareholders' Funds.
4. Net Retention Ratio (Net Premium divided by Gross Premium).
5. Net Commission Ratio (Net Commission divided by Net Premium).
6. Expenses of Management to Gross Direct Premium Ratio (with or without single premium).

7. Combined Ratio.
8. Technical Reserves to Net Premium Ratio.
9. Underwriting Balance Ratio.
10. Operating Profit Ratio.
11. Liquid Assets to Liabilities Ratio.
12. Net Earnings Ratio.
13. Return on Network.
14. Available Solvency Margin Ratio to required Margin Ratio.
15. Non-Performing Assets Ratio (both Gross and Net).

Key Analytical Ratios (for General Insurance Companies)

1. Gross Premium Growth Rate.
2. Gross Premium to Shareholders' Funds.
3. Gross Rate of Shareholders' Funds.
4. Net Retention Ratio.
5. Net Commission Ratio.
6. Expenses of Management to Gross Direct Premium Ratio.
7. Combined Ratio.
8. Technical Reserves to Net Premium Ratio.
9. Underwriting Balance Ratio.
10. Operating Profit Ratio.
11. Liquid Assets to Liabilities Ratio.
12. Net Earnings Ratio.
13. Return on Net Worth.
14. Available Solvency Margin Ratio to required Solvency Margin Ratio.
15. NPA (Gross/Net).

Cash Flow Analysis

Cash and funds flow statements are mandatory for all companies under AS 3. IRDA laid down to prepare cash flow statement according to direct method. Some companies show figures in rupees and some show in dollars, so comparison is not possible either for ratios or cash flows. The format of a cash flow and funds flow statements of an insurance (life) company is given below:

Cash Flow Form Operations

(a) *Underwriting activities*

Premium received
Reinsurance premium paid
Claims paid
Reinsurance and other recoveries received

Commission paid
Commission received
Net cash flow from underwriting activities.

(b) *Other Operating activities*
Income tax paid
General management expenses paid
Other operating payments
Loans advanced/repayment received
Other receipts in respect of operating assets
Net case flow from other operating activities
Total Cash flow from operating activities.

(c) *Investment activities*
Interest/Dividend received
Payments for investments
Proceeds for disposal of investments
Fixed capital expenditures
Proceeds from disposal of fixed assets
Total Cash flow from investing activities.

(d) *Financing activities*
Unclaimed Dividend paid
Long-term borrowings
Tax on dividend paid
Total Cash flow from Financing activities
Net cash inflow/outflow from all activities
Cash and cash equivalent at the beginning of the year
Cash and cash equivalent of the end of the year.

Fund Flow Statement

Sources of Funds

Shareholder's Funds:

(a) Share Capital
(b) Reserve and Surface.

Policyholder's Funds:

(a) Policy liabilities (participating/non-participating business annuities participating, linked business)
(b) Insurance Reserve (participating/non-participating/reserve)
(c) Liabilities for linked business.

Application of Funds

1. Investment
   Shareholders'
   Policyholders
   Assets held to cover linked business
2. Fixed Assets
3. Current Assets
   Less current liabilities and provisions
   Net current Assets
4. Profit and Loss A/c (Dr./Cr. Balance).

Budgeting

Budgets are used for financial planning purposes. Different approaches are used to prepare budgets in general e.g. Top down budgeting, bottom up budgeting and zero base budgeting. The branch budget of an insurance company may be divided into 3 categories.

(i) Socio-economic Data
(ii) Growth budget
(iii) Financial budget
(iv) Divisional budget
(v) Zonal budget.

(i) *Socio-economic data*. The information elicited will give Socio-Economic Profile of branch area. The information to be obtained from Census Report and Lead Bank Report. From the information available in this format, branch will be able to plan business in each market segment.

(ii) *Growth budget*. The budget for "Growth" covers the New Business Growth, the growth in each segment, number of lives to be covered, the agency growth, the quality of Agents in terms of termination/recruitment. Human Resources in terms of Development officers and growth plan of performance of the agent and Development officers. This will also cover the urban/rural, female insurance; Pension insurance, Mutual Fund, Group insurance schemes that can be initiated by the branch office. This work is done by Sales Department of the branch under the guidance of the ABM(s) Assistant Branch Manager (Sales).

(iii) *Financial budget*. The following budgets will be prepared by the branch:

(a) Income budget
(b) Expenditure budget
(c) Cash Flow budget
(d) Customer Service budget
(e) Capital budget

(a) *Income budget.* Keeping growth and new policies in mind the income budget has to be prepared in the following manner:

(i) The Average First Premium for the total business as well as segmental business.

(ii) The average First Year Renewal Premium.

(iii) The Renewal Premium Income of the previous financial year.

(iv) The income from loan interest and other sources have also to be estimated.

(b) *Expenditure budget.* This budget is prepared by Accounts Department in liaison with the other Department on the basis of Indices for certain items of expenditure. The major item of expenditure is the expenditure on the "Human Resources" so for as salary is concerned. The share of commission to premium, so far as the Agents Commission is concerned and the growth of development officer and his average remuneration. The other expenses on the basis of the experience.

(c) *Cash flow budget.* Planning Cash Flow, the total estimated income, the total expenditure and also the outgo has to be found out and the disposable income arrived at. The Cash Flow should be planned as percentage to the disposable income and theoretically this should not be less than the disposable income.

(d) *Customer service budget.* This budget should normally cover all the important areas of service, it covers the new business completion and issue of policies, budget of which has to be prepared by new business, department or the service side. It covers claims, sub-classified into death claims and maturity claims. It covers the Deposit clearance since outstanding deposits are an indication of the premium pending for adjustment. Adjustment is an important activity which should be planned as a part of budget.

(e) *Capital budget.* Capital budget is meant to plan for the basic requirements needed for efficient functioning of the branch offices in terms of fixed Assets such as:

Plant and Machinery, Furniture and Fixtures.

The budget has to be prepared by the Heads of Departments of the branches in consultation with the branch manager and other Heads of Department. The budget has to be discussed by all the heads of Department along with the Branch Manager and then submitted to divisional office.

(iv) *Divisional budget.* The Divisional budget consists of collective budget of all the branches. The Divisional budget has to be discussed by all the heads of Department with the Divisional Manager in charge and then the budget should be submitted to Zonal Manager.

(v) *Zonal budget.* The Divisional Budgets are consolidated and the Zonal expenditure budgets are added to it and that will form Zonal Budget which will be discussed by the Zonal Budget Management Committee. Similar exercise will take place at the Central Office where Corporate Budget will be prepared.

Risk Measurement—Variance Analysis

An insurance company, like a bank or mutual fund company, is a financial intermediary, as they are involved in both savings and investment functions. All financial intermediaries seek an adequate return. So management has to focus on—return and risk. The greater the risk of an investment, greater is the expected return. How to balance between these two goals?

One of the challenge facing an insurer in management is control of risk. Risk can be classified and managed is several ways.

A common quantitative measure of risk is standard deviation. The standard deviation (δ) is the square root of the variance. Variance is the weighted average squared deviations of each possible return from expected return. Cash flows in an insurance company from operations are from investments and from financing and other sources. Calculation of expected future cash flows is not an easy task. Cash flow in insurance is affected by economic conditions, policyholder's behaviour and market response to investments.

Example. Suppose HDFC standard life is considering offering an annuity plan, which will cost ₹ 10,00,000. The future cash flows depend on the state of economy and are estimated as follows:

State of Economy	Probability	Cash flows	Percentage returns	
Recession	20%	₹ 10,00,000	10%	Cash flows
Moderate growth	30%	₹ 12,00,000	12%	÷
Strong growth	50%	₹ 14,00,000	14%	Investment

The expected cash flow will be—

(0.2) (₹ 10,00,000) + (0.3) (₹ 12,00,000) + (0.5) (₹ 14,00,000)

= ₹ 12,60,000

The expected rate of return will be weighted average of all possible returns—the weighted average is 12.6%.

Suppose an insurer holds 1/3rd of its portfolio in above investment whose expected return is 12.6% and 1/6 whose return is 6% and 1/2 in debentures with expected return of 10%. The portfolio expected return will be 10.2%, as follows:

$$\left[\left(\frac{1}{3}\times 0.120\right)+\left(\frac{1}{6}\times 0.06\right)+\left(\frac{1}{2}\times 0.10\right)\right]=10.2\%$$

Calculation of standard deviation

Col. 1	Col. 2	Col. 3	Col. 4	Col. 5 (Col. 3 × Col. 4)
₹ 12,60,000	$(10,00,000 - 12,60,000)^2$	67,600	0.2	13,520
₹ 12,60,000	$(12,00,000 - 12,60,000)^2$	3600	0.3	1080
₹ 12,60,000	$(14,00,000 - 12,60,000)^2$	19,600	0.5	9800
			Variance	24,400

$$\delta = \sqrt{24,400} = 15.6$$

Range is 1.64 as per normal distribution. So $\overline{X} \pm 1.648\ \delta$ i.e. 12.6 + 1.64 × 15.6 = 222,144.

12.6 – 1.64 × 15.6 = 1,70,976

Diversification reduces risk. In providing services there are risks from actuarial point of view. They are asset depreciation risk, price inadequacy risk and interest rate risk. From financial point of view risk relate to market (systematic) risk, credit risk, liquidity, operational risk and legal risk.

In some cases, insurers transfer risk to third parties through a combination of re-insurance, pricing and product (plan) design. In other case they eliminate or mitigate both actuarial and financial risks through proper business practices. In general, an insurer relies on variety of risk management techniques such as standards, reports, underwriting authority limits and investment guidelines, incentive contracts and compensation design.

The insurers' capital from economist point of view is difference between market value of assets and its liabilities. The other view of regulators is that capital is the difference between book or historical value of assets and liabilities. Market valuation of the Balance sheet shows an economically accurate view of an insurer's net worth. It is better to find the ratio between market value and book value of assets and liabilities to know the degree of discrepancy between as reflected in capital market and its book value as per generally accepted accounting principles (GAAP).

Book value = (Par value + Contributed surplus + Retained earnings + Special Reserve) ÷ Number of shares outstanding.

Market Value = (Market capitalization) ÷ Number of shares outstanding.

Valuation of Assets and Liabilities

IRDA has laid own regulations 2000 relating to solvency margin. The regulations are given below.

An insurance company has to first value its assets and liabilities. **The difference between assets and liabilities in called "available solvency margin".** It is then compared with required solvency margin as prescribed by IRDA.

Insurance companies must hold liquid assets (gilt and AAA rated bonds) worth 1.5 times the insurance cover they have extended. If solvency margin falls below 1.5, the company would not be allowed to issue new policies. Even they may be forced to merge with high solvency insurance company.

Sections 64V and 64VA of the Insurance Act, 1938 deal with valuation. They are reproduced below:

Section 64V(1): For the purpose of ascertaining compliance with the provision of Section 64VA:

(i) Assets shall be valued at values not exceeding their market or realisable value and the assets hereafter mentioned shall be excluded to the extent indicated namely:

(a) agents' balances and outstanding premium in India, to the extent they are not realised within a spread of thirty days;

(b) agents' balances and outstanding premium outside India, to the extent they aren't realisable;

(c) sundry debts, to the extend they are not realisable;

(d) advances of an unrealisable character;

(e) furniture, fixtures, dead stock and stationery;

(f) deferred expenses;

(g) profit and loss appropriation account balance and any fictitious assets other than pre-paid expenses;

(h) such other asset or assets as may be specified by the regulations made in this behalf.

(ii) A proper value shall be placed on every item of liability and liabilities in respect of share capital, general reserve and other reserves of similar nature not created to meet specific liabilities and investment reserve, reserve for bad and doubtful debts, and depreciation fund shall be excluded and liabilities hereafter mentioned shall be included to the extent indicated, namely:

(a) provision for dividends declared or recommended, and outstanding dividends in full;

(b) **reserves for unexpired risks** in respects of:

(i) fire and miscellaneous business, 50 per cent, and

(ii) marine cargo business, 50 per cent, and

(iii) marine hull business, 100 per cent of the premium, net of re-insurances during the preceding twelve months;

(c) estimated liability in respect of outstanding claims, in full;

(d) amount due to insurance companies carrying on insurance business, in full;

(e) amounts due to sundry creditors, in full;

(f) provision for taxation, in full;

(g) such other liability which may be made in this behalf to be included for the purpose of clause (ii).

Explanation. In the case of an insurer whose principal place of business or domicile is outside India, where, in the accounts filed with the public authority of the country in which the insurer is constituted, incorporated or domiciled, in respect of marine insurance business, the provisions for unexpired risk and outstanding claims are not shown separately, the liabilities under items (b) and (c) of clause (ii) in respect of marine insurance business shall be taken together at a figure of not less than the total premium less re-insurance so in respect of that class of business during the preceding twelve months.

Every insurer shall furnish to the Authority with his returns under Section 15 or Section 16, as the case may be, a statement certified by an auditor approved by the Authority in respect of general insurance business, or an actuary approved by the Authority in respect of life insurance business, as he case may be, of this assets and liabilities assessed in the manner required by this section as on the 31st day of March of the preceding year.

Every insurer shall value his assets and liabilities in the manner required this section and in accordance with the regulations which may be made by the Authority in this behalf.

Note: In insurance premium is received in advance, but the claim may arise any time, e.g. fire insurance policy is issued for a year on the date of balance sheet, we cannot say that risk is reduced by 1/12 of the total risk. Even on last day of balance sheet risk is as high as on date of policy. The provision made on Balance Sheet date will be shown on the debit side of Revenue A/c instead of deducting it from premium. The balance of provision appears on liability side under heading "Balance of Funds & A/cs". The balance of provision is transferred to credit side of Revenue A/c.

Sufficiency of Assets

Section 64[VA]. An insurer shall, at all times [before the commencement of the Insurance Regulatory and Development Authority Act, 1999], maintain an excess of the value of his assets over the amount of his liabilities of not less than the amount arrived at as follows (hereafter in this section referred to as the "relevant solvency"), namely:

Solvency margin is calculated on any of following methods:

1. Based on mathematical Reserve and sum of Risk case of life insurance (Table 1).
2. Assets of policyholders funds in case of life insurance (Table 2).
3. Net premium and net incurred claims in case of general insurance.

(i) In the case of an insurer whose total premium income less reinsurances in respect of general insurance business (hereafter in this sub-section referred to as the "said income") in the preceding twelve months did not exceed five crores of rupees, one-fifth of the said income subject to a minimum of:

(a) Five lakhs of rupees in the case of an insurer who is a cooperative society registered under the Co-operative Societies Act, 1912 (2 of 1912), or any other law for the time being in force in any State relating to co-operative societies, or

(b) Ten lakhs of rupees in the case of any other insurer, and

(ii) In the case of an insurer whose said income in the preceding twelve months exceeding five crores of rupees, the aggregate of one-fifth of the first five crores of rupees of the said income and one-tenth of the amount by which the said income in the preceding twelve months exceed five crores of rupees:

Where a number of insurers occupying the status of parent and subsidiary companies prepare, under the laws of the country of origin of the parent company, a consolidated balance-sheet, the provisions of this sub-section shall apply to such of them as are not members of any group as if the constituted a single insurer, subject to the further condition that the relevant amount shall, in no case, be less than a sum equal to:

(i) The number of such insurers multiplied by ten lakhs of rupees, or

(ii) Where all the insurers are co-operative societies registered under the Co-operative Societies Act, 1912 (2 of 1912), or any other law for the time being in force in any State relating to co-operative societies, the number of such insurers multiplied by five lakhs of rupees:

If in respect of any insurer the Central Government is satisfied that either by reason of an unfavourable claim experience or because of a sharp increase in the volume of new business, or for any other reason, compliance with the provisions of this sub-section would cause undue hardship to the insurer, it may direct that for such period and subject to such conditions as it may specify, the provisions of this sub-section shall apply to that insurer with the modification that instead of the proportion of one-fifth, wherever mentioned in this sub-section, such other proportion being not less than one-tenth as may be specified by the government shall be applicable to that insurer:

In the case of an insurer carrying on insurance business at the commencement of the Insurance (Amendment) Act, 1968, it shall be sufficient compliance with the provisions of this sub-section until the 31st December 1972 or until such subsequent date, not being later than 31st December

1976, as the Central Government may, at its discretion, allow for any particular insurer, if the progressively brings up the excess of the value of his assets over the amount of his liabilities, in such manner as may be prescribed, to the relevant amount.

Note: Every insurer shall, at all times, on or after the commencement of the Insurance Regulatory and Development Authority Act, 1999, maintain an excess of the value of his assets over the amount of his liabilities of not less than the amount arrived at as follows (hereinafter referred to in this section as the "*required solvency margin*", namely:

(i) In the case of an insurer carrying on life insurance business, the required solvency margin shall be the higher of the following amounts:

(a) Fifty crores of rupees (one hundred crores of rupees in case of re-insurers); or

(b) The aggregate sums of the results arrived at in items (I) and (II) stated below:

(I) The aggregate of the results arrived at by applying the calculation described in item (A) below (Step I) and the calculation described in items (B) below (Step II):

(A) For Step I:

(A.1) There shall be taken, a sum equal to a percentage determined by the regulations not exceeding five per cent of the mathematical reserves for direct business and re-insurance acceptances without any deduction for re-insurance cessions;

(A.2) The amount of mathematical reserves at the end of the preceding financial year after the deduction of re-insurance cessions shall be expressed as a percentage of the amount of those mathematical reserves before any such deduction; and

(A.3) The sum mentioned in item (A.1) above shall be multiplied:

(A.3-1) Where the percentage arrived at under item (A.2) above is greater than eighty-five per cent (or in the case of a re-insurer carrying on exclusive re-insurance business, fifty per cent), by that greater percentage; and

(A.3-2) In any other case, by eighty-five per cent (or in the case of a re-insurer carrying on exclusive re-insurance business, by fifty per cent);

(B) For Step II:

(B.1) There shall be taken, a sum equal to a percentage determined by the regulations made by the Authority not exceeding one per cent of the sum at risk for the policies on which the sum at risk is not a negative figure,

(B.2) The amount of sum at risk at the end of the preceding financial year for policies on which the sum at risk is not a negative figure after the deduction of re-insurance cession shall be expressed as a percentage of the amount of that sum at risk before any such deduction, and

(B.3) The sum arrived at under item (B.1) above shall be multiplied:

(B.3-1) Where the percentage arrived at under item (B.2) above is greater than fifty per cent, by the greater percentage; and

(B.3-2) In any other case, by fifty per cent.

(II) A percentage determined by the regulations made by the Authority of the value of assets determined in accordance with the provisions of Section 64V;

(ii) In the case of an insurer carrying on general insurance business, the required solvency margin, shall be the highest of the following amounts:

(a) Fifty crores of rupees (one hundred crores of rupees in case of reinsurer); or

(b) A sum equivalent to twenty per cent of net premium income; or

(c) A sum equivalent to thirty per cent of net incurred claims,

subject to credit for re-insurance in computing net premiums and net incurred claims being actual but a percentage, determined by the regulations, not exceeding fifty per cent:

If in respect of any insurer, the Authority is satisfied that either by reason of an unfavourable claim experience or because of sharp increase in the volume of the business, or for any other reason, compliance with the provisions of this sub-section would cause undue hardship to the insurer, the Authority may direct, for such period and subject to such conditions, such solvency margin not being less than the lower of the amount mentioned as the case may be,

(i) **"Mathematical Reserves"** means the provision made by an insurer to over liabilities (excluding liabilities which have fallen due and liabilities arising from deposit back arrangement in relation to any policy whereby an amount is deposited by re-insurer with the cedent) arising under or in connection with policies or contracts for life insurance business. Mathematical reserves also include specific provision for adverse deviations of the bases, such as mortality and morbidity rates, interest rates, and expense rates, and any explicit provisions made, in the valuation of liabilities, in accordance with the regulations made by the Authority for this purpose;

(ii) "net incurred claims" means the average of the net incurred claims during the specified period of not exceeding three preceding financial years;

(iii) "sum at risk", in relation to a life insurance policy, means sum which is:

(a) In any case in which an amount is payable in consequence of death other than a case falling within sub-clause (b) below, the amount payable on death, and

(b) In any case in which the benefit under the policy in question consists of the making, in consequence of death, of the payments of annuity, payment of a sum by instalments or any other kind of periodic payments, the present value of that benefit, less in either case the mathematical reserves in respect of the relevant policies.

(2) An insurer who does not comply with the provisions of sub-section (1) shall be deemed to be insolvent and may be wound up by the court.

'[(2A) If, at any time an insurer does not maintain the required solvency margin in accordance with the provisions of this section, he shall, in accordance with the directions issued by the Authority, submit a financial plan, indicating a plan of action to correct the deficiency to the Authority within a specified period not exceeding three months.

(2B) An insurer who has submitted a plan under sub-section (2A) to the Authority shall propose modifications to the plan if the Authority considers it inadequate, and shall give effect to any plan accepted by the Authority as adequate.

(2C) An insurer who does not comply with the provisions of sub-section (2A) shall be deemed to be insolvent and may be wound up by the court.]

(3) The Authority shall be entitled at any time to take such steps as he may consider necessary for the inspection or verification of the assets and liabilities of any insurer or for securing the particulars necessary to establish that the requirements of this section have been complied with as on any date and the insurer shall comply with any requisition made in this behalf by the Authority, and if he fails to do so within two months from the receipt of the requisition, he shall be deemed to have made default in complying with the requirements of this section.

(4) This section does not apply to an insurer specified in Section 2(9)(c).

(5) In applying the provisions of sub-section (1) to any insurer, who is a member of a group, the relevant amount for that insurer shall be an amount equal to that proportion of the relevant amount which that group, if considered as a single insurer, would have been required to maintain as the proportion of his share of the risk on each policy issued by the group bears to the total risk on that policy:

When a group of insurers ceases to be a group, every insurer in that group who continues to carry on any class of insurance business in India, shall comply with the requirements of sub-section (1) as if he had not been an insurer in a group at any time:

It shall be sufficient compliance with the provisions of the foregoing proviso if the insurer brings up the excess of the value of his assets over the amount of his liabilities to the required amount within a period of six months from the date of cessation of the group:

The Central Government may, on sufficient cause being shown, extend the said period of six months by such further periods as it may think fit, so however that the total period may not in any case exceed one year.

(6) The Central Government may, by notification in the Official Gazette, reduce the sum of ten lakhs of rupees or five lakhs of rupees, as the case may be, referred to in sub-section (1) to a lower figure not less than one hundred thousand rupees in respect of a country craft insurer or in respect of an insurer not having a share capital and carrying on only such insurance business as, in the opinion of the Central Government, is not carried on ordinarily by insurers under separate policies.

(7) Every insurer shall furnish to the Authority his returns under Section 15 or Section 16, as the case may be, in case of life insurance business a statement certified by an actuary approved by the Authority, and in case of general insurance business a statement certified by an auditor approved by the Authority, of the required solvency margin maintained by the insurer in the manner required by sub-section (1A).

No Risk to be Assumed Unless Premium is Received in Advance

(1) No insurer shall assume any risk in India in respect of any insurance business on which premium is not ordinarily payable outside India unless and until the premium payable is received by him or is guaranteed to be paid by such person in such manner and within such time as may be prescribed or unless and until deposit of such amount as may be prescribed, is made in advance in the prescribed manner.

(2) For the purposes of this section, in the case of risks for which premium can be ascertained in advance, the risk may be assumed not earlier than the date on which the premium has been paid in cash or by cheque to the insurer.

Explanation: Where the premium is tendered by postal money order or cheque sent by post, the risk may be assumed on the date on which the money order is booked or the cheque is posted, as the case may be.

(3) Any refund of premium which may become due to an insured on account of the cancellation of a policy or alteration in its terms and conditions or otherwise shall be paid by the insurer directly to the insured by a crossed or order cheque or by postal money order and a proper receipt shall be obtained by the insurer from the insured, and such refund shall in no case be credited to the account of the agent.

(4) Where an insurance agent collects a premium on a policy of insurance on behalf of an insurer, he shall deposit with, or dispatch by post to, the insurer, the premium so collected in full without deduction of his commission within twenty-four hours of the collection excluding bank and postal holidays.

(5) The Central Government may, by rules, relax the requirements of sub-section (1) in respect of particular categories in insurance policies.

(6) The authority may, from time to time, specify, by the regulations made by it, the manner of receipt of premium by the insurer.

Assets, Liabilities and Solvency Margin of Insurers Regulations—Valuation of Assets

Every insurer shall prepare a statement of the value of assets in Form IRDA-Assets-AA in accordance with Schedule II.

Determination of Amount of Liabilities

Every insurer shall prepare a statement of the amount of liabilities in accordance with Schedule II-A, in respect of the life insurance business, and in Form HG in accordance with Schedule II-B, in respect of general insurance business, as the case may be.

Determination of Solvency Margin

Every insurer shall prepare a statement of solvency margin in accordance with Schedule III-A, in respect of life insurance business, and in Form KG in accordance with Schedule III-B, in respect of general insurance business, as the case may be. All three Government Insurance Companies are below solvency margin.

Health Insurance Business

Where the insurer transacts health insurance business, providing health covers, the amount of liabilities shall be determined in accordance with the principles specified under these Regulations.

Business Outside India

Where the insurer transacts insurance business in a country outside India, and submits statements or returns or any such particulars to a public authority of that country, he shall enclose the same along with the Forms specified in accordance with these Regulations and the Insurance Regulatory and Development Authority (Actuarial Report and Abstract) Regulations, 2000.

If the appointed actuary is of the opinion that it is necessary to set additional reserves over and above the reserves shown in the statements or returns or any such particulars submitted to the public authority of a county outside India, he may set such additional reserves.

Furnishing of Forms

The Forms, namely, Form IRDA-Assets-AA, for HG, and Form KG, shall be furnished separately for Business within India and Total Business transacted by the insurer.

Personal Visit of Appointed Actuary to the Authority

The Authority may, if considered necessary and expedient, ask the appointed actuary to make a personal visit to the office of the Authority to elicit from him any further information.

SCHEDULE I

Valuation of Assets

1. Interpretation

In this Schedule, unless the context otherwise requires, 'non-mandated investments' means those investments that are neither approved securities nor approved investments.

2. Values of Assets

(1) The following assets should be place with value zero:

(a) Agent's balances and outstanding premiums in India, to the extent they are not realised within a period of thirty days;

(b) Agents' balances and outstanding premiums outside India, to the extent they are not realisable;

(c) Sundry debts, to the extent they are not realisable;

(d) Advances of an unrealisable character;

(e) Furniture, fixtures, dead stock and stationery;

(f) Deferred expenses;

(g) Profit and loss appropriation account balance and any fictitious assets other than pre-paid expenses;

(h) Reinsurer's balance outstanding for more than three months; and

(i) Preliminary expenses in the formation of the company.

(2) The value of computer equipment including software shall be computed as under:

(i) Seventy-five per cent of its cost in the year of purchase;

(ii) Fifty per cent of its cost in the second year;

(iii) Twenty-five per cent of its cost in the third year; and

(iv) Zero per cent thereafter.

(3) All other assets of an insurer have to be valued in accordance with the Insurance Regulatory and Development Authority (Preparation of Financial Statements and Auditor's Report of Insurance Companies) Regulations, 2000.

3. Statement of Assets

Every insurer shall prepare a statement of assets in Form IRDA-Assets-AA.

FORM IRDA-ASSETS-AA

Insurance Regulatory and Development Authority (Assets, Liabilities, and Solvency Margin of Insurers) Regulations, 2000

Statement of Assets as at 31st March 20____.

Form Code: [][][][][][][][][][]

Name of Insurer: Registration Number: Date of registration:

Classification: Business Within India/Total Business

Item No. (1)	Category of Asset (2)	Policyholders' funds: Amount (in rupees lakhs) as per (a) below (3)	Shareholders' funds: Amount (in rupees lakhs) as per (a) (4)
01	Approved Securities		
02	Approved Investments		
03	Deposits		
04	Non-mandated Investments		
05	Other Assets, specify		
06	Total		
07	Fair Value Change Account		
08	Adjusted Value of Assets: (6) – (7)		

I certify that the statement has been prepare in accordance with Schedule I.

Place: .... Name and Signature of
Appointed Actuary.
(in case of a life insurer)

Date.................. Name and Signature of Auditor
(in case of a general insurer)

Note: The statement shall show the value of the above-mentioned categories of assets in accordance with Regulation 2 in Schedule I.

SCHEDULE II-A

Valuation of Liabilities-Life Insurance

1. Interpretation

In this Schedule:

(a) "Valuation date", in relation to an actuarial investigation, means the date to which the investigation relates.

(b) "Universal life contracts" means those contracts that are presenter in an unbundled form. The contracts where policyholders have an option to invest in units of insurer's segregated fund(s) shall be treated as "linked business"; and others shall be treated as "non-linked business".

2. Method of Determination of Mathematical Reserves

(1) Mathematical Reserves shall be determined separately for each contract by a prospective method of valuation in accordance with sub-paras (2) to (4).

(2) The valuation method shall take into account all prospective contingencies under which any premiums (by the policyholder) or benefits (to the policyholder/beneficiary) may be payable under the policy, as determined by the policy conditions. The level of benefits shall take into account the reasonable expectations of policyholders (with regard to bonuses, including terminal bonuses, if any) and any established practices of an insurer of an insurer for payment of benefits.

(3) The valuation method shall take into account the cost of any options that may be available to the policyholder under the terms of the contract.

(4) The determination of the amount of liability under each policy shall be based on prudent assumption of all relevant parameters. The value of each such parameter shall be based on the insurer's expected experience and shall include an appropriate margin for adverse deviations (hereinafter referred to as MAD) that may result in an increase in the amount of mathematical reserves.

(5) (i) The amount of mathematical reserve in respect of a policy, determined in accordance with sub-para (4), maybe negative (called "negative reserves") or less than the guaranteed surrender value available (called "guaranteed surrender value deficiency reserves") at the valuation date.

(ii) The appointed actuary shall, for the purpose of Section 35 of the Act, use the amount of such mathematical reserves without any modification.

(iii) The appointed actuary shall, for the purpose of Sections 13, 49, 64V and 64VA of the Act, set the amount of such mathematical reserve to zero, in case of such negative reserve, or to the guaranteed surrender value, in case of such guaranteed surrender value deficiency reserves, as the case may be.

(6) The valuation method shall be called "Gross Premium Method".*

(7) If in the opinion of the appointed actuary, a method of valuation other than the Gross Premium Method of valuations is to be adopted, then, other approximations (e.g., retrospective method) may be used:

---

* See p. 21.

The amount of calculated reserve is expected to be at least equal to the amount that shall be produced by the application of Gross Premium Method.

(8) The method of calculation of the amount of liabilities and the assumptions for the valuation parameters shall not be subject to arbitrary discontinuities from one year to the next.

(9) The determination of the amount of mathematical reserves shall take into account the nature and term of the assets representing those liabilities and the value placed upon them and shall include prudent provision against the effects of possible future changes in the value of assets on the ability of the insurer to meet its obligations arising under policies as they arise.

3. Policy Cash Flows

The gross premium method of valuation shall discount the following future policy cash flows at an appropriate rate of interest:

(a) Premiums payable, if any, benefits payable, if any, on death; benefits payable, if any, on survival; benefits payable, if any, on voluntary termination of contract, and the following, if any:

- (i) Basic benefits,
- (ii) Rider benefits,
- (iii) Bonuses that have already been vested as at the valuation date,
- (iv) Bonuses as a result of the valuation at the valuation date, and
- (v) Future bonuses (one year after valuation date) including terminal bonuses (consistent with the valuation rate of interest);

(b) Commission and remuneration payable, if any, in respect of a policy (This shall be based on the current practice of the insurer). No allowance shall be made for non-payment of commissions in respect of the orphaned policies;

(c) Policy maintenance expenses, if any, in respect of a policy, as provided under sub-para (4) of para 5;

(d) Allocation of profit to shareholders, if any, where there is a specified relationship between profits attributable to shareholders and the bonus rates declared for policyholders:

Provided that allowance must be made for tax, if any.

4. Policy Options

Where a policy provides built-in options, that may be exercised by the policyholder, such as conversion or addition of coverage at future date(s) without any evidence of good health, annuity rate guarantees at maturity of contract, etc., the costs of such options shall be estimated and treated as special cash flows in calculating the mathematical reserves.

5. Valuation Parameters

(1) The valuation parameters shall constitute the bases on which the future policy cash flows shall be computed and discounted. Each parameter shall have to be appropriate to the block of business to be valued. An appointed actuary shall take into consideration the following:

(a) The value(s) of the parameter shall be based on the insurer's experience study, where available. If reliable experience study is not available, the value(s) can be based on the industry study, if available and appropriate. If neither is available, the values may be based on the bases used for pricing the product. In establishing the expected level of any parameter, any likely deterioration in the experience shall be taken into account.

(b) The expected level, as determined in clause (a) of this sub-para, shall be adjusted by an appropriate Margin for Adverse Deviations (MAD), the level of MAD being dependent on the degree of confidence in the expected level, and such MAD in each parameter shall be based on the Guidance Notes issued by the Actuarial Society of India, with the concurrence of the Authority.

(c) The values used for the various valuation parameters should be consistent among themselves.

(2) Mortality rates to be used shall be by reference to a published table, unless the insurer has constructed a separate table based on his own experience:

Such published table shall be made available to the insurance industry by the Actuarial Society of India, with the concurrence of the Authority:

Such rates determined by reference to a published table shall not be less than hundred per cent of that published table:

Such rates determined by reference to a published table may be less than hundred per cent of that published table if the appointed actuary can justify a lower per cent.

(3) Morbidity rates to be used shall be by reference to a published table, unless the insurer has constructed a separate table based on his own experience:

Such published table shall be made available to the insurance industry by the Actuarial Society of India, with the concurrence of the Authority:

Such rates determined by reference to a published table shall not be less than hundred per cent of that published table.

Such rates determined by reference to a published table may be less than hundred per cent of that published table if the appointed actuary can justify a lower per cent.

(4) Policy maintenance expenses shall depend on the manner, in which they are analysed by the insurer, viz., fixed expenses and variable expenses. The variable expenses shall be related to sum assured or premiums or benefits. The fixed expenses may be related to sum assured or premiums or benefits or per policy expenses. All expenses shall be increased in future years for inflation, the rate of inflation assumed should be consistent with the valuation rate of interest.

(5) Valuation rates of interest, to be used by appointed actuary:

(a) Shall be not higher than the rates of interest, for the calculation of the present value of policy cash flows referred to in para 4, determined from prudent assessment of the yields for existing assets attribute to blocks of life insurance business, and the yields which the insurer is expected to obtain from the sums invested in the future, and such assessment shall take into account:

(i) The composition of assets supporting the liabilities, expected cash flows from the investment on hand, the cash flows from the block of policies to be valued, the likely future investment conditions and the reinvestment and disinvestment strategy to be employed in dealing with the future net cash flows;

(ii) The risks associated with investment in regard to receipt of income on such investment or repayment of principal;

(iii) The expenses associated with the investment functions of the insurer;

(b) Shall not be higher than, for the calculation of present value of policy cash flows in respect of a particular category of contracts, the yields on assets maintained for the purpose such category of contracts;

(c) In respect of non-participating business, shall recognise the risk of decline in the future interest rates;

(d) In respect of participating, shall be based on the assumption (with regard to future investment conditions), that the scale of future bonuses used in the valuation is consistent with the valuation rate of interest; and

(e) In respect of single premium business, shall take into account the effect of changes in the risk-free interest rates.

(6) Other parameters, may be taken into account, depending on the type of policy. In establishing the values of such parameters, the considerations set out in this Schedule shall be taken into account.

6. Applicability to Reinsurance

(1) The Schedule shall also apply to the valuation of business in the books of re-insurers.

(2) As regards the business ceded by insurers, this Schedule shall be applicable to the net sums at risk retained by the insurer.

(3) Reinsurance arrangement with an element of borrowing in the form of deposit or credit of any kind from insurer's re-insurers without the prior approval of the Authority shall not be treated as credit for reinsurance for the purpose of determination of required solvency margin.

7. Additional Requirements for Linked Business

(1) Reserves in respect of linked business shall consist of two components, namely, unit reserves and general fund reserves.

(2) Unit reserves shall be calculated in respect of the units allocated to the policies in force at the valuation date using values at the valuation date.

(3) General fund reserves' (non-unit reserves) shall be determined using prospective valuation method set out in this Schedule, which shall take into account of the following, namely:

(a) Premiums, if any, payable in future;

(b) Death benefits, if any, provided by the general fund (over and above the value of units);

(c) Management charges paid to the general fund;

(d) Guarantees, if any, relating to surrender values or minimum death and maturity benefits;

(e) fund growth rates and management charges. (The values of these parameters, along with others, shall be determined in accordance with para 5);

(f) negative reserves, if any, shall be dealt with in accordance with sub-para (5) of para 2.

8. Additional Requirements for Provisions

The appointed actuary shall make aggregate in respect of the following, where it is not possible to calculate mathematical reserves for each policy, in the determination of mathematical reserves:

(a) Policies in respect of which extra premiums have been charged on account of underwriting of under-average lives that are subject to extra risks such as occupation hazard, over-weight, under-weight, smoking history, health, climatic or geographical conditions;

(b) Lapses policies not included in the valuation but under which a liability exists or may arise;

(c) Options available under individual and group insurance policies;

(d) Guarantees available to individual and group insurance policies;

(e) The rates of exchange at which benefit in respect of policies issued in foreign currencies have been converted into Indian Rupees and what provision has been made for possible increase of mathematical reserves arising from future variations in rates of exchange;

(f) Other, if any.

9. Statement of Liabilities

An insurer shall furnish a statement of liabilities in accordance with the Insurance Regulatory and Development Authority (Actuarial Report and Abstract) Regulations, 2000.

SCHEDULE II-B

(*See Regulation* 4)

Valuation of Liabilities (General Insurance)

1. Interpretation

In this schedule:

(a) "Reserve for claims incurred but not reported (IBNR)" means the reserve for claims incurred but not reported on the balance sheet date, and includes reserve for claims which may be inadequately reserved; [IBINR]

(b) "Reserve for outstanding claims" means the reserve for outstanding claims as mentioned in para 2(1)(b)(iii) of this Schedule;

Note:

IBNER - incurred but not enough reported

IBNR, IBINR and IBNER all are outstanding claims.

2. Determination of Liabilities

An insurer shall:

1. Place a proper value in respect of the following items, namely:
   (a) Provision for bad and doubtful debts,
   (b) Reserve for dividends declared or recommended, and outstanding dividends in full,
   (c) Amount due to insurance companies carrying on insurance business, in full,

(d) Amount due to sundry creditors, in full,

(e) Provision for taxation, in full, and

(f) foreign exchange reserve.

2. Determine the amount of following reserves, in the manner specified herein below for each reserve:

☞(a) **Reserve for unexpired risk, shall be, in respect of:**

(i) Fire business, 50 per cent;

(ii) Miscellaneous business, 50 per cent;

(iii) Marine business other than marine hull business, 50 per cent; and

(iv) Marine hull business, 100 per cent,

of the premium, net of re-insurances, received or receivable during the preceding twelve months;

(b) **Reserve for outstanding claims** shall be determined in the following manner:

(i) Where the amounts of outstanding claims of the insurers are known, the amount is to be provided in full;

(ii) Where the amounts of outstanding claims can be reasonably estimated according to the insurer, he may follow the 'case by case method' after taking into account the explicit allowance for changes in the settlement pattern or average claim amounts, expenses and inflation;

(c) **Reserve for claims incurred but not reported** (IBNR) shall be determined using actuarial principles. In such determination, the appointed actuary shall follow the Guidance Notes issued by the Actuarial Society of India, with the concurrence of the Authority, and any directions issued by the Authority, in this behalf.

3. Statement of Liability

Every general insurer shall prepare a statement of liabilities in Form HG, certified by an auditor approved by the Authority in accordance with Section 64V of the Act, and also certified by its appointed actuary in respect of IBNR reserves. The statement shall be furnished to the Authority along with the returns mentioned in Section 15 of the Act.

FORM HG

(*See Regulation* 4)

Insurance Regulatory and Development Authority (Assets, Liabilities and Solvency Margin) Regulation, 2000

Table I: Statement of Liabilities as at 31st March, 20___.

Form Code:[][][][][][][][][][]

Name of Insurer: Registration Number: Date of registration:

Classification: Business Within India/Total Business

Item	Description	Reserves for unexpired risks	Reserve for out-standing claims	IBNR Reserves	Total Reserves
(1)	(2)	(3)	(4)	(5)	(6)
01	Fire				
02	Marine sub-class: Marine Cargo Marine Hull				
03	Miscellaneous Sub-class: Motor Engineering Aviation Liabilities Rural insurance Others				
04	Health Insurance				
05	Total Liabilities				

Certification from Auditor (approved by the Authority)

I Certify that the above statement represents the liabilities of the insurer which have been determined in the manner prescribed in the Insurance Regulatory and Development Authority (Assets, Liabilities and Solvency Margin of Insurers) Regulations, 2000 and the amounts of such liabilities are fair and reasonable. I also further certify that the above statement includes the IBNR reserves which have been determined by the appointed actuary and his certificate is furnished herein below.

Qualifications, if any (in regard to the determination of liabilities):

Place:

Date: Name and Signature of the Auditor

Certification from the Appointed Actuary

I certify that the IBNR reserves in the statement above represent, in my opinion, true and fair amount.

Qualifications, if any (in regard to the determination of IBNR reserves):

Place:

Date: Name and Signature of the Auditor

SCHEDULE III-A

(*See Regulation* 5)

Determination of Solvency Margins—Life Insurers

1. Interpretation

In this Schedule:

(a) 'Available Solvency Margin' means the excess of value of assets (furnished in IRDA-Form-AA) over the value of life insurance liabilities [furnished in Form H as specified in Regulation 4 of Insurance Regulatory and Development Authority (Actuarial Report and Abstract) Regulations, 2000] and other liabilities of policyholders' fund and shareholders' funds;

(b) "Solvency Ratio" means the ratio of the amount of Available Solvency Margin to the amount of Required Solvency Margin.

2. Determination of Solvency Margin

Every insurer shall determine the required solvency margin, the available solvency margin, and the solvency ratio in Form K as specified under Insurance Regulatory and Development Authority (Actuarial Report and Abstract), Regulations, 2000.

Table I: Required Solvency Margin Based on Mathematical Reserves and sum at Risk

Item No.	Description	Mathematical Reserves before Re-insurance	Mathematical Reserves Re-insurance	KI	Sum at Risk before Re-insurance	Sum at Risk after Re-insurance	K2	First factor	Second Required	Required Solvency Margin
(1)	(2)	(3)	(4)	(5)	(6)	(7)	(8)	(9)	(10)	(11)
	Category: Non Linked									
	Division: Individual									
01.	Sub-class Life Business									
02.	Sub-class General Annuity									
03.	Sub-class Pension									
	Division: Group Business:									
04.	(a) Premiums Guaranteed for not more than one year									
05.	(b) Premiums guaranteed for more than one year									
06.	Sub-class: General Annuity									
07.	Sub-class: Pension Category: Linked **Division: Individual** Sub-class: Life Business									
08.	(a) With guarantees									
09.	(b) Without guarantees Sub-class: General Annuity									
10.	(a) With guarantees									
11.	(b) Without guarantees									

(*Contd...*)

Item No.	Description	Mathematical Reserves before Re-insurance	Mathematical Reserves Re-insurance	KI	Sum at Risk before Re-insurance	Sum at Risk after Re-insurance	K2	First factor	Second Required	Required Solvency Margin
(1)	(2)	(3)	(4)	(5)	(6)	(7)	(8)	(9)	(10)	(11)
	Sub-class: Pension									
12.	(a) With guarantees									
13.	(b) Without guarantees									
	Division: Group Business									
	Sub-class: Life Business									
14.	(a) With guarantee									
15.	(b) Without guarantees									
	Sub-class: General Annuity									
16.	(a) With guarantees									
17.	(b) Without guarantees									
	Sub-class: Pension									
18.	(a) With guarantees									
19.	(b) Without guarantees									
	Category: Health Insurance									
	Division: Individual									
	Sub-class: Linked									
20.	(a) With guarantees									
21.	(b) Without guarantees									
	Sub-class: Non-Linked									
	Division: Group Business									
22.	Sub-class: Linked									
23.	(a) With guarantees									
24.	(b) Without guarantees									
	Sub-class: Non-linked									
25.	(a) Premiums guaranteed for not more than one year									
26.	(b) Premiums guaranteed for more than one year									
27.	**Total**									

Notes:

1. K1 = 0.85° or (Mathematical Reserves after Reinsurance/Mathematical Reserves before reinsurance), [0.50 in case of reinsurers, carrying on life insurance business]
2. K2 = 0.5 or (Sum a Risk after reinsurance/Sum at risk before reinsurance), whichever is higher,
3. Col.(11) = [Col.(3) × Col.(5) × Col.(9)] + [Col.(8) × Col.(8) × Col.(10)]
4. In the computation of the total sum at risk, ignore the contracts for which the sum at risk is a negative figure or does not exist.
5. Details of first and second factors.

Item	First Factor	Second Factor
	Non-linked Business	
Individual Business:		
01: Life Business	4%	0.3%
02: General Annuity	4%	0%
03: Pension	4%	0%
04: Health	4%	0%
Group Business:		
Life: Premium guaranteed for:		
05: not more than one year	1%	0.2%
06: more than one year	3%	0.3%
07: General Annuity	4%	0%
08: Pension	4%	0%
Individual Business:		
Life Business—		
09: With guarantees	2%	0.2%
10: Without guarantees	1%	0.2%
General Annuity		
11: With guarantees	2%	0%
12: Without guarantees	1%	0%
Pension		
13: With guarantees	2%	0%
14: Without guarantees	1%	0%
Group Business:		
Life Business—		
15: With guarantees	2%	0.3%
16: Without guarantees	1%	0.2%
Generally Annuity		
17: With guarantees	2%	0%
18: Without guarantees pension	1%	0%
Pension		
19: With guarantees	2%	0%
20: Without guarantees	1%	0%
	Health Insurance	
Individual Business		
Linked Business		
21: With guarantees	2%	0%
22: Without guarantees	1%	0%
23: Non-Linked business	4%	0%
Group Business		
Linked		
24: With guarantees	2%	0%
25: Without guarantees	1%	0%
Non-Linked		
26: Premiums guarantees for not more than one year	2%	0%
27: Premiums guarantees for more than one year	3%	0%

Table II: Required solvency margin Based on Assets of Policyholder's Fund

					Form Code: [][][][][][][][][]
Name of Insurer: Registration Number: Date of registration: _____					
Classification: Business within India/Total Business					
	Classified Code { }				

Item No.	Category of Asset	Notes	Amount (see Notes below) ₹	Third %	Required Solvency Margin
	(1)	(2)	(3)	(4)	(5)
	Non-Mandated investments				
	Corporate Bonds				
01	AAA or equivalent				
02	AA or equivalent				
03	A or equivalent				
04	BBB or equivalent				
05	BB or equivalent				
06	B or equivalent				
07	Lower than B				
08	Unrated mortgages				
09	Residential				
10	Commercial: Real State				
11	Residential				
12	Commercial: Preference shares				
13	Listed preference shares				
14	Unlisted preference shares equity				
15	Listed ordinary shares				
16	Unlisted ordinary shares				
17	Total				

Notes:

1. Column (5) = Column (3). Column (4);
2. Column (4) = zero until further intimation from the Authority;
3. The Table should show the Amount (In Column) (3) which is balance sheet value in respect of the above-mentioned category of asset [where the balance sheet is prepared in accordance with Insurance Regulatory and Development Authority (Preparation of Financial Statements and Auditor's Report of Insurance companies) Regulations, 2000].
4. All the Figures in Columns (3) and (5) should be in Indian Rupees lakhs.

Table III: Available Solvency Margin and Solvency Ratio

Form Code: [][][][][][][][][][]

Name of Insurer: Registration Number: Date of registration: _____

Classification: Business within India/Total Business

Classified Code { }

Item	Description	Notes No.	Adjusted Value
(1)	(2)	(3)	(4)
01	Available Assets in Policyholder's Fund		
	Deduct:		
02	Mathematical Reserves		
03	Other Liabilities		
04	Excess in Policyholders Fund: (01-02-03)		
05	Available Assets in Shareholders Fund:		
	Deduct:		
06	Other Liabilities of Shareholder's Fund		
07	Excess in Shareholder's Fund (05 – 06)		
08	Total ASM (04) + (07)		
09	Total RSM		
10	Solvency Ratio (ASM/RSM)		

Certification

I, ..., the Appointed Actuary, certify that the above statements have been prepared in accordance with the Section 64VA of the Insurance Act, 1938, and the amounts mentioned therein are true and fair to the best of my knowledge.

Place: Name and Signature of Appointed Actuary

Date:

Notes:

1. Item No. 01 shall be the amount of the Adjusted Value of Assets as mentioned in form IRDA-Assets—AA as specified under Schedules I of Insurance Regulatory and Development Authority (Assets, Liabilities, and Solvency Margin of Insures) Regulations, 2000;
2. Item No. 02 shall be the amount of Mathematical Reserves as mentioned in Form H;
3. Item Nos. 03 and 06 shall be the amount of other liabilities as mentioned in the Balance sheet;
4. Item No. 05 shall be the amount of the Total Assets as mentioned in Form IRDA-Assets-AA as specified under Schedule I of Insurance Regulatory and Development Authority (Assets, Liabilities and Solvency Margin of Insurers) Regulations, 2000.

SCHEDULE III-B

(*See Section* 5)

Determination of Solvency Margins—General Insurers

1. Interpretation

In this Schedule:

(a) 'Available Solvency Margin' means the excess of value of assets (furnished in Form IRDA-Assets-AA) over the value of liabilities (furnished in Form HG), with further adjustments as shown in Table III of Form KG.

(b) "Solvency Ratio" means the ratio of the amount of Available Solvency Margin to the amount of Required Solvency Margin.

2. Determination of Solvency Margin

Every insurer shall determine the required solvency margin, the available solvency ratio in Form KG.

FORM KG

(*See Regulation* 5)

Insurance Regulatory and Development Authority (Assets, Liabilities and Solvency Margin) Regulation, 2000

Table I: Statement of Solvency Margin: (General Insurers) as at 31st March 20___.

Form Code: [][][][][][][]

Name of Insurer: Registration Number: Date of registration:_____

Classification: Business within India/Total Business

Classification Code: [ ]

Table I: Required Solvency Margin Based on Net Premium and Net Incurred Claims

(In ₹ Lakhs)

Item No.	Description (Class of business)	Gross Premi.	Net Premi.	Gross Incu. claims	Net Incu. claims	RSM-1	RSM-2	RSM
(1)	(2)	(3)	(4)	(5)	(6)	(7)	(8)	(9)
01	Fire							
02	Marine: Marine Cargo							
03	Marine Hull							
04	Miscellaneous: Motor							
05	Engineering							
06	Aviation							
07	Liability							

(*Contd...*)

08	Rural Insurance							
09	Others							
10	Health Insurance							
11	Total							

Notes:

(1) RSM-1 in the above table means Required Solvency Margin based on net premiums, and shall be determined as twenty per cent of the amount which is the higher of the Gross Premiums multiplied by a Factor A as specified below and the Net Premiums.

(2) RSM-2 in the above table means Required Solvency Margin based on net incurred claims, and shall be determined as thirty per cent of the amount which is the higher of the Gross Net Incurred Claims multiplied by a Factor B as specified below and the Net Incurred Claims:

Item No.	**Description (Class of business)**	**A**	**B**
(1)	(2)	(3)	(4)
01	Fire	0.5	0.5
02	Marine: Marine Cargo	0.6	0.6
03	Marine Hull	0.5	0.5
04	Miscellaneous: Motor	0.75	0.75
05	Engineering	0.5	0.5
06	Aviation	0.9	0.9
07	Liability	0.75	0.75
08	Rural Insurance	0.5	0.5
09	Others	0.7	0.7
10	Health	0.75	0.75

(3) RSM means Required Solvency Margin and shall be the higher of the amounts of RSM-1 and RSM-2.

Table II: Available Solvency Margin and Solvency Ratio

Item	**Description**	**Notes No.**	**Amount**
(1)	(2)	(3)	(4)
01	Available Assets in Policyholders' Funds:		
	Deduct:		
02	Liabilities		
03	Other Liabilities		
04	Excess in Policyholders' funds (01-02-03)		
05	Available Assets in Shareholders Funds:		
	Deduct:		
06	Other Liabilities		
07	Excess in Shareholders' funds: (05-06)		
08	Total ASM (04) + (07)		
09	Total RSM		
10	**Solvency Ratio (Total ASM/Total RSM)**		

Certification

I, ..., the Auditor, certify that the above statements have been prepared in accordance with the Section 64VA of the Insurance Act, 1938, and the amounts mentioned therein are true to the best of my knowledge.

Place: Name and Signature of the Auditor

Date:

Countersignature: Principal Officer:

Guidelines on Mathematical Estimation of IBNR Claims Provision

(*Reserve for Claims incurred but not reported*)

1. Introduction

1.1 The purpose of these guidelines is to specify an approach to the determination of IBNR in a logical manner and for compilation of data required for such determination.

1.2 These guidelines are relevant to determination of IBNR provisions for direct insurance and facultative reinsurance accepted business. Estimation of IBNR on treaty accepted and Excess Loss accepted business requires other methods more appropriate to the nature of the portfolio and its claims development pattern. Likewise, estimation of IBNR for specialized business such as crop insurance or credit guarantee insurance will require other methods more appropriate to the nature of business.

1.3 In these guidelines, the term IBNR covers both provisions for claims not reported as well as inadequate provision for reported claims, called IBNER. It is not necessary to establish separate reserves for IBNR and for IBNER so long as the method used will take into account both elements.

1.4 There are several possible methods for determination of the provision for IBNR claims. The method most appropriate in a particular case will depend on the nature of the business and claims development pattern. The method stated in these guidelines is the preferred method and is generally suitable to most sets of data. Where the Appointed Actuary considers the method stated in these guidelines to be not suitable, he should set out the reasons for such conclusion and provide justification for the alternative method proposed to be used, being considered more appropriate. Where the method used is not one of the well-known methods, the Appointed Actuary should also describe the method and the underlying assumption in that method.

1.5 Every mathematical method of estimation is based on a set of assumptions. So, the validity of the assumptions underlying the method proposed to be used should be fully set out and validated sufficiently to lend credibility to the exercise.

1.6 Calculation of provision for IBNR should be done separately for each year of occurrence and the figures should be aggregated to arrive at the total amount to be provided.

1.7 When the mathematics produces a negative value for the estimate of IBNR provision for any year of occurrence, it is incorrect to automatically assume that the company is over-providing. The validity of the underlying assumptions should be re-examined. Other tests of credibility of the results should be applied. The incurred claims ratios derived after the estimation of IBNR should be reviewed in the general background of the ratios for the insurer concerned over the years and also the ratios for other insurers in the market for the same years. There should be a logically identifiable reason to support the findings. It is prudent to ignore negative values of IBNR provision.

2. Examination and Validation of Basic Data

2.1 Integrity and completeness of data is essential to an acceptable estimation of IBNR provision based on such data. Therefore, an examination of the data should precede the work of estimation of IBNR provision. Although it is the responsibility of the management of the insurer to provide an accurate data as required by the Appointed Actuary, the Appointed Actuary should apply such checks as practically possible, to ensure the quality and completeness of the data.

2.2 As suggested in the guidance note on collection of data on claims department, it is important to ensure homogeneity of data with regard to nature business and claims development pattern. Therefore, data should be examine separately for each of the classes set out in the guidance notes. If data of any class is aggregated with data for another class, care should be taken to see that the two classes are homogeneous in nature. In respect of motor insurance business, it may be possible to compile data separately by class of vehicle and by scope of cover and by nature of claim. Provided the quantum of data is statistically adequate for projection work, this may be done. In respect of a long-term insurance policies, the Appointed Actuary should adopt an appropriate basis to ensure that the earned premium for the year alone is used in the calculations. In respect of insurance plans including cover in more than one sub-class such as Householders' Comprehensive insurance, the system adopted by the insurer for classification of the business and the related premium should be consistently applied to data for all years used in the estimation process.

2.3 The underwriting policy of an insurer has a material effect on the nature of it portfolio and consequently, on the claims development pattern. Therefore, the Appointed Actuary should first examine the changes in underwriting policy over the period of observation and in particular, the changes made in current underwriting policy. The impact of such changes on the claims development pattern and claims ratio should be examined.

2.4 In the above context, the progression of premium over the recent years should be examined. Where the premium income shows significant fluctuation, the reasons for it should be examined. In particular, the impact of the types of risks being underwritten more actively, on the claims development should be taken into account. One of the important underwriting factors is the extent of policy deductible. If the average level of deductible has undergone material change over the recent years, its impact on the claims development should taken into account.

2.5 In respect of motor insurance business, the composition of the portfolio by type of vehicle is material to the claims development pattern. Where the portfolio has changed materially, over recent years, its impact on the overall claims development should be taken into account unless data is split into several sub-divisions.

2.6 Compilation of data on and underwriting year basis instead of year of occurrence basis may be proposed in some cases. Where this basis is followed the Appointed Actuary should support the reason for change of basis on objective reasons.

3. Claims Handling Practices

3.1 A detailed review of the claims handling practices from the following aspects should be made. Where material changes are identified, their impact on the claims development pattern should be taken into account.

3.2 Although the law requires every claim to be recognized on first intimation, the way this is implemented in practice may differ from one company to another. The impact of inadequate provision for claims-on-claims development will be significant and should be taken into account.

3.3 Besides recognition of claims, the practice followed by the insurer to determine the provision to be made and the mechanism to review such provision as the claim develops are also important factors in claims development. Also, if the insurer has the practice of downsizing the claims provision in cases where there has been no movement in the claim over a certain period, it will be an important factor in claims development.

3.4 Besides studying the practice with regard to recognition, reserving and review of reserve, the claims settlement practice of the insurer should be studied. In particular, the company's practice in speed of processing for settlement, fairness in settlement offers, attitude to litigation, approach to interim payments and effectiveness of recovery action both by sale of salvage and through recoveries from third parties, are all material to the claims development pattern. For example, financial problems can get reflected in slower development of claims paid and unless interpreted properly, they will lead to significant underestimation of ultimate claims incurred ratios.

3.5 When studying the above aspects, it should be remembered that any set of practices that have been stable, will be reflected in the claims development pattern. Hence they may not present as much of a problem in estimation as any material changes in practices. The impact of such changes should be evaluated.

3.6 Methods that work on incurred claims are subject to far more uncertainties than methods that rely on progression of paid claims due to the uncertainties of claims estimation and reserving. Hence the Appointed Actuary should invariably work on paid claims data as the core basis of the estimation-process. However, the Appointed Actuary may do another calculation using incurred claims as a point of comparison, if he so desires.

3.7 The claims development pattern can be materially affected by the occurrence of unusual events over the period of observation such as:

- Individual large claims;
- Catastrophic events causing a large number of claims;
- Changes in law affecting the incidence and size of claims; and
- Impact of external factors on the average size of claims.

3.8 When looking at estimation of IBNR on a "net of reinsurance" basis, note should be taken of any change in reinsurance protection and change in size of retentions over recent years.

4. Allowance for Trends

4.1 In order to make adequate allowance for trends, the following aspects should be studied:

(i) Composition of portfolio;

(ii) External factors such as economic environment, inflation, changes in legal, political or social conditions;

(iii) Insurer's underwriting policy; and

(iv) Insurer's claims settlement practice.

4.2 A significant indicator of claims experience is the frequency of claims occurrence and the average size per claim paid and per claim outstanding. These should be studied and any variations observed should be looked into.

5. Preferred Method for Estimation of IBNR

5.1 Based on data submitted for successive years, the cumulative development of claims picture should be compiled. It can be tabulated as shown in Form IBNR-B-1/2.

5.2 The cumulative claims paid as at the end of 24 months in respect of claims relating to events that occurred in the year from 1 April, 2002 to 31 March, 2003 is the total of claims relating to the "current year" in the statement of claims for the year ending 31 March 2003 and claims paid in the "first preceding year" in the statement of claims for the ending 31 March 2004; and so on. The cumulative statement is thus built up by putting together information from statement of claims for successive years.

5.3 The cumulative statement of claims development shows the way the claims paid picture develops over time. Assuming that the pattern of claims development will remain stable, it is possible to project to the completely developed claims amount using the progression of "link ratios" derived from the available data. The amount of IBNR will be the estimated ultimate claims cost less the amounts paid so far and amount provided as outstanding on the date of estimation.

5.4 If there were changes in portfolio or underwriting or claims settlement practices, it may be better use the latest available year's link ratios rather than the average ratios.

5.5 The estimation process should not discount the estimated future development of paid claims to the current date nor should it load the claims outstanding specifically to provide for inflation in the future cost of claims, other than the factor already inherent in the estimation process.

6. Tests of Credibility

6.1 The exercise of estimating the provision for IBNR will not be complete without applying the tests of credibility to the results produced. These include looking at the frequency of claims occurrence, ultimate incurred claims ratios, average cost per claim and per claim outstanding etc.

6.2 The ultimate incurred claims ratio for the successive years should be credible as compared to ratios of other insurance in the market and for the same insurer overtime. There should be logical explanations for any variations or sharp fluctuations. If the calculations produce progressively reducing ultimate claims ratios, they indicate a deficiency of the mathematical model. It may then be necessary to override the results by alternative methods such **as ultimate loss ratio method or Bornhuetter-Ferguson method.***

6.3 Since insurers do not normally consciously over-provide for claims and since event with utmost diligence there will be claims that have occurred but have not yet been intimated to the

---

* See p. 20.

insurer, it is inappropriate to accept any negative values for IBNR produced by the mathematics. To avoid such an error, estimation of IBNR should be made separately for each year of occurrence. Negative values of IBNR for any year should be ignored.

6.4 An essential check on the credibility of the estimation exercise is to see how the claims developed during the preceding twelve months as compared to the projection and estimation made last year. The outstanding claims provision and provision for IBNR made at the last Balance Sheet date should be compared with the aggregate of claims paid during the year, claims provided as outstanding at the end of the year and the provision for IBNR claims produced by the formula.

6.5 Most estimation methods produce less reliable results for the most recent years. Hence the results for the more recent years have to be revised based on the Actuary's knowledge of the business, the company's portfolio and claims settlement practices and the claims ratios of other insurers in the market.

Report of the Appointed Actuary on the Estimation of Reserve for IBNR Claims as at 31 March

Name of Insurer:

Name of Appointed Actuary:

Class of Business:

Section 1: The Insurer and its Business

1.1 How active is the insurer in that class of business? Has the growth of premium income been steady and reasonable? Fluctuations in growth rates or high or low growth rates may be indicative of a change in the composition of business or changes in underwriting policy.

1.2 What is the underwriting policy of the insurer in respect of:

(i) Selection of risks

(ii) Rates and deductibles

(iii) Delegation of underwriting authority.

1.3 Has the underwriting policy remained stable over the last six years? Have there been any changes in key underwriting personnel and how would that have impacted on the underwriting policy of the insurer?

1.4 What has been the claims processing and settlement policy of the insurer in the matter of:

(i) First recognition of claim;

(ii) Provision for a claim where no information or inadequate information on facts is available;

(iii) Periodicity of review of the provision for a claim;

(iv) Negotiation of bodily injury claims relating to motor accidents;

(v) Processing and settlement of claims; and

(vi) Pursuit of recovery or sale of salvage.

1.5 Has the claims processing and settlement policy remained the same over the past six years? Have there been any changes in key claims personnel and how would that have on the claims settlement practice of the insurer? If so, comment on how the impact of these changes have been taken into account?

1.6 Has the insurer passed through cash flow or financial problems over the observation period? If so, has it affected the insurer's underwriting or claims settlement practices? Was there a significant slowing down in claims settlements?

1.7 Were the observed claims data affected by catastrophic events such as earthquake, flood, windstorm, individual large claims, etc.? Were there significant changes in the business environment such as a severe economic recession that would have affected the business experience? If so, how have they affected the observed claims figures?

1.8 Was there any change in the general business and insurance industry conditions in matters such as legislative environment, competition, consumerism, levels of court awards, etc.? If so, the impact of these changes should be commented upon.

Section 2: The Data

2.1 If the data is not separately compiled for each of general insurance business as required by the guidance notes, then please comment on the reasons for variation.

2.2 Please comment on the source of data and steps taken to ensure that the data is consistent, reliable, complete and tallies with the audited accounts.

2.3 Please comment on the observed trends in the growth of premiums, frequency of loss occurrence, average cost per claim paid and per claim outstanding, speed of emergence of claims and speed of settlement. Please also state how these have been taken into account in the selection of the process of estimation.

2.4 Did any individually large claims affect development figures? If so, how are they taken note of in the estimation process?

2.5 Is the estimation of IBNR done on a "net of reinsurance" basis? If not, describe the process followed to determine the amount to be provided net of reinsurance. Was there any material change in the insurance programme? If so, describe the manner in which it was allowed for in the estimation process. If data on net of reinsurance basis is not readily available, it is open to the actuary to work on the IBNR estimate on a gross basis and work on the estimate of IBNR for the share of reinsurance ceded, if that is more easily possible.

Section 3: The Method

3.1 Please describe the method used for estimation of IBNR. If the method used now is different from the method used previously, please state the reason for change.

3.2 Please state the assumptions underlying the method and to what extent the validity of the assumptions was verified.

3.3 Where the method used is not commonly understood, please explain the methodology and provide adequate working sheets to understand the calculations and results.

3.4 Please cross-check the result using another method, preferably, the chain-ladder method and comment on the outcome. However, if the Appointed Actuary chooses to use the chain-ladder method for estimation, then he may check on the estimate using any other method considered by him to be suitable for the purpose.

Section 4: Evaluation of the Results

4.1 Please describe the tests of logic applied to the results and the results of the tests.

4.2 How do the figures of outstanding claims as per the estimation process compare with the actual provisions? If the calculated estimates are lower than the actual provisions, please advise the further tests applied to evaluate the validity of the results.

Section 5: Incurred Claims Ratios

Comment on calculated incurred claims ratios for the insurer over the years and also as compared to other insurers in the market. In particular, please comment whether the claims ratios for the more recent years are logical. If not, please state how the estimation process was modified to achieve more credible results.

Section 6: Attachments

The data collected for the database of the insurer, the compiled cumulative figures, the calculation sheets and the final results should be attached to the report.

Section 7: Certification

7.1 The Appointed Actuary should not put forward or certify any figures, which lack credibility, with serious reservations.

7.2 The Appointed Actuary should certify that he has checked the data to the best of his ability and is satisfied that they are consistent, reliable and complete and that the assumptions underlying the method used for estimation of IBNR are valid.

7.3 The report should be signed with the date by the Appointed Actuary. The Appointed Actuary should also secure a certificate from the Principal Officer as under and attach it to his report:

Certification

I certify that full and accurate particulars of every policy and claim have been furnished to the appointed actuary........... (name) for the purpose of the determination of IBNR Reserves as on the 31st day of March of....... (date of investigation).

Name of Insurer:

Name of Principal Officer:

Signature of Principal Officer:

Place:

Date:

Financial Disclosure and Reporting

As per the provisions of Section 211(3B) of the Act, where in the preparation of Profit & Loss Account and Balance Sheet any deviation has been made from the accounting standards, such deviation has to be disclosed in the Profit & Loss Account and Balance Sheet.

In addition, this sub-clause requires the deviations to be also reported in Corporate Governance Report in more representative of the true and fair view of underlying business transaction.

Accounting Standard as existing and applicable to Enterprises carrying on Insurance Business (like ours) are listed below for our ready reference:

AS 1 – Disclosure of Accounting Policies.
AS 3 – Cash Flow Statement.
AS 4 – Contingencies and/or events occurring after the Balance Sheet date.
AS 5 – Prior Period Items and changes in accounting Policies.
AS 6 – Depreciation Accounting Methods.
AS 10 – Accounting, Disclosure and Revaluation of Fixed Assets.
AS 11 – Accounting for the effects of changes in Foreign Exchange Rates.
AS 13 – Accounting for Investment.
AS 15 – Accounting for Retirement Benefits in the Financial Statements of Employees.
AS 17 – Segment Reporting.
AS 18 – Related Party Disclosures.
AS 22 – Accounting for Taxes on Income.
AS 26 – Recognition and Accounting of Intangible Assets.
AS 28 – Impairment of Assets.
AS 29 – Provisions, Contingent Liabilities and Contingent Assets.

Marketing Management

"One who can sell insurance can sell everything" so goes a saying. Insurance does not offer any tangible product. Insurance product continues to exist for a long period. Thirdly Secondly the seller (insurer) has not only to sell his product but also to keep the contract in force by continues and efficient serving i.e., sales and service go together. Moreover, in India insurance market is a seller market (it should be buyer market). This is because seller, the insurer has to decide whom to sell insurance product.

According to Philip Kotler marketing management means "analysis, planning, implementation and control of programmes designed to create, build and maintain beneficial exchange with target buyers for purpose of achieving organisational goals". Marketing management process for services is depicted below:

The insurance marketing management is discussed as under:

(1) Marketing Approach to Insurance

(2) Marketing Mix

(3) Marketing Channels

(4) Factors Effecting Insurance Marketing

Marketing Approach to Insurance

Insurance, particularly life insurance, is a personalised service-oriented sector. Hence, it should provide services that satisfy the customer's needs and wants. The marketing approach in relation to life insurance refers basically to four steps:

1. research to determine customers' financial insecurity;
2. design new services (policies) or innovate old ones;
3. market services to the customer for whom they were researched and designed (pricing, promotion and distribution) at a profit; and
4. in doing so, satisfy the customer's needs.

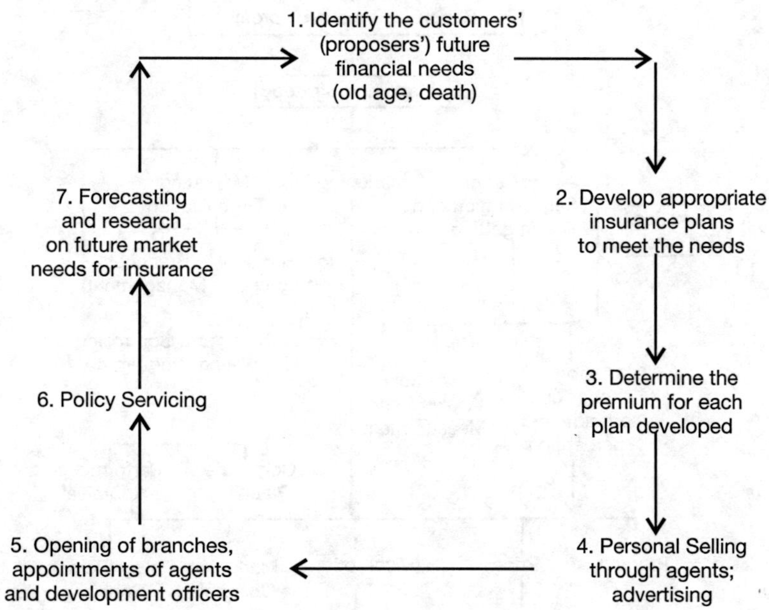

Marketing Strategy

The objective of the marketing process is profitable sale of services that satisfy customers financial requirements and needs. It puts emphasis on customer's need satisfaction, at a profit to the life insurance marketer. The marketing approach to life insurance services is presented in the 1. As can be seen, it starts and concludes with identifying and satisfying customers' needs. Stages 2 through 6 of the process is called the marketing mix. A marketing mix is a term used to describe a blend of decisions about service, place, promotion and price. It must not be forgotten that these decisions act on each other while they are being 'mixed' together. For example, a decision on price (premium) affects decision on promotion. If the total marketing programmes is to succeed, an evaluation of these decisions should be made continuously. Because of the tremendous importance of customer service, Policy Servicing in case life insurance has been treated as a separate 'p'. The marketing strategy (see below Chart) for life insurance company includes:

- a very clear definition of marketing objectives;
- a very clear definition of target customers;
- the development of a marketing mix to satisfy the customers at a profit;
- planning for each of the 'source' markets and each of the 'use' markets; and
- organisation and administration.

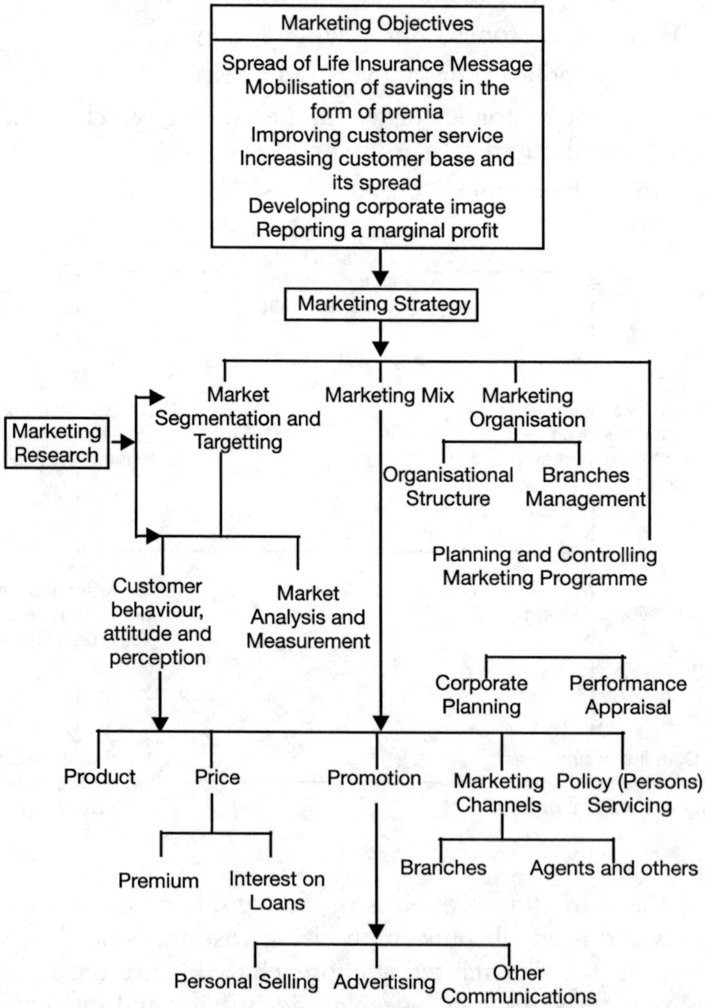

All the elements together with marketing research and their relationships with the insurance company objectives as depicted in chart suggested the overall life insurance marketing strategy. The development of an appropriate marketing mix implies first the recognition of target market. The traditional market for life insurance was the salaried white-collar workers of institutions.

With a shift from the product and selling concepts to marketing concept, the insurance companies appear to have begun analyse market opportunities and to develop new target markets through market segmentation.

Marketing Mix

(1) *Product*

A commercial product is sold in attractive colours, and packages with a view to create an awareness about the existence and more importantly to create an interest in the mind of the consumer. The same product may appear under different brands. Product differentiation is also occasionally made to meet varying needs of the consumer. Similarly, life insurance as product has also to be designed, keeping in view these basic requisites, in case of life insurance the needs are in the form of two broad economic contingencies, viz., death of the breadwinner and the subsequent financial insecurity of his dependents, and secondly, longer Life insurance is sold as term assurance and whole life policies, and various pension plans and annuities.

On the basis of market analysis and feedback from the market, the product (insurance plans) are developed from time to time to cater to the specific needs of customers. Policies with varied benefits as regards the premium payment, claims during and after the term, bonus, accident benefit, facility for taking loans, etc., have been developed by the insurance companies to later to the varying needs of the people of different segments. In the past only rich people with a regular high income had the access to the benefits of life insurance. But now sales workers, service workers, labourers, cultivators and agricultural, labourers have been brought within the life insurance fold. For example, group insurance plan was developed mainly for organised group of insurance. The product modification also takes place in case of life insurance product. Each plan is being tried and wherever necessary features attached to it are adapted according to the changing needs of the customers.

(2) *Price*

Premium is the price which the person seeking insurance pays to the insurer for purchasing in the life insurance policy. It is nothing but the 'cost' of insurance from purchaser's point of view. It is the consideration paid by each insured for building up a certain asset called the assured/insured sum with the insurer. The amount of premium has a bearing on the risk involved in covering a life. The risk, in turn, has a bearing on the age of the life to be covered, his/her habits, sex, family, race, habitat, food habits, education, etc. Life insurance premium increases with age since the probability of death increases. However, the insurers, for the convenience of the clientele and their own administrative conveniences, charge a level premium uniform throughout the contract period. Actually, slightly more premia being paid at the initial stages, along with investment returns on it, will be set off against the stages, along with investment returns on it, will be set off against the increases in premia at later ages. The actual process of accepting the person for life insurance and quoting him appropriate premium is known as underwriting. The premium may be paid in lump sum or over a period of yearly, half-yearly, quarterly or monthly basis.

Promotion and Place

As life insurance is a personalised service, personal selling plays an important role in promoting the same. Place and promotion are being highlighted here since the agents and development officers who for the pillars of the life insurance market structure discharge these two important functions. Agents are public relations men of insurance companies at the grassroot level. Their role in building up good customer relations is crucial. They work under the guidance and direct supervision of the development officers. They together sell the right type of policies suitable to the needs of the prospects for the right amount at the right time (age). The agents render various other services and also play a vital role in policy servicing. The development officers under each branch office beside guiding and supervising the activise of the agents are also responsible for their recruitment and training so as for develop a stable agency force. They activate the existing agents and motivate the new ones. Also they render all such services to the policyholders as will produce better policy servicing. Agents and development officers, as the intermediaries in the distribution system of the whole, develop and increase the life insurance business in a planned way.

For promoting life insurance business sales promotion activities are also carried out by the agents. In practice, however, it is observed that some agents lack sincere endeavour to update their knowledge of the latest developments regarding all plans of insurance, tax structure, saving and investments and underwriting which are very much relevant to their growth and ultimately to the growth of the insurance company.

Policy Servicing (People)

Customer satisfaction predominates the success of an enterprise. In the service industry where intangibles are marketed, the importance of customer satisfaction is all the more significant. Service is said to be the sharpest edge of any marketing strategy. Sales and Service are the two powerful wings of any insurance company. The emphasis should not be concentrated only on the sales but on service aspects too. Besides a supportive role in promoting sales effort, servicing influences the institutional image. Prompt and effective service boosts the morale of the sales force to present a bold form and hold their prospects. Service encompasses the service rendered to clients before, during, and after sales. Some of the activities in relation to life insurance marketing which come under each phase are given below:

Nature of Service during the Various Phases

Phase	Name of the service
(a) Before the Insurance Contract	1. Analysis of financial needs of the prospects. 2. Studying the family background. 3. Studying profession, vocation, etc. 4. Studying income, etc.
(b) During the Policy Term	1. Timely dispatch of first premium receipt. 2. Prompt dispatch of policy documents. 3. Prompt issue of premium notices. 4. Acceptance of remittances. 5. Issue of official receipts for premium/loan interest/repayment. 6. Prompt recording of change of address. 7. Transfer of policy records to another office, when needed. 8. Facilitating loans.
(c) After Sales (Policy-Becoming a Claim)	1. Completing the claim papers for immediate processing. 2. Getting claim amount with least delay. 3. Getting surrender payment when arising.

Source: Sahoo, S.C. *Marketing of Life Insurance in India* (HPH).

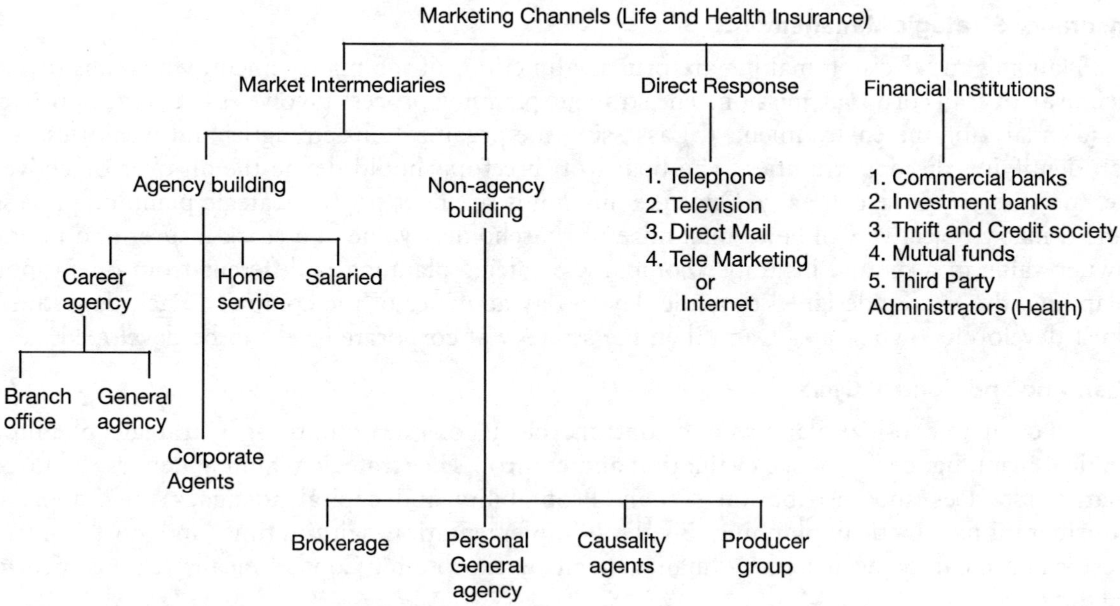

Factors Effecting Insurance Marketing

Three factors effect insurance marketing (1) distribution reach, (2) persistency and conservation, (3) speed and efficiency.

(1) Distribution reach: This depends upon agency model that currency exists 8% of business is contributed by 20% agents who are highly professional in their approach. Bank insurance is also an efficient channel. The huge strata of society call "Samanya" or "Shadarshi" i.e. above poverty segment requires focus on both customer acquisition and retention.

(2) Persistency and conservation: Customer awareness about has increased. Even then average Indian is still underinsured. IT helps in tracking customer retention and persistency. To achieve persistency three steps are necessary (a) understanding customer needs and delivering them the right product, (b) continuously following up with them, (c) and efficient trained sales force. Persistency starts from the selling point and ends up at claim stage.

(3) Speed and efficiency: Not only agents to be move efficient in terms of delivery, but also there is need for product growth. The customer satisfaction, product innovation (e.g. from non-UHIP to UHIP), and operational efficiency are areas that effect efficiency. To drive product innovation, the role of sales distribution agent, the marketing person and fund management are important, besides of actuary and underwriter. Operational efficiency is very important at claim service point. Highest number of grievances that come to ombudsman relate to claim settlement. All above three points are linked to customers delight.

Insurance industry has a huge potential at present. Only 2% of population has been tapped. But remember it is too optimistic to expect a linear growth in insurance sector. Information technology plays a vital role in above three cover areas of insurance. So for it is limited to servicing side only. Lastly IRDA has adopted "International Financial Reporting standards and solvency II" towards reducing financial risks in insurance sector.

Insurance Strategic Management

Planning and decision-making are primary functions of top management, which has to also define an overall corporate mission. The strategic planning process involves systematic approach to (a) analyzing the environment, (b) assessing the organizations strengths and weakness, and (c) identifying the opportunities. The board of directors should define the all over objectives, i.e. the mission of the company. Once the mission is set, next step is strategic planning process. The primary objective will be to maximize of shareholders value in a stock insurer and policy-owner value in a mutual insurance company. Strategic planning is different from operational planning, the later is designed to guide day-to-day activities of the company. Each department must develop its own strategy, and then the strategy at corporate level can be developed.

Planning and Control Cycle

All companies utilize planning and control cycle. It consists of four stages strategic: planning, tactical planning, performance evaluation and control. The strategic planning defines the target market, services and distribution system. Profitability and capital adequacy are important considerations. Tactical planning involves implementation within time and cost control. Performance can be evaluated by 'management by exception'. Control means readjustment of tactics.

The management of a life insurers' capital resources is very important for successful achievement of the mission. Value based planning is increasingly used in insurance as a tool for analyzing issues and establishing long range strategy. Value based planning focuses the economic net worth of a company and its relative increase from one planning period to another planning period. The values of a company consists of three elements:

(a) current capital and surplus with contingency reserve,

(b) value of expected future net flows arising from present business,

(c) expected future cash flows from future business. The present value of future cash flows at a particular rate of cost of capital is compared with present values.

8

Regulation of Investments

Definitions

'Financial Derivatives' means a derivative as defined under clause (aa) of Section 2 of the Securities Contracts (Regulation) Act, 1956, and includes a contract which derives its value from interest rates of underlying debt securities and such other derivative contracts as may be stipulated by the Authority, from time to time.

Money Market Instruments

Money Market Instruments shall comprise of short-term funds with maturity not more than one year comprising of the following instruments:

1. Certificate of deposit rated by a credit rating agency registered under SEBI (Credit Rating Agencies) Regulations, 1999.
2. Commercial paper rated by a credit rating agency registered under SEBI (Credit Rating Agencies) Regulations, 1999.
3. Repo, Reverse Repo.
4. Treasury Bills.
5. Call, Notice, Term Money.
6. CBLO as per Schedules I and II of these Regulations.
7. Any other instrument as may be prescribed by the Authority.

Regulation of Investments

Life business: In terms of the Explanation to Section 27A of the Act, the Authority has determined that assets relating to Pension business, Annuity business and all categories of Unit Linked business shall not form part of the controlled Fund for the purpose of that section.

Without prejudice to Section 27 or 27A of the Act, every insurer carrying on the business of life Insurance, shall invest and at all times keep invested his Investment Assets (other than funds relating to pension and general annuity business and all categories of Unit linked business) in the following manner:

No.	Type of Investment	Percentage
(i)	Government Securities of the fund	Not less than 25%
(ii)	Investments as specified in Section 27A of Insurance Act, 1938 and Schedule I of these Regulations, subject to Exposure/ Prudential Norms specified in Regulations 5;	Not less than 50% of the fund (incl. (i) above)
	(a) Approved Investments and Other Investments (Out of (ii)) a 'other investment' specified under Section 27A (2) of the Act, shall not exceed 15% of the fund.	Not exceeding 35% of the fund
	(b) Investment in housing and infrastructure by way of subscription or purchase of: 1. Bonds/debentures of HUDCO and National Housing Bank 2. Bonds/debentures of Housing Finance Companies either duly accredited by National Housing Banks, for house building activities, or duly guaranteed by Government or carrying current rating of not less than 'AA' by a credit rating agency registered under SEBI (Credit Rating Agencies) Regulations, 1999 3. Asset Backed Securities with underlying housing loans, satisfying the norms specified in the guidelines issued under these regulations.	Not less than 15% of the fund [(iii) b and c taken together]
	(c) Investment in Infrastructure: (*Explanation*: subscription or purchase of Bonds/Debentures, Equity and Asset Backed Securities) with underlying infrastructure assets would quality for the purpose of this requirement. 'Infrastructure facility' shall have the meaning as given in clause (h) of regulation 2 of Insurance Regulatory and Development Authority (Registration of Indian Insurance Companies) Amendment Regulation, 2008.	

Pension and general annuity business: Every Insurer shall invest and at all times keep invested funds belonging to his Pension and General Annuity Business in the following manner:

No.	Type of Investment	Percentage
(i)	Government Securities 20%	Not less than 20% of the fund
(ii)	Government Securities or 40% Other Approved Securities	Not less than 40% of the fund (incl. (i) above)
(iii)	Balance to be invested in Approved investments, as specified in schedule, subject to Exposure/ prudential norms specified in Regulation 5.	Not exceeding 60% of the fund

Note: For the purposes of this sub-regulation no investment falling under "Other investments" as specified under Section 27A(2) of Insurance Act, 1938 shall be made. However, funds pertaining to group Insurance Business, except One Year Renewable Pure Group B Term Assurance Business (OYRGTA) shall form part of Pension and General Annuity Fund. OYRGTA Funds shall follow the pattern of Investment of Life Business.

Unit linked insurance business: Every insurer shall invest and at all times keep invested his sedated fund of unit linked business as per pattern of investment offered to and approved by the policyholders where the units are categories of assets which are both marketable and easily realizable 27A(2) of Insurance Act, 1938, category shall at no time exceed 25% of such fund(s).

General insurance business: Without prejudice to Section 27B of the Act, every insurer carrying on the business of General Insurance shall invest and at all times keep invested his investment assets in the manner set out below.

No.	Type of Investment	Percentage
(i)	Government Securities	Not less than 20% of Investment assets
(ii)	Governor Securities or Other Approved Securities	Not less than 30% of Investment Assets (incl. (i) above)
(iii)	Investments as specified in Section 27B of Insurance Act, 1938 and Schedule II subject to Exposure/ prudential Norms specified in Regulation 5:	
	(a) Approved Investment and Other Investments (Out of (iii) a 'Other investment' specified under Section 27B(3) of the Act, shall not exceed 25% of Investment Assets)	Not exceeding 55%
	(b) Housing and loans to State Government for housing and firefighting equipment, by way of subscription or purchase of: 1. Bonds/debentures of HUDCO and National Housing Board 2. Bonds/debentures of Housing Finance companies either duly accredited by National Housing Banks, for house building activities, or duly guaranteed by Government or carrying current rating of not less than 'AA' by a credit rating agency registered under SEBI (Credit Rating Agencies) Regulation, 1999. 3. Asset Backed securities with underlying housing loans, satisfying the norms specified in the guidelines issued under these regulations.	Not less than 5%
	(c) Investment in Infrastructure: (*Explanation*: subscription or purchase of Bonds/ Debentures, equity and assets backed securities with underlying infrastructure assets would qualify for the purpose of this requirement.) 'Infrastructure facility' shall have the meaning as given in clause (h) of regulation 2 of Insurance Regulatory and Development authority (Registration of Indian Insurance Companies) (Amendment Regulations, 2008)	Not less than 10%

Reinsurance business: Every re-insurer carrying on re-insurance business in India shall invest and at all times keep invested his investment assets in the same manner as set out in sub-regulation (1), until such time, separate regulations in this behalf are formed by the Authority.

Notes. For the purpose of Regulations 3 and 4:

1. All investment in assets or instruments, which are capable of being rated as per market practice, shall be made on the basis of credit rating of such assets or instruments. No investment shall be mould in instruments, if such instruments are capable of being rated, but are not rated.
2. The rating should be done by a credit rating agency registered under SEBI (Credit Rating Agencies) Regulations, 1999.
3. Corporate bonds or debentures rated not less than AA or its equivalent and P1 or equivalent ratings for short-term bonds, debentures, certificate of deposit and commercial paper, by a credit rating agency, registered under SEBI (Credit Rating Agencies) Regulations, 1999 would be considered as approved Investments.
4. The rating of a debt instrument issued by All India Financial Institutions recognized as such by RBI shall be of '4A' or equivalent rating. In case investments of this grade are not available to meet the requirement of the investing insurance company, and Investment Committee's of the investing insurance company is fully satisfied about the same, then, for the reasons to be recorded in the Investment Committees minutes, the Investment Committee may approve investments in instruments carrying current rating of not less than '4+' or equivalent as rated by a credit rating agency, registered under SEBI (Credit Rating Agencies) Regulations, 1999, would be considered as approved Investments.
5. Approved Investments under points 3 and 4 above, which are downgraded below the minimum rating prescribed should be automatically re-classified under 'Other Investments' category for the purpose of pattern of investment.
6. Investments in equity shares listed on a registered stock exchange should be made in actively traded and liquid instruments viz., equity shares other than those defined as thinly traded as per SEBI Regulations and guidelines.
7. Not less than 7596 of debt instruments excluding Government and Other approved Securities—fund-wise, in the case life insurer and Investment Assets in the case of general insurer—shall have a rating of AM or equivalent rating for long-term and P1 or equivalent for short-term instruments. This shall also apply to Unit linked fund(s).
8. Notwithstanding the above, it is emphasized that rating should not replace appropriate risk analysis and management on the part of the Insurer. The Insurer should conduct risk analysis commensurate with the complexity of the product(s) and the materiality of their holding, or could also refrain from such investments.

Types of Investment	Limit for Investee Company	Limit for the entire 'group' of the investee company belong	Limit for industry Sector to which investee
1	2	3	4
(a) Investment in 'equity,' preference share, convertible debentures	10% of outstanding equity shares (face value) of 10% of the respective fund in the case of life insurer/ investment assets in the case of general insurer (including) reinsurer whichever is lower.	Not more than 10% of the respective fund in the case of life insurer/ investment assets in the case of general insurer (including reinsurer).	Investment by the insurer in any industrial sector shall not exceed 10% of its total investment exposure to the Industry sector as a whole.
(b) Investments in debt/ loans and any other permitted investments as per Act/Regulations, other than item 'a' above.	10% of the paid-up share capital, free reserves and debenture/ bonds of the investee company or 10% of respective fund in the case of life insurer/ investment assets in the case of general insurer (including reinsurer) whichever is lower.	The above percentage shall at 25% in the case of Unit linked funds.	The above percentage shall stand at 25% in the case of Unit linked funds. (Classification of industrial sectors shall be done by insurer on the lines of class signification by National Industrial classification Code for Extra Territorial Organization and Bodies in India (NIC) or any other system which adopts NIC classifications)

Notes:

1. Investments in equity including preference shares and convertible part of debentures shall not exceed 50% of above exposure norms as mentioned in the above table.
2. Investment in immovable property covered under Section 27A(1)(n) of Insurance Act, 1938 shall not exceed, at the time of investment. (a) 5% of Investment Assets in the case of general insurer, and (b) 5% of Investment Assets of funds relating to life funds, pension and general annuity funds in case of life insurer.

Exposure/Prudential Norms

Without prejudice to anything contained in Sections 27A and 27B of Insurance Act, 1938, every insurer shall limit his investment based on the following exposure norms:

1. Exposure norms for life (including unit linked business), general Insurance (including reinsurance) business for both Approved Investments as per Insurance Act, 1938 Schedules I and II of these Regulations, and Other Investments as permitted under Sections 27A(2) and 27B(3) of the Insurance Act, 1938.
2. Subject to exposure limits mentioned in the table above, an insurer shall not have investments of more than:

(i) 5% in aggregate of its total investments in companies belonging to the promoters' groups, if invested out of Life, Pension and General Annuity funds or General insurance funds; and

(ii) 12.5% in aggregate of its total investments in companies belonging to the promoters groups, if invested out of Unit linked funds, for the purpose of these regulations 'Group' shall have the same meaning as defined under these regulations.

3. In the case of Life, Pension and General Annuity Business the percentage and General Insurance business the 10% of group and industry sector exposure shall be raised upto to 15% with the prior approval of Investment Committee. The Investment Committee should exercise due care keeping in view the possible concentration and other related risks, in the interest of the policyholders. Exposure norms applicable for investments, for which specific circulars/guidelines are issued, shall be guided by such circulars/guidelines.
4. The exposure limit for financial and banking sector shall stand at 25% investment assets for all insurers.
5. Investment in fixed deposit, term deposit and certificate of deposit of a Scheduled Bank shall be made in terms of the provisions of Section 27A(9) and Section 27B(10) of the Insurance Act, 1938 such investments would not be deemed as exposure to banking sector, however, investments in such fixed deposit, term deposit and certificate of deposit in a bank falling under the promoter group of the insurer, shall continue to be subject to promoter group exposure norms as per point 3 of Note of this regulation.

Returns to be Submitted by an Insurer

Every insurer shall submit to the Authority the following returns within such time, at such intervals and verified/certified in such manner as indicated there against:

No.	Form	Description	Periodicity of returns	Time limit for submission	Verified/Certified by
1.	Form 1	Statement of Investment and Income on Investments	Quarterly	Within 45 days for the end of the Quarter	Chief Executive Officer/Chief of Investments
2.	Form 3A (Part A, B, C)	Statement of Downgraded Investments	Quarterly	Within 45 days for the end of the Quarter	Chief Executive Investments
3.	Form 3B	Statement of Investments (Life Insurers)—Compliance Report	Quarterly	Within 45 days for the end of the Quarter	Chief Executive Officer/Chief of Investments
4.	Form 3B	Statement of Investments (General Insurer)—Compliance Report	Quarterly	Within 45 days for the end of the Quarter	Chief Executive Officer/Chief of Investments

No.	Form	Description	Periodicity of returns	Time limit for submission	Verified/Certified by
5.	Form 4	Exposure and other norms—Quarterly compliance certificate	Quarterly	Within 45 days for the end of the Quarter	Chief Executive Officer/Chief of Investments
6.	Form 4A	Statement of Investment Subject to Exposure Norms Investee Company	Quarterly	Within 45 days for the end of the Quarter	Chief Executive Officer/Chief of Investments
7.	(Part A, B, C)	Description Statement of Investment Reconciliation	Quarterly	Within 45 days for the end of the Quarter	Chief Executive Officer/Chief of Investments
8.	Form 5	Statement of Mutual Fund Investments	Quarterly	Within 45 days for the end of the Quarter	Chief Executive Officer/Chief of Investments
9.	Form 6	Certificate under Sections 28(2A), 28(2B) and 28B(3) of the Insurance Act, 1938	Quarterly	Within 45 days for the end of the Quarter	Chief Executive Officer/Chief of Investments
10.	Form 7	Confirmation of Investment Portfolio Details	Quarterly	Within 45 days for the end of the Quarter	Chief Executive Officer/Chief of Investments
11.	Form 7A	Statement of Non-Performing Assets	Quarterly	Within 45 days for the end of the Quarter	Chief Executive Officer/Chief of Investments

Note: All returns for the quarter ending March shall be filed within the period stipulated above based on provisional figures and later resubmitted with Audited figures within 15 days of adoption of accounts by the Board of Directors.

Dealing in Financial Derivatives

(1) Every Insurer carrying on the business of life insurance or general insurance may deal in financial derivatives only to the extent permitted and in accordance with the guidelines issued by the Authority in this regard from time to time.

(2) Any margin or unamortized premium paid by any insurer in connection with the financial derivatives to the extent they are reflected as asset position in the balance sheet of the insurer in accordance with the guidelines issued by the Authority, shall be treated as approved Investment under Schedule I and Schedule II to these Regulations, only to the extent the derivative position constitutes a hedge for the underlying investment or portfolio which itself is treated as an approved investments under these regulations. All other margins or unamortized premium paid, to the extent reflected in the balance sheet of the insurer in accordance with the guidelines issued by the Authority in this regard from time to time, shall be treated as 'Other Investments'.

SCHEDULE - I

(*See Regulation* 3)

List of Approved Investments for Life Business

'Approved Investments' for the purposes of Section 27A of the Act shall consist of the following:

(a) All investments specified in Section 27A of the Act except,

(i) clause (b) of sub-section (1) of Section 27A of the Act;

(ii) first mortgages on immovable property situated in another country as stated in clause (m) of sub-section (1) of Section 27A of the Act;

(iii) immovable property situated in another country as stated in clause (n) of sub-section (1) of Section 27A of the Act.

(b) In addition the following investments shall be deemed as approved investments by the Authority under the powers vested in it vide clause(s) of sub-section (1) of Section 27A of the Act.

(i) All loans secured as required under Insurance Act, 1938, secured-debentures, secured bonds and other debt instruments rated as per Note appended to Regulations 3 and 4. Equity shares and preference shares and debt instruments issued by all India Financial Institutions recognized as such by Reserve Bank of India—investments shall be made in terms of investment policy guidelines, benchmarks and exposure norms, limits approved by the Board of Directors of the insurer.

(ii) Bonds or debentures issued by companies rated not less than AA or its equivalent and P1 or equivalent ratings for short-term bonds, debentures, certificates of deposits and commercial papers by a credit rating agency, registered under SEBI (Credit Rating Agencies) Regulations, 1999 would be considered as 'Approved Investments'.

(iii) Subject to norms and limits approved by the Board of Directors of the insures deposits (including fixed deposits as per Section 27A(9) of Insurance Act, 1938) with banks (e.g. in current account, call deposits, notice deposits, certificated of deposits, etc.) included for the time being in the second schedule to Reserve Bank of India Act, 1934 (2 of 1934) and deposits with primary dealers duly recognized by Reserve Bank of India as such.

(iv) Collateralized Borrowing and Lending Obligations (CBLO) created by the Clearing Corporation of India Ltd. And recognized by the Reserve Bank of India and exposure to gilt, G Sec and Liquid mutual fund forming part of Approved Investments as per Mutual Fund Guide Guidelines issued under these regulations and money market instrument/investment.

(v) Asset Backed Securities with underlying Housing loans or having infrastructure assets as underlying as defined under 'infrastructure facility' in clause (h) of regulation 2 of Insurance Regulatory and Development Authority (Registration of Indian Insurance Companies Amendment Regulations, 2008).

(vi) Commercial papers issued by a company or All India Financial Institution recognized as such by Reserve Bank of India having a credit rating by a credit rating agency registered under SEBI (Credit Rating Agencies) Regulations, 1999.

(vii) Money Market instruments as defined in Regulation 2(cc) of these Regulations.

Explanation

1. All conditions mentioned in the 'note' appended to Regulations 3 and 4 shall be complied with.

SCHEDULE – II

(*See Regulation* 4)

List of Approved Investments for General Business

'Approved Investments' for the purpose of Section 27B of the Act shall consist of the following:

(a) All investments specified in Section 27B of the Act except,

(i) Clause (b) of sub-section (1) of Section 27A of the Act;

(ii) Immovable property situated in another country as stated in clause (n) of sub-section (1) of Section 27A of the Act;

(iii) First mortgages on immovable property situated in another country as stated in clause (i) of sub-section (1) of Section 27B of the Act.

(b) In addition the following investments shall be deemed as approved investments by the Authority under the powers vested in it vide clause (j) of sub-section (1) of Section 27B of the Act:

(i) All loans secured as per Insurance Act, 1938, secured-debentures, secured bonds and other debt instruments rated as per Note appended to Regulations 3 and 4. Equity shares, preference shares and debt such by Reserve Bank of India—investments shall be made in terms of investment policy guidelines, benchmarks and exposure norms, limits approved by the Board of Directors of the insurer.

(ii) Bonds or debentures issued by companies rated not less than AA or its equivalent and P1 or equivalent ratings for short-term bonds, debentures, certificate of deposits and commercial papers by a credit rating agency, registered under SEBI (Credit Rating Agencies) Regulations, 1999 would be considered as 'Approved Investments'.

(iii) Subject to norms and limits approved by the Board of Directors of the insurers deposits (including fixed deposits as per Section 27B(10) of Insurance Act, 1938) with banks (e.g. in current account, call deposits, notice deposits, certificate of deposits etc.) included for the time being in the Second Schedule to Reserve Bank of India Act, 1934 (2 of 1934) and deposits with primary dealers duly recognized by Reserve Bank of India as such.

(iv) Collateralized Borrowing and Lending Obligations (CBLO) created by the Clearing Corporation of India Ltd. and recognized by the Reserve Bank of India and exposure to Gilt, G Sec and Liquid mutual fund forming part of approved Investments as per Mutual Fund Guidelines issued under these regulations and money market instrument/ investment.

(v) Asset Backed Securities with underlying Housing loans or having infrastructure assets as underlying as defined under 'infrastructure facility' in clause (h) of regulation 2 of Insurance Regulatory and Development Authority (Registration of Indian Insurance Companies Amendment Regulations, 2008).

(vi) Commercial paper issued by a company or All India Financial Institution recognized as such by Reserve Bank of India having a credit rating by a credit rating agency registered under SEBI (Credit Rating Agencies) Regulations, 1999.

(vii) Money Market Instruments as defined in Regulation 2(cc) of this regulation.

Explanation

1. All conditions mentioned in the 'note' appended to Regulations 3 and 4 shall be complied with. Every insurer shall invest and at all times keep invested funds belonging to his Pension Business, General Annuity Business in the following manner:

Guidelines for Mutual Fund Investments

As the term "Mutual Fund" is neither covered under Insurance Act, 1938 or by IRDA (Investment) Regulations, 2000 any Investment made in Mutual Funds will fall under the residuary category of investments namely "Other than Approved Investments" which in turn shall be subject to the limits prescribed in IRDA (Investment) Regulations, 2000 and the norms mentioned below:

Norms for Mutual Fund Investments

The investment shall be restricted to Investment of temporary surpluses of the Insurer which may be placed in schemes of Mutual Funds comprising of Liquid Funds. Gilt or Debt Funds and the same shall be governed by the following norms:

(i) The Mutual Fund should be registered with SEBI and be governed by SEBI (Mutual Funds) Regulations, 1996.

(ii) The insurer shall AT ALL TIMES ensure that the investments in Mutual Funds are diversified among the various Mutual Funds.

(iii) The Board of the insurer shall lay down proper Guidelines for selection of Mutual Funds and schemes permissible including exposure Norms to a Single Mutual Fund and to each Scheme of Mutual Fund so as to avoid concentrated of investment in a particular scheme.

(iv) Where, the schemes of mutual funds in which such investment is made by an Insurer is managed by an Investment Manager who is under the direct or indirect management or control of the Insurer or its promoter the same shall NOT exceed 20% of the amount of Investments falling under "Other than approved Investments" subject to provision referred under clause 5, pertaining to "Group" under IRDA (Investment) Regulations, 2000.

(v) The Insurer shall NOT make any investment in shares or debentures of any private limited company in which investment, if any, is made by the Mutual Fund.

FORM 1

Company Name and Code: Name of the Fund: ....

Statement as on:

Statement of Investment and Income on Investment

Periodicity of submission: Yearly

₹ In lakhs

Current Year							Previous Year			
No.	Category of Investment	Cat. Code	Investment (₹)	Income on Investment (₹)	Gross Yield (%)[1]	Net Yield (%)[2]	Investment (₹)	Income on Investment (₹)	Gross Yield (%)[1]	Net Yield (%)[2]
	Total									

Certification

Certified that the information given herein are correct and complete to the best of my knowledge and belief and nothing has been concealed or suppressed.

Signature ....

Full Name and Designation

Date:

Note: Category of investment shall be as per Guidelines.

1. To be calculated as prescribed in IRDA (Actuarial Report) Regulations, 2000 under Section 3(1) on an Annualised basis.
2. Yield netted for tax.
3. In the case of Life Insurance Business Form-I shall be prepared in respect of each fund.

Overall Investment/Exposure Limit

The investment in Mutual Funds AT ANY POINT OF TIME shall not exceed 50% of Investment falling under "Other than Approved Investment" for both Life and General Insurance Companies.

Note: For Public Sector Insurers the limit mentioned shall be 1/5th of the specified percentage.

The Authority would review the exposure limit periodically.

Valuation of Mutual Fund Investments

For each of the Quarter, Mutual Fund units shall be reported at Weighted Average Cost. Also, the insurer shall mention the Market Value of such Mutual Funds (which shall reflect the increase/decrease in the NAV) in Form 3B of IRDA (Investment) Regulations, 2000.

A separate fair value change account segregated for each of the Mutual Fund Investment shall be maintained.

The unrealized gains/losses arising due to changes in fair value of the Mutual Funds shall be taken to "Fair Value Change—Mutual Fund" account. The Profit/Loss on sale of Mutual Fund units, shall include accumulated changes in the Fair value previously recognized in Mutual Funds under the heading "Fair Value Change—Mutual Fund" in respect of a particular Mutual Fund and being recycled to Revenue/Profit and Loss Account on actual sale of Mutual Fund units.

The Insurer shall assess, on each Balance Sheet date, whether any impairment has occurred to the investment. An impairment loss shall be recognised as an expense in Revenue/Profit and Loss Account to the extent of the difference between the re-measured fair value of the Investment and its Weighted Average Cost as reduced by any previous impairment loss recognised as expenses in Revenue/Profit and Loss Account. Any reversal of impairment loss earlier recognized in Revenue/Profit and Loss Account shall be recognized in Revenue/Profit and Loss Account. In case of unit Linked business, mutual fund units shall be valued at NAV.

Investments in Equity Share Through IPOs

As per the current regulations, Investment in Equity Shares issued through Initial Public Offer (IPO) has to be categorised as "Other than Approved Investments". However, in the context of IPO issues, by well-known Corporates, where the issue size is fairly large and the (issuer) Corporates are known to have good performance record and sound financial, suggestions have been received to consider some relaxation in respect of Equity Shares of such Corporates, through IPO issue so as to categorise under "Approved Investments".

Arising out of this suggestion the following criteria are proposed after considering the comments received from Insurers in this matter. Equity shares offered through IPOs which satisfy all of the following criteria may be categorised as "Approved Investments".

1. Equity Shares are being "listed" through IPO.
2. Size of the issue of Equity Shares through IPO, including offer for sales is not less than ₹ 500 crores.
3. Number of shares offered is not less than 5 million shares.
4. The company issuing shares through IPO shall belong to a financially sound group with good performance record, for which the Insurer's Board shall lay down the criteria.
5. Performance track record of the company including Earnings and Dividend record, Dividend Criteria is satisfied:
   (a) for at least 7 past years as "unlisted" company as prescribed in the Insurance Act (Section 27A) in the case of Life Insurance Companies;
   (b) for at least 3 past years are "unlisted" company as prescribed in the Insurance Act (Section 27B) in the case of General Insurance Companies:

   Provided, in the case of Investee Companies, formed out of 'demerger' of a parent company, issuing shares through IPO, the performance track record would apply with reference to the parent company.
6. The Investment in Equity Shares should comply with prudential and exposure norms as prescribed and in particular. Note No. 7 to Sections 3 and 4 of IRDA (Investment)

Regulations, 2000 (as emended) i.e., "actively" and "liquid instrument" conditions should be satisfied within 3 months from the date of listing.

7. Such investments shall be subject to periodical review, particularly as to Approved status.
8. The Board of the Insurers shall empower its Investment Committee to approve Investment in equities through IPOs, satisfying the above criteria.

Any investment made in IPOs, which do not satisfy the above conditions, shall fall under "Other than Approved Investments".

The detail of all investments in Equity Shares through IPOs shall be filed with the Authority within 30 days thereof.

Entry Guidelines for Entry of NBFCS Into Insurance—Issued On June 9, 2000

1. Any non-banking financial company (NBFC) registered with RBI having net owned fund of ₹ 2 crores would be permitted to undertake insurance business as agent of insurance companies on fee basis, without any risk participation.

2. All NBFCs registered with RBI which satisfy the eligibility criteria given below will be permitted to set up a joint venture company for undertaking insurance business with risk participation, subject to safeguards. The maximum equity contribution such an NBFC can hold in the joint venture company will normally be 50 per cent of the paid-up capital of the insurance company. On a selective basis, the Reserve Bank of India may permit a higher equity contribution by a promoter NBFC initially, pending divestment of equity within the prescribed period [see Note (1) below]. The eligibility criteria for joint venture participant will be as under, as per the latest available audited balance sheet:

(i) The owned fund of the NBFC should not be less than ₹ 500 crores.
(ii) The CRAR of the NBFC engaged in loan and investment activities holding public deposits should be not less than 15% and for other NBFCs at 12% irrespective of their holding public deposits or not.
(iii) The level of net non-performing assets should be not more than 5% of the total outstanding leased/hire purchase assets and advances taken together.
(iv) The NBFC should have net profit for the last three continuous years.
(v) The track record of the performance of the subsidiaries, if any, of the concerned NBFC should be satisfactory.
(vi) Regulatory compliance and servicing public deposits, if held.

The provisions of RBI Act would be applicable for such investments while computing the net owned funds of the NBFC.

3. In case where a foreign partner contributes 26 per cent of the equity with the approval of Insurance Regulatory and Development Authority/Foreign Investment Promotion Board, more than one NBFC may be allowed to participate in the equity of the insurance joint venture. As such participants will also assume insurance risk, only those NBFCs which satisfy the criteria given in paragraph 2 above, would be eligible.

4. No NBFC would be allowed to conduct such business departmentally. A subsidiary or company in the same group of an NBFC or of another NBFC engaged in the business of a

non-banking financial institution or banking business will not normally be allowed to join the insurance company on risk participation basis.

5. NBFCs registered with RBI which are not eligible as joint venture participant, as above can make investments up to 10 per cent to the owned fund of the NBFC or ₹ 50 crores, whichever is lower, in the insurance company. Such participation shall be treated as an investment and should be without any contingent liability for the NBFC. The eligibility criteria for these NBFCs will be as under:

(i) The CRAR of the NBFC (applicable only to those holding public deposits) should not be less than 12 per cent if engaged in equipment leasing/hire purchase finance activities and 15 per cent if it is a loan or investment company;

(ii) The level of net NPA should be not more than 5 per cent of total outstanding leased/hire purchase assets and advances;

(iii) The NBFC should have not profit for the last three continuous years.

6. All NBFCs registered with RBI entering into insurance business as agents or investors or on risk participation basis will be required to obtain prior approval of the Reserve Bank. The Reserve Bank will give permission to NBFCs on case to case basis keeping in view all relevant factors. It should be ensured that risks involved in insurance business do not get transferred to the NBFC and that the NBFC business does not get contaminated by any risks which may arise from insurance business.

Notes:

1. Holding of equity by a promoter NBFC in an insurance company or participation in any form in insurance business will be subject to compliance with any rules and regulations laid down by the IRDA/Central Government. This will include compliance with section 6AA of the Insurance Act as amended by the IRDA Act, 1999, for divestment of equity in excess of 26 per cent of the paid up capital within a prescribed period of time.
2. For applications received during the financial year 2000-2001, any fresh capital infused after the audited balance sheet date for 1999-2000 would also be taken into account. The unaudited and certified balance sheet as on a latest date may be reckoned for determining the eligibility criteria and the audited balance sheet for the above date would be submitted to RBI as soon as possible.
3. For subsequent years, the eligibility criteria would be with reference to the latest available audited balance sheet for the previous year.

Note:

W.e.f. 1-10-2013 IRDA has allowed insurances to invest in category I Alternative Investment Funds (AIF). They are infrastructure fund, SME Fund, Venture Capital Fund and Social Venture Fund. In category II, at least 51% of the funds of such AIF shall be invested in either of the infrastructure entities or SHE entities or venture capital undertakings or social venture entities.

9

Distribution of Profits

For purposes of distribution of profits the insurer shall prepare a statement of policyholders' fund as specified under IRDA (actuarial report) Regulations, 2000. This statement shall show:

(a) The valuation date. The date on which valuation (investigation) is done;

(b) New products. A brief description of new products is introduced during the inter-valuation period giving salient features;

(c) Foreign operations. A brief descriptions of the foreign operations of the insurer, during the inter-valuation period;

(d) Valuation method. A brief description of:

(i) the methods adopted in the determination of mathematical reserves in respect of insurance products;

(ii) the method by which age at entry, premium term, maturity date, valuation age, period from the valuation date to the maturity date, have been treated for the purpose of valuation;

(iii) the method of allowing for:

(I) incidence of premium income; and

(II) premiums payable otherwise than annually;

(e) Valuation bases:

(i) Valuation parameters used in the valuation shall be furnished in the manner as specified in the following table;

(ii) Expenses related to premiums, sum assured, annuity, etc., and per policy shall be specified separately under column (5) of the table;

(iii) Items such as terminal bonus, in case of with profit contracts, management charges, etc. in respect of linked business, shall be specified under column (8) of the table;

Description	Mortality basis used	Morbidity basis used	Inflation rate	Interest rate	Expenses	Future bonuses, if any	Others please specify	Remarks
(1)	(2)	(3)	(4)	(5)	(6)	(7)	(8)	(9)
(a) Insurance Product: (i) Regular Premium (ii) Single premium and Fully paid up (iii) Reduced paid up								
(b) Insurance Product: (i) Regular Premium (ii) Single premium and Fully paid up (iii) Reduced paid up								

(f) Other adjustments (provisions). The methods by which provision, if any, has been made for the following matters, including a statement of bases wherever necessary:

(i) Policies in respect of which extra premiums have been charged on account on underwriting of under-averages lives that are subject to extra risks such as occupation hazard, over-weight, under-weight, smoking history, health, climatic or geographical conditions;

(ii) Lapsed policies not included in the valuation but under which a liability exists or may arise;

(iii) Options available under individual and group insurance policies;

(iv) Guarantees available to individual and group insurance policies;

(v) The rates of exchange at which benefits in respect of policies issued in foreign currencies have been converted into Indian Rupees and what provision has been made for possible increase of mathematical reserves arising from future variations in rates of exchange;

(g) Further information. The following information shall be appended:

(i) Returns on assets.

(ii) Distribution of surplus.

(iii) Principles adopted in distribution of surplus.

(iv) Negative Reserves and Guaranteed Surrender Value Deficiency Reserves.

(v) Miscellaneous information.

Returns on Assets

(1) The average gross rates of interest yielded by the assets may be determined expressing the investment income as percentage of the mean fund, [i = 2 × I/ (A + B – I)]; where i is the gross yield; I = Investment Income; A = the assets at the beginning of the financial year; and B = the assets at the end of the financial year. Investment Income (shown in the Revenue Account) should include the amount of the unrealised gain taken into revenue account, A and B have to be adjusted value of assets shown in the Balance Sheet.

(2) The average gross rates of interest, referred to under sub-regulation (1), shall be furnished for each fund maintained by an insurer.

Distribution of Surplus

The basis adopted in the distribution of surplus as between the shareholders and the policy holders, and whether such distribution was determined by the instruments constituting the company, or by its regulations or by-laws or how otherwise shall be mentioned.

Principles Adopted in Distribution of Profits

The general principles adopted in distribution of profits among policyholders, including statements on following points, shall be furnished:

(i) Whether the principles were determined by instruments constituting the insurer, or by its regulations or by-laws or how otherwise;

(ii) The number of years premium to be paid, period to elapse and other conditions to be fulfilled before a bonus is allotted;

(iii) Whether the bonus is allocated in respect of each year's premium paid, or in respect of each calendar year or year of assurance of how otherwise; and

(iv) Whether the bonus vests immediately on allocation, or, if not, conditions of vesting.

Statement of Composition of Surplus and Distribution of Surplus in Respect of Policyholders' Funds

A statement, showing total amount of surplus arising during the inter-valuation period, and the allocation of such surplus, shall be furnished separately for participating business and for non-participating business, with the particulars as mentioned below:

Composition of Surplus:

(a) Surplus shown;

(b) Interim Bonuses paid during the inter-valuation period;

(c) Terminal Bonuses paid during the inter-valuation period;

(d) Loyalty Additions or other forms of bonuses, if any, paid during the inter-valuation period;

(e) Sum transferred from shareholders' funds during the inter-valuation period;

(f) Amount of surplus, from policyholders' funds, brought forward from preceding valuation;

(g) Total Surplus [total of the items (a) to (f)].

Distribution of Surplus:

Policyholders' Fund:

(a) To Interim Bonuses paid;

(b) To Terminal Bonuses;

(c) To Loyalty Additions or any other forms of bonuses, if any;

(d) Among policyholders with immediate participation giving the number of policies which participated and the sums assured thereunder (excluding bonuses);

(e) Among policyholders with deferred participation giving the number of policies which participated and the sums assured thereunder (excluding bonuses);

(f) Among policyholders in the discounted bonus class giving the number of policies which participated and the sums assured thereunder (excluding bonuses);

(g) To every reserve fund or other fund or account (any such sums passed through the accounts during the inter-valuation period to be separately stated);

(h) As carried forward un-appropriated;

Shareholders' Fund:

(i) To the shareholders' funds (any such sums passed through the accounts during the inter-valuation period to be separately stated);

Totals:

(j) Total Surplus allocated: [total of the items (a) to (i)].

Specimen of Bonuses allotted to policies for one thousand rupees together with the amounts apportioned under the various manners in which the bonus is receivable, for each type of participating product, shall be furnished. A brief description of treatment adopted for negative reserves and guaranteed surrender value deficiency reserves shall be furnished.

Limitation of Expenses of Management in Life Insurance Business

(1) Every insurer transacting life insurance business in India shall furnish to the Authority, within such time as may be prescribed, statements in the prescribed form certified by an actuary on the basis of premiums currently used by him in regard to new business in respect of mortality, rate of interest, expenses and bonus loading.

(2) After the 31st day of December, 1950, no insurer shall, in respect of life insurance business transacted by him in India, spend as expenses of management in any calendar year an amount in excess of the prescribed limits and in prescribing any such limits regard shall be had to the size and age of the insurer and the provision generally made for expenses of management in the premium rates of insurers:

Provided that where an insurer has spent such expenses in any year an amount in excess of the amount permissible under this sub-section, he shall not be deemed to have contravened the provisions of this section, if the excess amount so spent is within such limits as may be fixed in respect of the year by the Authority after consultation with the Executive Committee of the Life Insurance Council constituted under Section 64F, by which the actual expenses incurred may exceed the expenses permissible under this sub-section.

(3) In respect of any statement mentioned in sub-section (1), the Authority may require that it shall be submitted to another actuary appointed by the insurer for the purpose and approved by the Authority, for certification by him, whether with or without modifications.

(4) Every insurer transacting life insurance business in India shall incorporate in the revenue account—

(a) a certificate signed by the chairman and two directors and by the principal officer of the insurer, and an auditor's certificate, certifying that all expenses of management in respect of life insurance business transacted by the insurer in India have been fully debited in the revenue account as expenses, and

(b) if the insurer is carrying on any other class of insurance business in addition to life insurance business an auditor's certificate certifying that all charges incurred in respect of this life insurance business and in respect of his business other than life insurance business have been fully debited in the respective revenue accounts.

Explanation

(a) "calendar year" or "year" means, in relation to an insurer who is required to furnish returns in accordance with sub-section (2) of Section 16, the period covered by the revenue account furnished by such insurer under clause (b) of the sub-section.

(b) "expenses of management" means all charges wherever incurred whether directly or indirectly, and includes—

- (i) commission payments of all kinds,
- (ii) any amount of expenses capitalised,
- (iii) in the case of an insurer having his principal place of business outside India, a proper share of head office expenses which shall not be less than such percentage as may be prescribed of the total premiums (less re-insurances) received during that year in respect of life insurance business transacted by him in India, but does not include in the case of an insurer having his principal place of business in India any share of head office expenses in respect of life insurance business transacted by him outside India.

Limitation of Expenses of Management in General Insurance Business

After the 31st day of December 1949, no insurer shall, in respect to any class of general insurance business transacted by him in India, spend in any calendar year as expenses of management including commission or remuneration for procuring business an amount in excess of the prescribed limits and in prescribing any such limits regard shall be had to the size and age of the insurer:

Where an insurer has spent as such expenses in any year an amount in excess of the amount permissible under this sub-section, he shall not be deemed to have contravened the provisions of this section, if the excess amount so spent is within such limits as may be fixed in respect of the year by the Authority after consultation with Executive Committee of the General Insurance Council constituted under Section 64F, by which the actual expenses incurred may exceed the expenses permissible under this sub-section.

Every insurer as aforesaid shall incorporate in the revenue account a certificate signed by the chairman and two directors and by the principal officer of the insurer, and by an auditor certifying that all expenses of management wherever incurred, whether directly or indirectly, in respect of the business referred to in this section, have been fully debited in the revenue account as expenses.

(a) "calendar year" shall have the meaning assigned to it in Section 40B;

(b) "expenses of management" means all charges, wherever incurred whether directly or indirectly, including commission payments of all kinds and, in the case of an insurer having his principal place of business outside India, a proper share of head office expenses, which shall not be less than such percentage as may be prescribed, of his gross premium income (that is to say, the premium income without taking into account premiums or re-insurance ceded or accepted) written direct in India during the year, but in computing the expenses of management in India the following, and only the following, expenses may be excluded, namely:

  (i) in the case of an insurer having his principal place of business in India, a share of head office expenses in respect of general insurance business transacted by him outside India not exceeding such percentage of his gross direct premium written outside India as may be prescribed;

  (ii) in the case of an insurer having his principal place of business outside India, a share of the expenses of his office in India in respect of general insurance business transacted by him outside India through his office in India, not exceeding such percentage of his gross direct premium written outside India through his office in India, as may be prescribed;

  (iii) any expenses debited to profit and loss account relating exclusively to the management of capital, and dealings with shareholders and a proper share of managerial expenses calculated in such manner as may be prescribed; and

  (iv) any expenses debited to claims in the revenue account in Form F of Part II of the Third Schedule;

(c) "insurance business transacted in India" includes insurance business wherever effected relating to any property situate in India or to any vessel or aircraft registered in India.

Prohibition of Rebates

No person shall allow or offer to allow, either directly or indirectly, as an inducement to any person to take out or renew or continue an insurance in respect of any kind of risk relating to lives or property in India, any rebate of the whole or part of the commission payable or any rebate of the premium shown on the policy, nor shall any person taking out or renewing or continuing a policy accept any rebate, except such rebate as may be allowed in accordance with the published prospectuses on tables of the insurer:

Acceptance by an insurance agent of commission in connection with a policy of life insurance taken out by himself on his own life shall not be deemed to be acceptance of a rebate of premium within the meaning of this sub-section if at the time of such acceptance the insurance agent satisfies the prescribed conditions establishing that he is a bona fide insurance agent employed by the insurer.

Any person making default in complying with the provisions of this section shall be punishable with fine which may extend to five hundred rupees.

Restriction on Dividends and Bonuses

No insurer, who carries on the business of life insurance or any other class or sub-class of insurance business shall, for the purpose of declaring or paying any dividend to shareholders or any bonus to policyholders or of making any payment in service of any debentures, utilize directly or indirectly any portion of the life insurance fund or of the fund of such other class or sub-class of insurance business, as the case may be, except a surplus shown in the valuation [balance sheet in such form as may be specified by the regulations made by the Authority] submitted to the Authority as part of the abstract as a result of an actuarial valuation of the assets and liabilities of the insurer; nor shall be increase such surplus by contributions out of any reserve fund or otherwise unless such contributions have been brought in as revenue through the revenue account applicable to that class or sub-class of insurance business on or before the date of the valuation aforesaid, except when the reserve fund is made by solely of transfers from similar surpluses disclosed by valuation in respect of which returns have been submitted to the Authority.

The payments made out of any such surplus in service of any debentures shall not exceed fifty per cent of such surplus including any payment by way of interest on the debenture, and interest paid on the debentures shall not exceed ten per cent of any such surplus except when the interest paid on the debentures is offset against the interest credited to the fund or funds concerned in deciding the interest basis adopted in the valuation disclosing the aforesaid surplus.

The share of any such surplus allocated to or reserved for the shareholders (including any amount for the payment of dividends guaranteed to them, whether by way of first charge or otherwise), shall not exceed such sums as may be specified by the Authority and such share shall in no case exceed ten per cent of such surplus in case of participating policies and in other cases the whole thereof.

The actual amount of income-tax deducted at source during the period following the date as at which the last preceding valuation was made and preceding the date as at which the valuation in question is made may be added to such surplus after deducting an estimated amount for income-tax on such surplus, such addition and deduction being shown in [an abstract of the report of the actuary referred to in sub-section (1) of Section 13].

Life Funds

With effect from 1st April, 2003:

A life insurer registered under Section 3 of the Insurance Act, 1938 shall be required to maintain separately:

(a) a life fund for participating policyholders, and

(b) a life fund for non-participating policyholders.

A failure to comply with the requirements of sub-regulation (1) above shall mean that the life fund maintained by the insurer shall be for the benefit of the participating policyholders only.

Procedure for Distribution of Surplus

A life insurer may, on the advice of his appointed actuary, reserve a part of the actuarial surplus (also referred to as valuation surplus) arising out of a valuation of assets and liabilities made for a financial year in accordance with Insurance Regulatory and Development Authority (Actuarial Report and Abstract) Regulations, 2000, to its shareholders, which shall be:

(a) one hundred per cent, in case of a life fund maintained for non-participating policyholders;

(b) one-ninth of the surplus allocated to policyholders in case of a life fund maintained for participating policyholders.

An insurer shall, however, be required to obtain prior approval of the Authority in cases where the said allocation is not the one-ninth of the surplus.

An insurer shall not allocate or reserve exceeding ten per cent, of the said actuarial surplus to its shareholders.

10

Protection of Policyholders' Interests and Foreign Exchange Management (Insurance) Regulations

Protection of Policyholders' Interests—Regulations, 2017*

Board Approved Policy for Protection of Interests of Policyholders:

1. Every insurer shall have in place a board approved policy for protection of policyholders' interests which shall at the minimum, include:

(i) steps to be taken for enhancing Insurance Awareness so as to educate prospects and policyholders about insurance products, benefits and their rights and responsibilities.

(ii) service parameters including turnaround times for various services rendered.

(iii) procedure for expeditious resolution of complaints.

(iv) steps to be taken to prevent mis-selling and unfair business practices at point of sale and service.

(v) steps to be taken to ensure that during policy solicitation and sale stages, the prospects are fully informed and made aware of the benefits of the product being sold vis-a-vis the product features attached thereto and the terms and conditions of the product so that the benefits/returns of the product are not mis-stated/mis-represented.

2. Every insurer shall display the service parameters and turnaround times as approved by the Board in its website and keep the same updated as and when the service parameters are revised by the Board.

Point of Sale

1. A prospectus of any insurance product shall clearly state:

(i) (a) the Unique Identification Number (UIN) allotted by the Authority for the concerned insurance product;

(b) the scope of benefits;

* *Source*: https://taxguru.in/corporate-law/irda

(c) the extent of insurance cover;

(d) warranties, exclusions/exceptions and conditions of the insurance cover along with explanations.

(ii) (a) a description of the contingency or contingencies to be covered by insurance;

(b) the class or classes of lives or property eligible for insurance under the terms of such prospectus;

(c) a full statement of the circumstances, if any, in which rebates of the premiums quoted in the prospectus or table shall be allowed on the effecting or renewal of a policy, together with the rates of rebate applicable to each case; and

(d) a copy of Section 41 of the Act but not including the proviso to sub-section (1) thereof.

(iii) the allowable riders or add-on covers on the insurance products shall be clearly spelt out with regard to their scope of benefits;

(iv) the premium pertaining to health related or critical illness riders shall not exceed 100% of premium under the basic product, the premiums under all other life insurance riders put together shall not exceed 30% of premiums under the basic product and any benefit arising under each of the above-mentioned riders shall not exceed the sum assured under the basic product;

(v) in case of life insurance, whether the product is participating (with-profits) or non-participating (without-profits).

Provided that the benefit amount under riders in a life insurance policy shall be subject to Section 2(11) of the Insurance Act, 1938.

Explanation: The rider or riders attached to a life insurance policy shall bear the nature and character of the main policy, viz. participating or non-participating and accordingly the life insurer shall make provisions, etc., in its books.

2. An insurer or its agent or other intermediary shall provide all material information in respect of a proposed cover to the prospect to enable the prospect to decide on the best cover that would be in his or her interest.

3. Where the prospect depends upon the advice of the insurer or his agent or an insurance intermediary, such a person must advise the prospect dispassionately.

4. Where for any reason, the proposal and other connected papers are not filled in by the prospect, the insurer or the distribution channel shall explain the contents of the form, and a certificate shall be incorporated at the end of the proposal form from the prospect that the contents of the proposal form and connected documents have been fully explained to him and he has fully understood the significance of the proposed contract.

5. The insurers shall ensure, that a sale executed over distance-marketing modes such as Internet, SMS, Tele Marketing, interactive electronic medium etc., shall be undertaken by authorized and qualified sales persons who are specified in this behalf by the Authority. It is mandatory that the consent of the prospect be obtained before canvassing. Care should be exercised to ensure that the prospect contacted has clarity as to the identity of the insurer, the distribution channel, the product, benefits and conditions of offer etc. The canvassing so made shall not involve compulsion, inconvenience or nuisance of any kind to the prospect.

Products on Offer/Products Withdrawn

1. Every insurer shall place in its website the terms and conditions of every insurance product that is offered for sale by the insurer as it was approved by the Authority under File and Use procedure or filed with the Authority under Use and File procedure, including products modified or products withdrawn. The UIN allotted by the Authority to every insurance product shall also be mentioned against each product.

2. The insurer shall keep the list updated at all times.

Proposal for Insurance

1. Except in case of a marine insurance cover, or such other covers approved by the Authority exempting usage of proposal form, a proposal for grant of insurance cover, either for life insurance business or for general insurance business or for health insurance business, must be evidenced by a document in written or electronic or any other format as approved by the Authority. It is the duty of the insurer to furnish to the insured, free of charge, within 30 days of the acceptance of a proposal, a copy of the proposal submitted by the Insured.

2. In case of marine insurance cover or other insurance covers where a proposal form is not used, the insurer shall record the information obtained orally or in writing or electronically, and confirm it within a period of 15 days thereof with the prospect and incorporate the information in its cover note or policy. Where the insurer claims that the prospect suppressed any material information or provided misleading or false information on any matter material to the grant of a cover, then the onus of proof rests with the insurer only in respect of any information not so recorded.

3. Any proposal form seeking information for grant of life cover shall prominently state therein the requirements of Section 45 of the Act.

4. While answering the questions in the proposal form for obtaining life insurance cover, the prospect is to be guided by the provisions of Section 45 of the Act.

5. Wherever the benefit of nomination is available to the proposer, in terms of the Act or the conditions of policy, the insurer or the distribution channel shall draw the attention of the proposer to it and encourage the proposer to avail the facility and inform him of the provisions of Section 39 of the Act.

6. Insurer shall process the proposals with speed and efficiency and the decision on the proposal thereof, shall be communicated in writing to the proposer within a reasonable period but not exceeding 15 days from the date of receipt of proposals or any requirements called for by the insurer.

7. Where a proposal deposit is refundable to a prospect under any circumstances, the same shall be refunded within 15 days from the date of underwriting decision on the proposal.

Matters to be Stated in Life Insurance Policy

1. A life insurance policy shall clearly state:

(i) the name and UIN allotted by the Authority for the product governing the policy, its terms and conditions; name, code number, contact details of the person involved in sales process;

(ii) whether it is participating in profits or not, whether it is linked or non-linked;

(iii) the manner of vesting or payment of profits such as cash bonus, deferred bonus, simple or compound reversionary bonus;
(iv) the benefits payable and the contingencies upon which these are payable and the other terms and conditions of the insurance contract;
(v) the name of Nominee(s), age of nominee(s) and their relationship and name of guardian in case of minor nominees;
(vi) the details of the riders being attached to the main policy;
(vii) the date of commencement of risk, the date of maturity and the date(s) on which survival benefits, if any, are payable;
(viii) the premiums payable, periodicity of payment, grace period allowed for payment of the premium, the date of last instalment of premium, the implication of discontinuing the payment of an instalment(s) of premium and also the provisions of guaranteed surrender value;
(ix) the details of revival schemes provided for reviving a lapsed policy and requirements to be submitted for revival there under. The insurers shall use term "revival" which is in vogue for renewing a lapsed insurance policy;
(x) Name, Address, Date of birth and age of the insured as at the date of commencement of the policy;
(xi) the policy conditions for
   (a) conversion of the policy into paid up policy,
   (b) surrender,
   (c) foreclosure,
   (d) non-forfeiture,
   (e) discontinuance provisions in case of Linked Policies;
(xii) contingencies excluded from the scope of the cover, both in respect of the main policy and the riders;
(xiii) the provisions for nomination, assignment, loans on security of the policy and a statement that the rate of interest payable on such loan shall be as prescribed by the insurer at the time of taking the loan;
(xiv) any special clauses, exclusions or conditions imposed on the policy;
(xv) the address, email id of the insurer to which all communications in respect of the policy shall be sent;
(xvi) the notes to policyholder highlighting the significance of notifying timely the change of his/her address;
(xvii) details of insurer's Internal Grievance Redressal Mechanism along with address and contact details of Insurance Ombudsman within whose territorial jurisdiction the branch or office of the insurer or the residential address or place of residence of the policyholder is located;
(xviii) the list of documents that are normally required to be submitted by a claimant in case of a claim under the policy.

Free Look Cancellation of Life Insurance Policies

1. (i) The insurer shall inform clearly by the letter forwarding the policy to the policyholder that he has a free look period of 15 days from the date of receipt of the policy document and

period of 30 days in case of electronic policies and policies obtained through distance mode, to review the terms and conditions of the policy and where the policyholder disagrees to any of those terms or conditions, he has the option to return the policy to the insurer for cancellation, stating the reasons for his objection, then he shall be entitled to a refund of the premium paid subject only to a deduction of a proportionate risk premium for the period of cover and the expenses incurred by the insurer on medical examination of the proposer and stamp duty charges.

(ii) In respect of a linked insurance product, in addition to the deductions under sub-regulation (i) above, the insurer shall also be entitled to repurchase the units at the price of the units on the date of cancellation.

(iii) A request received by insurer for free look cancellation of the policy shall be processed and premium refunded within 15 days of receipt of the request, as stated at sub-clause (i), (ii) above.

Matters to be Stated in General Insurance Policy

1. A general insurance policy shall clearly state:

(i) the name(s) and address(es) of the insured and of any bank(s) or any other person having financial interest in the subject matter of insurance, UIN of the product, name, code number, contact details of the person involved in sales process;

(ii) full description of the property or interest insured;

(iii) the location or locations of the property or interest insured under the policy and, where appropriate, with respective insured values;

(iv) period of Insurance; III 21

(v) sums insured;

(vi) perils covered and not covered;

(vii) any franchise or deductible applicable;

(viii) premium payable and where the premium is provisional subject to adjustment, the basis of adjustment of premium be stated;

(ix) policy terms, conditions and warranties, exclusions, if any;

(x) action to be taken by the insured upon occurrence of a contingency likely to give rise to a claim under the policy;

(xi) the obligations of the insured in relation to the subject matter of insurance upon occurrence of an event giving rise to a claim and the rights of the insurer in the circumstances;

(xii) any special conditions attaching to the policy;

(xiii) the grounds for cancellation of the policy which in the case of a retail policy, for the insurer, can be only on the grounds of mis-representation, non-disclosure of material facts, fraud or non co-operation of the insured.

Explanation: Products approved as retail policies under File and Use guidelines notified by the Authority from time to time fall within the purview of retail policy referred above.

Provided that in the case of Commercial policies alone, other circumstances under which the policy may be cancelled be given, along with the manner of calculation of refund and notice period for cancellation.

(xiv) the address of the insurer to which all communications in respect of the insurance contract should be sent;

(xv) the details of the endorsements, add-on covers attaching to the main policy;

(xvi) that, on renewal, the benefits provided under the policy and/or terms and conditions of the policy including premium rate may be subject to change; and

(xvii) details of insurer's internal grievance redressal mechanism along with address and contact details of Insurance Ombudsman within whose territorial jurisdiction the branch or office of the insurer or the residential address or place of residence of the policyholder is located.

Matters to be Stated in a Health Insurance Policy

1. A health insurance policy shall clearly state:

(i) The name of the policyholder and the names of each beneficiary covered, UIN of the product, name, code number, contact details of the person involved in sales process;

(ii) Date of birth of the insured and corresponding age in completed years;

(iii) The address of the insured;

(iv) The period of insurance and the date from which the policyholder has been continuously obtaining health insurance cover in India from any of the insurers without break;

(v) The sums Insured;

(vi) The sub-limits, Proportionate Deductions and the existence of Package rates if any, with cross-reference to the concerned policy section;

(vii) Co-pay limits if any;

(viii) The pre-existing disease (PED) waiting period, if applicable;

(ix) Specific waiting periods as applicable;

(x) Deductible as applicable—general and specific, if any;

(xi) Cumulative Bonus, if any;

(xii) Periodicity of payment of premium instalment;

(xiii) Policy period;

(xiv) Policy terms, conditions, exclusions, warranties;

(xv) Action to be taken on the occurrence of a claim for cashless and reimbursement options separately;

(xvi) Details of TPA, if any engaged, their address, toll free number, website details;

(xvii) Details of Grievance Redressal mechanism of insurer;

(xviii) Free look period facility and portability conditions;

(xix) Policy migration facility and conditions where applicable;

(xx) that, on renewal, the policy could be subject to certain changes in terms and conditions including change in premium rate;

(xxi) Provision for cancellation of the policy; and

(xxii) Address and other contact details of Ombudsman within whose territorial jurisdiction the branch or office of the insurer or the residential address or place of residence of the policyholder is located.

General Principles Governing Issuance of General and Health Insurance Policies

1. In stipulating the exclusions of the policy, insurers shall endeavour to classify the exclusions, wherever possible as under:

(i) Standard exclusions applicable in all policies;
(ii) Exclusions specific to the policy which cannot be waived;
(iii) Exclusions specific to the policy, which can be waived on payment of additional premium.

2. The insurers may also endeavour to broadly categorize policy conditions into following, so as to give clarity and understanding of the conditions to the policyholder:

(i) Conditions precedent to the contract;
(ii) Conditions applicable during the contract;
(iii) Conditions when a claim arises;
(iv) Conditions for renewal of the contract.

3. Every insurer shall keep the insured informed on the requirements to be fulfilled regarding lodging of a claim arising in terms of the policy and the procedures to be followed by him so as to settle claim early.

Claims Procedure in Respect of a Life Insurance Policy

1. A life insurer, upon receiving a death claim, shall process the claim without delay. Any queries or requirement of additional documents, shall be raised all together and not in a piece-meal manner, within a period of 15 days of the receipt of the claim.

2. (i) A death claim under a life insurance policy shall be paid or be rejected or repudiated giving all the relevant reasons, within 30 days from the date of receipt of all relevant papers and required clarifications. However, where the circumstances of a claim warrant an investigation in the opinion of the insurer, it shall initiate the same at the earliest and complete such investigation expeditiously, in any case not later than 90 days from the date of receipt of claim intimation and the claim shall be settled within 30 days thereafter. III 23

(ii) If there is delay on the part of Insurer beyond the timelines mentioned in sub-regulation (i) above, the insurer shall pay interest at a rate, which is 2% above bank rate from the date of receipt of last necessary document.

(iii) Except in the case of claims where an application is made under Section 47 of the Act to the court, if a claim is ready for payment but the payment cannot be made due to any reasons of proper identification of the payee, the life insurer shall pay interest on the claim amount at the bank rate from the date on which claim is ready for payment.

(iv) In respect of Maturity, Survival Benefit claims and Annuities, the Life Insurer shall initiate the claim process by sending intimation sufficiently in advance or send post-dated cheque or give direct credit to the bank account of claimant through any electronic mode approved by RBI, so as to pay the claim on or before the due date. In case of any delay on the part of the insurer in settling the claim on due date, the life insurer shall pay interest at a rate, which is 2% above bank rate from the due date of payment or date of receipt of last necessary document from the insured/claimant, whichever is later.

(v) In respect of free look cancellation, surrender, withdrawal, request for refund of proposal deposit, refund of outstanding proposal deposit if any, shall be processed and paid within 15 days of receipt of request or last necessary document, failing which the insurer shall pay penal interest at a rate, which is 2% above bank rate from the date of request or receipt of last necessary document if any whichever is later, from the insured/claimant.

Explanation: Administration of Health Insurance Policies issued by Life Insurers shall also be governed by Chapter IV of IRDAI (Health Insurance) Regulations, 2016.

(vi) The interest payments referred above in sub regulations (ii), (iii), (iv), (v) shall be paid by the Life Insurer suo moto without waiting for specific demand from the insured/claimant.

Claim Procedure in Respect of a General Insurance Policy

1. An insured or the claimant shall give notice to the insurer of any loss arising under contract of insurance at the earliest or within such extended time as may be allowed by the insurer. On receipt of such a communication, a general insurer shall respond immediately and give clear information to the insured on the procedures that he should follow. In cases where a surveyor has to be appointed for assessing a loss/claim, it shall do so immediately, in any case within 72 hours of the receipt of intimation from the insured. Insurer shall communicate the details of the appointment of surveyor, including the role, duties and responsibilities of the surveyor to the insured by letter, email or any other electronic form immediately after the appointment of the surveyor.

2. The insurer/surveyor shall within 7 days of the claim intimation, inform the insured/claimant of the essential documents and other requirements that the claimant should submit in support of the claim. Where documents are available in public domain or with a public authority, the surveyor/insurer shall obtain them.

3. The surveyor shall start the survey immediately unless there is a contingency that delays immediate survey, in any case within 48 hours of his appointment. Interim report of the physical details of the loss shall be recorded and uploaded/forwarded to the insurer within the shortest time but not later than 15 days from the date of first visit of the surveyor. A copy of the interim report shall be furnished by the insurer to the insured/claimant, if he so desires.

4. Where the insured is unable to furnish all the particulars required by the surveyor or where the surveyor does not receive the full cooperation of the insured, the insurer or the surveyor, as the case may be, shall inform in writing to the insured under information to the insurer about the consequent delay that may result in the assessment of the claim. It shall be the duty equally of the insurer and the surveyor to follow up with the insured for pending information/documents guiding the insured with regard to submissions to be made. The insurer and/or surveyor shall not call for any information/document that is not relevant for the claim.

5. (i) The surveyor shall, subject to sub-regulation 4 above, submit his final report to the insurer within 30 days of his appointment. A copy of the surveyor's report shall be furnished by the insurer to the insured/claimant, if he so desires. Notwithstanding anything mentioned herein, in case of claims made in respect of commercial and large risks the surveyor shall submit the final report to the insurer within 90 days of his appointment. However, such claims shall be settled by the insurer within 30 days of receipt of final survey report and/or the last relevant and necessary document as the case may be.

(ii) Where special circumstances exist in respect of a claim either due to its special/complicated nature, or due to difficulties associated with replacement/reinstatement, the surveyor shall, seek an extension from insurer for submission of his report. In such an event, the insurer shall give the status to the insured/claimant fortnightly wherever warranted. The insurer may make provisional/on account payment based on the admitted claim liability.

6. If an insurer, on the receipt of a survey report, finds that it is incomplete in any respect, he shall require the surveyor, under intimation to the insured/claimant; to furnish an additional report on certain specific issues as may be required by the insurer. Such a request may be made by the insurer within 15 days of the receipt of the final survey report.

Provided that the facility of calling for an additional report by the insurer shall not be resorted to more than once in the case of a claim.

7. The surveyor, on receipt of this communication, shall furnish an additional report within three weeks from the date of receipt of communication from the insurer.

8. On receipt of the final survey report or the additional survey report, as the case may be, and on receipt of all required information/documents that are relevant and necessary for the claim, an insurer shall, with in a period of 30 days offer a settlement of the claim to the insured/claimant. If the insurer, for any reasons to be recorded in writing and communicated to the insured/claimant, decides to reject a claim under the policy, it shall do so within a period of 30 days from the receipt of the final survey report and/or additional information/documents or the additional survey report, as the case may be.

9. In case, the amount admitted is less than the amount claimed, then the insurer shall inform the insured/claimant in writing about the basis of settlement in particular, where the claim is rejected, the insurer shall give the reasons for the same in writing drawing reference to the specific terms and conditions of the policy document.

10. In the event the claim is not settled within 30 days as stipulated above, the insurer shall be liable to pay interest at a rate, which is 2% above the bank rate from the date of receipt of last relevant and necessary document from the insured/claimant by insurer till the date of actual payment.

Claim Procedure in Respect of a Health Insurance Policy

1. Every insurer shall adhere to the procedure laid down under Insurance Regulatory and Development Authority of India (Health Insurance) Regulations, 2016 for settlement of health insurance claims.

(i) An Insurer shall settle the claim within 30 days from the date of receipt of last necessary document in accordance with the provisions of Regulation 27 of IRDAI (Health Insurance) Regulations, 2016.

(ii) In the case of delay in the payment of a claim, the insurer shall be liable to pay interest from the date of receipt of last necessary document to the date of payment of claim at a rate 2% above the bank rate.

2. However, where the circumstances of a claim warrant an investigation in the opinion of the insurer, it shall initiate and complete such investigation at the earliest, in any case not later than 30 days from the date of receipt of last necessary document. In such cases, insurer shall settle the claim within 45 days from the date of receipt of last necessary document. III 25

(i) In case of delay beyond stipulated 45 days the insurer shall be liable to pay interest at a rate 2% above the bank rate from the date of receipt of last necessary document to the date of payment of claim.

3. Return of premium on cancellation during Free Look Period shall be processed in accordance with the provisions of Regulation 14 of IRDAI (Health Insurance) Regulations, 2016. Any refund shall be processed with speed and shall be refunded within 15 days from the date of receipt of request for free look cancellation.

Explanation: Health Insurance claims for the purpose of this Regulation shall be claims arising under all insurance policies issued by Life, General and Health Insurers in respect of Health Insurance Business as defined in Section 2(6C) of the Act.

Grievance Redressal Procedure

Every insurer shall have in place proper procedures and effective mechanism to resolve complaints and grievances of policyholders, claimants efficiently and with speed.

1. A complainant who wishes to make a complaint against insurer, intermediary, insurance intermediary, distribution channel or other regulated entities involved in insurance sales and services shall approach the respective grievance redressal officer of insurer. In case either grievance redressal officer of insurer does not respond or the resolution provided by him is not to the satisfaction of the complainant he may register a complaint in grievance redressal management system of the Authority. The Authority facilitates re-examination of the complaint so as to provide final resolution by insurer.

2. Every insurer shall have in place an effective grievance redressal procedure to address complaints of policyholders efficiently and with speed and communicate the action taken by the insurer on the complaint to the complainant along with the information in respect of Insurance Ombudsman as may be necessary.

3. Grievance Redressal Officer

(i) Every insurer shall have a designated Grievance Redressal Officer (GRO) of a senior level at the corporate office. The GRO at the corporate office will be the contact person for the Authority.

(ii) Every other office of the insurer shall also have a designated Grievance Officer who shall be head of that office. The details of the GRO/designated Grievance Officer along with the contact details in full shall be published in the website of the insurer and the name and contact details of designated Grievance Officer of respective office and the other Grievance Officers in hierarchy up to GRO at corporate office shall also be displayed in the notice board of respective offices.

(iii) Every office of the insurer shall also display in prominent place, the name, address and other contact details of the insurance ombudsman within whose jurisdiction the office falls.

4. Grievance Redressal System/Procedure

(i) Every insurer shall have a system including IT systems and a procedure for receiving, registering and disposing of grievances in each of its offices. Every insurer shall publicize its grievance redressal procedure and ensure that it is specifically made available on its website.

(ii) All insurers shall necessarily form part of the Integrated Grievance Management System (IGMS) put in place by the Authority to facilitate the registering/tracking of complaint on-line by the policyholders. The Insurer's system, shall involve, mirroring of the Grievance database, of Insurers with IGMS and shall also facilitate analysis of complaints, mitigation, improvement of processes and system, through constant review.

(iii) Insurers shall also have in place system to receive and deal with all kinds of calls including voice/e-mail, relating to grievances, from prospects and policyholders. The system shall enable and facilitate the required interfacing with the Authority's system of handling calls/e-mails.

5. Closure of complaint/grievance:

(i) A complaint shall be considered as disposed of and closed when

(a) The insurer has acceded to the request of the complainant fully.

(or)

(b) Where the complainant has indicated in writing, acceptance of the response of the insurer.

(or)

(c) Where the complainant has not responded to the insurer within 8 weeks of the insurer's written response.

(ii) Where the grievance is not resolved in favour of the policyholder or partially resolved in favour of the policyholder, the insurer shall inform the complainant of the option to take up the matter before insurance ombudsman giving details of the name and address of the Ombudsman of competent jurisdiction.

General Principles

1. Every life insurer shall inform policyholders whose participating policies are in force, at least once in a year, the bonus accrued to their policies or the value of their ULIP policies as the case may be, through a letter/e-mail/any other electronic mode.

2. The requirements of "disclosure of material information" regarding a proposal or policy apply, under these regulations, both to the insurer and the insured. As far as the insured is concerned, wherever required, he shall co-operate with the distribution channels to ensure this.

3. The policyholder shall assist the insurer, if the insurer so requires, in any prosecution, proceeding or in the matter of recovery of claims by the insurer against third parties.

4. The policyholder shall furnish all information that is sought from him by the insurer, either directly or through the distribution channels, which the insurer considers as having a bearing on the risk to enable the insurer to assess properly the risk covered under a proposal for insurance.

5. Insurers shall at all times maintain total confidentiality of policyholder information, unless it becomes necessary to disclose the information to statutory authorities due to operation of any law.

6. Any breach of the obligations cast on an insurer or distribution channels or surveyors in terms of these regulations may enable the Authority to initiate action against each or all of them, jointly or severally, under the Act and/or the Insurance Regulatory and Development Authority Act, 1999.

Source: https://taxguru.in/corporate-law/irda-protection-of-policyholders-interests-regulations-2017html

Foreign Exchange Management (Insurance) Regulations, 2000

In exercise of the power conferred by sub-section (2) of section 47 of the Foreign Exchange Management Act, 1999 (42 of 1999), the Reserve Bank makes the following regulations with respect to the holding by a person resident in India of a general or life insurance policy issued by an insurer outside India, namely:

Short Title and Commencement

1. (i) These regulations may be called the Foreign Exchange Management (Insurance) Regulations, 2000.
   (ii) They shall come into force on 1st day of June, 2000.

Definitions

2. In these regulations, unless the context otherwise, requires—
   (i) 'Act' means the Foreign Exchange Management Act, 1999 (42 of 1999).
   (ii) The words and expressions used but not defined in these regulations shall have the same meanings respectively assigned to them in the Act.
3. Permission to take or hold a general insurance policy issued by an insurer outside India.
   (i) A person resident in India may take or continue to hold a general insurance policy issued by an insurer outside India, provided that, the policy is held, under a specific or general permission of the Central Government.
   (ii) A person resident in India may continue to hold any general insurance policy issued by an insurer outside India when such person was resident outside India.

Provided that where the premium due on a general insurance policy has been paid by making remittance from India, the policyholder shall repatriate to India through normal banking channels, the maturity proceeds or amount of any claim due on the policy, within a period of seven days from the receipt thereof.

4. Permission to take or hold a life insurance policy issued by an insurer outside India.
   (i) A person resident in India may take or continue to hold a life insurance policy issued by an insurer outside India, provided that, the policy is held, under a specific or general permission of the Reserve Bank of India.
   (ii) A person resident in India may continue to hold any life insurance policy issued by an insurer outside India when such person was resident outside India.

Provided that where the premium due on a life insurance policy has been paid by making remittance from India, the policyholder shall repatriate to India through normal banking channels, the maturity proceeds or amount of any claim due on the policy, within a period of seven days from the receipt thereof.

GIM

Memorandum of Exchange Control Regulations Relating to General Insurance in India

Introduction

General insurance business in India is undertaken by insurance companies which are registered with Insurance Regulatory and Development Authority (IRDA).

Scope of Memorandum

Exchange Control Regulations governing general insurance business written in India are set out in this Memorandum.

Directions contained in this Memorandum have been issued under Section 10(4) and Section 11(1) of Foreign Exchange Management Act, 1999 (42 of 1999).

Definitions

For the purpose of this Memorandum, the terms "Person resident in India" and "Foreign Currency" will have the same meaning as defined under Foreign Exchange Management Act, 1999.

Bank Encasement Certificates

Where insurers have been permitted to issue policies expressed in foreign currency against premium payable in foreign currency, they should insist on submission of suitable document to satisfy themselves that the premium has been received by foreign exchange remittance through banking channels or in rupees derived by sale of foreign exchange to an authorised dealer in foreign exchange or an authorised money-changer.

Direct Insurance Outside India by Residents

Persons, firms, companies, etc. resident in India are not permitted to take insurance cover of any kind with insurance companies in foreign countries without the prior permission of Reserve Bank. Besides, permission of Government of India under General Insurance Business (Nationalisation) Act, 1972, is also required to be taken in such cases.

Transaction in Nepal and Bhutan

Indians, Nepalese and Bhutanese resident in Nepal and Bhutan as well as offices and branches of India, Nepalese and Bhutanese firms, companies or other organisations in these two countries are treated as resident in India for purposes of transactions in Indian rupees. Payment of claims to such persons against marine or non-marine policies may be freely made in rupees. Payments in foreign currency towards claims under marine or non-marine policies require prior approval of Reserve Bank, except where premiums thereon were also collected in foreign currency.

The Memorandum is divided into four parts as under:

PART A - Marine Insurance

PART B - Non-Marine Insurance

PART C - Reinsurance

PART D - Foreign Currency Accounts And Investments Abroad.

PART A: Marine Insurance

Currency in which Marine Policies may be Issued

Marine insurance policies on coastal shipments may be issued only in Indian rupees.

Marine insurance policies on shipments between India and other countries as also between two points outside India may be issued in rupees or in any foreign currency.

Premiums on Marine Policies Covering Exports

Payment of premium on a marine insurance policy on exports from India may be accepted in rupees provided exporter furnishes to the insurer a certificate to the effect either (a) that insurance charges on the shipment in question have to be borne by him in terms of contract with overseas buyer and that he is not making the payment on behalf of any non-resident, or (b) that he is defraying insurance charges on the shipment in question on account of overseas buyer of the goods and he undertakes to add the amount on the invoice and recover the payment so made from the buyer in an approved manner.

Notes:

A. Overseas buyers may sometimes approach Insurers directly or through their overseas offices/agents for extension of cover for additional risks or for extended transit risks necessitated by circumstances not envisaged when the marine insurance was originally covered in India with the Insurers. Such extensions may be made by Insurers provided the additional premiums are collected from overseas buyers in foreign currency.

B. Certain countries operate restrictions requiring importers in their countries to obtain marine insurance cover from local insurers, settlement under which may not be possible in the event of cargo getting lost before reaching port of destination due to Exchange Control Regulations governing remittances against imports into those countries. Insurers may issue in such cases, contingency marine insurance policies to exporters to protect their interest till goods are paid for. The policies should be issued with a condition that they will not be assignable to overseas buyer or any other non-resident party. Claims on such policies should be paid only to exporters in India.

Premiums on Marine Policies Covering Imports

Payment of premium on a marine insurance policy on imports into India may be accepted in rupees provided importer furnishes to the insurer a certificate to the effect that (a) the insurance charges are required to be borne by him in terms of the contract with the overseas seller and (b) where the import is made against an Import License, he undertakes to ensure that the amount of insurance premium is endorsed on the import license in due course.

In case of import by the public sector (viz.), Central Government, any State Government, Statutory or public bodies and Government undertakings), payment of insurance premium in rupees may be freely accepted.

In all other cases, where payment of premium in respect of imports is offered in rupees, prior approval of Reserve Bank will be required. Applications for the purpose should be made by letter (in duplicate) furnishing full particulars.

Premiums on Marine Policies Covering Shipments between Countries Outside India

Premiums on marine insurance policies covering shipments between countries outside India must ordinarily be received in foreign currency, but payment in rupees may be accepted provided a certificate from an authorised dealer in foreign exchange is produced to show that the rupees are derived by a remittance from abroad in an approved manner.

Note: Overseas offices of the Insurers may grant marine insurance cover for trade-between China and third countries and receive premium/settle claims through foreign currency accounts maintained by their overseas offices without prior approval of Reserve Bank.

Sometimes, firms and companies in India finance merchanting trade i.e., goods shipped from one foreign country to another and financed by an intermediary in India. In some of these cases goods may be purchased on f.o.b./c.&f. terms and/or sold on c.i.f. terms, the marine insurance cover being arranged by the intermediary in India. Insurance companies registered with IRDA may issue policies covering transit risks between the loading and the destination ports in rupees or in any foreign currency in such cases, against payment of premium in rupees by the intermediary, after satisfying themselves that the contract provides for marine insurance being taken by intermediary.

Claims Against Marine Policies

Claims against marine insurance policies, when payable to persons, firms or companies in India should be paid on in rupees, irrespective of the currency in which relative policies had been issued. Where claimant is not a resident of India, Insurers may settle the claim out of foreign currency balances held by them, provided they are satisfied that ownership of the goods lost, damaged etc., vests in such claimant and that the latter is not making the claim merely as agent of the real owner of the goods in India.

Remittance of Claims on Exports

In the case of marine claims against exports, remittances of claim will be permitted by authorised dealers in foreign exchange on application on form A2 provided the Insurer has satisfied himself that the ownership of the goods on which claim has arisen vests in the non-resident claimant. Applications should be supported by following documents:

(a) Statement of claim duly certified by an official authorised by the insurance company registered with IRDA for this purpose.
(b) Insurance policy.
(c) Survey report or other customary proof of loss.
(d) Bills of lading/Airway bill.
(e) Certified copy of invoice.
(f) Any other documents ordinarily required to support the claim.

Where original documents are not available for any reason, photo copies may be produced to authorised dealer together with reasons for non-availability of the original documents. This provision does not apply to remittances for replenishment of foreign currency balances which will require specific approval of Reserve Bank.

Note: Insurers may settle claims in rupees in favour of Indian exporters even in cases where title to the goods has passed to foreign buyer, if a request to that effect has been made by the non-resident claimant. A certificate indicating full particulars of the transaction including number of relative GR/PP Form and amount paid in settlement of claim should be issued to the exporter to enable the latter to obtain necessary approval from Reserve Bank for making replacement shipments.

Claims against marine insurance policies covering exports may also be settled through the overseas claims settling agents, if so desired by Insurers. Authorised dealers have been permitted to open revolving letters of credit in favour of established claims-setting agents abroad and reimburse claims under the credit on verification of the necessary documentary evidence, viz. statement of claim, survey report or other documentary evidence of loss/damage, original policy or certificate of insurance, etc.

Payment in Foreign Currency of Certain Import Claims

Although it is a basic rule that marine claims on imports should be settled locally in rupees in favour of importer in cases where ownership of the goods lost, damaged, etc. vests in the importer. Insurers may settle claims from their foreign currency balances in favour of overseas suppliers in the following categories of imports, in order to facilitate early replacement of the lost, damaged, etc. goods, on request being received in this regard from importers:

(a) Imports by Government Departments and public sector undertakings.

(b) Imports by private sector undertakings against foreign credits provided the terms of the foreign credit require that insurance cover should be taken in foreign currency for replacement of lost/damaged goods.

(c) In all other cases, where the ownership of the goods lost/damaged etc. vests with the overseas supplier and no payment has been made towards any part of the cost of the goods.

These provisions are applicable not only to marine policies, but also to marine-cum-erection policies, whether issued separately or combined.

Claims on Policies Covering Merchanting Trade

Claims arising from marine insurance policies covering merchanting trade financed through India may be settled by Insurers from their foreign currency balances only if:

(a) The ownership of the goods vests with the overseas party, and

(b) Where the claim is proposed to be settled in favour of the overseas supplier, payment for the goods has not been made to the supplier and where claim is proposed to be settled in favour of the overseas buyer, payment for the goods has been received by the Indian intermediary from the buyer.

PART B: Non-Marine Insurance

Assets in India

Insurance cover on risks inside India (including All Risks Insurance) on assets in India owned by residents of India may be issued only in rupees. This is also applicable to assets of Indian branches/offices of foreign companies, banks, etc.

Assets Outside India

Non-marine risks in respect of assets in India owned by residents of India may be covered in rupees or in foreign currency provided that in respect of immovable property held outside India by Indian nationals, permission of Reserve Bank for holding the property had been obtained (where necessary). Settlement of claims under such policies should be made only in rupees locally. Foreign currency policies providing for payment of claims in foreign currency in the foreign currency out of eligible foreign currency assets held by Indian nationals/persons of Indian origin who have returned to India from abroad after a minimum continuous stay abroad for at least one year or out of funds held in their RFC accounts with authorised dealers in India. Issue of foreign currency policies in other cases will require prior approval of Reserve Bank.

Policies in Foreign Currency Approved by Reserve Bank—Settlement of Claims

Request for issue of policies in foreign currency which are not covered by the above guidelines are examined on merits by RBI. For such request where RBI grants specific approval for issue of policy in foreign currency, acceptance of premium in foreign currency and settlement of claim in foreign currency, insurers may approach A.D. for remittance of claims under policies subject to the following conditions:

(a) The policy has been issued in foreign currency with specific approval of RBI;
(b) The claim has been admitted by the competent authority of the insurance company;
(c) The claim has been settled as per the surveyors report and other sustaining documents;
(d) Claims on account of reinsurance are being lodged with reinsurers and will be received as per reinsurance agreement;
(e) The remittance is being made to the non-resident beneficiary under the policy. For resident beneficiaries the claim may be settled in Rupee equivalent of foreign currency due. Under no circumstances payment in foreign currency be made to a resident beneficiary.

Insurers may submit, to the Regional Office of RBI under whose jurisdiction it operates, a report on quarterly basis of the claims settled in foreign currency along with sustaining documents of each claim settled by them. These reports may be submitted within 15 days from the end of each quarter of the calendar year.

Baggage and Valuables in Transit

Insurance cover on baggage or valuables in transit between India and other countries or between two countries outside India may be issued in rupees or in foreign currency.

Premiums on such policies may be collected in rupees only if the owner of the baggage or other valuables is either an Indian national or is normally resident in India. In other cases, premiums should be received in foreign currency or in rupees derived by surrender of foreign currency to an authorised dealer in foreign exchange or authorised money-changer; such payments should be supported by a certificate from the authorised dealer/money-changer in the prescribed form.

Claims on such policies may be paid only in rupees in India except where the policyholder is a person normally resident outside India and premiums against the policy had been collected either in foreign currency or in rupees derived by surrender of foreign currency. Remittances of claims in foreign currencies in other cases will require prior approval of Reserve Bank.

Remittances towards claims on personal baggage reshipped from India by foreign nationals on completion of their assignments in India may be allowed by insurers, if they are eligible for or have been accorded remittance facilities at the time of retirement from India.

War etc. Risks Insurance on Marine Hulls

Insurance on Indian marine hulls covering All Risks against was and other allied risks arising out of civil commotion, political or labour disturbances etc. are required to be obtained from the Insurers in India only.

Personal Accident Insurance

Personal accident policies may be issued only in rupees and claims thereon settled only in rupees, in case of Indian nationals and persons of Indian origin normally resident in India. In other cases, personal accident policies may be issued in foreign currency, provided premiums thereon are paid either in foreign currency or in rupees derived by surrender of foreign currency to an authorised dealer or authorised money-changer. Claims in these cases may be settled in currency of the policy or in rupees as desired by the policyholder.

Note: Indian companies executing construction and turnkey contracts in foreign countries may at times desire to obtain personal accident cover from Indian Insurers for the workmen and technical staff actually engaged in the overseas contracts providing for settlement of claims in foreign currency. Insurers may permit such insurance being taken provided premiums will be paid by remittances in foreign currency from out of the foreign currency earnings generated by the contracts. Claims in such cases may be settled in foreign currency or if so desired, in rupees locally.

Overseas Medical Insurance Scheme for Indians Travelling Abroad

Policies may be issued in India under the Overseas Medical Insurance Schemes as approved by Reserve Bank to Indian residents travelling abroad for any approved visits viz., business study tour, specialised training, conferences, employment or higher studies. Premiums on such policies, other than for visits for employment, may be collected in rupees and for employment in foreign currency. Insurers may also open a revolving letter of credit with an Indian bank in London for settlement of its share in the claims that may eventually arise under the policies.

Miscellaneous

Insurers may issued product liability policies for exports and Errors and Omissions Policy in respect of computer software exports in foreign currency against receipt of premium in rupees and settle claims if any in foreign currency in respect of such policies.

Claims arising outside India against policies issued under Workmen's Compensation Act and Merchant Shipping Act may be paid in appropriate foreign currency. Remittances will be allowed for meeting specific claims on application by the Insurers furnishing full details of the claims.

PART C: Reinsurance

As per the extant Government of India's instructions, reinsurance arrangement of the insurance companies registered with IRDA are to be decided by the companies themselves on an annual basis, which is to be approved by the respective insurance company's Boards in consultation with IRDA. Authorised dealer, designated by these insurance companies may allow remittances falling due under such approved reinsurance arrangements, by the insurers in accordance with the terms and conditions laid down by their Boards.

Remittance of Reinsurance Premia by Local Brokers

Wherever local brokers arrange the reinsurance on behalf of insures, local brokers may remit the premia through the branch of the authorised designated by the insurance company in terms of para above subject to the production of undernoted documents:

(i) Relative debit notes from overseas insurance company.

(ii) Detailed statement of premia settled by the individual insurance company, along with a certificate to the effect that the amount of reinsurance business is within the overall limit approved by the insurance company's Board and the that the risks covered under the reinsurance arrangements are within the scope of the Reinsurance Programme, approved by the insurance company's Board in consultation with IRDA.

(iii) A certificate from the Chartered Accountant of the local broker, prepared on the basis of certificates and statements obtained from the insurance companies, to the effect that the proposed remittance of reinsurance premia sought, is in agreement with the various statements/certificates obtained from the insurance company companies.

PART D: Foreign Currency Accounts and Investments Abroad

Foreign Currency Accounts Abroad

Insurers may open, hold and maintain with a bank outside India foreign currency accounts for facilitating transactions and expenses relating/incidental to general insurance business undertaken in foreign countries in accordance with regulations laid down in this Memorandum. Insurers should endeavour to keep in their foreign currency accounts only the minimum balances required for normal business and transfer to India regularly all surplus funds held at foreign centres.

Investments Abroad

Renewal of existing investments, reinvestment of redemption proceeds of existing investments and fresh investment out of funds abroad, in Government/semi-Government securities and bank deposits may be made by Insurers freely without prior approval of Reserve Bank, provided they are for meeting statutory requirements in the foreign country concerned. All other investments will require prior approval of Reserve Bank of India.

LIM-Revised Instructions Under LIM

1. Attention of authorized dealers is invited to the Notification No. FEMA 12/2000-RB, dated May 3, 2000 viz., Foreign Exchange Management (Insurance) Regulations, 2000. The memorandum of Exchange Control Regulations relating to Life Insurance in India (LIM) since brought out is enclosed. The major changes in procedure as per Memorandum are summarized in the Annexure.

2. Necessary amendments to the Foreign Exchange Management Regulations, 2000 are being issued separately.

3 . Authorised Dealers may bring the contents of this circular to the notice of their constituents concerned.

4. The directions contained in this circular have been issued under Section 10(4) and Section 11(1) of the Foreign Exchange Management Act, 1999 (42 of 1999).

ANNEXURE

Major Changes Proposed in the Revised LIM

Sl. No.	Subject Matter	Changes
1.	Scope of Memorandum	The earlier instructions of LIM covered only LIC which was the only instruction permitted to undertake the business of Life Insurance. The present instructions contained in the Memorandum are applicable to LIC as well as Life Insurance Companies which are registered with IRDA.

Sl. No.	Subject Matter	Changes
2.	Re-insurance arrangement	The re-insurance arrangement of Life Insurance Companies registered with IRDA are to be decided by the Company's Board themselves and IRDA is to be kept informed. Authorised Dealers designated by these insurance companies are now permitted to make remittances falling due under such approved re-insurance arrangements.
3.	Settlement of claims in foreign currency favouring residents and crediting the same to RFC Accounts	In the LIM issued under FERA, residents were not permitted to retain any receipts in foreign currency as the same had to be surrendered to the authorized dealer within 7 days. Under FEMA resident beneficiaries of foreign currency life insurance policies are being permitted to retain the proceeds in foreign currency in RFC Accounts.
4.	Permitting credit of foreign currency claims favouring non-residents to NRE/FCNR Accounts	In the revised LIM the proceeds of policies denominated in foreign currency or the rupee policies for which premia are paid in foreign currency or out of NRE/FCNR Accounts are now permitted to be credited to NRE/FCNR Account of non-resident without prior approval of Reserve Bank.
5.	Restrictions on Issue of rupee policies to foreign nationals	The restrictions on issue of rupee policies maturing within 7 years to foreign nationals not permanently resident in India have been withdrawn.
6.	Export of policies	The restrictions in regard to export of policies have been withdrawn under revised LIM.
7.	Instruction addressing Exchange Control Concerns	The revised LIM is modified in such a manner whereby only issues of exchange control concern are addressed. Other operational instructions not relating to exchange control have been excluded.

LIM

Memorandum of Foreign Exchange Regulations Relating to Life Insurance in India

1. *Introduction*

Life insurance business in India can be undertaken by insurance companies registered with Insurance Regulatory and Development Authority (IRDA) and as per the regulations notified by Reserve Bank of India under Notification Nos. 1 and 12/2000-RB, dated May 3, 2000.

2. *Scope of Memorandum*

Exchange Control Regulations governing issue of life insurance policies in rupees and foreign currencies to non-residents, collection of premia, settlement of claims, maintenance and operations of foreign currency accounts abroad, reinsurance, investment of surplus funds abroad and allied matters are set out in this Memorandum. The receipt and payment of foreign exchange shall be as per Notification FEMA 14/2000-RB, dated May 3, 2000 i.e., Foreign Exchange Management (Manner or Receipt and Payment) Regulations. For current account transactions, insurers may be guided by the rules notified by Government of India vide G.S.R. 381(E), dated May 3, 2000, as amended from time to time and the various notification issued under FEMA, 1999 by Reserve Bank.

3. *Definitions*

For the purpose of this Memorandum the terms "Person resident in India", "Person resident outside India" and "foreign currency" will have the same meaning as defined under Foreign Exchange Management Act, 1999 (42 of 1999).

"Foreign nationals" will have the same meaning as defined in Regulation 4 of FEMA Notification No. 12/2000-RB, dated May 3, 2000.

"Person of Indian Origin" will have the same meaning as defined in FEMA Notification No. 5/RB-2000, dated May 3, 2000.

4. *Issue of Policies and Collection of Premia*

(a) **Residents**

(i) Policies may be issued in foreign currency to resident persons of Indian nationality or origin who have returned to India after being non-resident provided the premia are paid out of remittances from foreign currency funds held by them abroad or from their Resident Foreign Currency (RFC) account with authorized dealers in India.

(ii) Policies denominated in foreign currency or rupees may be issued to foreign nationals not permanently resident in India provided the premia are paid out of foreign currency funds or from their income earned in India or repairable superannuation/pension fund in India.

(iii) Conversion of Rupee policies on the lives of persons resident in India into foreign currency or transfer of records of such policies to a country outside India is not permitted without prior approval of Reserve Bank.

(b) **Non-Residents**

(i) Insurers may issue policies denominated in foreign currency through their offices in India or abroad to non-residents provided the premia are collected in foreign currency from abroad or out of NRE/FCNR accounts of the insured or his family members held in India.

(ii) For policies denominated in rupees issued to non-residents, funds held in NRO accounts can be accepted towards payment of premia.

(iii) Policies issued to Indian nationals are persons of Indian origin resident abroad by overseas office by overseas offices of insurers may be transferred to Indian register, together with the currency policies in such circumstances shall be converted into rupee policies except in case where the policy has been in force for at least 3 years prior to policyholder's return to India and the policyholder wishes to retained continue the foreign currency policy. Request received for payment in foreign currency towards premia on such policies may be permitted by authorized dealers provided the policyholder undertakes to repatriate to India the maturity proceeds or any claim amounts due on the policy through normal banking channels.

5. *Settlement of Claims*

(i) The basic rule for settlement of claims on rupee life insurance policies in favour of claimants resident outside Indian is the payments in foreign currency will be permitted only in proportion in which the amount of premia paid in foreign currency in relation to the total premia payable.

(ii) Non-resident beneficiaries of insurance claims/maturity/surrender value settled in foreign currency may be permitted to credit the same to NRE/FCNR account, if they so desire.

(iii) Resident beneficiaries of insurance claims/maturity/surrender values settled in foreign currency may be permitted to credit the same to RFC accounts, if they so desire.

(iv) Claims/maturity proceeds/surrender value in respect of rupee life insurance policies issued to non-resident Indians for which premia have been collected in non-repairable rupees only be paid only in rupees by credit to NRO account of the beneficiary. They would also apply in cases of death claims being settled in favour of non-resident assignees/ nominees.

(v) Claims/maturity proceeds/surrender value in respect of rupee policies issued to foreign nationals not permanently resident in India may be paid in rupees or may be allowed to be remitted abroad, if the claimant so desires.

6. *Commission to Overseas Agents*

Insurers may pay commission to their agents who are permanently resident outside India regardless of the fact that part of the business booked by them may be on the lives of persons resident in India and relative premia are paid in rupees in India. Remittances of commission from India to such agents abroad will be governed by instructions contained in Government Notification No. G.S.R. 381(E), dated May 3, 2000 relating to Current Account Transactions as amended from time to time.

7. *Reinsurance*

In terms of the existing instruction, reinsurance arrangements for the insurance companies registered with IRDA are to decided by the companies themselves on an annual basis and approved by the respective insurance company's Board in consultation with IRDA. Authorised a dealer, designated by these insurance companies may allow remittances for the reinsurance arrangements in accordance with the terms and conditions laid down by the respective Board of insurance companies.

8. *Foreign Currency Accounts*

Insurances may open, hold and maintain with a bank outside India foreign currency accounts for facilitating transactions and expenses relating/incidental to life insurance business undertaken in foreign countries in accordance with regulations laid down in the Memorandum. Insurers should transfer to India regularly all surplus funds held at foreign centres and endeavour to keep in their foreign currency accounts only minimum balances required for normal business.

9. *Investments Abroad*

Renewal of existing investments, reinvestment of redemption proceeds of existing investments and fresh investments out of funds held abroad, in Government/Semi-Government securities and bank deposits may be made by insurers freely without prior approval of Reserve Bank provided they are for meeting statutory requirements in the foreign country concerned. All other investments will require prior approval of Reserve Bank.

10. *Utilisation of Foreign Currency Funds*

(i) Insurers may freely use its foreign currency balances for meeting all the normal expenses of its overseas offices inclusive of taxes and other dues in connection with maintenance and upkeep of building and properties held by insurers in foreign countries as well as purchase of cars for official use.

(ii) Insurers may also freely use their overseas funds for settlement of provident fund, gratify and other retirement benefits to retiring employees of overseas offices.

(iii) Insurers may grant loans, without prior permission of Reserve Bank, to employees of their overseas offices (other than Indian nationals who had been deputed or posted from India) against provident fund balances held in the country concerned provided loan recoveries will be made in foreign currency.

Clarification

1. Attention of Authorised Dealers is invited to A.P. (DIR Series) Circular No. 72, dated January 17, 2003 enclosing the Memorandum of Exchange Control Regulations relating to Life Insurance in India (LIM). In terms of paragraph 5 (iii) of the Memorandum relating to settlement of claims, Authorised Dealers were advised that Resident beneficiaries of insurance claims/maturity/surrender value settled in foreign currency may be permitted to credit the proceeds thereof to Resident Foreign Currency (RFC) Account, if so desired.

2. On a review, it has been decided that:

(i) Resident beneficiaries of the insurance claims/maturity/surrender value in foreign currency may be permitted to open and credit the proceeds thereof of their RFC (Domestic) Account instead of RFC Account as advised earlier.

(ii) Non-resident India Policyholders who are beneficiaries of insurance claims/maturity or surrender value settled in foreign currency in respect of policies issued by Insurance Companies in India and registered with Insurance Regulatory and Development Authority to conduct insurance business may be permitted to credit the proceeds to the RFC Account opened by them on their becoming residents.

3. Authorised Dealers may bring the contents of this circular to the notice of their constituents concerned.

4. The directions contained in this circular have been issued under Sections 10(4) and 11(1) of the Foreign Exchange Management Act, 1999 (42 of 1999).

Source: AP(DIR Series) (2003-2004) Circular No. 51, dated 15-12-2003.

Major C Ranges Proposed in Revised GIM (General Insurance Memorandum)

Sl. No.	Subject Matter	Changes
1.	Scope of Memorandum	The earlier instructions of GIM covered only public sector general insurance companies. The present instructions contained in the Memorandum are applicable to public sector general insurance companies as well as general insurance companies which are registered with IRDA.
2.	Reinsurance Arrangement	The reinsurance arrangement of public sector general insurance companies registered with IRDA are not to be decided by the respective Boards of the insurance companies and IRDA is to be kept informed. ADs designated by these insurance companies are now permitted to make remittances falling under such approved reinsurance arrangements without reference to the Reserve Bank.
3.	Remittance of Re-insurance premia by local brokers	Ads have been permitted to allow remittance of reinsurance premia by local brokers of insurance companies after verifying debit notes from the overseas insurance company, statement of account and CA's certificate of broker certifying the sum etc.
4.	Foreign currency accounts abroad	Public sector general insurance companies and general insurance companies registered with IRDA are permitted to open, maintain and hold a foreign currency bank account with a bank outside India for the purpose of facilitating transactions and expenses relating/incidental to general insurance business undertaken in foreign countries.
5.	Settlement of claims in foreign currency	For settlement of claims in foreign currency in respect of policies issued in foreign currency, insurance companies are now permitted to make remittances subject to certain condition as stipulated in the Memorandum, without reference to Reserve Bank as required in the past.

11

Fire Insurance

Introduction

Fire Insurance is of late origin as compared to marine insurance. The Great Fire of London in 1666 prompted the formation of fire insurance companies in England, though fire insurance as a suggestion was made in 1609 in Germany. The first London fire insurance company was formed in 1667, by a builder (though physician), called Dr. Nicholas Barbon. Between 1710 to 1750 many fire insurance companies came up. In India Britishers formed fire insurance companies and earliest known such company was Sun Insurance Ltd. (1710). After independence Indian known insurance companies were National Insurance Co. Ltd., Calcutta, New India Assurance Company Ltd., Bombay, Oriental Fire and General Insurance Co. Ltd., New Delhi, and United India Fire and General Insurance Co. Ltd., Madras. In May 1971, fire insurance companies were nationalised (64 Indian and 42 foreign), along with life and marine insurance companies (LIC of India took over 245 Companies). But in 1999 the insurance sector has been denationalised and Insurance Regulatory Authority has been formed.

Fire Insurance Contract

The law relating to fire insurance is found in the Insurance Act, 1938. Section 2(6A) of the Act defines a fire insurance business as "the business of effecting, otherwise than incidentally to some other class of business, contracts of insurance against loss by or incidental to fire, or other occurrence customarily included among risks insured against the fire insurance policies".

This definition is very exhaustive and it covers loss by fire and incidental to fire. A fire insurance contract is a contract where one person, called insurer, agrees in consideration of a sum of money called premium, to indemnify for any loss or damage to the insured property or goods of the insured caused by fire. The contract specifies the subject matter insured, the amount of policy and circumstances of under which insurance is not liable. A fire insurance contract is for one year by law and can be extended before the expiry of the year. The premium can be paid as a lump sum or in installments. The "policy" is the document containing terms and conditions of fire insurance. The contract should satisfy all the requirements of a valid contract.

Characteristics of a Fire Insurance Contract

Following are the characteristics of fire insurance contract:

1. Indemnity contract. It is a contract of Indemnity because in case of loss, the insured can recover only the actual loss and not more than the loss. The maximum amount of loss to be compensated shall be the value for which the policy has been taken. Under standard fire policy losses are settled on the basis of market value of the property on the date of fire.

2. Utmost good faith. Fire insurance is a contract of utmost good faith (uberrimae fidei). Both the insured and insurance company have to disclose everything which is in their knowledge and which may affect the contract. The disclosure of every material facts must be full and fair.

3. Period. A fire insurance contract is only for one year. It can be renewed, after making payment of the premium within the days of grace.

4. Insurable interest. In case of fire insurance, the insured has to show insurable interest, proprietary or pecuniary in the subject matter. It should be present both at the time of taking the policy as well as at the time of loss. Owners, bailees, mortgagees and a carrier have all insurable interest. Owners have proprietary interest and bailee or mortgagee has pecuniary interest. The later can insure every without the knowledge of the owner, and to the extent of full value of goods or property.

5. The risk covered by the insurance contract is the loss resulting from fire or some other cause which is the proximate cause of damage.

6. Subrogation and contribution. These two principles apply to fire insurance.

7. There is no surrender value in case of fire policy.

8. A fire policy can be assigned as an actionable claim under Transfer of Property Act, 1882.

Meaning of "Fire" and Loss or Damage by Fire

*Meaning of "Fire"**

The word "fire" literally means a "condition of burning" and is used in its popular sense to mean a friendly fire used for domestic or manufacturing purposes. It is confined within the proper limits and does not break bound. In insurance by fire means only "hostile" fire in a place where it has broken bounds. The word fire in fire insurance is given its plain and ordinary meaning and not any restricted meaning. Fire, in this sense, means that: (a) there must be actual fire or ignition and (b) it must be accidental or fortuitous in origin so far as the insured is concerned. Thus, to form a valid claim under the policy there must be actual ignition which was accidental.

1. There must be Actual Fire or Ignition. Fire means the production of light and heat by combustion (burning) and unless there is actual ignition there is no fire within the meaning of the term in an ordinary policy. In this sense, heating not accompanied by ignition is not fire. Loss occasioned by fire means loss by ignition of the articles consumed or by ignition is not fire. Loss occasioned by fire means loss by ignition of the articles consumed or by ignition of that part of the premises storing them. For example, if sugar is spoiled by excessive heat due to the closing a ventilator in the chimney and there is no actual ignition, the insurer is not liable. Likewise, the heat of the sun often contracts timber but that would not be considered a loss by

* Mohd. Arif Khan, *Ibid.*, p. 102.

fire. In fact, we call a thing as fire when there is a flame ending in conflagration (burning) and there can be no flame unless the heat applied or generated rises to the ignition point. Fire, in order to come within the policy must result from actual ignition and the resulting loss must be proximately caused by such ignition. Damages from lightning are not included in fire risk, but if lightning causes ignition, the loss would be fully covered. The same rule applies to loss or damage caused by electricity or as a result of smoke or of putting out the fire. Thus, if in the process of putting out a fire, goods are spoiled by water, or some articles of furniture are thrown out of the window, or a neighbouring house is destroyed by explosion for arresting fire, all will be covered under the fire policy. Also, loss by theft during a fire is covered as a fire disconnected or damaged stove pipe and the fire never left the stove, the insurer is not liable. However, if the chimney catches fire, the insurer is liable. Similarly, if paper is discoloured due to smoke and heat from a flue the insured cannot claim. Generally, certain causes for which insurers are not prepared to accept the liability, as for example, earthquake, riot, or civil commotion are excluded from the purview of fire policy. Ignition is, therefore, the acid test of "fire" and as such, there can be "no claim without flame".

2. Actual Fire (Ignition) must be Accidental or Fortuitous. Secondly, the fire must be accidental or fortuitous in its origin so far as the insured is concerned. Unless, the fire owes its origin to an accident, it is not a fire within the meaning and intention of the policy. Thus, a fire lit in an ordinary stove or gas-burner or in the furnace of a boiler where a process requiring the application of heat is carried on is not an accidental fire. The cause of fire is immaterial unless it was the deliberate act of the insured. In such cases the insured cannot recover any loss caused by his own willful misconduct. However, if fire is intentionally lit for the purpose of cooking which accidentally goes beyond control, then it will also come within the definition of fire. Even loss by fire caused by negligence of insured, his servant or strangers is covered. In *Harris* vs. *Poland* H. hid his jewellery in her grate (metal frame for holding cola etc. in a fire place) under the coal. Later, having forgotten this, she unintentionally lit the fire and the jewellery was damaged. In this case insurer Poland is liable to pay. In *Staney* vs. *Western Insurance* Co., S's Car was insured against fire and not against collision. Fire broke due to short circuit. To control fire S lost control of car and fire destroyed the whole car. S can recover the total loss. In short, the object of the contract, of fire insurance is to indemnify the insured against accidental loss by fire, and so long as the property is accidentally burnt, it will come within the policy cover. It does not matter whether the fire comes to the insured property, or the insured property comes to the fire, their effects being the same, viz., subject matter of insurance burnt which ought not to have burnt.

Principle of Causa Proxima

It is clear that to constitute a "fire" within the meaning of a fire insurance policy, there must be actual ignition and the fire must be accidental or fortuitous in origin so far as the insured is concerned. Hence, in order to establish a claim under the policy, it is not sufficient merely to prove that the loss is attributable to fire. But what is actually required is that the fire must be the efficient proximate cause of the loss and not merely a remote or indirect cause which brought into action various elements which, though acted independently, caused the loss. In other words, the fire must be the immediate cause or dominant factor, and not the remote or distant cause i.e., the principle is "*causa proxima non remota spectatur*". It should, however, be remembered that the term "immediate cause" does not always means that the fire must be nearest to the loss in a sequence of events. Even if the fire is not nearest to the loss in a sequence of events. Even if the fire is not nearest to the loss in a sequence and if the other events in the sequence are merely contributory of it, and the fire is a dominating cause, then such fire will come within the preview of a fire. For example, if after the outbreak of a fire in a cinema house, the walls of the shops in the adjacent market fall, then in this case the fire is the dominant effective cause. This is obviously because the fall of the walls being incidental to the fire and a natural consequence of it, even though the walls may not have been touched by a flame of fire, the insurer will be liable to compensate for the damages. In the same way, the loss of goods or property due to the smoke from the fire, damage done due to water in the process of extinguishing a fire, damage during the salvage operations, blistering, searching or cracking of adjoining property by the heat from the fire, or loss arising due to the theft caused by confusion during fire and loss arising due to removal of property from the place of fire, are recoverable as losses covered by a fire policy, as the fire is the dominant effective cause in all these cases. However, if the loss is indirect consequence of fire the loss incurred due to fire will not be considered as a result of proximate cause but of remote cause. If after a fire the walls are left standing, though posing a threat to the life and later on are blown down by a violent gale, causing damage to adjoining property, then in this case, the proximate cause of loss is "gale" and not fire. Likewise, if a mob breaks the windows of a shop in the neighbourhood of a fire for purposes of looting, the proximate cause of loss in the act of mob and not fire.

The following losses have been held to be caused proximately by fire:

1. Loss which is the necessary consequence of fire in the sense that if there had been no fire it would not have happened.
2. Loss which is the reasonable and probable consequence of fire in that it results in the ordinary course of events from the happening of fire.
3. Loss caused by water used to extinguish fire, destroying property or by fire brigade in the execution of their duties.
4. Loss arising as a consequence of removal of the property from the building in which fire is raging with the intention of saving it, or loss due to theft during the confusion caused by the fire.
5. Wages period to persons engaged for extinguishing fire.

Loss Caused in Extinguishing Fire

Generally, when there is fire, a crowd of people gather around in order to help the removal of goods from the place or some may help to extinguish the fire. During the course of these operations, if any loss occurs, it is regarded as a loss resulting from fire.

In determining the extent of the insurance company's liability, the cause of fire is immaterial, unless it has been deliberately brought about by the insured. The general rule of law is that the insurer is liable on a fire policy if the subject matter insured are destroyed or damaged by fire except when the fire is caused by the willful act of the assured or of somebody with his private or consent. However, the insurer is liable on a fire policy if the insured goods are inadvertently (thoughtlessly) set fire to by the assured himself or where the fire is caused by the negligence of the assured himself.

Following losses are not covered by fire policy:

1. Loss by theft during or after fire.
2. Loss to property by its own characteristics, e.g., a bomb exploiting itself.
3. Loss by burning of property by order of any public authority.
4. Loss caused by thunder.
5. Loss by Act of God or by civil disorder and wages paid to persons engaged for extinguishing fire.

Rights of Insurer

Under a fire insurance contract, the insurer has various rights such as the right of avoiding the contract for non-disclosure or concealment of any material fact, right of control over the property, right of entering the property, right of subrogation, salvage and reinstatement, right of contribution, etc. which have been discussed below:

1. Right of to avoid contract. A fire insurance contract, like any other contract, is a contract of good faith (*uberrimae fidei*). The assured is bound to disclose to the insurer before the conclusion of the contract every material circumstance which, in the ordinary course of business, ought to be known by him. If the assured fails to make such disclosure the insurer is entitled to avoid the contract of the fire insurance. If the assured mis-states any fact or withholds any material fact the insurer can avoid the contract.

2. Right of control over the property. Under the fire insurance contract, the insurer has an implied right to assume control over the damaged property. It is the insurer who is ultimately to suffer the loss under the fire insurance contract. In order to mitigate further loss he can, therefore, adopt any means he likes.

3. Right of entering the property. The insurer is entitled to enter upon the premises insured or wherein the things insured are. But in order to enable him to do so, the assured is required to give an immediate notice of the fire with the particulars of damage done.

4. Right to salvage. When the insured property is destroyed or damaged by fire, the insurer has a right to take possession of the salvage, i.e., the property or things saved after fire. This right of the insurer is absolute because fire insurance the contract of indemnity.

5. Right of reinstatement. The insurer has a right instead of paying the loss to the policyholder in cash to replace or repair the property, which is known as the insurer's right of reinstatement. This right gives option to the insurer either to pay the indemnity money in cash or to restore to the assured the property damaged or destroyed by fire. The insurers may insist the right to reinstate if he is required to do so as per the contract or if he has any suspicion of fraud or arson. He can insist if he is required to do by any person, other than the assured who is interested in or entitled to the premises damaged by fire.

6. Right of subrogation. Subrogation is a right which equity has given in order to enable the insurer to recover so far as may be, his loss under the contract. Subrogate means 'to take the place of' or to step in shoes of. The insurer is also entitled to recover from the assured the value of any benefit received by him by way of compensation from other sources in excess of his actual loss, as well as the full value of any right or remedies against third parties which have been renounced by him and to which, but for such renunciation, the insurer would have a right to be subrogated.

7. Right of contribution. When the same property has been insured with more than one insurer and if in case of loss one of the insurers has paid the full amount of loss to the insured, the insurer has a right to claim contribution from the other co-insurers, in rateable proportion.

Comparison between Fire and Marine Insurance

There are some points of similarity and differences between fire insurance and marine insurance. Both these forms of insurance have two common features. Firstly, all fire insurance contracts are contracts of indemnity like marine insurance contracts, except in case of valued policy. Secondly, both these policies are issued only for a short period, fire insurance policy for one year and marine insurance policy either for a particular voyage or time. The following are the differences between the two.

1. Insurable interest. In case of fire insurance policy, insurable interest must exist both at the time of the insurance as well as at the time of loss. But in marine insurance contract insurable interest must exist at the time of the loss and need not exist when the insurance is taken.

2. Transfer. A fire insurance policy cannot be transferred without the permission of the insurance company whereas a marine policy can be freely transferred.

3. Loss. Under the fire insurance, the actual loss or the amount insured, whichever is less, is indemnified. But, under a marine insurance policy the insured is given a profit up to 10 to 15 per cent of the insured amount.

4. Responsibility. The moral responsibility of the insured is an important factor in the case of a fire policy but such a responsibility of the insured (cargo-owner) does not exist in case of marine insurance.

Procedure of Talking Out Fire Insurance Policy

When an individual or businessman wants a fire insurance policy, the following is the procedure:

1. Selection of company. First of all, the person who wants to effect fire insurance should select the company or a broker with whom insurance is to be effected.

2. Proposal form. When the office from which a policy is to be purchased is decided upon, the next step is to fill in a proposal form which furnishes the basis of the contract. Maximum possible care should be taken in filling it up. The proposal form contains details like the name and address of the proposer, his business situation and construction of building, occupation of building, amount assured and other terms of the contract. The proposer can take different types of policies, i.e., specific policy, comprehensive policy, valued policy on floating policy. While indicating the value of the property or the goods, the insured should give the market value because the company takes into account the current make value of the subject-matter at the time of settling the claim. A little margin added to such value for likely appreciation in its market value.

3. Evidence of credibility. By purchasing a policy for setting fire to the property, the insured might get a large sum of temptation to "incendiarism". If the proposer is a well-known figure, then the risk is assumed without any enquiry but in case of new proposers or strangers of doubtful integrity, the company may ask the proposer to furnish some reasonable evidence of his creditability, honesty and integrity.

4. Survey of the property. The next step in fire insurance is a survey of the property proposed to be insured through qualified experts known as surveyors. These surveyors are deputed to inspect the property carefully and to estimate the degree of risk involved. It is on the basis of their report that the company accepts or rejects the proposal and quotes the rates of premiums.

5. Acceptance of the proposal forms. On the basis of the proposal form and the surveyor's report, the risk is considered by the company. If the company is satisfied with the report of the surveyor it accepts the proposal and intimates the proposer accordingly.

6. Commencement of risk. The usual practice of giving the acceptance by the insurer to the insured to demand the payment of premium. The risk will commence only when premium has been paid, unless the contract provides otherwise.

7. Cover note. The insurance company may accept the risk unconditionally or subject to certain conditions and may give a provisional protection to the assured through a document, known as cover note. It is in the nature of interim policy.

8. Policy. After that the company issues the fire insurance policy.

Renewal, Cancellation and Assignment of Fire Policy

As fire insurance policy is issued for a period of one year, if the insured wants to renew the policy he can do so within renewal period. Days of grace are 15 days usually to pay the premium for renewal of the policy. If fire breaks out during days of grace, the insurance company is liable to pay the loss. If the insured has no intention to renew the contract, insurer is not liable to pay the loss. While renewing the policy, the insured has to make a full disclosure of all material facts i.e., any change or increase or decrease in the risk. The insurer may revise the premium rates in case of such a change. The insured may increase the insured amount as well.

If a policy is not renewed, it is automatically cancelled. Even during the period of policy, either party can cancel the contract. The policy may be forfeited in following cases:

1. Non-payment of premiums.
2. Misleading or false description of risk i.e., violation of principal of good faith.
3. Intentional or willful burning of property.
4. Inability of furnish evidence of loss.
5. Transfer of property without insurer consent.
6. Alteration in property.

In English law a policy of fire insurance can be assigned only with the consent of the insurer. In India, a fire policy can be assigned like a chose-in-action under Transfer of Property Act, 1882. The assignment must be endorsed on the policy or by a separate deed of assignment. A notice to the insurer must be given of assignment by the insured. The consent of the insurer for assignment is not needed if it is due to "will" of the insured or by operation of law, e.g., death or insolvency of the insured.

The assigner is the transferor, assignee in the transferee and assignment means transfer of legal right or interest in the policy. Sections 49 and 135 of the Transfer of Property Act, 1982, deal with assignment of a fire policy and are given below:

"Where immovable property is transferred for consideration, and such property or any part thereof is at the date of the transfer insured against loss or damage by fire, the transferee, in case of such loss or damage may in the absence of a contract of the contrary, require any money which the transferor actually receives under the policy or so much thereof as may be necessary to be applied in reinstating the property."—Section 49

"Every assignee, by endorsement or other writing of a policy of marine insurance or of a policy of insurance against fire, in whom the property in the subject insured shall be absolutely vested at the date of assignment shall have transferred and vested in him all rights of suit as if the contract contained in the policy had been made with himself." —Section 135

More than One Fire Policy

It is no use of taking more than one fire policy.

When the same property suffers more than one fire, the insurer is bound to pay in all upto the insured sum stated in the policy. For example, a property valued at ₹ 10,00,000 is insured for ₹ 60,000. The insurer will pay the actual loss. Say if the fire causes loss ₹ 20,000 and second fire causes loss of ₹ 45,000. The insurer will pay first ₹ 20,000 and for second fire only ₹ 40,000. If insured wants to cover entire risk, he can reinstate the sum to the original amount by paying a fresh premium on a *pro rata* basis to the date of expiry.

In case of more than one policy, the **principle of contribution** applies. If a property is insured with A and then with B for ₹ 1,00,000. If loss is ₹ 40,000, A and B shall share it equally and in no case the insured can recover more than ₹ 40,000 from both. If A pays the entire amount of ₹ 40,000. We can recover from B the share which B has to pay of ₹ 20,000.

Types of Fire Policies

The main type of fire policies are four:

(1) Unvalued policy,

(2) Valued policy,

(3) Average policy, and

(4) Floating policy.

Besides there are subsidiary types of policies like, Reinstatement or Replacement Policy, Consequential Loss Policy, Comprehensive Policy, Declaration Policy, Excess Policy, Sprinkler Leakage Policy, Adjustable Policy, Maximum Value with Discount Policy, Blanket Policy, Rent Policy, Transit Policy and Policies on Buildings in course of erection. They are explained below:

1. Unvalued policy. A unvalued policy is that which insures risk not for a fixed amount. Under this policy, insurer will pay the actual loss or insured amount whichever is less. In this policy the value of the property has no relevance in arriving at the liability. Such policy is a case of UNDER INSURANCE and does not penalize the under insured except when there is a total loss.

2. Valued policy. In such policy, a fixed amount will be paid whatever may be the loss. This policy violates the principle of Indemnity and cannot be legally challenged. At the time of loss, market value of the property is not taken into account.

3. Average policy. A fire policy containing an average clause is called an average policy. An average policy requires the insurer to pay that proportion of actual loss as the insurance bears to the actual value of the property at the time of loss. This condition applies if the insured is UNDER INSURED.

Example. If the actual value of the property is ₹ 5,00,000 and is insured for ₹ 4,00,000 and actual loss is ₹ 1,00,000. The insured will get 4,00,000/5,00,000 × 1,00,000 = ₹ 80,000. The balance of ₹ 20,000 shall be born by himself. If the insured amount is equal to the value of the property more than that, the insured will get the entire loss of ₹ 1,00,000.

4. Floating policy. It is a policy that covers different types of goods lying in different places under one sum and for one premium e.g. An exporter or importer keeps goods in a warehouse from time to time and it is difficult for him to take a policy every time. An average rate of premium is fixed. If goods are insured under marine policy against fire, this policy becomes in-operative, he can recover loss only in marine insurance policy.

5. Reinstatement or replacement policy. Under this policy the property or plant, in the event of total destruction by fire, is replaced by similar type of property or plant. If they are damaged then the repair of the damaged property or plant is done.

6. Consequential loss policy or loss of profit policy. It is a policy that covers loss of profits due to temporary stoppage or suspension of business after the outbreak of fire. It also covers any expenses that are incurred during this period as well as necessary expenses incurred in minimizing the loss e.g., employing extra person to rewrite records or to hire a temporary accommodation.

7. Comprehensive policy. This policy gives many forms of cover in one single policy like fire, explosion, floods, riots, storm, strikes, burglary, labour disturbances, etc. This policy is different from 'Blanket' policy. Blanket policy covers several different properties (current and fixed assets) under one insurance located at different places, belonging to one person.

8. Erection all risk policy (EAR). In fire insurance, in modern times, EAR policy is issued. Under this policy two aspects are applied (a) "Minimum Computing Requirement" i.e., where sum assured exceeds ₹ 50 crores, the insured must maintain a fire engine, and (b) Additional fire protection requirements, e.g. in case of highly hazardous risks such as plastic Chemicals, Cotton, etc. risks are covered by one more warranty e.g. Flame Proof Electrical equipment.

Fire Policy Conditions

A condition is a stipulation essential to the main purpose of the contract the breach of which gives rise to treat the contract cancelled and claim damages. In an insurance contract such conditions and stipulations are of two types, (a) Implied conditions and (b) Express conditions.

Implied conditions. Such conditions may or may not be stated in the policy. They are implied by law even if not mentioned in the policy. These conditions are:

1. Existence of the subject matter at the time of insurance.
2. Identification of the subject matter according to the description given in the policy when claim arises.
3. Existence of the insurable interest both at the time of taking the policy and at the time of loss by fire.

4. The insured has observed the principle of good faith at all material times and in all material particulars. The above three implied conditions arise because of principle of indemnity and this one because of principle of *Uberrimae Fedei*.

Express Conditions

Such conditions are expressly indicated in writing in the policy, failing which the insured cannot be held guilty of non-compliance such conditions can be grouped under two headings:

(A) Relating to Principle of Good Faith

1. Misdescription. According to this condition the policy is voidable in case of misstatement or misrepresentation or misdescription, non-disclosure or concealment of any material fact by the insured. The fact is material fact that affects the estimating of risk of affects the judgement of the insurer, if disclosed.

2. Double insurance. The insured should disclose if he has insured or subsequently insured the same property, against same period and or same interest with other company. This is to apply the contribution clause amongst insurers.

3. Alterations and removals. The policy shall be avoided in respect of any item in regard to which there shall be an alteration by removal or where the risk of destruction or damage is increased or where the insured's interest ceases, except by will or by operation of law, e.g. if a property is unoccupied for a period of one month is alteration of circumstances.

4. Forfeiture. All benefits are forfeited if it is found that insured made a false declaration or guilty of fraud or damage is caused by willful act or in connivance with any other person.

(B) Relating to Payment of Premium

1. Fallen buildings. The insurance shall cease if building falls or is displaced except in case of earthquake or by fire itself. Such fall or displacement should either increase the risk of fire or is otherwise material.

2. Risks not covered. Fire Insurance does not cover certain risks like loss by theft during or after fire, burning of property by public authority or sub-terranean (underground) fire, or damage by natural heating or combustion or fermentation.

3. Perils excluded. The fire policy excludes certain perils, e.g., earthquake, typhoon, tornado, cyclone, etc. or war, invasion or act of enemy, civil commotion, material law, rebellion. They are abnormal conditions.

4. Risk not covered unless expressly included. Fire insurance can cover certain risk if the insurer wants by payment of extra premium, e.g., bullion, precious stones, drawings and designs, explosives, goods held in trust, securities stamps, paper money, etc.

5. Marine clause. This clause excludes from fire policy any indemnity for property which is also covered by marine policy.

Procedure in the Event of Loss

1. Occurrence of Fire. The insured should give a notice in writing to the insurance company on occurrence of fire. He should fire claim supported by required documents, e.g., certificate from fire brigade.

2. Arbitration. Any difference of opinion may be settled by arbitration clause is given in the policy.

3. Time limit. The insured should file the claim within the time limit given in the policy.

General

1. The receipt of premium must be signed by an officer or any agent duly authorised, with stamp of the company.
2. Any party can terminate the contract by giving a notice in writing.
3. The right of subrogation and contribution rests in the insurer after payment of loss.
4. Any salvage left after fire shall be the property of the insurer.

Insurance Claim and Settlement

In case of loss by fire, the insured has to notify immediately to the insured and should file the claim. The claim may be settled by the insurer by paying cash or may replace or repair the damaged property or may reinstate the property.

Following steps are taken to recover the claim procedure:

1. Notice. First the insured should give a written notice of loss to the insurer.

2. Evidence. The insured should produce a proof that loss by fire has occurred, e.g. certificate from fire brigade authority or police report in case of arson.

3. Form. The insured should fill the prescribed form given by the insurer along with documents asked for and attestations required.

4. Inspection. The insurer assessing staff, loss assures or loss surveyors, will inspect the loss and give their estimate of loss.

5. Under or double insurance. In case of under insurance, the insurer shall pay the loss by applying 'average clause', e.g., if insured value of a property is ₹ 20,000, it has been insured for ₹ 12,000 and loss is ₹ 10,000 then the payment will be

$$\frac{12,000}{20,000} \times 10,000 = ₹6000.$$

If the subject matter has been insured with two or more insurers, the contribution clause will apply. The insurer may recover the whole loss from one insurer and in that case that insurer will proportionately recover the share from other insurers. For example, if a building is insured with A for ₹ 10,000, B for ₹ 8000 and C for ₹ 2000 then each will share the loss in the ratio 50%, 40% and 10%. The insurer can recover the respective share from each insurer himself.

6. More than one fire. The actual loss will be paid, but in no case more than the insured value. If the property is insured for ₹ 30,000 (actual value) and there are three fires in one year and loss each time is ₹ 10,000, ₹ 8000 and ₹ 12,000. If it is insured for ₹ 10,000 then loss shall be paid as follows: First fire $\frac{10,000}{30,000} \times 10,000 =$ ₹ 3333; Second fire $\frac{10,000}{30,000} \times 8000 =$ ₹ 2666 and Third fire ₹ 4000 (not ₹ 5000) because total insured value is ₹ 10,000.

7. Rejection. The insurance company may reject the claim. Save times, ex-gratia payment is also made. If the books of account have been destroyed, then the basis is to take record of old account books for estimation, e.g. last year closing stock will be opening stock of the year, credit sales can be found out from creditors.

8. Payment. The insurer will pay the loss. Sometimes, "ex-gratia" payment is also made.

Rating and Credibility Theory

The word "rating" means the evaluation of the moral and other risks of an individual or organisation and thereby making of insurance rates. It is used for assessing the appropriate premium for different risks. Rating in fire insurance has developed into a highly technical and sophisticated process and is based on past experience by applying mathematical principles. The actual process of rating consists of three steps: (i) Classification, (ii) Discrimination and (iii) Rate-fixing.

Classification. The first stage in the rating process is classification which means rating group into which a particular risk is placed. This is based on the collective experience of all offices for a fairly long period. In India, risks of building construction are divided into three classes: (i) Class I Fire-proof or Pucca Construction, (ii) Class II Ordinary Construction and (iii) Class III Kutcha-pucca Construction.

Discrimination. Discrimination means the process of differentiation of the risk from each other according to their merits and demerits. The factors which affect the discrimination of various rates for individual risks in a particular class are: (i) Occupancy, (ii) Location of the property, (iii) Contraction, and (iv) Protection of building, etc.

Rate-fixing. The last step is to work out the actual rate of premium on the basis of the individual features (good-will) of the subject-matter of insurance. In order to make the result fairly representative, a sufficiently long period from as wide a field as possible should be taken, so that the experience of good as well as bad years may be taken into account. The total loss figures include all the expenses of management like staff salaries, cost of buildings, printing costs, a margin for reserves, commission and reasonable profits. This is represented by L (total loss) V stands for the total sum insured while R stands for average rate per cent.

Average Rate per cent: $R = \frac{L}{V} \times 100$

This method is called "Loss Ratio method".

Types of rate fixing. Rate fixing is of three broad types: (i) Judgement rating or individual rating: where each risk is rated on its own merits. (ii) Manual or class rating: it represents the sorting out of large group of similar risks, each risk of a particular class is charged the same rate. (iii) Merit rating: charging from different insured persons in the same manual classification varying rates. Merit rating consists of Schedule rating, experience rating or retrospective rating.

(a) Schedule rating. Various Physical elements of a risk are analysed. The system is based on the theory that the aggregate hazard of any risk is capable of ultimate analysis into component factors, e.g. each building is considered separately and a rate is established for it. Lower rate is given for features in form of on listing or schedule.

(b) Experience rating. It is based on an individual or specific company's record for a specific risk. The hazards effecting insured's operation are sufficiently within insured's control and can be reduced special efforts. Insurance permitted or lower rate of insurance for coming period. They are used in graph health workers compensation and auto insurance. Both (a) and (b) may be combined. In that case the rates are determined on the basis of tabulation of statistical data.

(c) Retrospective rating. That is permitting adjustments between maximum and minimum limits for the period just ended. The premium is determined by actual record of loss suffered by the insured during the year.

Credibility Theory

This theory is attached to experience rating formulas that were convex combinations (weighted average) of individual and class estimates of the individual risk premium. This theory covers more broadly linear estimation and prediction in latest variable needed. Mr. Whitney propounded this theory in 1918. The problem of assessing risk premium $\bar{m}$ is defined as the expected claim expenses from a portfolio of similar risks. The premium rate will be weighted average.

Formula $\bar{m} = z\hat{m} + (1 + z)\mu$

z = variable, $\hat{m}$ = observed mean claim amount per unit of risk exposed for the individual contract and μ is a corresponding overall mean in the insurance portfolio. Risk premium is a random variable. Today, it is a function m(–) of a random element Θ representing the unobservable characteristic of the individual risk. The random nature of Θ expresses the notion of heterogeneity. The individual risk is a random selection from a portfolio of similar but not identified risks and the distribution Θ describes the variation of individual risk characteristic across the portfolio.

Thus, credibility theory is a method by which the premium charged by an insurance company from a policyholder (or a group of policyholders) can be adjusted, given the new information on the policyholder's experience.

Example. A insures his house against fire. How does the insurance company will work out appropriate premium? The company does not have information about A as well his house. The best way for company is to assume that A is an average policyholder and the house is an 'average' house and charge A the premium suitable for an average building.

Suppose A has not made any claim for last five years. Does it mean that A is a better risk for the insurance company and charge a lower premium or A is an exception of randomness. Creditability theory allows the insurance company to assign a "Credibility Factor" on A's past experience so that A's past experience plays a role in calculating the future premium (or credibility premium), $\bar{m}$ and μ are premium estimates from two sources, one policyholder's past experience and the premium for whole group of policyholders respectively. Z is the credibility factor of $\bar{m}$. The actual calculation of credibility premium depends on the type of information available. Z = 1 denotes a fully credible group where the current experience is regarded as self-sufficient for rating purposes, z = 0 shows a group where the current experience is too small to be useful for rating purposes.

Rate making of combined risks. When the risks of various classes are combined and the insured wishes to have a joint insurance policy of such risks of more than one class, the rate-makers apply two methods: (i) they charge the highest rate of premium, which includes all the lower rates, (ii) all the rates are combined together and the actual rate is fixed somewhere between the highest rate and the combined rate.

Under-insurance and its effects on rating. When the insured effects under-insurance, the rates of premiums have to be increased. Thus, the person who have taken insurance not for full value are penalised in the form of higher premiums.

Also, the insured in case of loss will loss by way of under-insurance because they get proportionately under-payment from the insurer to the extent of under-insurance.

Average Clause

In fire insurance, the word "average" refers to a practice used to combat under-insurance. The term is used to meet *pro rata* distribution, i.e., in the event of loss the insurer shall be liable for not more than that proportion of the loss which the amount of the insurance-under the policy bears to a specified percentage of the actual cash value of the property insured. Generally, there are three types of averages: (i) The *pro rata* condition of average: the insured is penalized exactly proportionately to the degree of under insurance that exists. (ii) The special condition of average: under-insurance is not penalized unless the sum insured represents less than 75 per cent of the value at risk. (iii) The two conditions of average: the first condition is the normal *pro rata* condition of average and the second condition is an exclusion of property more specifically insured, except to the extent that the other insurance may be inadequate.

Co-insurance clause. The clause is extensively used in the USA whereby the property owner is to carry insurance upto an amount determined in accordance with the provisions of the policy. This is usually a stated percentage of the value of the property, in return for which he pays a lower premium.

Rates of Premium in India. The rates of premium for different classes of constructions differ from region to region, area to area and the nature of the goods stored in the buildings. Hazardous goods are not generally accepted by the insurance company, except on a very high premium rates. The entire work of framing and enforcing tariff rules, regulations and rates and other terms and conditions has been entrusted to Tariff Advisory Committee, which is a body corporate having perpetual succession and a common seal.

Reinsurance

Reinsurance means taking out another insurance policy again by the insurance company of the risk already insured by it. Thus, the risk of loss spread and a disproportionately large loss under a single policy does not fall on one company. The main purpose of effecting reinsurance is exactly the same as that of the original contract of insurance, viz. the risk to be borne is greater than the insurer wishes to retain.

Types of Reinsurance

Reinsurance may be effected by three methods: (i) Facultative Reinsurance, (ii) Treaty Reinsurance, and (iii) Reinsurance Pools.

Facultative reinsurance. It means optional i.e., accept or decline. It is the oldest method of reinsurance and involves the consideration of each risk separately. The insurer has to make specific enquiry from the reinsurer, who may accept the offer, decline it or require further clarification. If the reinsurer is obliged accept, facultative obligatory reinsurance.

Treaty reinsurance. It is a formal, legally binding agreement between the principal and the reinsurer that the reinsurer shall accept without the option of rejecting, a specified proportion of the excess on any risk over the insurer's limit of retention. There are three kinds of treaty insurance: (a) Quota share treaty, (b) Surplus treaty, (c) Excess of loss treaty or non-proportional. The insurer retains some portion and balance to be transferred to reinsurance. It is in non-proportional basis. In blind treaty details of each risk that is reinsured in not given.

Reinsurance pools. A group of insurance companies that have joined together for the purpose of sharing certain risks on an agreed upon basis.

Advantages of Reinsurance

1. Spreads the risks. It continues the basic principle of insurance by spreading the risk over an even wider field, which reduces the impact of loss on any one person. It further helps in stabilising the incomes of insurance companies and provides facilities to gain experience in the incidence of loss and to find a common basis for rating the risks.

2. Protects the insurance funds. It protects the insurance funds of the original insurer and gives additional security to the policyholders and insuring community.

3. Limits the liability. Reinsurance enables the insurers to undertake risks and to spread them. It, therefore, helps in limiting the liability of the insurer to the maximum amount.

4. Encourage new enterprises. Reinsurance is of particular importance to the new underwriters who in their early period of development, have limited retentive capacity. In the absence of reinsurance facility, the tremendous growth of new enterprises is doubtful.

5. Reduction in profit fluctuations. The reinsurance plans reduce, to a considerable extend, the violent fluctuations in the profits of the companies. If, on the other hand, heavy risks are retained by the original insurer, his profits are greatly upset due to a heavy single loss.

6. Minimum dealings. Due to the reinsurance schemes, the insured is required to indulge in the minimum dealings with only one insurer. Without reinsurance facility, the insurer would have to contact several insurers to enter into various individual insurance agreement on the same property. This involves considerable cost, loss of precious time and slows down the pace of protection cover.

7. Brings stability. Reinsurance facilities are helpful in bringing the stability in the insurance market. These facilities also bring stability in the value of the shares of such companies on the stock exchange.

8. Prevents rate cutting. Finally, the reinsurance prevents the rate cutting and acceptance of undesirable risks to a great extent. This is obviously because the actions of the rare fixing office are always subject to audit and scrutiny and thorough examination by the guaranteeing office for its satisfaction. This leads to check various unhealthy and undesirable practices and promotes a healthy spirit of competition amongst the insurers.

Problems

1. A, the owner, insured his house against fire. He sold the house to B, but did not assign the policy to B. The house is damaged by fire. Can B recover the loss from the insurer?

Ans. No, because the policy has not been assigned either endorsement or by a separate instrument to B. See Section 135 of Transfer of Property Act in the text.

2. An exporter has kept his cargo in a warehouse on rent. The cargo is insured. The cargo is burnt. The exporter recovers the loss from the insurer as well as from warehouse-keeper. What can insurer do?

Or

A seller of a house told to a purchaser that the house was insured against fire. There was not mention of the insurance in the agreement. After a week the house was damaged by fire and the seller received the loss from the insurer. Later, the sale deed was completed without deducting the amount of loss received from the purchase price, what can insurer do?

Ans. According to the principle of subrogation the insurer can recover the amount paid from the exporter/seller of house. The cannot make profit of their loss. The facts of this problem are similar to the case of *Castellan* vs. *Preston*.

3. A travel bus company insured a truck against fire. In the proposal form the address at which the truck was to be parked usually was given unknowingly wrong. The clause of the policy read that proposal form will be the basis of contract. The truck is destroyed by fire. Is the insurer liable?

Ans. No, because the insured did not observe the principle of good faith.

4. A theft is committed during the confusion, following outbreak of fire. Is the insurer liable for loss by theft?

Ans. Yes, if the loss by theft was a loss proximately caused by fire.

5. A took a fire policy on his goods. The wife of A, during quarrel with A set fire to the goods. Can A recover the loss from the insurer?

Ans. Yes, because the proximate cause of loss was fire, irrespective who caused the loss.

Or

A insured his house against fire R. While smoking a cigarette, A fell asleep and the house was on fire. A escaped unhurt. Can A claim the loss?

Ans. Yes. The loss was not caused intentionally.

6. X insured his house against fire. During insanity X killed his wife, injured his son and set fire to the house. Late X died in the fire. Can the son, the survivor, recover the loss from the insurer?

Ans. Yes, because X did not cause fire knowingly, but during insanity.

7. A bus was insured against fire, but not against collision. There broke a fire due to short circuit in electric wire. The driver, while to put it out lost control of bus. As a result, the bus collided with a tree and the fire spread which destroyed the entire bus. The loss due to fire was estimated to be ₹ 20,000 and due to collision ₹ 5,00,000. The bus was insured for ₹ 6,00,000. How much the insurer will pay?

Ans. Full loss. The loss due to collision was direct result of fire.

8. In case of *Harris* vs. *Poland*, the Plaintiff has put her jewellery, jewellery in her furnace ground. She forgot after it. Once she lit the fire and jewellery was damaged. She claimed the loss under fire policy. Can she recover the loss?

Ans. Yes, because there is negligence but it is not willful and deliberate.

9. While trying to mitigate the loss by fire, an insured threw his furniture from the window down outside. The furniture was broke. Can he cover the loss of furniture?

Ans. Yes, because the furniture loss is consequential loss by fire.

10. Three buildings A, B, and C were insured against fire. Fire broke out in building A, which spread and destroyed building B and C. Can insures of building B and C recover from insure of building A or each will pay separately?

11. A owned 90% shares of a private company dealing in timber. He insured the timber in his own name belonging the loss on ground of substantial creditor and shareholder of the company. Can he succeed?

Ans. No, he has no insurable interest as he is neither the owner nor the possessor of the subject matter.

12. A insured his shop merchandise against fire. For ₹ 16,000 worth ₹ 20,000. The fire damaged the merchandise worth ₹ 10,000. How much he can recover if there is an average clause or no average clause? Will it make any difference if he insures the goods for ₹ 25,000?

Ans. (a) $\frac{16,000}{20,000} \times 10,000$ = ₹ 8000.

(b) If there is not average clause, then he recover ₹ 10,000.

(c) He can recover the loss upto ₹ 20,000 or the actual loss, whichever is less.

13. A residential house was insured against fire. But later par of it was given on rent for commercial purposes. Insurance coy was not informed claim rejected.

14. Insured took a fire and special peril policy for stock in shop. Flood water damage the goods and government authorities reduced to destroyed damaged stock due to foul smell which was hazard for health. The surveyor reported these was no stock found damaged. He arrived after government order held to pay claim.

12

Marine Insurance

Introduction

Marine insurance is the oldest form of insurance. It developed alongside trade and commerce during transportation on high seas, rivers and canals. Thus it is divided into two branches—(a) Ocean marine insurance and (b) Inland marine insurance.

It started in Italy, Spain, Belgium and came to England in 15th century. In 1774, an association of insurers emerged, called Lloyd's association. It started where merchants and mariners used to meet at Lloyds coffee house to narrate their adventures.

The subject matter of marine insurance these days are three: (1) Hull or ship, (2) Cargo or goods, and (3) Freight. The procedure to take out a marine policy is simple. After selecting an insurance company (underwriter), through an agent, a marine declaration form is filled. The insurer assess the risk and on payment of premium, a Cover Note is issued. After formalities are compiled with the company the policy is issued.

Upto 1963, in India, British Marine Insurance Act, 1906 applied and the usual form of policy issued was based on issued by Lloyds. The Indian Navy and Indian Shipping have undergone considerable expansion since independence. The insurance contracts in India also became subject to Indian Contract Act, 1872. The insurance policy form used in India was the English form based on mercantile customs and business conventions. The practice appears to be in conflict with the Indian Contract Act, 1872. The result was that courts have to put their own interpretations. There was obviously unsatisfactory position. For smooth development of Indian Marine Insurance the Marine Insurance Act, 1963 was enacted consistent with Indian conditions.

The Marine Insurance Act, 1963 contains 92 Sections (Section 92 repealed) and one schedule (Form of policy).

Marine Insurance and Fire Insurance Compared

1. Transferability. A marine policy can be freely transferred. A fire policy cannot be transferred without the consent of the insurance company.

2. Insurable Interest. In marine insurance insurable interest must exist at the time of loss. In fire insurance it must exist both at the time when insurance contract is made and at the time of loss.

3. Period. A fire insurance is for one year only. A marine insurance may for a shorter period (time policy) or for a destination (voyage policy).

4. Form. A marine insurance policy has a standard form as given in the Marine Insurance Act, 1963. A form of fire insurance policy is not given in any law.

Definitions

1. "freight" includes the profit derivable by a ship-owner from the employment of his ship to carry his own goods or other movables as well as freight payable by a third party, but does not include passage money; 2(b).

2. "insurable property" means any ship, goods or other movables which are exposed to maritime perils; 2(c).

Marine insurance policy covers perils of the sea but perils contemplated do not include ordinary action of winds and waves.

3. "marine adventure" includes any adventure where:

(i) Any insurable property is exposed to maritime perils;

(ii) The earnings or acquisition of any freight, passage money, commission, profits or other pecuniary benefit, or the security for any advances, loans, or disbursement is endangered by the exposure of insurable property to maritime perils;

(iii) Any liability to a third party may be incurred by the owner of or other person interested in or responsible for, insurable property by reason of maritime perils;

In a contract of marine insurance, non-delivery of goods not due to maritime perils and no marine adventure took place, Insurance company is not liable for non-delivery of goods.

4. "maritime perils" means the perils consequent on, or incidental to, the navigation of the sea, that is to say, perils of the sea, fire, was perils, pirates, rovers, thieves, captures, seizures, restraints and detainments of princes and people, jettisons, barratry and any other perils which are either of the like kind or may be designated by the policy; 2(e).

Barratry includes every wrongful act willfully committed by the masters or crew of a ship to the prejudice of the owner or, as the case may be, the charterer; jettison is the throwing overbroad of goods from necessity to lighten the vessel in a storm, or to prevent capture or any other sufficient cause. It is the simplest and oldest instance of general average.

The burden to proof that loss of cargo was due to perils of the sea lies on the consignor.

5. "movables" means any movable tangible property, other than the ship, and includes money, valuable securities and other documents; 2(f).

6. "ship" includes every description of vessel used in navigation; 2(h).

7. Marine Insurance Contract. A contract of marine insurance is an agreement whereby the insurer undertakes to indemnify the assured, in the manner and to the extent thereby agreed, against marine losses, that it to say, the losses incidental to marine adventure (Section 3).

The losses against which a merchant or shipowner is not protected by insurance in England in the usual form are: (i) Acts of the Government; (ii) Breaches of revenue law; (iii) Breaches of the law of nations; (iv) Consequences of deviation; (v) All loss arising from unseaworthiness;

(vi) All loss arising out of unusual protraction of the voyage; (vii) All loss to which the shipowner is liable when he does damages to others; (viii) Average clause.

The Marine Insurance Policy merely denotes the time during which the policy would remain in force and the expression. "Warehouse to warehouse" in policy merely indicates the period during which the policy would remain in force and has nothing to do about the type of the risk policy covered.

Mixed sea and land risks. A contract of marine insurance may, by its express terms, or by usage of trade, be extended so as to protect the assured against losses on inland waters or on any land risk which may be incidental to any sea voyage.

Where a ship in course of building or the launch of a ship, or any adventure analogous to a marine adventure, is covered by a policy in the form of a marine policy, the provision of the Act, in so far as applicable, shall apply thereto, but, except as by this section provided, nothing in the Act shall alter or affect any rule of law applicable to any contract of insurance other than a contract of marine insurance as by the Act defined.

Explanation. An adventure analogous to a marine adventure includes an adventure where any ship, goods or other movables are exposed to perils incidental to local or inland transit (Section 4). Transit by land can be a subject-matter of marine insurance. A contract of marine insurance under the Act may cover mixed sea and land risks.

Insurance Company undertaking to carry the goods to the places of destination by railway, motor and lorry, etc., covering various risks including non-delivery, intended to do marine insurance business within the meaning of Section 2(13-A) of the Insurance Act, 1938 and so the policies must be regarded as marine insurance policies and so they must be governed by the provisions of Section 135-A of the Transfer of Property Act. Marine insurance business under Section 2(13-A) of Insurance Act, 1938 means "the business of effecting contracts of insurance upon vessels of any description, including cargoes, freights and other interests which may be legally be insured, or in relation to such vessels cargoes and freights, goods, wares, merchandise and property of whatever description insured for any transit by land or water or both and whether or not including warehouse risks or similar risks in addition or as incidental to such transit and includes any other risks customarily included among the risks insured against in marine insurance policies."

Principles of Marine Insurance

The general principles of insurance also apply to Marine Insurance. They are:

1. Principle of Insurable Interest
2. Principle of Good faith
3. Principle of Indemnity

We shall discuss them one by one.

Insurable Interest

Avoidance of wagering contracts. Every contract of marine insurance by way of wagering is void.

A contract of marine insurance is deemed to be wagering contract:

(a) Where the assumed has not an insurable interest as defined by the Act and the contract is entered into with no expectation of acquiring such an interest; or

(b) Where the policy is made "interest or no interest", or "without further proof of interest than the policy itself", or "without benefit of salvage to the insurer", or subject to any other like term. The Act prohibits what are called "P.P.I." (Policy Proof of Interest) policies.

However, where there is no possibility of salvage, a policy may be effected without benefit of salvage to the insurer (Section 6).

Insurable interest defined. Every person is deemed to have insurable interest who is interested in a marine adventure.

In particular a person is interested in a marine adventure where he stands in any legal or equitable relation to the adventure or to any insurable property at risk therein, in consequence of which he may benefit by the safety or due arrival of insurable property, or may be prejudiced by its loss, or by damage thereto, or by the detention thereof, or may incur liability in respect thereof (Section 7).

A person who has not obtained the possession of the bills of lading by endorsement thereon and who has not paid for the goods cannot be said to have got insurable interest in the goods. Thus, cargo owner, shipping company shipowner and lender of money or ship or cargo have insurable interest.

When interest attach, i.e., must be present. The assured must be interested in the subject-matter insured at the time of the loss, though he need not be interested when the insurance is effected:

Provided that, where the subject-matter is insured "lost or not lost", the assured may recover although he may not have acquired his interest until after the loss, unless at the time of effecting the contract of insurance the assured was aware of the loss, and the insurer was not.

Where the assured has no interest at the time of the loss, he cannot acquire interest by any act or election after he is aware of the loss (Section 8). A policy known as "Warehouse to Warehouse Policy" covers all risks commencing from the point of time when the goods leave the warehouse of the exporter until the point of time when it reaches the warehouse of the assured. If the policy covers all risks, the enumeration of the various risk thereafter would be mere illustrative and not exhaustive. Where one of the perils insured against was "rust" and rusting took place after the goods left the warehouse of the exporter but before it reached the warehouse of the assured, the insurance company was held liable.

Defeasible or contingent interest. A defeasible interest is insurable, and also a contingent interest.

In particular, where the buyer of goods has insured them, he has an insurable interest, notwithstanding that he might, at his election, have rejected the goods, or have treated them as at the seller's risk, by reason of the latter's delay in making delivery or otherwise.

A. **Partial interest.** A partial interest of any nature is insurable (Section 10).

B. **Reinsurance.** The insurer under a contract of marine insurance has an insurable interest in his risk, and may reinsure in respect of it.

Unless the policy otherwise provides, the original assured has not right or interest in respect of such reinsurance (Section 11).

C. **Bottomry.** The lender of money on bottomry or respondentia has an insurable interest in respect of the loan [Section 12(1)]. Bottomry is a species of mortgage or hypothecation of a ship by which her keel or boom is pledged, while respondentia means the hypothecation of cargo or goods on board a ship as security, for the repayment of a loan. The term respondentia is now seldom used and the expression 'bottomry' is generally employed whether the vessel or the cargo or both be the security.

D. **Master's and seamen's wages.** The master or any member of the crew of a ship has an insurable interest in respect of this wages (Section 13).

E. **Advance freight.** In the case of advance freight, the person advancing the freight has an insurable interest, in so far as such freight is not repayable in case of loss (Section 14). Where a bill of lading states that freight has been prepaid by the consignee and the assured does not show that he had supplied the consignor with the necessary amount of money to advance the freight, it is the consignor who would have insurable interest within Section 14.

F. **Charges of insurance.** The assured has an insurable interest in the charges of any insurance which he may affect (Section 15).

G. **Quantum of interest.** Where the subject-matter insured is mortgaged, the mortgagor has an insurable interest in the full value thereof, and the mortgage has an insurable interest in respect of any sum due or to become due under the mortgage.

A mortgage, consignee, or other person having an interest in the subject-matter insured may insure on behalf and for the benefit of other persons interested as well as for his own benefit.

The owner of insurable property has an insurable interest in respect of the full value thereof, notwithstanding that some third person may have value agreed, or be liable to indemnify him in case of loss (Section 16). An ensured is not required to prove absolute ownership of the goods in order to satisfy the test of having an insurable interest. When it was established that the assured was a consignee of the goods in question, he had an insurable interest in the goods by virtue of Section 16(2).

Assignment of interest. Where the assured assigns or otherwise parts with his interest in the subject-matter insured, he does not thereby transfer to the assignee his rights under the contract of insurance, unless there be an express or implied agreement with the assignee to that effect.

But the provisions of this section do not affect transmission of interest by operation of law (Section 17).

Insurable Value

Measure of insurable value. Subject to any express provision or valuation in the policy, the insurable value of the subject-matter insured must be ascertained as follows:

1. In insurance on ship, the insurable value is the value, at the commencement of the risk, of the ship, including her outfit provisions, and stores for the officer and crew, money advanced for seamen's wages, and other disbursements if any incurred to make the ship fit for the voyage or adventure contemplated by the policy, plus the charges of insurance upon the while,

The insurable value, in the case of a steamship, includes also the machinery, boilers, and coals and engine stores if owned by the assured; in the case of a ship driven by power other than steam includes also the machinery and fuels and engine stores, if owned by the assured; and in the case of a ship engaged in a special trade, includes also the ordinary fittings requisite for that trade;

2. In insurance on freight, whether paid in advance or otherwise, the insurable value is the gross amount of the freight at the risk of the assured, plus the charges of insurance;
3. In insurance on goods or merchandise, the insurable value is the prime cost of the property insured, plus the expenses of and incidental to shipping and the charges of insurance upon the whole;
4. In insurance on any other subject-matter, the insurable value is the mount at the risk of the assured when the policy attaches, plus the charges of insurance (Section 18).

Disclosure and Representations

Contract of good faith (Uberrimae Fidei). A contract of marine insurance is as contract based upon the utmost good faith, and if the utmost good faith be not observed by either party, the contract may be avoided by the other party (Section 19). A contract is said to be *uberrimae fidei* when the promise is bound to communicate to the promisor every fact or circumstance which may influence him in deciding whether to enter into the contract or not. Such contracts are those entered into between persons of a particular relationship, as guardian and ward, solicitor and client, insurer and insured.

Disclosure by assured. Subject to the provisions of the section, the assured must disclose to the insurer, before the contract is concluded, every material circumstance which, is known to the assured, and the assured is deemed to know every circumstance which, in the ordinary course of business, ought to be known to him. If the assured fails to make such disclosure, the insurer may avoid the contract.

Every circumstance is material which would influence the judgement of a product insurer in fixing the premium, or determining whether he will take the risk.

In the absence of inquiry the following circumstances need not be disclosed namely:

(a) Any circumstance which diminishes the risk;

(b) Any circumstance which is known or presume to be known to the insurer. The insurer is presumed to known matters of common notoriety or knowledge, and matters which an insurer in the ordinary course of his business as such ought to know;

(c) Any circumstance as to which information is waived by the insurer;

(d) Any circumstance which it is superfluous to disclose by reason of any express or implied warranty.

Whether any particular circumstance, which is not disclosed, be material or not, is, in each case, a question of fact.

The term "circumstance" includes any communication made to, or information received by, the assured (Section 20). Non-disclosure is an offence of suppression or be untrue, then it is not a case of omission or *suppress-omission* to do something. If what is stated turns out to vision of anything.

Disclosure by agent effecting insurance. Subject to the provisions of the preceding section as to circumstances which need not be disclosed, where an insurance is effected for the assured by an agent, the agent must disclose to the insurer:

(a) Every material circumstance which is known to himself, an agent to insure is deemed to know every circumstance which in the ordinary course of business ought to be known by, or to have been communicated to, him; and

(b) Every material circumstance which the assured is bound to disclose, unless it comes to his knowledge too late to communicate it to the agent (Section 21).

Representations pending negotiation of contract. Every material representation made by the assured or his agent to the insurer during the negotiations for the contract, and before the contract is concluded, must be true. If it be untrue the insurer may avoid the contract.

A representation is material which would influence the judgement of a prudent insurer in fixing the premium, or determining whether he will take the risk.

A representation may be either as to a matter of fact, or as to a matter of expectation or belief.

A representation as to a matter of fact is true, if it be substantially correct, that is to say, if the difference between what is represented and what is actually correct would not be considered material by a prudent insurer.

A representation as to a matter of expectation or belief is true it if be made in good faith.

A representation may be withdrawn or corrected before the contract is concluded.

Whether a particular representation be material or not, is, in each case, a question of fact (Section 22).

When contact is deemed to be concluded. There is no specific proposal form specified for marine insurance. A contract of marine insurance is deemed to be concluded when the proposal of the assured is accepted by the insurer, whether the policy be then issued or not; and for the purpose of showing when the proposal was accepted, reference may be made to the slip, covering note or other customary memorandum of the contract, although it be unstamped (Section 23). Proposal form in marine insurance is not mandatory.

There was concluded contract regarding monsoon coverage between the plaintiff-owner of fishing boat and the Insurance Company on the very fact that the premium amount was accepted with the endorsement of monsoon coverage policy for one month.

Where in a suit for recovery of sum as compensation for loss of the cargo dispatched by ship the plaintiff was neither the holder of the bills of lading nor was liable to pay the value of goods to the seller, it cannot be said that the plaintiff had suffered any loss or damages by virtue of the loss of the goods covered by the bills of lading.

The Policy

Contract must be embodied in policy. A contract of marine insurance shall not be admitted in evidence unless it is embodied in a marine policy in accordance with this Act. The policy may be executed and issued either at the time when the contract is concluded, or after words (Section 24). A Liberian Corporation, whose business was carried on from Dubai insured their Small Cargo vessel against war and marine risks under a policy issued by the Kuwaiti Insurance

Company. The form of policy was based upon the Llyod's Standard from of marine policy with modifications but gave Kuwait as the place of issue and provided the claims to be payable there. There was no provision in the policy as to the law which was to govern the contract. The vessel was detained by Saudi Arabian authorities for an offence of attempting to smuggle oil and the master and the crew imprisoned for some months. Corporation claimed the total constructive loss of the vessel under the Institute War and Strike Clauses which formed part of the policy. Held that the proper law of contract was English Law since the provisions of the policy taken as a whole by necessary implication led to the inevitable conclusion that it was the parties intention that their mutual rights and obligations under it should be determined in accordance with the English Law of marine insurance.

What policy must specify. A marine policy must specify:

1. The name of the assured, or of some person who affects the insurance on his behalf;
2. The subject-matter insured and the risk insured against;
3. The voyage, or period of time, or both, as the case may be covered by the insurance;
4. The sum of sums insured;
5. The name or names of the insurer or insurers (Section 25).

Marine insurance policy. Added words in printed policy override printed words and express final intention of parties.

Where the insurance cover note was in the printed form of marine insurance but he contents thereof indicating that the goods were to be transported throughout by road and all details thereof had been mentioned in the said cover note, the provisions of the Act would not be applicable.

If shipowners insuring the fleet of vessels against loss of freight caused by perils of the sea under a time policy of marine insurance which incorporated the time Clause (cl. 8) of the Institute Times Clauses (Freight Time Charter clause exempting the insurers from liability in respect of any claim "consequent on loss of time" arising from a peril of the sea) during the currency of the policy, the vessels sustaining damage by peril of the Sea namely breakdown of machinery and stranding and had to be repaired. During the period of repairs the vessel was off-hire. Held that the loss of freight by shipowners during such period was consequent on loss of time within the meaning of time charter clause and shipowners' claim for lost hire was excluded from the cover of the policy by virtue of the time charter clause.

Signature of insurer. A marine policy must be signed by or on behalf of the insurer.

Where a policy is subscribed by or on behalf of two or more insurers, each subscription, unless the contrary be expressed, constitute a distinct contract with the assured (Section 26).

Types of Marine Policies

First note that marine cargo policies are freely assignable for which prior consent of insured is not necessary. Even a blank endorsement on the back of the policy is sufficient. As such marine policy is a negotiable instrument.

The policies are of following types:

1. Voyage Policy
2. Time Policy

3. Mixed Policy
4. Valued Policy
5. Open or Unvalued Policy
6. Floating Policy
7. Wagering or Honour Policy
8. Comprehensive/Composite Policy.

Voyage and time policies. Where the contract is of insure the subject-matter at and from, or from one place to another or others, the policy is called a "voyage policy", and where the contract is to insure the subject-matter for a definite period of time, the policy is called a "time policy". A contract for both voyage and time may be included in the same policy, called mixed policy. A time policy which is made for any time exceeding twelve months is invalid (Section 27). "Sea-worthiness warranty" does not apply in time policy.

WAREHOUSE TO WAREHOUSE POLICY i.e., from the exporter's warehouse till the importer's warehouse. It is a type of time policy.

Ship insured "at and from or for the period" from April 21, 1975 to April 20, 1976—Policy containing inter alia a warranty as follows: (a) trading within Persian Gulf but including one delivery from Singapore to Persian Gulf on its own steam sailing on or about April 21, 1975, (b) Panamanian load lien and maintained, (c) Subject to satisfactory condition survey by approved surveyors—Ship encountering rough weather between Singapore and Colombo where she had incurred extensive repairs at Colombo and subsequently left for Daman on Sept. 8, 1975 some 15 miles off the coast of Iran. The vessel ran aground and listed to portside and capsized—Total loss as a result of the perils of the sea not disputed. Held, that unseaworthiness will only be a defense available to underwriters if the ship was insured under a voyage policy and not a time policy and that the policy in the case was not a time policy simpliciter but was a **mixed policy** affording a cover of 12 months attaching as from and on the voyage from Singapore or Persian Gulf.

An open policy covering all the equipments and machines despatched from time to time during the period of coverage is not pure and simple time policy so as to attract provision of Section 27(2).

Designation and subject-matter. (a) The subject-matter insured must be designated in a marine policy with reasonable certainty.

(b) The nature and extent of the interest of the assured in the subject-matter insured need not be specified in the policy.

(c) Where the policy designates the subject-matter insured in general terms, it shall be construed to apply to the interest intended by the assured to be covered.

(d) In the application of this section regard shall be had to any usage regulating the designation of the subject-matter insured (Section 28).

Valued and unvalued policy. A policy may be either valued or unvalued (open policy).

A valued policy is a policy which specifies the agreed value of the subject-matter insured.

Subject to the provisions of the Act, and in the absence of fraud, the value fixed by the policy is, as between the insurer and assured, conclusive of the insurable value of the subject intended to be insured, whether the loss be total or partial.

Unless the policy otherwise provides, the value fixed by the policy is not conclusive for the purpose of determining whether there has been a constructive total loss (Section 29).

When there was no evidence showing that any fraud was practised by the complainant when the agreed value of boat was fixed at the time of entering into a contract of insurance, then it could not be said that the valuation as on the date of the contract was either more or less than the figure mentioned in the policy as the agreed value.

Unvalued policy. An unvalued policy is a policy which does not specify the value of the subject-matter insured, but subject to the limit of the sum insured, leaves the insurable value to be subsequently ascertained, in the manner herein before explained (Section 30).

Floating policy. A floating policy is a policy which describes the insurance in general terms, and leaves the name or names of the ship or ships and other particulars to be defined by subsequent declaration.

The subsequent declaration or declarations may be made by endorsement on the policy, or in other customary manner.

Unless the policy otherwise provides, the declarations must be made in the order of despatch or shipment. They must, in the case of goods, comprise all consignments within the terms of the policy, and the value of the goods or other property must be honestly stated, but an omission or erroneous declaration may be rectified even after loss or arrival, provided the omission or declaration was made in good faith.

Unless the policy otherwise provides, where a declaration of value is not made until after notice of loss or arrival, the policy must be treated as an unvalued policy as regards the subject-matter of that declaration (Section 31). This is a policy issued to cover all shipments of goods of the assured by any vessel between specified places. It is a policy generally issued to factors or warehouse-men to cover their limited interest in property of which they have charged.

Wagering policy. Such policy is not recognised by law, but by insurance companies. That is why they are called 'Honour Policy'. Such policies do not need insurable interest. "P.P.I", i.e., Policy Proof of Interest is one such policy.

Composite or collective policy. When two or more underwriters insure the same subject-matter a composite policy is issued. A comprehensive policy is a policy when two or more types of insurance are undertaken by insured, e.g. life with accident policy or Marine with fire policy. A composite insurance is not double insurance. The former is one by insurers, the latter by insured.

Construction of terms in policy. A policy may be in the form as given in the Schedule.

Subject to the provisions of the Act, and unless the context of the policy otherwise requires, the terms and expressions mentioned in the Schedule shall be construed as having the scope and meaning assigned to them in the Schedule (Section 32).

Premium to be arranged. Where an insurance is effected at a premium to be arranged, and no arrangement is made, a reasonable premium is payable. Where an insurance is effected on the terms that an additional premium is to be arranged in a given event, and that event happens but no arrangement is made, then a reasonable additional premium is payable (Section 33).

Rates of premium vary according to degree and exposure of loss or damage. Pure premium refers to premium that covers actual past loss or is insufficient to pay losses.

Where the insurance policies in respect of cargo coming into force the moment the cargo leaves the warehouse, extend up to the place of destination and there was no specific exclusion regarding jettisoning and the firms exporting the cargo had clearly established that after the boats left the wharf with the cargo to unload them into the ship and were waiting to do so, the weather conditions worsened resulting in the boat being tossed about and rendered leaky and that with a view to save the boats as well as the crew, jettisoning of the cargo had to be done in the manner spoken to by the light house supported by their reports as well as protest notes, the insurance company could not deny its liability in respect of jettisoned goods.

When the voyage from one place to another and other destinations was insured in respect of cargo of exporting firms and there was neither any change contemplated at any point of time in the destination nor was there any departure from the accustomed course of voyage, then no question of change of voyage or deviation arises merely because the boats carrying cargo returned from steamer back to shore without loading cargo into steamer and, therefore, the insurance company could not deny its liability for loss of goods in such voyage on ground that extra-premium had not been arranged for a change of voyage.

Double Insurance

Where two or more policies are effected by or on behalf of the assured on the same adventure and interest or any part thereof, and the sums insured exceed the indemnity allowed by this Act, the assured is said to be over-insured by double insurance.

Where the assured is over-insured by double insurance:

(a) The assured, unless the policy otherwise provides, may claim payment from the insurers in such order as he may think fit, provided that he is not entitled to receive any sum in excess of the indemnity allowed by the Act;

(b) Where the policy under which the assured claims is a valued policy, the assured must give credit as against the valuation, for any sum received by him under any other policy, without regard to the actual value of the subject matter-insured;

(c) Where the policy under which the assured claims is an unvalued policy he must give credit, as against the full insurable value, for any sum received by him under any other policy;

(d) Where the assured receives any sum in excess of the indemnity allowed by the Act, he is deemed to hold such sum in trust for the insurers, according to their of contribution among themselves (Section 34).

Warranties

Nature of Warranty. A warranty, means a promissory warranty, that is to say a warranty by which the assured undertakes that some particular thing shall or shall not be done, or that some condition shall be fulfilled, or whereby the affirms or negatives the existence of a particular state of facts.

A Warranty may be Express or Implied

A warranty, as above defined, is a condition which must be exactly complied with, whether it be material to the risk or not. If it be not so complied with, then, subject to any express provision in the policy the insurer is discharged from liability as from the date of the breach of warranty but without prejudice to any liability incurred by him before that date (Section 35).

Where suit for compensation against insurance company was filed by boat owner whose fishing boat was found to be missing in heavy rains without complying the warranty clause in the insurance policy, the boat owner would not be entitled to decree for compensation against insurance company.

When breach of warranty excused. Non-compliance with a warranty is excused when, by reason of a change of circumstances, the warranty ceases to be applicable to the circumstances of the contract, or when compliance with the warranty is rendered unlawful by any subsequent law.

Where a warranty is broken, the assured cannot avail himself of the defence that the breach has been remedied, and the warranty complied with before loss.

A breach of warranty may be waived by the insurer (Section 36).

Express warranties. An express warranty may be in any form of words from which the intention to warrant is to be inferred.

An express warranty must be included in, or written upon, the policy, or must be contained in some document incorporated by reference into the policy.

An express warranty does not exclude implied warranty, unless it be inconsistent therewith (Section 37).

Implied Warranties

1. Warranty of neutrality. Where insurable property, whether ship or goods, is expressly warranted neutral, there is an implied condition that the property shall have a neutral character at the commencement of the risk, and that so far as the assured can control the matter, its neutral character shall be preserved during the risk.

Where a ship is expressly warranted "neutral", there is also an implied condition that, so far as the assured can control the matter, she shall be properly documented, that is to say, that she shall carry the necessary papers to establish her neutrality, and that she shall not falsify or suppress her papers, or use simulated papers. If any loss occurs through breach of this condition, the insurer may avoid the contract (Section 38).

2. No implied warranty of nationality. There is no implied warranty as to the nationality of a ship, or that her nationality shall not be changed during the risk (Section 39).

3. Warranty of good safety. Where the subject-matter insured is warranted "well" or "in good safety" on a particular day, it is sufficient if it be safe at any time during that day (Section 40).

4. Warranty of seaworthiness of ship. In a voyage policy there is an implied warranty that at the commencement of the voyage the ship shall be seaworthy for the purpose of the particular adventure insured.

Where the policy attaches while the ship is in port, there is also an implied warranty that she shall, at the commencement of the risk, be reasonably fit to encounter the ordinary perils of the port.

Where the policy relates to a voyage which is performed in different stages, during which the ship requires different kinds of or further preparation or equipment, there is an implied warranty that at the commencement of each stage the ship is seaworthy in respect of such preparation or equipment for the purposes of that stage.

A ship deemed to be seaworthy when she is reasonably fit in all respects to encounter the ordinary perils of the seas of the adventure insured.

In a time policy there is not implied-warranty that the ship shall be seaworthy at any stage of the adventure, but where, with the privity of the assured, the ship is sent to sea in an unseaworthy state, the insurer is not liable for any loss attribute to unseaworthiness (Section 41).

5. No implied warranty that goods are seaworthy. In a policy on goods or other movable there is no implied warranty that the goods or movables are seaworthy.

In a voyage policy on goods or other movables there is an implied warranty that at the commencement of the voyage the ship is not only seaworthy as a ship, but also that she is reasonably fit to carry the goods or other movables to the destination contemplated by the policy (Section 42).

6. Warranty of legality. There is an implied warranty that the adventure insured is a lawful one, and that, so far as the assured can control the matter, the adventure shall be carried out in a lawful manner (Section 43). When in a insurance claim for loss of cargo there was neither any delay on the part of consignor nor the cargo in question had any inherent vice and the damage was caused to cargo because of abandonment by crew of the ship, then the insurance company would be liable to pay the amount of Insurance covered by the policy.

The Voyage

Implied conditions as to commencement of risk. Where the subject-matter is insured by a voyage policy "at the from" or "from" a particular place, it is not necessary that the ship should be at that place when the contract is concluded but there is an implied condition that the adventure shall be commenced the insurer may avoid the contract (Section 44).

The implied condition may be negatives by showing that the delay was caused by circumstances known to the insurer before the contract was concluded, or showing that he waived the condition.

Alteration of port of departure. Where the place of departure is specified by the policy, and the ship instead of sailing from that place sails from any other place, the risk does not attach (Section 45).

Sailing for different destination. Where the destination is specified in the policy, and the ship, instead of sailing for that destination, sails for any other destination, the risk does not attach (Section 46).

Change and Deviation of Voyage

Change means changing the destination. Deviation means change of route.

Change of voyage. Where, after the commencement of the risk, the destination of the ship is voluntarily changed from the destination contemplated by the policy, there is said to be a change of voyage.

Unless the policy otherwise provides, where there is a change of voyage, the insurer is discharged from liability as from the time of change, that is to say, as from the time when the determination to change it is manifested, and it is immaterial that the ship may not in fact have left the course of voyage contemplated by the policy when the loss occurs (Section 47).

Deviation. Where a ship, without lawful excuse, deviates from the voyage contemplated by the policy, the insured is discharged from liability as from the time of deviation, and it is immaterial that the ship may have regained her route before any loss occurs.

There is a deviation from the voyage contemplated by the policy:

(a) Where the course of the voyage is specifically designated by the policy, and that course is departed from; or

(b) Where the course of the voyage is not specifically designated by the policy, but the usual and customary course is departed from.

The intention to deviate is immaterial; there must be a deviation in fact to discharge the insurer from his liability under the contract (Section 48).

Several ports of discharge. Where several ports of discharge are specified by the policy, the ship may proceed to all or any of them, but, in the absence of any usage or sufficient cause to the contrary, she must proceed to them, or such of them as she goes to in the order designated by the policy. If she does not there is a deviation (Section 49).

Where the policy is to "ports of discharge", within a given area, which are not named, the ship must, in the absence of any usage or sufficient cause to the contrary, proceed to them, or such of them as she goes to, in their geographical order. If she does not there is a deviation.

Delay in voyage. In the case of a voyage policy, the adventure insured must be prosecuted throughout its course with reasonable despatch, and, if without lawful excuse it is not so prosecuted, the insurer is discharged from liability as from the time when the delay became unreasonable (Section 50).

Excuse for deviation or delay. Deviation or delay in prosecuting the voyage contemplated by the policy is excused:

(a) Where authorised by any special term in the policy; or

(b) Where caused by circumstances beyond the control of the master and his employer; or

(c) Where reasonably necessary in order to comply with an express or implied warranty; or

(d) Where reasonably necessary for the safety of the ship or subject-matter insured; or

(e) For the purpose of saving human life or aiding a ship in distress where human life be a danger; or

(f) Where reasonably necessary for the purpose of obtaining medical or surgical aid for any person on board the ship; or

(g) Where caused by the barratrous conduct of the matte or crew, if barratry be one of the perils insured against.

When the cause excusing the deviation or delay ceases to operate, the ship must resume her course, and prosecute her voyage, with reasonable dispatch (Section 51). When the voyage from one place to another and other destinations, was insured in respect of cargo of exporting firms and there was neither any change contemplated at any point of time in the destination nor was there any departure from the accustomed course of voyage, then no question of change of voyage or deviation arises merely because the boats carrying cargo returned from steamer back to shore without loading cargo into steamer and, therefore, the insurance company could not deny its liability for loss of goods in such voyage on ground that extra premium had not been arranged for a change of voyage.

Assignment of Policy

When and how policy is assignable. A marine policy may be transferred by assignment unless it contains terms expressly prohibiting assignment. It may be assigned either before or after loss.

Where a marine policy has been assigned so as to pass the beneficial interest in such policy, the assignee of the policy is entitled to sue thereon in his own name; and the defendant is entitled to make any defence arising out of the contract which he would have been entitled to make if the suit had been brought in the name of the person by or on behalf of whom the policy was effected.

A marine policy may be assigned by endorsement thereon or in other customary manner (Section 52).

Such a policy not being an incident to the property insured, the transfer of the property insured does not *per se* effect the transfer of a policy to the assignee.

Where the deed of subrogation gives the insurers nothing more than what they would have under sub-section (3) of Section 135-A of Transfer of Property Act, it cannot be held that there was any assignment of the subject-matter of insurance by the document, and would not entitle them to a file suit for damages in their own name.

Examples based on cases:

1. An assignee could not have sued in his own name unless such right was conferred on the assignee.

2. Goods were damaged in transit. Insurance company paying compensation to owner. The owner assigning right to claim damages from carrier in favour of insurance company. Held suit by company against carrier is maintainable.

3. Insured transferred to the insurer all its rights, title and interest in such of the goods as had not been delivered by the railways concerned. This does not effect an assignment of the insurance policies—Petitioner (insurer) not entitled to come under Section 135A(1) of T.P. Act.

4. Assignment of rights under policy of marine insurance—Suit for damages for wrongful non-delivery of certain goods entrusted to railway for carriage—Consigned goods comprised mica blocks and condenser films—At destination the delivery was found short by 17 mds 12 ch—This would be 'total loss of an apportionable part' however it may be case of partial loss with reference to the entire consignment—Payment by insurer to the insured person for the loss of goods—The insurer is subrogated to all rights and remedies of the insured person and in respect of that subject-matter as for the time of the casualty causing the loss. Held Insurance can file a suit in his own name.

5. In case of the goods which were sent by Sea and were covered by marine insurance policy wherein a 'Sure & Labour' Clause was mentioned but the insured persons were not indemnified and insurance wasn't subrogated to rights and remedies of assured and the insurer was not asking for assignment but insisting upon for filing claim against the carrier but where the suit regarding the recovery of damages has been filed by plaintiff and no damages were paid by insurer. Under circumstances it was held that it shows the conduct of the insurer. Under circumstances it was held that is shows the conduct of the insurance company that it was never willing to pay and get subrogated as required by law nor did it every offer to take assignment which would require payment of loss.

6. Where in a suit for recovery of amount under policy by Exporting firms the insurance policies were issued in favour of Marketing Federation and the Federation endorsing and transferring rights under policy in favour of Exporting firms, the suit would not be bad for non-joinder of Federation.

Assured who has no interest cannot assign. Where the assured has parted with or lost his interest in the subject-matter insured, and has not, before or at the time of so doing expressly or impliedly agreed to assign the policy, any subsequent assignment of the policy is inoperative:

Provided that nothing in this section affects the assignment of a policy after loss (Section 53).

The Premium

When premium payable. Unless otherwise agreed, the duty of the assured or his agent to pay the premium and the duty of the insurer to issue the policy to the assured or his agent, are concurrent conditions, and the insurer is not bound to issue the policy until payment or tender of the premium (Section 54).

Loss and abandonment

Included and excluded losses. 1. Subject to the provisions of the Act, and unless the policy otherwise provides, the insurer is liable for any loss proximately caused by a peril insured against, but, subject as aforesaid, he is not liable for any loss which is not proximately caused by a peril insured against.

2. In particular:

(a) The insurer is to liable for any loss attributable to the willful misconduct of the assured, but, unless the policy otherwise provides, he is liable for any loss proximately caused by a peril insured against, even though the loss would not have happened but for the misconduct or negligence of the master or crew;

(b) Unless the policy otherwise provides, the insurer on ship or goods is not liable for any loss proximately caused by delay, although the delay be caused by a peril insured against;

(c) Unless the policy otherwise provides, the insurer is not liable for ordinary wear and tear, ordinary leakage and breakage, inherent vice or nature of the subject-matter insured, or for any loss proximately caused by rats or vermin, or for any injury to machinery not proximately caused by maritime perils (Section 55).

Points to Note

Warehouse to Warehouse policy—Covers all risks commencing from the point of time when the goods leave the warehouse of the exporter until the point of time when it reaches the warehouse of the assured.

Where a ship insured against the perils of capture, seizure, detention in consequence of hostilities is captured by any enemy nation and condemned by the Prize Court of that nation, the insurers cannot avoid the responsibility to pay the agreed sum on the ground that there was no formal declaration of war by the capturing State or on the ground that the war and, hence, the condemnation were illegal when the insurers have not protected themselves from the consequence of an unlawful or an undeclared or an informal war and have not taken any of the pleas relating to the character of the war. A capture is an act of State and its legality cannot be questioned in an action for recovery of insured sum. The insurers are bounded by the terms and conditions of the policy.

Where even according to the plaintiffs assured, what happened was that the vessel was drifted out to the sea, perhaps, because of the break of the cable of the anchor, the plaintiffs could not sustain an action and would not entitled to recover the amount under the policy.

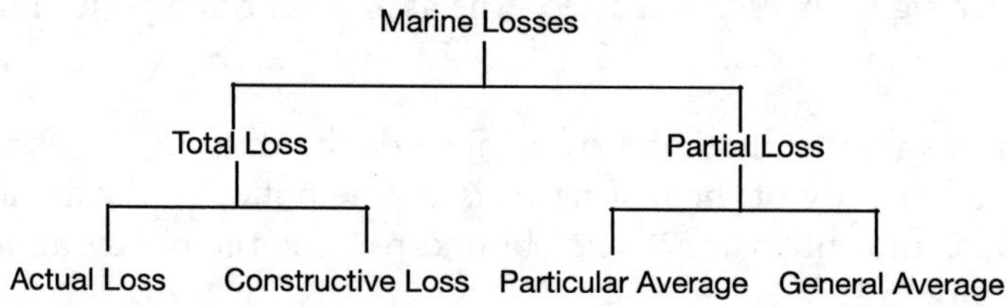

Partial and total loss. A loss may be either total or partial. Any loss other than a total loss, as hereinafter defined, is a partial loss.

A total loss may be either ran actual loss, or a constructive total loss.

Unless a different intention appears from the terms of the policy, an insurance against total loss includes a constructive, as well as an actual, total loss.

Where the assured brings a suit for a total loss and the evidence proves only a partial loss, he may, unless the policy otherwise provides, recover for a partial loss.

Where goods reach their destination in specie, but by reason of obliteration of marks, or otherwise, they are incapable of identification, the loss, if any, is partial and not total (Section 56).

(a) 'Loss' does not mean same things as 'loss' under Carriage of Goods by Sea Act (1924). Article 4, Cl. 2.

(b) "Total Loss"—No evidence that due to 'perils at sea' plaintiff was permanently deprived of his control over goods—No evidence that goods were of a perishable nature—No evidence that plaintiff had no means of recovering the goods by 'insuperable obstacles'—Goods cannot be considered as totally lost, or even constructively lost.

Actual total loss. Whether the subject-matter insured is destroyed, or so damaged as to cease to be a thing of the kind insured, or where the assured is irretrievably deprived thereof there is an actual total loss.

In the case of an actual total loss no notice of abandonment need be given (Section 57).

The loss which is produced by the direct efficient and predominating cause is the proximate cause of the loss in the law of Marine Insurance. Mere intrusion of a new cause is of no moment so long it does not wither away the efficiency of the direct, efficient and predominating cause. Merely because a cause has intervened, does not make it a nova cause superveniens.

The expression "covering total loss only" does not exclude loss of the entire cargo on account of jettisoning which was inevitable in the circumstances.

Where the insurance policies in respect of cargo coming into force the moment the cargo leaves the warehouse, extend up to the place of destination and there was no specific exclusion regarding jettisoning and the firms exporting the cargo had clearly established that after the boats left the wharf with the cargo to unload them into the ship and were waiting to do so, the weather conditions worsened resulting in the boats being tossed about and rendered leaky and that with a view to save the boats as well as the crew, jettisoning of the cargo had to be done in the manner spoken to by the tindels supported by their reports as well as protest notes, the insurance company could not deny if liability in respect of jettisoned goods.

Missing ship. Where the ship concerned in the adventure is missing, and after the lapse of a reasonable time no news of her has been received, an actual total loss may be presumed (Section 58).

Effect of transhipment, **etc.** Where, by a peril insured against, the voyage is interrupted at intermediate port or place, under such circumstances as, part from any special stipulation in the contract of affreightment to justify the master in landing and reshipping the goods or other movables, or in transhipping them, and sending them on to their destination, the liability of the insurer continues, notwithstanding the landing or transhipment (Section 59).

A contract made either by a charter party or a bill of lading by which a shipowner agrees to carry goods in his ship for reward. The person for whom the goods in his ship for reward. The person for whom the goods are carried is called the freighter and the sum paid by him for their carriage is called freight.

Constructive total loss defined. Subject to any express provision in the policy, there is a constructive total loss where the subject-matter insured is reasonably abandoned on account of its actual total loss appearing to be unavoidable, or because it could not be preserved from actual loss without an expenditure which would exceed its value when the expenditure had been incurred.

In particular, there is a constructive total loss:

(i) Where the assured is deprived of the possession of his ship or goods by a peril insured against, and

(a) It is unlikely that he can recover the ship or goods, as the case may be, or

(b) The cost of recovering the ship or goods, as the case may be, would exceed their value when recovered; or

(ii) In the case of damage to a ship, where she is so damaged by a peril insured against that the cost of repairing the damage would exceed the value of the ship when repaired.

In estimating the cost of repairs, no deduction is to be made in respect of general average contributions to those repairs payable by there interest, but account is to be taken of the expense of future salvage operations and of any future general average contributions to which the ship would be liable if required; or

(iii) In the case of damage to goods, where the cost of repairing the damage and forwarding the goods to their destination would exceed their value on arrival (Section 60).

(A) Abandonment is not defined in the Act. It means the relinquishment of and interest or claim. The Civil Law permitted a master who was sued for a slave's short to free himself from liability by abandoning the slave to the person injured.

(B) As capture of a ship followed by condemnation by the sentence of a Prize Court of competent jurisdiction extinguishes the title of the owner in the res, it amounts to actual loss to the owner. It is a judgement in *rem*. Seizure and capture followed by condemnation stand on the same footing and in both the cases the title in the res is vested in the capturing State. Where the res is restored to its former owner after condemnation it is a gift to him and a new title flows from the date of the grant.

(C) The words "their value on arrival" do not mean "their damaged value on arrival", but "their-conventional value as agreed by the parties".

(D) Vessel and cargo sustaining damage by perils of the sea—Claim that the cargo was a total constructive loss—Plaintiff failing to prove damage—Absence of detailed examination as to whether destination would exceed their value on arrival—No constructive total loss can be claimed.

Effect of constructive total loss. Where there is a constructive total loss the assured may either treat the loss as a partial loss, or abandon the subject-matter insured to the insured to the insurer and treat the loss as if it were an actual total loss (Section 61).

Insurance policy in respect of the transportation of a tractor—Policy covering total loss only—Tractor transported for loading on to a tongkang and while loading slipping into the river—Tractor subsequently salvaged and repaid—Assured claiming constructive total loss alleging that the cost of salvage and repairs exceeded the value of goods. Held that policy covered total loss and the assured having failed to prove a total constructive loss, the claim deserved dismissal.

Notice of abandonment. 1. Subject to the provisions of this section, where the assured elects to abandon the subject-matter insured to the insurer, he must give notice of abandonment. If he fails to do so the loss can only be treated as a partial loss.

2. Notice of abandonment may be given in writing, or by word of mouth, or partly in writing and partly by word of mouth, and may be given in any terms which indicate the intention of the assured to abandon his insured interest in the subject-matter insured unconditionally to the insurer.

3. Notice of abandonment must be given with reasonable diligence after the receipt of reliable information of the loss, but where the information is of a doubtful character the assured is entitled to a reasonable time to make enquiry.

4. Where notice of abandonment is properly given, the rights of the assured are not prejudiced by the fact that the insurer refuses to accept the abandonment.

5. The acceptance of an abandonment may be either express or implied from the conduct of the insurer. The mere silence of the insurer after notice is not an acceptance.

6. Where notice of abandonment is accepted the abandonment is irrevocable. The acceptance of the notice conclusively admits liability for the loss and the sufficiency of the notice.

7. Notice of abandonment is unnecessary where at the time when the assured receives information of the loss, there would be no possibility of benefit of the insurer if notices were given to him.

8. Notice of abandonment may be waived by the insurer.

9. When an insurer has reinsured his risk, no notice of abandonment need be given by him (Section 62).

Notice of abandonment, if conditional, is wholly invalid—Notice must be given in a reasonable time from the date of his knowledge of the actual state of affairs which entitles him to make such abandonment.

When in an insurance claim for loss of cargo there was neither any delay on the part of he consignor nor the cargo in question had any 'inherent vice' and the damage was caused to cargo because by abandonment by crew of the ship, then the insurance company would be liable to pay the amount of insurance covered by the policy.

Effect of abandonment. Where there is a valid abandonment the insurer is entitled to take over the interest of the assured in whatever may remain of the subject-matter, insured, and all proprietary rights incidental thereto.

Upon the abandonment of a ship, the insurer thereof is entitled to any freight in course of being earned, and which is earned by her subsequent to the casualty causing the loss, less the expenses of earning it incurred after the casualty; and, where the ship is carrying the owner's goods, the insurer is entitled to a reasonable remuneration for the carriage of them subsequent to the casualty causing the loss (Section 64).

Partial Losses

Particular average loss. A particular average loss is a partial loss of the subject-matter insured, caused by a peril insured against, and which is not a general average loss.

Expenses incurred by or on behalf of the assured for the safety or preservation of the subject-matter insured, other than general average and salvage charges, are called particular charges. Particularly charges are not included in particular average (Section 64).

Average is damage from perils of the sea. In the ordinary sense, average is where goods on board a ship, or part of the ship herself, are lost or damaged, general average is where any loss or damage in voluntarily or properly incurred in respect of the goods or of the ship or general safety of the ship and the cargo.

Average also denotes some petty charges, such as towage, beaconage, etc. which the owner or consignee of goods shipped on board a vessel is bound to reimburse to the master or shipowner.

Salvage is allowance or compensation made by maritime law to those by whose exertions ships or goods have been saved from the dangers of the seas, fires, pirates or enemies. The crew of a ship are not entitled to salvage or any unusual remuneration for extraordinary efforts they have made in saving her, it being duty as well as interest to contribute their utmost upon such occasions, the whole of their possible service being pledged to the master and owners.

Salvage charges. Subject to any express provision in the policy, salvage charges incurred in preventing a loss by perils insured against may be recovered as a loss by those perils.

"Salvage charges" means the charges recoverable under maritime law by a salvor independently of contract. They do not include the expenses of services in the nature of salvage rendered by the assured or his agents, or any person employed for hire by them, for the purpose of averting a peril insured against. Such expenses, where properly incurred, may be recovered as particular charges or as a general average loss, according to the circumstances under which they were incurred (Section 65).

General average loss. 1. A general average loss is a loss caused by or directly consequential on a general average act. It includes a general average expenditure as well as a general average sacrifice.

2. There is a general average act where any extraordinary sacrifice or expenditure is voluntarily and reasonably made or incurred in time of peril for the purpose of preserving the property imperiled in the common adventure.

3. Where there is a general average loss, the party on whom it falls is entitled, subject to the conditions imposed by maritime law, to a rateable contribution from the other parties interested, and such contribution is called a general average contribution.

4. Subject to any express provision in the policy, where the assured has incurred a general average or expenditure, he may recover from the insurer in respect of the proportion of the loss which falls upon him; and in the case of a general average sacrifice, he may recover from the insurer in respect of the whole loss without having enforced his right of contribution from the other parties liable to contribute.

5. Subject to any express provision in the policy, where the assured has paid, or is liable to pay, a general average contribution in respect of the interest insured, he may recover therefore from the insurer.

6. In the absence of express stipulation, the insurer is not liable for any general average loss or contribution where the loss was not incurred for the purpose of avoiding, or in connection with the avoidance of a peril insured against.

7. Where ship, freight, and cargo, or any two of those interests, are owned by the same assured, the liability of the insurer in respect of general average losses or contributions is to be determined as if those interests were owned by different persons (Section 66).

Measure of Indemnity

One of the principles of marine insurance is that it is a contract of indemnity.

Extent of liability of insurer for loss. 1. The sum which the assured can recover in respect of a loss on a policy by which he is insured, in the case of an unvalued policy to the full extent of the insurable value or in the case of a valued policy to the full extent of the value fixed by the policy, is called the measure of indemnity.

2. Where there is a loss recoverable under the policy, the insurer or each insurer if there be more than one, is liable for such proportion of the measure of indemnity as the amount of his subscription bears to the value fixed by the policy in the case of a valued policy, or to the insurable value in the case of an unvalued policy (Section 67).

Total loss. Subject to the provisions of the Act, and to any express provision in the policy, where there is a total loss of the subject-matter insured:

1. If the policy be a valued policy, the measure of indemnity is the sum fixed by the policy;

2. If the policy be an unvalued policy, the measure of indemnity is the insurable value of the subject-matter insured (Section 68).

Insurance policy covering total loss only—Loaded tractor during transportation slipped into river—Subsequently salvaged and repaired—Claim for constructive loss since cost of salvage and repairs exceeded value of goods on arrival—Plaintiff failing to prove constructive total loss—No partial loss, on the footing that the greater (total) includes the lesser (partial) can be claimed.

Partial loss of ship. Where a ship is damaged, but is not totally lost, the measure of indemnity subject to any express provision in the policy, is as follows:

1. Where the ship has been repaired, the assured is entitled to the reasonable cost of the repairs, less the customary deductions, but not exceeding the sum insured in respect of any one casualty.

2. Where the ship has been only partially repaired, the assured is entitled to the reasonable cost of such repairs, computed as above, and also to be indemnified for the reasonable depreciation, if any, arising from the unrepaired damage, provided that the aggregate amount shall not exceed the cost of repairing the whole damage, computed as above.

3. Where the ship has not been repaired, and has not been sold in her damaged state during the risk, the assured is entitled to be indemnified for the reasonable depreciation arising from the unrepaired damage, but not exceeding the reasonable cost of repairing such damage, computed as above.

4. Where the ship has not been repaired, and has been sold in her damaged state during the risk, the assured is entitled to be indemnified for the reasonable cost of repairing the damage, computed as above, but not exceeding the depreciation in value as ascertained by the sale (Section 69).

Partial loss of freight. Subject to any express provision in the policy, where there is a partial loss of freight, the measure of indemnity is such proportion of the sum fixed by the policy in the case of a valued policy or of the insurable value in the case of an unvalued policy, as the proportion of freight lost by the assured bears to the whole freight at the risk of the assured under the policy (Section 70). Freight is the reward payable to the carrier by sea for the safe carriage and delivery of goods. When freight is prepaid its nature differs considerably from that of ordinary freight, in that then it ceases to be dependent on the safe delivery of the goods, and therefore if the goods are lost the shipowners is not bound to refund the prepaid freight (see Sections 82, 83 infra).

Partial loss of goods, merchandise, etc. Where there is a partial loss of goods, merchandise, or other movable, the measure of indemnity, subject to any express provision in the policy, is as follows:

1. Where part of the goods, merchandise or other movable insured by a valued policy is totally lost, the measure of indemnity is such proportion of the sum fixed by the policy as the insurable value of the part lost bears to the insurable value of the whole, ascertained as in the case of an unvalued policy;

2. Where part of the goods, merchandise or other movable insured by an unvalued policy is totally lost, the measure of indemnity is the insurable value of the part lost, ascertained as in case of total loss;

3. Where the whole or any part of the goods or merchandise has been delivered damaged at its destination, the measure of indemnity is such proportion of the sum fixed by the policy in the case of a valued policy, or of the insurable value in the case of an unvalued policy, as the difference between the gross sound and damaged values at the place of arrival bears to the gross sound value;

4. "Gross value" means the wholesale price, or, if there be no such price, the estimated value, with, in either case, freight, landing charges, and duty paid beforehand; provided that, in the case of goods or merchandise customarily sold in bond; the bonded price is deemed to be the gross value. "Gross proceeds" means the actual price obtained at a sale where all charges on sale are paid by the sellers (Sec. 71).

Apportionment of valuation. 1. Where different species of property are insured under a single valuation, the valuation must be apportioned over the different species in proportion to their respective insurable values, as in the case of an unvalued policy. The insured value of any part of species is such proportion of the total insured value of the same as the insurable value of the part bears to the insurable value of the whole, ascertained in both cases as provided by this Act.

2. Where a valuation has to be apportioned, and particulars of the prime cost of each separate species, quality, or description of goods cannot be ascertained, the division of the valuation may be made over the net arrived sound values of the different species, qualities, or descriptions of goods (Section 72).

General average contributions and salvage charges. Subject to any express provision in the policy, where the assured has paid, or is liable for, any general average contribution, the measure of indemnity is the full amount of such contribution if the subject matter liable to contribution is insured for its full contributory value; if such subject-matter be not insured for its full contributory value, or if only part of it be insured, the indemnity payable by the insurer must be reduced in proportion, to the under insurance, and where there has been a particular average loss which constitutes a deduction from the contributory value, or if only part of it be insured, the indemnity payable by the insurer must be reduced in proportion to under insurance, and where there has been a particular average loss which constitutes a deduction from the contributory value, and for which the insurer is liable, that amount must be deducted from the insured value in order to ascertain what the insurer is liable to contribute (Section 73).

Where the insurer is liable for salvage charges the extent of his liabilities must be determined on the like principle.

Liabilities to third parties. Where the assured has effected an insurance in express terms against any liability to a third party, the measure of indemnity, subject to any express provision in the policy, is the amount paid or payable by him to such third party in respect of such liability (Section 74).

General provisions as to measure of indemnity. 1. Where there has been a loss in respect of any subject-matter not expressly provided for in the foregoing provisions of this Act, the measure of indemnity shall be ascertained as nearly as may be, in accordance with those provisions, in so far as applicable to the particular case.

2. Nothing in the provisions of this Act relating to the measure of indemnity shall affect the rules relating to double insurance, or prohibit the insurer from disproving interest wholly or in

part, or from showing that at the time of the loss whole or any part of the subject-matter insured was not at risk under the policy (Section 75).

Particular average warranties. 1. Where the subject-matter insured is warranted free from particular average, the assured cannot recover for a loss of part, other than a loss incurred by a general average sacrifice, unless the contract contained in the policy may recover for a total loss of any apportionable part.

2. Where the subject-matter insured is warranted free from particular average, either wholly or under a certain percentage, the insurer is nevertheless liable for salvage charges and for particular charges and other expenses properly incurred pursuant to he provisions of the suing and labouring clause in order to avert a loss insured against.

3. Unless the policy otherwise provides, where the subject-matter insured is warranted free from particular average under a specified percentage, a general average loss cannot be added to a particular average loss to make up the specified percentage.

4. For the purpose of ascertaining whether the specified percentage has been reached, regard shall be had only to the actual loss suffered by the subject-matter insured. Particular charges and the expenses of an incidental to ascertaining and proving the loss must be excluded (Section 76).

Successive losses. 1. Unless the policy otherwise provides, and subject to the provisions of the Act, the insurer is liable for successive loss, even though the total amount of such losses may exceed the sum insured.

2. Where, under the same policy, a partial loss, which has not been repaired or otherwise made good, is followed by a total loss, the assured can only recover in respect of the total loss:

Provided that nothing in this section shall affect the liability of the insurer under the suing and labouring clause (Section 77).

SUE and Labour Clause

1. Where the policy contains a suing and labouring clause, the engagement thereby entered into is deemed to be supplementary to the contract of insurance, and the assured may recover from the insurer any expenses properly incurred pursuant to the clause, notwithstanding that the insurer may have paid for a total loss, or that the subject-matter may have been warranted free from particular average, either wholly or under a certain percentage.

2. General average losses and contribution and salvage charges, as defined by the Act, are not recoverable under the suing and labouring clause.

3. Expenses incurred for the purpose of averting or diminishing any loss not covered by the policy are not recoverable under the suing and labouring clause.

4. It is the duty of the assured and his agents, in all cases, to take such measures as may be reasonable for the purpose of averting or minimising a loss (Section 78). This is a clause in the policy of marine insurance introduced to make it clear that the assured and his agents or servants, e.g., the master and the crew, can take every step to recover the insured property in peril without loss of the rights under the insurance and will be repaid any expenditure which may be incurred by the assured or high agents or servants to avert the loss. It is the duty of the assured and his agents so to act.

Rights of Insurer on Payments

Rights of subrogation. Section 79 of the Act defines subrogation as follows:

Where the insurer pays for a total loss, either of the whole, or in the case of goods of any apportionable part, of the subject-matter insured, he thereupon becomes entitled to take over the interest of the assured in whatever may remain of the subject-matter so paid for, and he is thereby subrogated to all the rights and remedies of the assured and in respect of that subject-matter as from the time of the casualty causing the loss.

Subject to the foregoing provisions, where the insurer pays for a partial loss, he acquires no title to the subject-matter insured, or such part of it as may remain, but he is thereupon subrogated to all rights and remedies of the assured and in respect of the subject-matter insured as from the time of the casualty causing the loss, in so far as the assured has been indemnified, according to this Act, by such payment for the loss (Section 79). Following points be noted:

1. Goods carried by sea or otherwise, covered by marine insurance policy—Insurance subrogated to rights and remedies of assured to the extent of the payment made to the assured on payment of partial loss under the policy—Insurer not entitled to sue carrier of gods or other wrong-doers or tort-feasors in his own name to recover compensation for loss or damage due to assured—The insurer cannot sue in his own name even when he pays for a total loss.
2. Loss of goods insured—Insurer compensating total loss to insured—Insured cannot bring suit against those responsible for loss or damages but insurer can.
3. A subrogee under Section 135A of the T.P. Act acquires rights only to the extent of his payment which may be less than the rights of the assured himself.
4. The right of subrogation is embodied in Section 79 of the Act. It does not require a deed. But assignment is by act of parties. It, therefore, requires a deed. The assignee can sue in his own name. The subrogee cannot. Then the subrogee can sue only for the sum paid. He cannot recover more than what he has paid. The doctrine of indemnification on which the rule of subrogation is founded says that the subrogee is entitled to no more than what he has paid to the insured.
5. Carriage of goods by Sea partial loss—Claim of consignee satisfied by Insurance Company—Suit for damages against carriers by consignee—Held not maintainable.
6. Goods carried by Sea—Covered by Marine Insurance Policy—Insurance was not subrogated—Insurer not asking for a assignment but insisting on filing claim against Carrier—Insured persons were not indemnified—Mentioning of 'sue and labour' clause in policy—Suit of Plaintiff for recovery of damages—Insurance Company not paying money and resisting the suit—Held it shows the tendency of Insurance Company that it was never willing to pay and get subrogated nor did it ever offer to take assignment which would require payment of loss.
7. Suit against Port Trust Board, Madras, under Section 110 of Madras Port Trust Act, 1905—Suit by owners of goods or by insurer as subrogee stands on same footing as regards starting of limitations—Time begins to run from date of loss—Plea that in case of insurer, it commences from the time he pays the assured overruled.

8. On general principle of subrogation the insurer can have only the rights and remedies of the assured and cannot claim by higher or better right which the assured does not have. Thus, where the suit claiming damages on account of collision of the ships of the insurer and that of the defendant was filed by the insurance company against the defendant on the basis of a letter of subrogation by the assured subsequent to the payment on account of the loss due to collision and the cause of action of assured against defendant was barred by Limitation, the suit would be liable to be dismissed.
9. Mere subrogation does not entitle insurer to sue in its own name—Right to sue either has to be conferred by statue or by the insured by way of assignment.
10. Assignment of rights under policy of marine insurance—Suit for damages for wrongful non-delivery of certain goods entrusted to railway for carriage—Case is one of marine insurance—Consigned goods at destination found short in weight—A case of total loss of apportionable part within Section 52(2)—Payment made by insurer to the insured person for the loss of goods—Insurer gets subrogated to the rights and remedies of the insured person—Insurer can file a suit in his own name.
11. Though the plaintiff in a suit for recovery of money for loss of goods booked had obtained a power-of-attorney from the insured but for some reason insured as Co-plaintiff and implead him as only defendant, then the suit would not be dismayed merely because insured is instead of being made Co-plaintiff made a defendant.

Types

Subrogation can be broadly classified into three categories:

(i) subrogation by equitable assignment;
(ii) subrogation by contract; and
(iii) subrogation-cum-assignment

In the first category, the subrogation is not evidenced by any document, but is based on the insurance policy and the receipt issued by the assured acknowledging the full settlement of the claim relating to the loss.

In the second category, the subrogation is evidenced by an instrument. To avoid any dispute about the right to claim reimbursement, or to settle the priority of inter-se claims or to confirm the quantum of reimbursement in pursuance of the subrogation, and to ensure co-operation by the assured in suing the wrong-doer, the insurer usually obtains a letter of subrogation in writing, specifying its rights vis-à-vis the assured. The letter of subrogation is a contractual arrangement.

The third category is where the assured executes a letter of subrogation-cum-assignment enabling the insurer retain the entire amount recovered (even if it is more than what was paid to the assured) and giving an option to sue in the name of the assured or to sue in its own name.

In all three types of subrogation, the insurer can sue the wrongdoer in the name of the assured. This means that the insurer requests the assured to file the suit/complaint and has the option of joining as co-plaintiff. Alternatively the insurer can obtain a special power of Attorney from the assured and then to sue the wrong-doer in the name of the assured as his attorney.

Examples:

Suppose the loss to the assured is ₹ 1,00,000. The insurer settles the claim of the assured for ₹ 75,000. The wrong-doer is sued for recovery of ₹ 1,00,000.

- If the suit filed for recovery of ₹ 100,000 is decreed as prayed, and the said sum of ₹ 1,00,000 is recovered the assured would appropriate ₹ 25,000 to recover the entire loss of ₹ 1,00,000 and the doctrine of subrogation would enable the insurer to claim and receive the balance of ₹ 75,000.
- If the suit filed for recovery of ₹ 1,00,000 is decreed as prayed for, but the assured is able to recover only ₹ 50,000 from the Judgment-Debtor (wrong-doer), the assured will be entitled to appropriate ₹ 25,000 (which is the shortfall to make up ₹ 100,000 being the loss) and the insurer will be entitled to receive only the balance of ₹ 25,000 even though it had paid ₹ 75,000 to the assured.
- Where, the suit is filed for recovery of ₹ 1,00,000 but the court assesses the loss actually suffered by the assured as only ₹ 75,000 (as against the claim of the assured that the value of goods lost is ₹ 1,00,000) and then awards ₹ 75,000 plus costs, the insurer will be entitled to claim and receive the entire amount of ₹ 75,000 in view of the doctrine of subrogation. Where the assured executes a letter of subrogation entitling the insurer to recover ₹ 75,000 (The suit is filed in the name of the assured or jointly by the assured and insurer).
- If the document executed by the assured in favour of the insured provides that in consideration of the settlement of the claim for ₹ 75,000, the assured has transferred and assigned by way of subrogation and assignment, the right to recover the entire value of the goods lost and retain the entire amount without being accountable to the assured for any excess recovered (over and above ₹ 75,000) and provides that the insurer may sue in the name of the assured or sue in its own name without reference to the assured, the instrument is a subrogation-cum-assignment and the insurer has the choice of either suing in the name of the assured or in its own name. Where the assured executes a letter of assignment in favour of a third party to sue and recover from the carrier, the value of the consignment.
- If the assured, having received ₹ 75,000 from the insurer, executes an instrument in favour of a third party (not being the insurer) assigning the right to sue 3 and recover from the carrier, damages for loss of the consignment, such a document will be an Assignment. The assignee cannot file a complaint before the consumer for a, as he is not a 'consumer'. Further, such a document being a transfer of a mere right to sue, will be void and unenforceable, having regard to Section 6(e) of Transfer of Property Act, 1882. It is well settled that a right to sue for unliquidated damages for breach of contract or for tort, not being a right connected with the ownership of any property, nor being a right to sue for a debt or actionable claim, is a mere right to sue and is incapable of being transferred.

Right of Contribution

1. Where the assured is over-insured by double insurance, each insurer is bound, as between himself and the other insurers, to contribute rateably to the loss in proportion to the amount for which he is liable under his contract.
2. If any insurer pays more than his proportion of the loss, he is entitled to maintain a suit for contribution against the other insurers, and is entitled to the like remedies as a surely who has paid more than his proportion of the debt (Section 80).

Effect of Under Insurance: Where the assured is insured for an amount less than the insurable value, or in the case of valued policy, for an amount less than the policy valuation, he is deemed to be his own insurer in respect of the uninsured balance (Section 81).

Return of Premium

Enforcement of return: Where the premium, or a proportionate part therefore, is, by this Act, declared to be returnable—

(a) if already paid, it may be recovered by the assured from the insurer, and

(b) if unpaid, it may be retained by the assured or his agent (Section 82).

Return by agreement: Where the policy contains a stipulation for the return of the premium, or a proportionate part thereof, on the happening of a certain event, and that event happens, the premium, or, as the case may be, the proportionate part thereof, is thereupon returnable to the assured (Section 83).

Return for Failure of Consideration

1. Where the consideration for the payment of the premium totally fails, and there has been no fraud or illegality on the part of the assured or his agents, the premium is thereupon returnable to the assured.

2. Where the consideration for the payment of the premium is apportionable and there is a total failure of any apportionable part of the consideration, a proportionate part of the premium is, under the like conditions, thereupon returnable to the assured.

3. In particular:

(a) Where the policy is void, or is avoided by the insurer as from the commencement of the risk, the premium is returnable, provided there has been no fraud or illegality on the part of the assured; but if the risk is not apportionable, and has not once attached, the premium is not returnable;

(b) Where the subject-matter insured, or part thereof, has never been imperiled the premium, or, as the case may be, a proportionate part thereof, is returnable.

Provided that where the subject-matter has been insured "lost or not loss", and has arrived in safety at the time when the contract is concluded, the premium is not returnable unless, at such time, the insurer knew of the safe arrival;

(c) Where the assured has no insurable interest throughout, the currency of the risk the premium is returnable, provided that the rule does not apply to a policy effected by way of wagering;

(d) Where the assured has a defensible interest which is terminated during the currency of the risk, the premium is not returnable;

(e) Where the assured has over-insured under an unvalued policy, a proportionate part of the premium is returnable;

(f) Subject to the foregoing provisions, where the assured has over-insured by double insurance, a proportionate part of the several premiums is returnable.

If the policies are effected at different times, and any earlier policy has at any time borne the entire risk, or if a claim has been paid on the policy in respect of the full sum insured thereby, no premium is returnable in respect of that policy, and when the double insurance is effected knowingly by the assured no premium is returnable (Section 84).

SCHEDULE

Form of Policy

(Section 24)

BE IT KNOWN THAT as well in the name as for and in the name and names of all and every other person or persons to whom the same doth, may, or shall appertain, in part on in all doth make assurance and cause and them, and every of them, to be insured lost, or not lost, at and from upon any kind of goods merchandises, and also upon the body, tackle, apparel, ordinance, munition, artillery, boat and other furniture, of and in the good ship or vessel called the whereof is master for this present voyage or whosoever else shall go for master in the said ship or by whatsoever other name or names the said ship, or the master thereof, is or shall be named or called; beginning the adventure upon the said goods and merchandises from the loading thereof aboard the said ship, upon the said ship, etc. and so shall continue and endure, during her abode there, upon the said ship, etc. And further, until the said ship with all her ordinance, tackle, apparel, etc. and goods and merchandises whatsoever shall be arrived at upon the said ship, etc. until the hath moored at anchor twenty-four hours in good safety; and upon the goods and merchandises, until the same be there discharged and safety landed. And it shall be lawful for the said ship, etc. in this voyage to proceed and sail to and touch and stay at any ports or places whatsoever without prejudice to this insurance. The said ship, goods and merchandises, etc., for so much as concerned the assured by agreement between the assured and assurers in this policy, are and shall be valued at touching the adventures and perils which we the assurers are contended to bear and do take upon us in this voyage; they are of the seas, men of war, fire, enemies, pirates, rovers, thieves, jettisons, letter of mart and countermart, surprisals, takings at sea, arrests, restraints, and detainments of all kings, princes, and people of what nation, condition, or quality so ever, barratry of the master and mariners, and of all other perils losses, and misfortunes that have or shall come to the hurt, detriment, or damage of the said goods and merchandises, and ship, etc. or any part thereof.

And in case of any loss or misfortune it shall be lawful to the assured, their factors, servants and assigns, to sue, labour, and travel for, in and about the defence, safeguards and recovery of the said goods and merchandises and ship, etc. or any part thereof, without prejudice to this insurance: to the charges whereof we, the assurers, will contribute each one according to the rate and quantity of his sum herein assured.

And it is especially declared and agreed that no acts of the insurer or insured in recovering, saving, or preserving the property insured shall be considered as a waiver, or acceptance of abandonment. And so we, the assurers, are contended, and do hereby promise and bind ourselves, each one for his own part, our heirs, executors, and goods to the assured, their executors, administrators, and assigns, for the true performance of the promises, confessing ourselves paid and the consideration due into us for this assurance by the assured, at and after the date of.

It witness whereof, we, the assurers, have subscribed our names and sums assured in MEMORANDUM. N.B.—Corn, fish, salt, fruit, flour, and seed are warranted free from average, unless general or the ship be stranded—sugar, tobacco, hemp, flax, hides and skins are warranted free from average, under five per cent and all other goods also the ship and freight, are warranted free from average, under three per cent, unless general or the ship be standard.

Rules for Construction of Policy

The following are the rules referred by the Act for the construction of a policy in the above or other like from, where the context does not otherwise require:

1. Lost and not lost. Where the subject-matter is insured "lost or not lost" and the loss has occurred before the contract is concluded, the risk attaches unless, at such time the assured was aware of the loss, and the insurer was not.

2. From. Where the subject-matter is insured "from" a particular place, the risk does not attach until the ship starts on the voyage insured.

3. At and from:

(a) Where a ship is insured "at and from" a particular place, and she is at that place in good safety when the contract in concluded, the risk attaches immediately.

(b) If she be not at that place when the contract is concluded, the risk attaches as soon as she arrives, there in good safety, and, unless the policy otherwise provides, it is immaterial that she is covered by another policy for a specified time after arrival.

(c) Where chartered freight is insured "at and from", a particular place, and the ship is at that place in good safety when the contract is concluded, the risk attaches immediately. If she be not there when the contract is concluded, the risk attaches as soon as she arrives there in good safety.

(d) Where freight, other than chartered freight, is payable without special conditions and is insured "at and from" a particular place, the risk attaches *pro rata* as the goods or merchandise are shipped; provided that if there be cargo in readiness which belongs to the shipowner, or which some other person has contracted with him to ship, the risk attaches as soon the ship is ready to receive such cargo.

4. From the loading thereof. Where goods or other movables are insured "from the loading thereof", the risk does not attach until such goods or movables are actually on board, and the insurer is not liable for them while in transit from the share to the ship.

5. Safety landed. Where the risk on goods or other movables continues they are "safety landed", they must be landed in the customary manner and within a reasonable time after arrival at the port of discharge, and if they are not so landed at the risk ceases.

6. Touch and stay. In the absence of any further license or usage, the liberty to touch and stay "at any port or place whatsoever", does not authorise the ship to depart from the course of her voyage from the port of departure to the port of destination.

Note: The ship should call the ports in the ordinary course of voyage or in geographical order and for a justifiable purpose.

7. Perils of the seas. The term "perils of the seas" refers only to fortuitous accidents or casualties of the seas. It does not include the ordinary action of the winds and waves.

8. Pirates. The term "pirates" includes passengers who mutiny and rioters who attack the ship from the shore.

9. Thieves. The term "thieves" does not cover clandestine theft or a theft committed by any one of the ship's company, whether crew or passengers.

10. Restraint of princes. The term "arrests, etc., of kings, princes, and people" refers to political or executive acts, and does not include a loss caused by riot or by ordinary judicial process.

11. Barratry. The term "barratry" includes every wrongful act willfully committed by the master of crew to the prejudice of the owner or, as the case may be, the charterer.

12. All other perils. The term "all other perils" includes only perils similar in kind to the perils specifically mentioned in the policy.

13. Average unless general. The term "average unless general" means a partial loss of the subject-matter insured other than a general average loss, and does not include "particular charges".

14. Stranded. Where the ship has stranded, the insurer is liable for the expected losses although the loss is not attributable to the stranding, provided that when the stranding takes place the risk has attached and, if the policy be on goods, that the damaged goods are on board.

15. Ship. The term "ship" includes the hull, material and outfit, stores and provisions for the officers and crew, and, in the case of vessels engaged in a special trade, the ordinary fittings requisite for the trade, and also in the case of a steamship, the machinery, boilers, and coals and engine stores, if owned by the assured and also in the case of a ship driven by power other than steam, the machinery, and fuels and engine store, if owned by the assured.

16. Freight. The term "freight" includes the profit derivable by a shipowner from the employment of his ship to carry his own goods or movables as well as freight payable by a third party, but does not include passage money.

17. Goods. The term "goods" means goods in the nature of merchandise, and does not include personal effects or provisions and stores for use on board.

In the absence of any usage to the contrary, deck cargo and living animals must be insured specifically, and not under the general denomination of goods.

Other Terms

(a) Jettison. It is throwing over board a part of the cargo or any part of equipment to heighten the ship in case of emergency.

(b) Letters of mart, countermarts, surprisals, taking at sea. The power granted by a government to an individual to attack the enemy in revenge for losses suffered is granted by letter of mart/

letter of counter mart refers to the power granted by opposing nation to resist and retaliate upon such attacks. Surprisals means capture of any ship or goods as a proof or by force or by shill. 'Taking at sea' refers to stopping and taking into port a ship for examination in case of suspicion.

Bottomery Bond and Respondentia Bond. These bonds are loan agreements taken on the security of ship or cargo. If captain, on voyage, is short of money, he can pledge the ship to any lender and the bond executed between them is called Bottomery Bond. If the owner of a ship borrows money on the security of cargo, it is called Respondentia Bond. These bonds were used in old days. These days these bonds have lost their importance because of fast increased communication and transfer of facilities.

Some Other Clauses

York-Antwerp rules. In 1864, an association of major maritime countries, called "The Association for Reform and Codification of the Law of Nations" held a meeting at York (England) and another meeting in 1877 at Antwerp (Belgium). The association adopted a code of rules called "York-Antwerp Rules". These rules relate to the procedure for settling a loss. These rules were revised in 1890, in 1924 and in 1950. The insurance policy can provide the "particular average loss" will be settled and these rules.

Inchmaree clause. This clause covers the perils other than perils of the sea. The clause is named after the name of vessel called "Inchmaree". This clause covers certain losses caused by: (a) the negligence of cover and the beam engaged in loading and unloading, (b) the explosions, bursting of boilers or by breakage of shaft, (c) by latent defect in any machinery or hull. The clause includes loss only by these reasons and not others.

Waiver clause. This clause declares that no act of an insurer or insured in recovering or preserving a subject matter of insurance shall be considered as a waiver or acceptance or abandonment. This clause supplements the 'Sure and labour' clause.

Attached clauses. These clauses are given at the end of the policy by which the insurer frees from liability. Some of them are given below and are self-explanatory:

(a) Free from particular average clause
(b) Free from capture and misuse of the ship during war
(c) Free from all averages
(d) Free from strikes, riots, and civil commotion clause
(e) Frustration clause i.e., the underwriter is not liable if the ship is prevented from carrying out the voyage.

Running down or collision clause. The underwriter will pay only 75% of loss in case the ship collides with another ship and the collision is due to the guilt of the ship insured. A part of loss is borne by the insured and the guild must be proved in a court.

Continuation clause. In case the time policy expires when the ship is in the sea, the insurer adds this clause by which the time policy is extended till the ship arrives at the port.

Claims Procedure

It is the duty of the Assured and their Agents, in all cases, to take such measures as may be reasonable for the purpose of averting or minimizing as loss and to ensure that all rights against

Carriers, Bailees or other third parties are properly preserved and exercised. In particular, the Assured or their Agents are required:

1. To claim immediately on the Carriers, Port Authorities or other Bailees for any missing packages.
2. In no circumstances, except under written protest, to give clean receipt where goods are in doubtful condition.
3. When delivery is made by Container, to ensure that the Container and its seals are examined immediately by their responsible official. If the Container is delivered damaged or with seals broken or missing or with seals other than as stated in the shipping documents, to clause the delivery receipt accordingly and retain all defective or irregular seals for subsequent identification.
4. To apply immediately for survey by Carrier or other Bailee's representative if any loss or damage be apparent and claim on the Carrier or other Bailee for any actual loss or damage found at such survey.
5. To give notice in writing to the Carriers or other Bailees within three days of delivery if the loss or damage was not apparent at the time of taking delivery.

Note: The Consignees or their Agents are recommended to make themselves familiar with the Regulation of the Port Authorities at the port of discharge. Instructions for survey in the event of loss or damage which may involve a claim under this insurance, immediate notice of such loss or damage should be given to and a Survey Report obtained from the Company's representatives at port of discharge or destination or if there be no representative of the Company, the nearest Lloyd's Agent. Documentation of claims to enable claims to be dealt with promptly, the Assured or their Agents are advised to submit all available supporting documents without delay, including when applicable.

(a) Original policy or Certificate of Marine Insurance.

(b) Original copy of Shipping Invoices, together with Packing List, and/or Weightment notes.

(c) Original Bill of Lading and/or other contract of carriage.

(d) Survey report and other documentary evidence, if available, to show the extent of the loss or damage.

(e) Landing Remarks/Account and Weightment notes at final destination.

(f) Correspondence exchanged with the Carriers and other Parties regarding their liability for the loss or damage.

Claims

Documents such as original insurance policy, copy of bill of lading, bill of entry, ship survey report estimate of repairs, customs certificate of loss/damage are to be submitted. Monetary claim against port authorities within seven days and suit within six months from the date of discharge must be filed.

(a) In order to recover under this insurance policy the Assured must have an insurable interest in the subject-matter insured at the time of the loss.

(b) Subject to above, the Assured shall be entitled to recover for insured loss occurring during the period covered by this insurance, notwithstanding that the loss occurred before contract of insurance was concluded, unless the Assured was aware of the loss and the Underwriters were not.

(c) Where, as a result of the operation of a risk covered by this insurance the insured transit is terminated at a port or place other than that to which the subject-matter is covered under this insurance policy, the Underwriters will reimburse the Assured for any extra charges properly and reasonably incurred in unloading storing and forwarding the subject-matter to the destination to which it is insured hereunder. This does not apply to general average or salvage and shall not include charges arising from the fault negligence insolvency or financial of the Assured or their servants.

(d) No claim for Constructive Total Loss shall be recoverable hereunder unless the subject-matter insured is reasonably abandoned either on account of its actual total loss appearing to be unavoidable or because the cost of recovering, reconditioning and forwarding the subject-matter to the destination to which it is insured would exceed its value on arrival.

(e) (i) If any Increased value insurance is effected by the Assured on the cargo insured herein the agreed value of the cargo shall be deemed to be increased to the total amount insured under this insurance and all Increased value insurance covering the loss, and liability under this insurance shall be in such proportion as the sum insured herein hears to such total amount insured. In the event of claim the Assured shall provide the Underwriters with evidence of the amounts insured under all other insurances.

(ii) Where this insurance is on Increased value the following clause shall apply: The agreed value of the cargo shall be deemed to be equal to the total amount insured under the primary insurance and all increased value insurances covering the loss and effected on the cargo by the Assured, and liability under this insurance shall be in such proportion as the sum insured herein bears to such total amount insured. In the event of claim the Assured shall provide the Underwriters with evidence of the amounts insured under all other insurances.

Benefit of Insurance

This insurance policy shall not insure to the benefit of the carrier or other bailee.

Minimising Losses

It is the duty of the Assured and their servants and agents in respect of loss recoverable hereunder:

(a) to take such measures as may be reasonable for the purpose of averting or minimizing such loss, and

(b) to ensure that all rights against carriers, bailees or other third parties are properly preserved and exercised and the Underwriter will, in addition to any loss recoverable hereunder, reimburse the Assure for any charge properly and reasonably incurred pursuance of these duties.

(c) measures taken by the Assured or the Underwriters with the object of saving, protecting or recovering the subject-matter insured shall not be considered as a waiver or acceptance of abandonment or otherwise prejudice the rights of either party.

Avoidance of Delay

It is a condition of this insurance that the Assured shall act with reasonable dispatch in all circumstances within their control.

Exclusions

(a) In no case shall insurance policy cover:

1. loss damage or expense attributable to willful misconduct of the Assured.
2. ordinary leakage, ordinary loss in weight or volume, or ordinary wear and tear of the subject-matter insured.
3. loss damage or expense caused by insufficiency or unsuitability of packing or preparation of the subject-matter insured. Packing shall be deemed to include stowage in a container or lift van but only when such stowage is carried out prior to attachment of this insurance or by the Assured or their servants.
4. loss damage or expense caused by inherent vice or nature of the subject-matter insured.
5. loss damage or expense proximately caused by delay, even through the delay be caused by a risk insured against.
6. loss damage or expense arising from insolvency or financial default of the owners, managers, charterers or operators of the vessel.
7. deliberate damage to or deliberate destruction of the subject-matter insured or any part thereof the wrongful act of any person or persons.
8. loss damage or expense arising from the use of any weapon of war employing atomic or nuclear fission and/or fusion or other like reaction or radioactive force or matter.

(b) 1. in no case shall this insurance cover loss damage or expense arising from unseaworthiness of vessel or craft, unfitness of vessel craft, unfitness of vessel craft conveyance container of lift van for the safe carriage of the subject-matter insured, where the assured or their servants are privy to such unseaworthiness or unfitness, at the time subject-matter insured is loaded therein.

2. the underwriters waive any breach of the implied warranties of the seaworthiness of the ship and fitness of the ship to carry the subject-matter insured to destination, unless the Assured or their servants are privy to such unseaworthiness or unfitness.

(c) In no case shall insurance cover loss damage expense caused by

1. civil war revolution rebellion insurrection, or civil strife arising therefrom, or any hostile act by or against a belligerent power.
2. capture seizure arrest restraint or detainment (piracy excepted), and the consequences thereof or any attempt thereat.
3. derelict mines, torpedoes, bombs or other derelict weapons of war.

(d) In case this insurance shall cover loss damage or expense:

1. cause by strikers, locked-out workmen, or persons taking part in labour disturbances, riots or civil commotions.

2. resulting form strikes, lock-outs, labour disturbances, riots or civil commotions.
3. caused by any terrorist or any person acting from a political motive.

Duration

(a) This insurance attaches from the time the goods leave the warehouse or place of storage at the place named herein for the commencement of the transit, continues during the ordinary course of transit and terminates either.
   1. on delivery to the consignees or other final warehouse or place of storage at the destination named herein,
   2. on delivery to any other warehouse or place or storage, whether prior to or at the destination named herein, which the Assured elect to use either, for storage other than in the ordinary course of transit or for allocation or distribution, or
   3. on the expiry of 60 days after completion of discharge overside of the goods hereby insured from the oversea vessel at the final port of discharge, whichever shall first occur.

(b) If, after discharge overside from the oversea vessel at the final port of discharge, but prior to termination of this insurance, the goods are to be forwarded to a destination other than that to which they are insured hereunder, this insurance, whilst remaining subject to termination as provided for above, shall not extend beyond the commencement of transit of such other destination.

(c) This insurance shall remain in force during delay beyond the control of the Assured, any deviation, forced discharge, reshipment or transshipment and during any variation of the adventure arising from the exercise of a liberty granted to shipowners or charterers under contract of affreightment.

(d) If owing to circumstances beyond the control of the Assured either the contract of carriage is terminated at a port of place other than the destination named therein or the transit is otherwise terminated before delivery of the goods as provided then this shall remain in force, subject to an additional premium if required by the Underwriters, either
   1. Until the goods are sold and delivered at such port or place, or unless otherwise specially agreed, until the expiry of 60 days after arrival of the goods hereby insured at such port or place, whichever shall first occur, or
   2. If the goods are forwarded within the said period of 60 days (or nay agreed extension thereof) of the destination named herein or to any other destination, until terminated in accordance with the provisions.

(e) Where, after attachment of this insurance, the destination is changed by the Assured, held covered at a premium and on conditions to be arranged subject to prompt notice being given to the Underwriters.

Underwriting of Marine Insurance

Marine Insurance started with insuring sea-going/water-borne vessels and cargo carried therein. The term "marine" means "concerned with or belonging to the sea". But no longer is Marine Insurance restricted to sea-going vessels or cargo carried on them. It has expanded to all forms of goods and commodities carried by all types of water-borne vessels, railway trains, trucks, airplanes, etc. for hire or reward. Apart from ships and other water-borne vessels written in the marine hull department, aircraft hull and associated liabilities also form part of the marine portfolio.

For a marine cover to be issued in respect of goods and commodities, the essential requirement is there has to be a "Contract of carriage". A contract of carriage also known as a "contact of affreightment" being a commercial contract has to have a consideration. In contracts of carriage, the consideration is the fee or the charge for carrying the goods. The evidence of a contract of carriage in respect of goods carried:

(i) By a ship or water-borne vessel is a bill of lading,
(ii) By a goods carrying vehicle like a truck is a lorry receipt,
(iii) By a goods or freight train is the railway parcel bill, and
(iv) By an airplane is the airway bill.

We may also send goods or a parcel through a courier or the India Post for which the receipt given by them is a valid contract of carriage.

A Policy which covers a ship or an airplane is a time policy which means it has a definite time of commencement and a definite time of expiry. On the other hand, a policy which covers goods consigned through a ship or truck or airplane is a voyage policy which has a date of commencement but no definite of expiry. Such a policy expires when the goods reach their destination and are taken over by the consignee or his or her authorized agent.

A voyage could take a few days or a few weeks or even a few months depending on the conditions of the sea or ocean through which it sails and the shipping line it takes. If, for any reason, a ship has to take refuse in a port for temporary repairs the voyage may get extended.

The provisions of Carriage by Air Act, 1972, Warsaw Convention and the Hague Protocol govern the liability in respect of all goods and commodities carried by air. For goods carried by surface transport, the provisions of the Carriers Act, 1865 are applicable. For goods consigned by water-borne vessels both coastal waters and international waters the provisions of Carriage by Sea Act are applicable and in addition the Institute Cargo Clauses, the Institute Time Clauses. York Antwerp Rules and Hague Visby Rules are applicable.

Underwriting of marine cargo risks is a complex process and needs good knowledge in various domains, particularly one need to know five major factors:

1. The vessel, its age, tonnage, and the flag it flies,
2. The voyage or the transit, particularly whether they are into tramp shipping,
3. The nature of cargo and its packing,
4. The perils, terms and conditions of insurance coverage, and
5. The reputation of the shipping company.

Regardless of the transit, once a consignor hands over the consignments to the shipping company's agent, the skipper has no control over the safety of the consignment. It is the master and crew of the vessel who have physical possession of the consignment. After the consignment is positioned in the holds of the ship, even they have no control over it. Hence the safety of the consignment largely depends on the way the consignment is stacked, seaworthiness and fitness of the vessel.

The fitness and seaworthiness of the vessel depends on the age and stage of maintenance of the vessel and whether it can withstand the hazards and the perils of the sea/ocean during the navigation. Regulation maintenance of the ship and sound management of the ship contributes in substantial measure to its state of fitness and seaworthiness of the vessel.

If the voyage is through familiar shipping lines, to a large extent it relieves the corners of all the interests. But at times because of factors like high tides, rough seas, hurricanes and whirlpools which are unpredictable, the master of the vessel may be compelled by force of circumstances to take deviation in the sailing of the vessel. Another serious threat which has cropped up of late is the sudden attack by hordes of rovers and pirates which many established shipping companies are forced to face, particularly the Somali pirates. Seaquakes triggered by earthquakes by distant lands are another source of worry for even for huge tankers.

Though detailed maps of underground earthquakes are made available to the ships, there is no knowing when a seaquake can erupt. The action of sea beds is most unpredictable. If the subterranean tectonic plates suddenly shift, they can trigger forces which travel underneath for miles and miles and suddenly erupt. The recent earthquake in Chile sent subterranean tsunami shock waves to countries as far as Japan. Despite all research and findings how ocean floors behave, still an ocean is an unknown factor whose dimensions are still a mystery.

The nature of cargo, whether it is fragile, what its dimensions are, how it is packed, whether it is cargo that can go easily into the holds of the ship or has to be taken as deck cargo, is it break-bulk or neo-bulk, or needs to be lashed etc. is a major risk factor.

A risk which any ship has to contend with is whether any item of cargo can shift during voyage caused by the pitching and swaying of the vessel triggered by wave action. With containerization becoming universal, many of the risks like jettisoning of cargo to save the adventure have been very largely mitigated. Still in respect of break-bulk cargo or on deck cargo like large machinery, turbines, huge automobiles and construction machinery even though securely lashed are not secure and can be washed overboard by gigantic waves. Massive hurricanes and cyclones like Hurricane Huge or Cyclone Nargis can topple over even huge container vessels.

The perils, terms and conditions of insurance are very relevant for underwriting. Particularly in marine cargo one could go for various types of covers as follows:

1. **Institute cargo clauses (ICC) (C):** This policy covers loss or damage caused by explosion, standing, grounding, sinking or capsizing of the vessel; overturning or derailment of land conveyance; collision or contact of the vessel with any external object other than water; discharge of cargo at any port of distress; jettison; general average sacrifice and salvage charges.
2. **Institute cargo clauses (ICC) (B):** In addition to what the ICC(C) policy covers loss or damage caused by earthquake, volcanic eruption or lightning; washing overboard; entry of seawater into the holds or the sea or place of storage; total loss any package lost overboard whilst loading or unloading from the vessel or the craft.

3. **Institute cargo clauses (ICC) (A):** This is an "all risks" policy. It covers all perils as covered by ICC(C) and ICC(B) policies and the addition some of the perils which are excluded in those policies. The term "all risks" is not to be understood in the sense any loss or damage however caused is covered. Only those fortuitously are covered.

All policies also cover War and Strikes, Riots, Civil Commotion (SRCC) risks for which premium has to be paid as per scale rates. The risk of terrorism and terrorist activities is another major exposure for which also cover is granted when applied for at additional premium.

Contract of Sale

A contract of sale is a bilateral contract. The seller and buyer of goods or services determine the terms of contract. Over the years certain conventions came into existence which later on became law, such as the Sale of Goods Act, 1930. When it comes to international sales, exports and imports, the common forms of sale are **Free on Board (FOB), Cost & Freight (C&F) and Cost, Insurance and Freight (CIF).**

In **FOB contracts,** the seller undertakes to deliver the goods contracted for sale over the ship's rail where the risk passes from the seller to the buyer. On taking over the goods, it is the buyer who is addition to payment of freight also has to arrange for the insurance required in respect of the goods in transit. FOB contracts are generally sought by importers in a country who might have a marine open policy or open cover with their insurer which gives them the facility of declaration of goods imported by them to the insurer as and when such imports take place. Also the importers might have negotiated with their insurers the rates of premium which their overseas vendors might not be able to provide.

Another advantage an FOB contract has is that the importer may sell the goods even when they are on high seas to a buyer who does not have the hassle of arranging insurance. Of course, this benefit is available in C&F and CIF contracts.

A&F contract is one where the seller pays the freight leaving the insurance in respect of the consignment to the buyer. One benefit a C&F contract has is that the vendor who might be a regular customer of the shipping company might be able to get more reasonable freight rates than the importer. The responsibility of insurance of the consignment still rests with the buyer. Otherwise, a C&F contract is similar to that of an FOB contract.

CIF contracts are quite common in all international commercial transactions. Most imports for projects which are on 'turn-key' basis are invariably on CIF terms. From the originating country till the goods are handed over to the ultimate buyer at the destination the vendor is responsible.

Another aspect of CIF contracts is most of them are on "warehouse to warehouse" basis. In a "warehouse to warehouse" transaction the vendor takes the responsibility of packing the goods contracted to be sold as per the specifications agreed at the warehouse of the country of origin, transporting the packed materials to the port of origin, loading the consignment on board the carrying ship, paying the freight arranging insurance mostly under an ICC(A) policy, unloading the consignment at the port of destination and arranging for transfer of the consignment to the buyer's warehouse at the destination.

Marine Hull Insurance

When we go back to the early history of marine insurance, what strikes us as most significant is that the seafaring merchants who had to encounter heavy losses and damage to their vessels and goods they carried caused by maritime perils like high tides, hurricanes, cyclones, fire, icebergs and the like and attack by pirates, rovers, thieves, freebooters and barratry in the course of their voyage thought of a mechanisms of creating a special fund to share their losses which later took the form of insurance.

It was George Lloyd who ran a coffee house in London agreed to become the trustee for the contributions the merchants made and to distribute the funds to those who suffered losses in their maritime adventure from out of the trust fund. How those initial forays into a form of insurance transformed into the modern day marine hull insurance is a long history which needs a special study.

Basically four main types of sea-going vessels are found in the current maritime channels, both coastal and international:

1. General Cargo Vessels
2. Dry Bulk Carriers
3. Liquid Bulk Carriers like tankers, VLCC and ULCC
4. Passenger Carriers.

This list does not include Coast Guard Ships, Naval Ships, Pilot Ships, Lighter Vessels, Dredgers of navigation channels and harbor basins and self-propelled tugs. Also boats that ply inland waters are not included in the list.

Ocean-going general cargo vessels are in the range of 5000 to 15,000 GRT. They include Container Ships, RO/RO vessels, Lighter Abroad Ship (LASH), Refrigerated Vessels, Livestock Carriers, Heavy Lift Vessels, etc. Vessels specially built for carrying petroleum crude and petroleum products with a DWT of even 500,000 or even a million tons are known as super tankers, very large crude carriers (VLCC), ultra large crude carriers (ULCC) are in great demand to transport crude from petroleum exporting countries to many of the world.

Dry bulk carriers are specially built with over 70,000 GRT for carrying iron ore, coal, grains, fertilizers, etc. Underwriters who are specialized in writing tankers, bulk carriers, VLCC, ULCC, etc. must be quite knowledgeable about the nature of cargo carried, sea lines through which they navigate, how stable they are, and in the event of distress where they could seek refuge for dry docking etc.

Container vessels are meant to carry fully laden container cargo and are engaged on a fast liner service between specific ports. They carrying capacity of container vessels referred to in terms of the number of TEUs (20-foot equivalent units up to 20 tons) or FEUs (40-foot equivalent units, i.e. 40 tons capacity).

Conclusion

Marine insurance is closely linked to international trade and commerce as banking. Banking relies heavily on insurance and in particular on marine insurance. Despite airplanes carrying quite some cargo world over, ocean marine transport of cargo is the most predominant means of transport in international trade.

Problems

1. A ship, insured under a time policy, was sent to sea unseaworthy. Its hull was unfit, and crew was inefficient. The assured knew about insufficiency of crew but not about unfit hull. The ship was lost. Is the insurer be liable to pay loss? (Yes, in time policy, the warranty of seaworthiness does not apply).
2. A ship was Chartered from Mumbai to Karachi and then to Dubai. The ship from Karachi went to Aden and then to Dubai. From Aden to Dubai, it was damaged due to storm. Can the loss be recovered from insurer? (No, there is deviation).
3. A bill of lading was endorsed to B by A. The bill of lading was for goods to be shipped from Mumbai to Russia. The ship deviated and enroute collided with a sea-rock. A part of cargo was damaged. The policy did not contain any route and deviation was to save some sick people. Is the underwriter liable to pay? (Yes, endorsee gets full rights like an endorser).
4. A ship, insured by a time policy, was hit by pirates and damaged. Is insurer liable for loss? (Yes, it is a loss by peril or sea).
5. Bales of cotton were shipped from Port Sudan by a ship. After the date when the goods suffered damage, but before the news of this reached him, the claimant acquired an interest in the cargo and insured it "lost or not lost". The insurer refuses to pay (No, the insurer is liable to pay).
6. Due to fire on board a ship some cargo of A was destroyed in putting out the fire by water and some cement bags of B were damaged. Who can recover loss? (B can claim general average contribution and A can claim loss from the insurer).
7. The cargo of rice insured from a voyage from Thailand to Saudi Arabia against 'perils of the sea' was damaged by heating due to closing of ventilators to prevent rain water entering store. Is the insurer liable for loss? (Yes, the proximate cause was peril of the sea).
8. In order to keep away the pirates, the captain of the ship offers some money to them. Can this loss of money be recovered from the insurer?
9. During a voyage a ship was damaged. To get it repaired the ship was taken on an island. The residents of the island took the shore cargo by force. Insured claims total loss (Yes, under Section 57 of the act).
10. A cargo of dates, insured, was shipped from Jeddah to Mumbai. During transit, due to rain and storm the dates were so badly damaged that were not for human consumption. But they were used for making wine. Is there any loss? (Yes, the loss can be treated as actual total loss).
11. A consignment of 100 bales of cotton was insured at ₹ 10,000, out of which ten bales were damaged. It was estimated that the damaged goods would fetch ₹ 500. But if they were not damaged they could have been sold in the market for ₹ 1000. Calculate the particular average.

Solution: Calculation of Particular Average

Insured value of the goods damaged	=	₹ 1000
Market value of the goods damaged	=	₹ 1000 (undamaged)
Actual value of goods damaged	=	₹ 500
Actual loss (₹ 1000 – ₹ 500)	=	₹ 500

Particular Average

∴ the insurer will pay ₹ 500 to the cargo-owner.

12. A cargo is insured for ₹ 30,000. It is damaged during the course of transition and is expected to realise ₹ 10,000. Had the cargo reached safely, it would have fetched ₹ 24,000 (gross). Calculate the particular average loss.

Solution: Computation of Particular Average Loss

		₹
Insured value of the goods damaged	=	1,000
Gross sound value on arrival	=	24,000
Gross damaged value on arrival	=	10,000
Actual loss or damage (24,000 – 10,000)	=	14,000

This damage of ₹ 14,000 is 14,000/24,000 or 7/12 of the gross sound value. Hence, the claim on policy will be 7/12 of ₹ 30,000 i.e., ₹ 17,500. If the insured value is ₹ 20,000, the underwriter will be liable to pay 7/12 of ₹ 20,000 i.e., ₹ 11,666 approximately.

13. A consignment of 1000 bales of jute valued and insured at ₹ 1,00,000 was shipped from Kolkata to London per S.S. Jabakusum of which 200 bales were damaged by seawater. It is estimated that the damaged bales will fetch ₹ 10,000, though they could have been sold for ₹ 22,000. Calculate the particular average.

Solution: Computation of Particular Average

		₹
Value of insured damaged goods	=	20,000
Market value of undamaged condition	=	22,000
Present value in damaged condition	=	10,000
Actual Loss (₹ 22,000 – ₹ 10,000)	=	12,000
Particular Average	=	10,909

14. A cargo consisting of 500 bags was insured for ₹ 5000, out of which 100 bags were damaged and could realise at the rate of ₹ 2 per bag. The insured also incurred the following expenses: (a) 1 per cent commission, (b) ₹ 10 survey fee, (c) ₹ 10 sales expenses.

You are required to prepare a Particular Average Statement, assuming that the goods would have realised at the rate of ₹ 10 per bag in their undamaged condition and the policy is valued.

Solution: Computation of Particular Average Loss		₹
Insured value of damaged goods	=	1000
Gross sound value on arrival (100 bags × ₹ 10)	=	1000
Gross damaged value on arrival (100 bags × ₹ 2)	=	200
Actual loss or damage (1000 – 200)	=	800
Particular Average	=	800

To this sum, the charges paid by the insured will be added:

		₹
Particular Average (as above)	=	800.00
Commission on sale (1% on ₹ 200)	=	2.00
Survey Fee	=	15.00
Sales Expenses	=	10.00
Total amount of claim		₹ 827. 00

15. A cargo of 10,000 boxes of turmeric was consigned from Cairo to Chennai. The insured value of cargo was ₹ 60,000. Out of this cargo 500 boxes were damaged to transit. Amount realised on the sales of damaged boxes amounted to ₹ 1500, and expenses on sale amounted to ₹ 130. The normal value of turmeric per box ₹ 8.00.

Calculate the particular average loss.

Solution: The insured value of damaged boxes.		₹
Insured value of damaged tins	=	₹ 3000
Market value of damaged cargo (500 × 8)	=	4000
Less gross sale proceeds	=	1500
Loss	=	2500
Loss on the market value of ₹ 4000	=	2500
∴ Loss on the market value of ₹ 3000	=	₹ 1875.

Total Loss = Loss on insured value ₹ 1875 + Expenses on sale ₹ 130 = ₹ 2005.

16. Six thousand tins of chilli powder @ ₹ 6 per tin and 4000 tins of butter @ ₹ 12 per tin were sent from Chennai to Dubai, the total invoice price being ₹ 84,000. The insured value of the whole cargo covered by one policy is ₹ 1,00,000. 500 tins of chilli were damaged. The damaged tins were sold for ₹ 1500 and expenses on sale amounted to ₹ 130.

    Calculate the particular average loss on the assumption that the normal market value of chilli powder is ₹ 8 per tin.

Solution: Since the total invoice price of ₹ 84,000 was insured for ₹ 1 lakh, the damaged goods would have been insured for ₹ 3571.42.

		₹
Market value of damaged cargo		
(500 tins × ₹ 8)	=	4,000
Less gross sale proceeds	=	1500
Loss	=	2500
Loss on market value of ₹ 4000	=	2500
∴ Loss on insured value of ₹ 2500	=	2232
Add expenses on sale		130
Total Loss		2,362

13

Automobile Insurance

Under Motor Vehicles Act, 1988, an automobile must be compulsorily insured. Four types of vehicles come under such insurance: (i) Private cars, (ii) Commercial vehicles (trucks, vans, tractors, buses, etc.), (iii) Motorcycles and scooters, (iv) Other like automobiles displayed at showrooms, ambulances, Government vehicles, trailers, bulldozers, armoured cars, petrol wagons, etc.

There are two types of risks covered under this insurance:

(i) Damage or loss of the automobile under this insurance.

(ii) Damage of property of a third party (called Third Party Insurance or Act only policy).

A COMPREHENSIVE POLICY may also be taken which includes personal accident, damage of vehicle, third party insurance and theft or fire, loss by riot, earthquake, flood, Terrorist activity of loss during transit, etc.

Insurance Against Third Party Risk

Third party insurance is compulsory on the part of the motor vehicle owner. Under the Motor Vehicles Act, 1988/under sections 140 and 141 the owners of vehicles are liable to pay compensation in certain cases on the "PRINCIPAL OF NO FAULT" in case of death or permanent disablement to a third party.

A bill called "Road Transport and Safety bill 2014" has been introduced in parliament to replace old Motor vehicle Act, 1988. Following are major changes proposed in the bill:

(1) Old provisions of "*No Fault Liability*" has been dropped.

(2) The definition of goods, passenger, transport vehicle and goods vehicle has been changed. Goods means any kind movable property, live stock and motor vehicle transported on another motor vehicle but does not include persons and their personal effects.

(3) The persons to be compulsorily covered are (i) even persons not using the vehicle of accident like pedestrian, (ii) driver driving the vehicle, (iii) owner of goods or his authorised representative carried in the vehicle, (iv) In case of public service vehicle passengers, conductor, ticket examiner in the vehicle and in goods vehicle workmen in that vehicle (formerly they were covered under workmen compensation Act, 1923).

(4) Duty and defences: The insurer shall have to pay inspite of that the insurer may be entitled to avoid or cancel or may have avoided or cancelled the policy, the sum assured. He can defend on following grounds:

(a) breach of a specified condition of the policy (except use of vehicle), (b) on contract date the vehicle was not covered by permit to ply for hire or reward, (c) for organised racing and speed testing, (d) transport vehicle used for purpose not allowed under the permit, (e) without side car being attached where the vehicle is motor cycle, (f) a condition excluding driving by a named person or person not duly licensed or who has been disqualified for a driving license or a condition excluding liability during war, civil war, riot or civil commotion or a, (g) the policy is void in ground that it was obtained by nondisclosure of material fact or by a representation of fact which was false in some material particular.

(5) Creation of Two more Funds: In addition to the existing **"Solution fund"** for payment of compensation in "Hit and Run" accident victim the two new funds created are (a) funds to provide treatment to the road accident victims during **"golden hour" Gold Hour** means that time period lasting from a few minutes to several ours following traumatic injury during which time there is higher likelihood of presenting death by provision of prompt medical care, (b) **Motor accident fund** to provide compulsory insurance cover to all road user in India.

Necessity for Insurance Against Third Party Risk

No person shall use, except as a passenger, or cause or allow other person to use, a motor vehicle in a public place, unless there is in force in relation to the use of the vehicle by that person or that other person, as the case may be, a policy of insurance complying with the legal requirements:

Provided that in the case of a vehicle carrying, or meant to carry, dangerous or hazardous goods, there shall also be a policy of insurance under the Public Liability Insurance Act, 1991.

A person driving a motor vehicle merely as a paid employee, while there is in force in relation to the use of the vehicle no such policy as is required by this sub-section, shall not be deemed to act in contravention of the sub-section unless he knows or has reason to believe that there is no such policy in force.

This shall not apply to any vehicle owned by the Central Government or a State Government and used for Government purposes unconnected with any commercial enterprise.

The appropriate Government may, by order, exempt from the operation of sub-section (1) any vehicle owned by any of the following authorities, namely:

(a) the Central Government or a state Government, if the vehicle is used for Government purposes connected with any commercial enterprise;

(b) any local authority;

(c) any State transport undertakings.

Provided that no such order shall be made in relation to any such authority unless a fund has been established and is maintained by that authority in accordance with the rules made in that behalf under this Act for meeting any liability arising out of the use of any vehicle of that authority which that authority or any person in its employment may incur to third parties (Section 229).

Requirement of Policies and Limits of Liability

1. In order to comply with the requirements a policy of insurance must be a policy which—

(a) is issued by a person who is an authorised insurer; and

(b) insures the person or classes of persons specified in the policy to the extent specified in the Act.

(i) against any liability which may be incurred by him in respect of the death of or bodily injury to any person, including owner of the goods or his authorised representative carried in the vehicle or damage to any property of a third party caused by or arising out of the use of the vehicle in a public place;

(ii) against the death of or bodily injury to any passengers of a public service vehicle caused by or arising out of the use of the vehicle in a public place:

Provided that a policy shall not be required:

(i) to cover liability in respect of the death, arising out of and in the course of his employment of the employee, of a person insured by the policy or in respect of bodily injury sustained by such an employee arising out of and in the course of his employment other than a liability arising under the Workmen's Compensation Act, 1928 in respect of the death of, or bodily injury to, any such employee—

(a) engaged in driving the vehicle, or

(b) if it is a public service vehicle engaged as a conductor of the vehicle or in examining tickets on the vehicle, or

(c) if it is a goods carriage, being carried in the vehicle, or

(ii) to cover any contractual liability.

Explanation: 1. For the removal of doubts, it is hereby declared that the death of or bodily injury to any person or damage to any property of a third party shall be deemed to have been caused by or to have arisen out of, the use of a vehicle in public place notwithstanding that the person who is dead or injured or the property which is damaged was not in a public place at the time of the accident, if the act or mission which led to the accident occurred in a public place.

2. A policy shall be of no effect for the purposes of the law unless and until there is issued by the insurer in favour of the person by whom the policy is effected a certificate of insurance in the prescribed form and containing the prescribed particulars of any condition subject to which the policy is issued and of any other prescribed matters; and different forms, particulars and matters may be prescribed in different cases.

3. Where a cover note issued by the insurer is not followed by a policy of insurance within the prescribed time, the insurer shall, within seven days of the expiry of the period of the validity of the cover note, notify the fact to the registering authority in whose records the vehicle to which the cover note rebates has been registered or to such other authority as the State Government may prescribe.

4. Notwithstanding anything contained in any law for the time being in force an insurer a policy of insurance under this section shall be liable to indemnify the person or classes of persons specified in the policy in respect of any liability which the policy purports to cover in the case of that person or these classes of persons (Section 230).

Validity of Policies on Insurance Issued in Reciprocating Countries

Where, in pursuance of an arrangement, between India and any reciprocating country, any motor vehicle registered in the reciprocating country operates on any route or within any area common to the two countries and there is in force in relation to the use of the vehicle in the reciprocating country, a policy of insurance complying with the requirements of the law of insurance in force in that country, then, notwithstanding anything contained in Section 230 but subject to any rules which may be made, such policy of insurance shall be effective throughout the route or area in respect of which, the arrangement has been made, as if the policy of insurance had complied with the requirements of the Act (Section 231).

Duty of Insurers to Satisfy Judgements and Awards Against Persons Insured in Respect of Third Party Risks

1. If, after a certificate of insurance has been issued in favour of the person by whom a policy has been effected, judgement or award in respect of any such liability as is required to be covered by a policy is obtained against any person insured by the policy, then, notwithstanding that the insurer may be entitled to avoid or cancel or may have avoided or cancelled the policy, the insurer shall, pay to the person entitled to the benefit of the decree any sum not exceeding the sum assured payable thereunder, as if he were the judgment-debtor, in respect of the liability, together with any amount payable in respect of costs and any sum payable in respect of interest on that sum by virtue of any enactment relating to interest on judgments.

2. No sum shall be payable an insurer in respect of any judgment or award unless, before the commencement of the proceedings in which the judgment or award is given the insurer had notice through the Court or, as the case may be, the Claims Tribunal of the bringing of the proceedings, or in respect of such judgment or award so long as execution is stayed thereon pending an appeal; and an insurer to whom notice of the bringing of any such proceeding is so given shall be entitled to be made a party thereto and defend the action on any of the following grounds, namely:

(a) that there has been breach of a specified condition of the policy, being one of the following conditions, namely:

(i) a condition excluding the use of the vehicle:

- for hire or reward, where the vehicle is on the date of the contract of insurance a vehicle not covered by a permit to ply for hire or reward, or
- for organised racing and speed testing, or
- for a purpose not allowed by the permit under which the vehicle is used, where the vehicle is a transport vehicle, or
- without side car being attached where the vehicle is a motor cycle; or

(ii) a condition excluding driving by a named person or persons or by any person who is not duly licensed, or by any person who has been disqualified for holding or obtaining a driving license during the period of disqualification; or

(iii) a condition excluding liability for injury caused or contributed to by conditions of war, civil war, riot or civil commotion; or

(b) that the policy is void on the ground that it was obtained by the non-disclosure of a material fact or by a representation of fact which was false in some material particular (Section 233).

Rights of Third Parties Against Insurers on Insolvency of the Insured

1. Where under any contract of insurance effected a person is insured against liabilities which he may incur to third parties, then:

(a) in the event of the person becoming insolvent or making a composition or arrangement with his creditors, or

(b) where the insured person is a company, in the event of a winding up order being made or a resolution for a voluntary winding-up being passed with respect to the company or of a receiver or manager of the company's business or undertaking being duly appointed, or of possession being taken by or in behalf of the holders of any debentures secured by a floating charge of any property comprised in or subject to the charge,

if, either before or after that event, any such liability is incurred by the insured person, his rights against the insurer under the contract in respect of the liability shall be transferred to and vest in third party to whom the liability was so incurred.

2. Where an order for the administration of the estate of a decreased debtor is made according to the law of insolvency, then, if any debt provable in insolvency is owing by the decreased in respect of a liability to a third party against which he was insured under a contract of insurance, the decreased debtor's rights against the insurer in respect of that liability shall, notwithstanding anything to the country in any provision of law, be transferred to and vest in the person to whom the debt is owing (Section 234).

Duty to Give Information as to Insurance

No person against whom a claim is made in respect of any liability shall on demand by or on behalf of the person making the claim refuse to stage whether or not he was insured in respect of that liability by any policy issued or would have been so insured if the insurer had not avoided or cancelled the policy, nor shall he refuse, if he was or would have been so insured, to give such particulars with respect to that policy as were specified in the certificate of insurance issued in respect thereof (Section 235).

Settlement between Insurers and Insured Persons

No settlement made by an insurer in respect of any claim which might be made by a third party in respect of any liability of the nature shall be valid unless such third party is a party to the settlement (Section 236).

Effect of Certificate of Insurance

When an insurer has issued a certificate of insurance in respect of a contract of insurance between the insurer and the insured person, then:

(a) If and so long as the policy described in the certificate has not been issued by the insurer to the insured, the insurer shall, as between himself and any other person except the insured, be deemed to have issued to the insured person a policy of insurance, conforming in all respects with the description and particulars stated in such certificates; and

(b) If the insurer has issued to the insured the policy described in the certificate, but the actual terms of the policy are less favourable to persons claiming under or by virtue of the policy against the insurer either directly or through the insurer than the particulars of the policy as stated in the certificate, the policy shall, as between the insurer and any other person except the insured, be deemed to be in terms conforming in all respects with the particulars stated in the said certificate (Section 239).

Transfer of Certificate of Insurance

Where a person in whose favour the certificate of insurance has been issued transfers to another person the ownership of the motor vehicle in respect of which such insurance was taken together with the policy of insurance relating thereto, the certificate of insurance and the policy described in the certificate shall be deemed to have been transferred in favour of the person to whom the motor vehicle is transferred with effect from the date of its transfer (Section 240).

Production of Certain Certificates, License and Permit in Certain Cases

1. Any person driving a motor vehicle in any public place shall, on being so required by a police officer in uniform authorised in this behalf by the State Government, produce:

(a) the certificate of insurance;

(b) the certificate of registration;

(c) the driving license; and

(d) in the case of a transport vehicle, also the certificate of fitness referred to in Section 56 and the permit, relating to the use of the vehicle.

2. If, where owing to the presence of a motor vehicle in a public place an accident occurs involving death or bodily injury to another person, the driver of the vehicle does not at the time produce of the certificates, driving license and permit referred to in sub-section (1) to a police officer, he shall produce the said certificates, license and permit at the police station at which he makes the report required.

3. No person shall be liable to conviction by reason only of the failure to produce the certificate of insurance if, within seven days from the date on which its production was required from the date of occurrence of the accident, he produces the certificate at such police station as may have been specified by him to the police officer who required its production or as the case may be, to the police officer at the site of the accident or to the officer in charge of the police station at which he reported the accident:

4. A copy of FIR and medical report or post-mortem report.

5. The owner of a motor vehicle shall give such information as he may be required by or on behalf of a police officer empowered in this behalf by the State Government to give for the purpose of determining whether the vehicle was or was not being given in contravention of law and on any occasion when the driver was required under this section to produce his certificate of insurance.

6. As soon as any information regarding any accident involving death or bodily injury to any person is recorded or report under this section is completed by a police officer, the officer in charge of the police station shall forward a copy of the same within thirty days from the date of recording of information or, as the case may be, on completion of, such report to the Claims Tribunal having jurisdiction and a copy thereof to the concerned insurer, and where a copy is made available to the owner, he shall also within thirty days of receipt of such report, forward the same to such Claims Tribunal and Insurer (Section 238).

The onus to prove that insured vehicle was being driven without a valid permit at the material time of accident is on the insurance company obtaining information from RTA [SC (2002) *Kamala M. Vayani* Vs *United India Insurance*]. A car is insured for three years as per IRDA.

Production of Certificate of Insurance on Application for Authority to Use Vehicle

A State Government may make rules requiring the owner of any motor vehicle when applying whether by payment of a tax or otherwise for authority to use the vehicle in a public place to produce such evidence as may be prescribed by those rules to the effect that:

On the date when the authority to use the vehicle comes into operation there will be in force the necessary policy of insurance in relation to the use of the vehicle by the applicant or by other persons on his order or with his permission.

Special Provisions as to Compensation in Case of Hit and Run Motor Accident

Notwithstanding anything contained in the General Insurance Business (Nationalisation) Act, 1972, or any other law for the time being in force or any instrument having the force of law, the General Insurance Corporation of India and the insurance companies for the time being carrying on general insurance business in India shall provide for paying in accordance with the provisions of M.V. Act and the scheme w.e.f. 1-7-1989 compensation in respect of the death of, or grieve is hurt to, persons resulting from hit and run motor accidents.

The compensation shall be paid:

(a) in respect of the death of any person resulting from a hit and run motor accident, a fixed sum of twenty-five thousand rupees;

(b) in respect of grievous hurt to any person resulting from a hit and run motor accident a fixed sum of twelve thousand and five hundred rupees.

Option to File Claim in Certain Cases

Where a person is entitled to claim compensation, he shall file the claim under either under Section 247 or Section 228 and not under both.

For computation of compensation to motor accident victims the principle applied is based on **'future prospective income'** that victim could have earned. There is another method called **'split multiplier'** method. This method is a corollary of first method. The method may be explained. Suppose death occurs of a government employee aged about 57 years earning about ₹ 10,000 P.M. the income of the deceased was calculated based on his monthly salary less professional tax plus income tax if any and personal expenses to the extent of 1/3, ½, ¾ based on size of family, which is called contribution to the family. The said amount is multiplied by the relevant multiplier as applicable to the age group of which the deceased belong provided in 2nd schedule of the Act or laid down by Supreme Court in Sarla Verma's case. Suppose he would have retired by age of 60. Considering his age 57, the applicable multiplier (see II Schedule) would be 11. Since he would have retired by 60 years, the 11 multiplier shall be split in two parts. Multiplier 3 shall have been applied for his actual income at the time of his death and multiplier 8 shall be made applicable to his pension which he would have received.

When a claim is filed, the insured usually claims for (a) Hospitalisation Bill, (b) Post hospitalisation medical expenses, (c) Income loss (explained above), (d) Pain and suffering, (e) In case of death claim for loss of partner and love of family. A claim must be settled within 30 days.

As decided by Supreme Court in *Sarla Verma* vs. *Delhi Transport Corporation* (2008) and *Santoshi Devi* vs. *National Insurance Company* (2012) for calculation, following principles are laid down?

1. The insurer will take into account the actual income at the time of death, and is a rule of thumb. Deviation is permissible in rare and exceptional cases.
2. A person over the age of 50 can be eligible for compensation based on future prospective income.
3. Even if a person who is self-employed or is engaged on fixed wages will get 30% increase in his total income over a period of time if he/she is victim of accident for calculating the amount of compensation.
4. If a person does not file claim before Motor accident claims Tribunal ₹ 5 lakhs will be paid in case of death and in case of others ₹ 2.5 lakhs.

Effecting of Motor Insurance

Any person who wishes to insure his motor vehicle has to fill up a proposal form. After the receipt of the proposal form, the insurance company has to determine the rate of the premium. The company will charge rates according to the schedule for a particular vehicle under a particular policy. The schedule castes wherein premium and any amount for an additional risk is added to the basic premium, while rebate allowed is subtracted from it. Horse Power and, to a lesser degree, the value of the vehicle are the main factors for determining the amount of premium.

After hearing from the insurance company, the proposer will pay the amount of the premium and the company will, after the receipt of the premium, issue a cover note along with a certificate of insurance. The Cover Note serves as an evidence of the acceptance of the risk by the insurance company till a final policy is issued. The certificate of insurance can be produced before the Regional Transport Authority as a proof of the insurance. These certificates of insurance are of various kinds, depending on the type of the vehicle, type of the policy, persons entitled to drive the vehicle, etc. This certificate contains various details about the vehicle and the insured.

The term of motor insurance is also usually for ONE YEAR excepting for any allowance given to the insured for the renewal of the policy. A motor insurance policy may be taken for a period shorter than a year but the rates of premium will be higher on such policies. If the insured wants to cover any extra benefits or cancel some limitations during the currency of the policy, it can be done by paying extra premium on PRO RATA basis and subject to any minimum premium fixed by the insurance company. If the insured wants to sell his insured car and replace it by a new one, the policy can be transferred to apply to the new car. The amount of premium, if necessary, can be adjusted proportionately.

Policies on Commercial Vehicle

Commercial vehicles refer to any type of mechanically driven vehicles used for business or trade purpose. They may be passenger vehicles, goods vehicles, line cars, single and double deckers, coaches, police vehicles, ambulances, or tractors. When the automobiles is used for earning a living like Taxi, the chances of risks will be more as it will be used for more kilometers in comparison to private cars. Generally, the policies on commercial vehicles cover third party risk and own damages. Other risks are provided for by endorsement according to the circumstances of each individual case by paying extra premium. The policy does not cover the damage from boiler explosion, passenger risk, riot and civil commotion risk, mechanical breakdown, unless otherwise provided. The procedure of settlement of claims is the same, as explained under private cars.

IRDA, in January 2012 has laid down that all general insurers registered to carry on motor insurance business shall collectively participate in a pooling arrangement to share in all motor third party insurance business underwritten by any of the registered general insurers in accordance with the following provisions:

"Motor Third Party Declined Risk Insurance Pool" for Commercial Vehicles

With effect from 31-3-2012, IRDA has dismantled the existing "Indian Motor Third Party Insurance Pool" (IMTPIP). IRDA has created 'Indian Motor Third Party Declined Risk Insurance Pool' (DR. Pool) w.e.f. 1-4-2012 in its place. Following guidelines have been issued by IRDA on 23-12-2011:

(i) All existing general insurers shall be admitted as a member of new pool. Any general insurer not willing to write the third party insurance shall refer to DR. Pool. Specialist insurer not licensed for motor insurance business shall not be member of the pool.

(ii) No insurer can refuse to write the risk.

(iii) DR. Pool shall apply to all commercial vehicles for stand alone third party insurance. No comprehensive motor insurance policy or part thereof shall be ceded to the pool. Miscellaneous and special class of vehicles (Class D, E, F & G) as per section 4 of erstwhile Indian motor tariff shall also be excluded from scope of the pool.

(iv) General Insurance Corporation shall act as administrator of the DR. Pool. GIC shall be paid a fee on actual cost basis.

(v) The member companies, called ceding company shall retain 20% of the gross premium to their account, cede as per obligatory cession to GIC (at present 10% of gross premium, and cede the balance (currently 70% of the gross premium) to DR. Pool.

(vi) The pool liability for the underwriting year will be extinguished on a clear cut basis at the end of every year with net cash payments being exchanged between the ceding and receiving companies on the basis of ultimate loss ratio (ULR) estimated by pool actuary. He will complete the estimate by end of MAY each year.

(vii) The estimates of ULR for business written by the insurer for DR Pool shall be as per (vi) above for all the three viz. net account, GIC account and pool account. However, the estimates of ULR for business written by the insurer to its on account fully may be as per its appointed actuary's estimate.

(viii) GIC Re shall not be a part of clear cut settlement as it has got a 10% share by way of obligatory cession.

(ix) The premium in pool shall be reviewed annually based on following formula and according to actuarial principles

$P(t) - CI(t) \times CII(t-1) + C2(t)$

$P(t)$ = Motor third party premium applicable to the financial year t

$CII(t-1)$ = cost inflation index for the year 't – 1' as notified by CBDT

$CI(t)$ and $C2(t)$ are the parameters applicable to the financial year 't' whose values shall be determined and notified by IRDA in each year based on the experience measured in terms of average claim amounts, frequency and expenses involved in servicing the motor TP business.

Trade Policies

Motor traders have special insurance requirements, as many of the vehicles on their premises do not belong to them, but are there for repairs or to be garaged or put in show rooms. For this purpose, trade policies are issued. These policies are similar to the policies on commercial vehicles with the exception that damage or loss by accident is usually confide to that by collision and only such damages or losses are covered as occur on the road, or in the garage. Third Party Risks are also accepted on the road in the similar way.

Policies on Motor Cycles and Scooters

Motor cycles and scooters are generally used and owned by young people with a zest for speed, and as such, this type of insurance has proved too costly to insurers. In case of motor cycles and scooters, auto-cycles or mechanically assisted pedal cycles, a comprehensive policy is generally issued which covers loss of or damage to it by fire, lightning, explosion, self-ignition, theft, larceny, malicious acts, transit and accidents. The policies also cover the accessories and spare parts against theft, it stolen with the motor cycle or scooter. Accidental or fire damage to the accessories is covered irrespective of the cycle being damaged with them or not. Types are covered if damaged with motor cycle or scooter. Motor cycles used for private and business purposes are rated on the cubic capacity of the engine and the area where the cycle is ordinarily garaged. Value of expensive machines is also taken into account. Pillion riders can also claim. Supreme Court hold in 1993 in case of Manam Yasovardhana that delay in filing FIR, absence of blood stains on offending vehicle, non-production of driving license and non-filling of claim by pillion rider is no ground for not granting claim. The policy can be issued for five years as per IRDA.

No-claim Bonus

Usually, insurers encourage "accident-free" insureds and allow them a no-claim bonus (a type of discount) from the premiums for private cars, commercial vehicles and motor cycles, where no claim has been made for the insured vehicle for one year or more. Of course, the amount of bonus varies widely from company to company and according to the number of claim-free years that there have been. The reductions are allowed off the net renewal premium in the event of no claims made or pending during the preceding years in respect of private motor cars. In a comprehensive policy bonus starts with 20% for first year, 35% in second year and maximum upto 50% by 4 years or more.

Personal Accident Insurance

We have discussed personal accident Insurance at the beginning of the chapter. IRDA has made mandatory for drivers to insure themselves.

Besides, personal accident insurance is an integral part of health insurance and is designed to replace a substantial part of earned income host through disability caused by accidental injury, and also may provide for payment of medical expenses for insured when he is in hospital occasioned by accidental injury and indemnity for death or loss of limbs or sight suffered through accident. In other words, under a personal accident insurance contract, the insurer agrees to pay the insured or to his heir or legal representatives in case of death, a stated sum of money in the event of his being killed, permanently disabled, temporary total or partial disablement by accident. Such insurance is of considerable importance in the modern industrialised society, where the rates of personal accidents have increased tremendously due to excessive use of modern mechanical equipments, fastest modes of transport and application of technology in every sphere of economic activity.

Supreme Court held that any person saving the accident victim on road must be given immunity from police harassment and hospital amount from identification.

Types of Insurance Policies

There are various attractive schemes of personal accident available to the insured, out of which the proposer has to select the type of cover most suited to his particular requirements and pocket, main classes of policy are:

(a) Accident only insurance,

(b) Accident and all sickness insurance,

(c) Short period travel insurance,

(d) Accident and specified diseases,

(e) Group accident,

(f) Permanent sickness and accident insurance, and

(g) Other special schemes.

All these policies, except short period travel insurance, are issued for one year and can be renewed after their expiry. However, beyond attaining a certain age say, 55 or 60 years, these policies are not renewed, as older people are more liable to suffer accident or contract disease and recovery may be retorted on account of reduced physical resistance. The premiums within the permitted age range is the same for the different ages as the element of age in personal accident insurance is not so important as in life insurance. Contrarily, with the increase in age, the insured shows greater prudence to avoid the risk of accident. Hence, the premiums do not vary according to the age of the insured but depends on the measure of benefits asked for and the occupation of the proposer.

Exclusion

The policy does not cover death, injury or disablement resulting from:

(a) Service on duty with any Armed Forces or while engaged or taking part in commotions or riots of any kind;

(b) Intentional self-injury, suicide or attempted suicide (whether felonious or not) provided assault, fighting (except in bona fide self-defence), or the influence or drink or drugs;

(c) Medical or surgical treatment (except where such treatment is rendered necessary by bodily injury caused accident within the scope of the policy);

(d) Aviation other than fare-paying passenger in an aircraft licensed for hire or owned and rated by a regular airline or established charter service;

(e) Mountaineering (necessitating the use of guides or ropes) or winter sports;

(f) Riding or driving in any kind of race, hunting and a big game shouting;

(g) Any consequence of war, invasion, act of foreign, enemy, hostilities (whether was be declared or not), civil war, rebellion, revolution, insurrection or military or usurped power.

Legal Cases—Accidents and Motor

Automobile Insurance and Accident Insurance

(1) Insured's car was stolen, which was insured for ₹ 55,000. The company paid ₹ 41,500 without giving reason for less payment than insured value. Held company was bond to pay ₹ 55,000 (*Shantanu Chatterji* vs. *United India Insurance Co.* Gurgaon).

(2) Mr. Ishwar Singh's motor cycle was met with accident. He lodged complaint with police and insurance company. The insurer rejected the claim on the ground that intimation of accident was given to police 21 days after and to the company after 25 days. Held the company was not justified in repudiating the claim because complaint was made in time (*Ishwar Singh* vs. *ICICI Lombard General Insurance Co.* Gurgaon).

(3) Complainant stated that his truck was insured met with an accident. He informed the insurer and filed claim. The vehicle was surveyed at Aligarh by a surveyor. His vehicle was taken to Delhi and again a final survey was made by another surveyor. He got claim of ₹ 70,680, whereas settlement was for ₹ 95,200. The company deducted the amount on ground that spot survey was not done. Held company was not justified for deduction of 25%. Hence payment of ₹ 24,520, the balance, was ordered to be paid (*Rajesh Kalra* vs. *Reliance General Insurance Co. Ltd.* Aligarh).

(4) Dilbag Rai met with an accident of 6-11-2009. Only bonnet cover was damaged on 7-11-2009, he gave vehicle to M/S Rana Motors, New Delhi on 14-11-2009 the workshop informed that the repair of the car was not cleared by the surveyor. He took the car to Ambala and gave it to M/S Ravi Motors. He paid the repair charges to ₹ 6564 in addition to surveyor fee ₹ 900. The surveyor estimated repairs to ₹ 6219. The company refused to pay on the ground that claims were filed both at Delhi and Ambala. Held that claim was payable because loss was during currency of policy (*Dilbag Rai* vs. *National Insurance* Ambala).

(5) The complainant had a Janata Personal accident policy. He informed insurer that his vision of both the eyes was lost due to accidental injury. Insurer contented that blindness was not solely and directly caused due to accident.

Two doctors certified that blindness is due to degenerative Retina. Held that accident caused by white ants as alleged by complainant, white cleaning roof is not confirmed. Repudiation was up held (*Bhupendra Kumar C. Shah* vs. *United India Insurance Co.* Ahmedabad).

(6) Mr. Saffiulla was covered under individual Janata Personal accident for ₹ 1 lakh for a period of five years. His wife Ammunisa was a nominee. After four years he died due to electrocution. The incident was not reported to police and no post-mortem was done. The insurer repudiated the claim on this ground. The death certificate was produced issued by a Muslim Sunnath committee which confirmed his death due to electric shock and his body was buried in Muslim graveyard.

The insurance company's investigator confirmed this. It is noted that post-mortem and FIR are not prerequisite of policy. The insurer was directed to settle the claim (*Mrs. J. Ammunisa* vs. *The Oriental Insurance Co.* Chennai).

(7) In *Sasanka Sekhar Maity* vs. *National Insurance* the son of the complainant died of accident being run by train. The post-mortem report stated "as per inquest report and post-mortem report the death was due to shock and haemorrhage by train accident." But insurer's investigator death was due to suicide. The claim was refused. Held the insurer was liable to pay claim and interest @2% above the prevailing bank rate for the period of delay.

(8) *Smt. Bindu Barman* vs. *National Insurance Co. Ltd.*, Guwahati. The complainant's husband procured a policy from the insurance company. The insured died due to vehicle accident. The insurance company repudiated the claim on the ground of non-submission of death intimation and relevant documents within specified time. Strict compliance of social condition is not a must in deserving cases. During hearing before Ombudsman the insurer remained absent. The complainant proved his ignorance of the existence of policy due to death, not intentionally. Claim was to be paid.

(9) The complainant's husband was insured under a long term JPA policy for ₹ 100,000 for a period of five years. The complainant's husband died due to electric shock. The insurer refused to pay the claim on the ground as it fell-under exclusion 4(d) of the policy for death arising or resulting from insured committing any breach of law with criminal intent. The deceased was a casual labour and cooked as a helper to assistant line man. While climbing pole for repair he sustained shock, fell from pole and died. The insurer contended that the deceased was employed as a private electrician and was not authorised to climb the electric pole. Complainant produced a group photo of the electricity department, in which he was present. All records show that the electricity department called the deceased for work. Held there was no breach of law. The insurer could not prove the breach of law. The claim was to be paid.

14

Home and Other Types of Insurance

Because of changes in the lifestyle in big cities, home insurance is important. In earlier days joint families ensured that the house was never left unoccupied. So the risk of thieves or succumbing to fire was minimised.

An individual can insure his house as the owner or even a tenant can insure its all contents not only against fire, theft, natural disasters, third party liability but also against even accidental death or injury. A comprehensive policy can be taken to cover all these risks. Such policy contains 10 to 15 Sections. A discount is given by insurance company upto 15% to 20%, if less number of sections of the policy are opted.

Before going for an insurance cover, one should make a detailed list of all the things. The list should include the quantity details, description, cost and the amount of loss associated with each item. The inventory list must be updated on a regular basis once in six months. Copies of bills, invoices and other papers should be kept along with the inventory list.

If there are any improvements added to the house then they should automatically be included in the coverage. Even if the improvements are still in progress, it is better to insure them just in case they are irreparably damaged before they are complete. The purchase date, serial number and price of all the electronic items should be kept in order for quick verification.

The insured should be sure to include component parts and the contents of drawers, shelves, closets, storage boxes and built-in cabinets. Remember that one may be covered for things that are not excluded in one's policy.

An agent might insist on the necessity of taking a complete Comprehensive Householder's Insurance Policy comprising of 10 or 15 Sections, but as an individual, be prudent in opting for the sections that are relevant even if it involves a tedious job of sorting and assessing each article. Out of the 10 or 15 Sections, the base policy (Section 1) has two sub-sections—one covers the building and the second sub-section protects its contents against damage from ruin and allied perils from fire, lightning, explosion of gas in domestic appliances, riots and natural calamities such as floods and earthquakes.

The comprehensive policy also called 'householders package policies' is divided into 10 Sections. The package includes the following sections:

1. Fire insurance of the building and contents (house-hold contents). Insurance of contents against fire risks is compulsory and a minimum of three covers is to be selected for issue of a package policy.
2. Burglary, house-breaking, larceny and theft insurance.
3. All risks insurance for jewellery, ornaments and other valuables.
4. Place glass accident insurance.
5. Breakdown of domestic appliances (electrical and mechanical failures).
6. Television including VCR, VCD, DVD and music systems.
7. Pedal cycle insurance.
8. Personal travel baggage insurance.
9. Personal accident with family package discount of 10%.

Item No. 1 is under Tariff and rest items fall in non-tariff category.

Some companies also offer insurance of household goods in case a person is shifting residence or a rent up to a specified period if a person is faced with some contingency.

Before taking the policy one should always enquire whether the area of his residence falls in the seismic zone. For example, Kolkata and Mumbai are least prone to earthquakes while Delhi, and Ahmedabad fall in the earthquake-prone regions, thereby commanding a higher premium on the policy. It is always prudent since tremors too are capable of destroying houses as had happened in Delhi a few years ago. The coverage of a Householder's Policy is exhaustive. The necessary covers include risk of fire and allied perils for the building and its contents, burglary, housebreaking, breakdown of appliances and television and public liability.

The need based or optional sections that one might opt for only if he deems it necessary include an All risk for cash and jewellery, plate glass, pedal cycle, baggage, personal accident. A break-up of the Comprehensive Householder's Policy will make it clear.

Valuables such as lot of cash and jewellery are safest in bank lockers, but if one does keep them at home, one should opt for cover which provides 'All risks' cover against loss or damage to jewellery and valuables and even cameras. It's important to provide a break-up and specific details of each insured item.

The policy may provide cover against accidental breakdown of electric, electronic and mechanical gadgets, including refrigerators, air-conditioners, microwave ovens, washing machines or motor pumps but not televisions.

A householder's policy requires the policyholder to insure the contents of his home for their full value. It is true that with each passing year the value of the contents in the house decreases, however, what needs to be remembered is that while purchasing the policy; one should cover the valuables and articles at their replacement value. For instance, if a five-year old refrigerator can be resold for ₹ 9,000, it will still cost an individual ₹ 18,000 to replace. However, unless the individual insures the refrigerator for ₹ 18,000, he will be ineligible for a full settlement on its breakdown claims.

The policy may cover the damage to television sets and VCDs/VCRs/VCPs and computers against all types of risks, fire and allied perils, theft and accidental breakdown. The cover also includes damage to the TV if it is accidentally dropped while moving it within the house. On computers, the cover applies to losses in excess of ₹ 2500.

Another section that should be included while taking the cover is insurance against public liability. It covers legal liability to a third party for personal injury or property damage. For instance, if the domestic help at someone's place falls down and breaks his legs while installing the fan, he needs to be compensated for the damage. In such instances, the third-party liability cover becomes useful.

Necessary Covers

Fire and allied perils	Cover	Premium
(a) Building	20,00,000	1000
(b) Contents (excluding cash and jewellery) Burglary, house-breaking, including:	5,00,000	250
Larceny and theft	5,00,000	1,200
Appliances	1,00,000	250
Television	25,000	250
One pays (after 15% discount of premium)		2507.50
Optional Covers		
All risk (cash and jewellery)	50,000	500
Plate glass	10,000	100
Pedal cycle	2000	40
Baggage	20,000	150
Personal Accident	10,00,000	2,000
Public Liability	20,000	10
One Pays (After 20% discount)		₹ 4,600

The Optional Covers

There are sections one can give a miss from following covers. For example, loss of or damage to baggage while travelling or loss of or damage to a bicycle and personal accident.

There are various companies offering household insurance in the country. Notable among them is Royal Sundaram Alliance, Tata-AIG General Insurance, ICICI Lombard, Bajaj Allianz General Insurance, Iffco-Tokio General Insurance and the public sector players including United India Insurance, New India Assurance, Oriental Insurance and National Insurance. There is hardly a 10% variation in premium among players. Loss of rent keys locker replacement, temporary resettlement, ATM with drawl robbery, less of wallet, dog insurance public-liebling and employees compensate.

Compensation Offered

Depending on the property insured, the insurance cover provides compensation equivalent to the market value or the cost of replacement. In cases, where the items are insured are susceptible to depreciation. The actual value is offered. Specifically to be public liability risk, the amount preferred is up to ₹ 25,000. The period of insurance may be from one year to three years.

Exclusions

The exclusions under the householder's insurance policy are specific to the item or property insured:

- Under the Fire tariff, the house must conform to Class 'A' construction norms.
- Personal computers do not qualify as contents to be insured. A separate electronic equipment policy has to be taken.
- Disk antennae are not covered under the policy.

ICICI Lombard's Home Insurance is provided over the counter. A unique feature of this policy is that it also provides expenses for temporary resettlement covering packing, unpacking, loading and unloading upto 4% of the content's sum insured. However, if the premise is unoccupied for more than 30 days, then the insurance is not applicable.

Bajaj Allianz's Householders' Insurance is a single policy providing protection for property and interests of the insured and his family members who permanently reside with him. The package policy covers 10 sections including fire, burglary, jewellery and/or precious stones all risks, plate glass, domestic appliances, electronic equipments, pedal cycles, baggage insurance, personal accident insurance and public liability. The unique feature of this policy is that group discounts can be availed by opting for more than 5 sections.

Tata AIG's Home Secure on the other hand, offers the policyholder the option to choose from 6 pre-packed policies. The 15-section policy includes purchase protection, against loss of money in transit and rent for alternative accommodation. Moreover, the sections of the policy become ineffective only if the premises have been unoccupied for more than 60 days.

Iffco-Tokio's Home and Family Protector Insurance Policy also provides protection against increased living expenses and loan payment. An automatic increase in the sum insured for a period of 15 days before and after a wedding of any family member is covered.

Claim Settlements

Insurance contracts are always based on the information provided in the proposal form and is verified at the time of a claim, when physical inspection of the property is done. In case of any misrepresentation, it is the prerogative of the insurance company to avoid a claim, or avoid the policy, or pay a claim for a reduced amount.

Here are some important points, which would help in the claims procedure:

- On receipt of claim intimation, the insurer will forward a claim form.
- The insurer will arrange for inspection of the damaged items to access the loss. In case of major losses, a specialist-licensed surveyor is deputed.
- The insured has to provide the required documents to substantiate the extent of loss.

In view of varied nature of policies, certain points distinct to individual policies, in addition to the above, are listed below:

Fire Claims

- The insured should take all possible steps to minimize the loss.
- The fire brigades may be intimated immediately.

- Lodge a police complaint in case of a fire arising out of rioting mob, striking workers, malicious damage by third parties, terrorist damage.
- Obtain a meteorological report in case of loss due to cyclone, flood and inundation and if the loss is localised like in the case of flood and inundation from a local water source, MRO report may be obtained.
- If the policy is on 'reinstatement basis', the claim is settled only after completion of repairs/replacement of the damaged items and submission of bills for claim payment.

Burglary Claims

- Immediately report to the police and obtain a non-traceable certificate that the items are not found.
- The insurers will insist upon a letter of undertaking on a stamp paper of appropriate value, for refunding the claim amount when the stolen property is recovered.

'All Risks' Policy for Jewellery and Valuables

- Report to the police and obtain a non-traceable certificate.

Breakdown of Domestic Appliances

- Notice of claim and estimated cost of repairs should be filed with the insurers to arrange for inspection. In case of partial losses, no depreciation is charged but when the items are not insured for its present-day replacement value, the items are treated as under insured and the claim amount is proportionately reduced. Depreciation is only applied for Total Loss claims.
- If an appliance is partially damaged, it should be repaired (on approval from insurance company) before it is put to use, as otherwise further loss is not covered.

TV Sets

- Notice of claim and estimated cost of repairs should be filed with the insurers to arrange for inspection.
- It is at the option of the insurers to repair/replace a damaged item and the insured has no option to insist upon Total Loss and abandon the set.
- In extraordinary circumstances, the insurers will arrive at the liability and pay it in cash leaving the option to the insured.

Household Goods in Transit

- In case any damage is suspected in transit, open delivery should be insisted upon the carrier and their certificate should be obtained.
- In case of loss/damage in transit, a monetary claim should be lodged with the carrier within the time limit to protect recovery rights, without which, the claim may not be admitted.

Household Insurance Cases

(1) The plaintiff has taken a householder policy for a period from 5-9-2007 to 4-9-2008 on 24-11-2007, the plaintiff along with his family was going to attend a marriage at Mohali. When

he reached the venue, he discovered that the pouch of his wife, containing six gold bangles, of ₹ 31,000 were missing from the car. He informed the police and lodged an FIR on 27-11-2007. He also intimated to the insurer on 26-11-2007. Missing purse could not be traced by police and issued a certificate on 4-3-2007 to that affect. The insurer repudiated the claim on ground that reasonable care was not taken. The theft took place when owner of bangles was present. Held that it was not a case of taking adequate care but misfortune. The insurer is liable to pay the loss (*G.C. Bhargava* vs. *Oriental Insurance* Co. Chandigarh).

(2) In *Smt. Padmaja Pathi* vs. *Oriental Insurance* Co. (Hyderabad) case the complainant purchased a burglary policy and cash insurance policy to cover money for a sum insured of ₹ 2,50,000 and stock-in-trade of ₹ 7,50,000. A burglary of part of stock and cash of ₹ 73,000 took place. Insurer was informed. The required documents were not produced before surveyor because complainant contended that police seized the account documents and cheque books. The surveyor went to police authorities who denied that account books were taken. A false FIR was lodged. Insurer's decision not to pay was up held.

(3) The complainant, owner of electronic shop insured his T.V. sets music system, radio etc. look from the insurer a Burglary and house breaking policy for a sum insured of ₹ 5,50,000. Burglars decamped with electronic goods worth ₹ 2,47,278. A FIR was lodged. **The surveyor asset a loss** of ₹ 41,558. The insurer settled the claim for ₹ 41,550. The insured was notable to produce the papers of purchases, sales and stock register as they were stolen by burglars. Held the claim settled by insurer was corrects in the absence of documents (*Shri Ranjan Kumar Dey* vs. *Oriental Insurance* Co. Orissa).

(4) Ravinder Kumar Verma, took a householders policy opting for all risk cover from Oriental Insurance Co. Ltd for a sum insured of ₹ 1,30,602 for a period 9-2-2007 to 8-2-2008. On 7-11-2007, while travelling on a motor cycle with his wife an child, a purse containing Jewellery fell down somewhere and could not be traced. The insurer refused to pay claim on ground of gross negligence of the insured. The circumstances leading to loss wave not convincing. The insured produced hills of bangles and said that he was carrying for repair. The bangles were bought on 7-2-2007. Repairs do not require normally for bangles bright six month back. He did not take any safeguards.

Miscellaneous Insurance

There are many other type of insurances in vogue in India. Some of them are:

1. Mediclaim insurance/overseas mediclaim insurance. The first is a scheme which pays for all hospital in patient expenses arising from unforeseen illness/diseases or accident. Tax benefit is available under Section 80D of Income Tax Act for such policy. The second policy provides for indemnity for expenses incurred for medical treatment for illness/diseases or injury sustained during overseas travel primarily in the nature of an emergency.

Mr. Paresh H. Desai vs. *Oriental Insurance Co. Ltd.* Ahmedabad, mediclaim was not repudiated on the ground that hospitalisation was for observation only. The insured met with an accident and sustained angle and back region injury. The treating doctor clearly stated that insured was admitted for observation and reassessment. The hospitalisation was as per-advice of a qualified doctor. The insurer brought out other procedural non compliance, which were rejected. A claim of ₹ 3629 was upheld.

An overseas mediclaim policy is not a general health insurance policy and is intended for use by the insured person in the event of a sudden and unexpected sickness or accident outside the Republic of India.

2. Professional indemnity insurance. The policy covers the risk under which insured became legally liable to pay as damage to third party in respect of errors and/or omissions on the part of insured whilst rendering professional services.

This is based on rule in *Hedley Byrne Co. Ltd.* vs. *Heller & Partners Ltd.* (164). Professional is liable in case of negligence irrespective of the existence of any contract between him 3rd party. In Satyam Scam (2009). The price water Co. auditors were convict with 7 year jail and five of ₹ 50 lakhs. Liability may be civil as well as criminal liable. The plaintiff has to prove against professional that:

(a) He owed a legal duty towards plaintiff
(b) He has breached the duty
(c) His action/inaction caused injury
(d) The plaintiff has suffered damage.

3. Shopkeeper's insurance. It is a comprehensive specially designed policy that seeks to minimise the losses arising out of wide variety of risks and perils. It lets a shopkeeper concentrate on running his business.

A credit insurance provides protection against failure of customers to pay their debt to the shopkeeper.

4. Students safety bima policy/scholar care. It includes vital medical insurance cover, travel inconvenience, study interruption and sponsor protection.

In *Smt. Prema Nagarajan* vs. *ICICI Lombard General Insurance Co. Ltd.*, Chennai, the plaintiff has taken a Travel Insurance policy for her visit to USA. The insurer informed that on his early return to India, she will be eligible for refund of the difference of the premium. She fell sick in USA and her claim was settled. She returned to Indian and claimed the refund of premium. The insurer rejected the claim of difference on the ground that she has already made a claim and was paid. Hence refund for early return will not be made. The court found that insurer acted as per terms of the policy. Hence complaint dismissed.

5. Combo policy. It is a comprehensive policy issued by LIC. It includes features of whole life, money back, endowment and maturity payment rolled into one.

6. Fidelity insurance. Fidelity (i.e., loyalty and honesty) insurance protects the covered employer against loss due to dishonesty, cheating or misappropriation of money or goods by the employee. The insurance company naturally has to make extensive inquiries about the employees, their personal history, employment records, reasons for leaving last jobs and gaps in employment. The discovery period, i.e., the date of misappropriation by the employee and the date when discovered is decided, usually it is 6 months to 2 years.

7. BPO—Data pilferage insurance. Business Process Out-sourcing firms have a risk of pilferage of personal data of foreign clients as well as intellectual property theft by existing employees. IFFCO-TOKIO General Insurance Co. Ltd. has included breach of contract as a feature in their policy specially designed to protect India's software and service companies. Under this insurance cover, BPO firms will be insulated against infringement of intellectual property, breach of confidence or infringement of right to privacy, defamation and payment for outstanding fees.

Four different forms of policies are in use: (a) individual policy, (b) collective policy, (c) floating policy, (d) blanket policy. While under individual policy only one employee is covered and under collective policy a number of employees are covered. Floating policy is also like collective policy where the total insured amount is mentioned instead of individual limits of guarantee. Blanket policy covers all employees without mentioning their names but only their position or status. The amount of premium depends upon the amount of guarantee, usually a fixed percentage of the guaranteed amount.

8. Aviation insurance. Such insurance course are available for aircrafts—both military and civil—Cargo military hardware and passengers (army personnel), as well as staff working in airlines and airports.

British Institute of insurance has framed policy clauses relating to cargo carried by air.

For example, institute cargo clauses (AIR) C/259 lays down "if after unloading from aircraft at the final place of discharge but prior to termination of the insurance, the subject matter is forwarded a destination other than that to which it insured here under the insurance, whilst remaining subject to termination as provide for shall not extend beyond the commencement of transit to such other destination." War clause no. 258 lays down "if during the insured transit the aircraft arrives at an intermediate place to discharge the subject-matter insured for on-carriage by aircraft. The insurance shall continue until the expiry of 15 days counting from midnight of the day of arrival of the aircraft at such place and thereafter reattaches the subject-matter insured. During the period of 15 days the insurance remains in force after discharge only at such intermediate place. If the air transit in the contract of carriage is terminated at a place other than the destination, that place shall be final place of discharge." Termination of transit clause (terrorism), which covers loss or damage to subject matter insured caused by any terrorist or person acting from political motive, lays down "in respect of air transit, on the expiry of 30 days after the unloading the subject-matter insured from the aircraft at the final place of discharge, on at consignee warehouse or place of whichever shall first occur."

9. Aviation insurance in India. Constitutes a miniscule percentage of the Indian insurance market accounting for 1.7% of premium underwritten by all non-life insurance companies. Globally the premiums have been falling since 2001 due to reduction in number of accidents. With the cost of claims soaring, the capacity reducing, the market becoming hard, the rates of premium are expected to rise. Indian aviation industry is fast growing and this will help to raise aviation insurance.

How to buy family travel insurance: Travelling abroad is expensive. A medical emergency or loss of baggage only add to costs. A family travel insurance policy thus covers these risks at a nominal price. It is mandatory to by such a policy visiting certain countries.

Types of policies: These plans come in different variants for single trip, multiple trips or year-long travel. If a single trip is plan is chosen, it is good idea to choose a policy duration which exceeds the trip duration, just in case there are any unforeseen delays while travelling.

Coverage: While choosing a policy find out the exact-amount covered and the heads under which these amounts are covered. Policy may offer benefits like emergency cash in advance.

Pre-existing medical conditions: It is important to declare pre-existing diseases, if any, at the time of taking the policy. Travel insurance policies typically do not cover pre-existing medical conditions. Except a few that cover life threatening medical conditions.

Deductibles: Along with the coverage and claim limits, it is important to check the deductibles amount from the cover in case of a claim. The amount mentioned as deductible is to be paid by insured before the insurance company pays the amount under the claim.

How to buy: Airline booking portals provide travel insurance cover as an add-on. One can also use an insurance aggregator website to view comparable quotes or visit insurance company website.

10. Political risk insurance. Political risk comes in various forms. There may be uncertainty about future viability of a hosts country's system. These may be ownership risk in the form of confiscation (governments take over of ownership without compensation), expropriation (government takes over ownership by paying some compensation) and domestication (organization). Besides ownership risk there is operation risk i.e. government may restrict the operation of a firm in production, marketing or finance or human resource management. The third type of risk is transfer risk, e.g. remittance of funds or assets outside a country. Firms adopt risk avoiding or risk shifting or risk reduction strategies.

Insurance is a risk shifting strategy. ECGC in India Issues political risk policies covering shipments by exporters both from the date of shipment or contract. It also provides overseas investment insurance cover. The risks of war, expropriation and restriction or remittance are covered by various schemes by it. In U.S.A. Overseas Private Investment Corporation provides cover against political risk. The Lloyds of London is the only private insurer against expropriation risks. Multinational Investment Guaranties Agency a member of world group, provides protection against political risks of international level through insuring investment of other national insurers.

11. Foreign exchange risk insurance. The foreign exchange exposure and risk is divided into two types: (a) accounting exposure, which may be transaction exposure and translation exposure. The exposure means the degree to which a firm is affected. Transaction exposure arises when a currency is converted to make or receive payment for goods and services or to repay loans and interest and to pay or-receive dividend on royalty. Translation exposure arises when financial statements are converted from one currency to another, (b) Economic or operating exposure. It occurs when currency fluctuations have impact on the cash flows of the firm in the years to come and which have impact on competitive posture of the firm.

12. Engineering insurance. The term is used to describe various types of policies for the protection of construction works, as well as erection and operation of machinery. There are two categories (a) Single project cover—non-renewable policies, and (b) renewable annually. They are also of two sub-categories (i) property, and (ii) business income protection policies. The later cover advance loss of profit or loss of profit due to machinery breakdown or deterioration of stock. Engineering reinsurance methods are same as of other classes of insurance like fire i.e. facultative, surplus reinsurance, and facultative obligatory reinsurance. It started in 19th century. Today it may cover all types of electronic equipment, computer configurations, perishable goods stored in cold storage, power stations and boilers and pressure vessels.

13. Liability insurance. Policies are issued to cover following liabilities:

(1) Liability of employer under employees compensation Act 1923 and employer liability 1938 and sale of goods Act 1930 motor vehicle Act 1988.

(2) Liability of industries dealing with hazardous substances listed in Public Liability Insurance Act, 1991.

The growth of hazardous industries, processes and operation has led to growing risk of accident, not only to the workers employed in such under takings, but also members of public who may be in the vicinity. Properties are damaged: Mostly economically weaker sections suffer great hardship. There is a low to protect workers, but not members of the public. So, it is mandatory public liability insurance. This will provide immediate relief to public, instead of going to courts. The Bhopal gas tragedy is an example. The Central Government has also established a fund called 'Environmental Relief Fund.' Every owner shall get such insurance policy.

(3) Liability to cover claim of third parties on account of bodily injury or property damage arising out of insured's product and combination of above no. 2 and 3.

(4) Errors and omission/Professional liability, i.e., injury to body or property damage due to service offered by insured like medical practitioners, C.A., architects, software firms and engineers.

(5) Legal liability of directors or officers, i.e., managing director, manager and secretary. SEBI has made mandatory insurance to cover all public listed companies and professional bodies (C.A., Company secretaries) to provide insurance cover for loss caused by Error and omission of directors or officers. IRDA has made insurance compulsory for errors and omissions committed by insurance brokers.

(6) Liability for negligence, nuisance and trespass negligence may arise either under a contract or under stature. If negligence of one person is attributed to another person, it is called vicarious liability or imputed liability, e.g. negligence of an employee may be imputed to the employer.

The liabilities of directors and officers of a company are based on common law principles. They are: (a) duty of care, (b) duty of loyalty to the company, (c) duty of disclosure, and (d) duty of compliance, i.e. of fiduciary relationships. Under company law liabilities arise for *ultra vires* acts, misrepresentation or misstatement or misleading statements, mismanagements of funds and failure to file required certificates and documents and lately sexual harassment claim and corporate governance.

There are three types of coverage under such policies (a) to protect individual managers from risk of shareholders litigation, (b) to reimburse corporation for its indemnification payments to its directors officers, and (c) protects the company from the shareholders litigation to which company itself a party. However, no claim is allowed for fraud, prior claims against company before issue of policy and when litigation is between parties who are both insured, and on non-disclosure of facts. Liability insurance can be classified into (a) claim made liability insurance, i.e. insurer is liable to the insured only when a third party makes a claim within insurance period and (b) occurrence based/trigger based liability i.e. insurer agrees to defend and indemnify the insured against, any loss which allegedly occurred as a result of an act of omission of the insured during insurance period.

Liability insurance requires CASE study i.e. circumstances, activity, security and event of the risk.

The insured had paid the premium for professional for past two years. In first year he received only the receipt and for second year even receipt was not received. The insurer did not issue policy document for both the years. The plaintiff contented that in 2005-06, he had not submitted any proposal and policy was issued. No doubt there is a laxity on the part of the field official of the insurer, but plaintiff, being a well-informed person and who required the insurance protection as part of his professional dealings with large-scale construction activities should have demanded a proposal form.

As per-records, an amount said to be premium has been deposited into the personal savings bank account of a company official, who is in charge of a 'one man office' of the insurer. Held the actions of a responsible official of a leading public sector insurer, has been thoroughly unprofessional. On the other hand, the transactions are of professional nature and are resolved between the individuals, the plaintiff's complaint is dismissed (*Mr. G. Vasiharan* vs. *United India Insurance Co. Ltd.* Chennai).

15

Various Types of Insurance Fraud

Commercial frauds in international trade are becoming more significant and adversely affecting the General Insurance Industry. There may never be perfect crime but there can be ideal crime with minimum risk, maximum profit, easily adaptable to prevail conditions, relatively very simple to operate, considerably difficult to defect but still more difficult to prosecute even if detected—all these qualities are in fact well included in insurance fraud.

Although in India there are specialized bodies like Fire Protection Association, Loss Prevention Association, etc., but there is nobody for crime prevention although in recent times this is keenly felt. It may be argued that increase in crime to some extent is due to defect in structure of society, i.e., increase in unemployment, severe depression faced by shipping industry all over the world resulting in huge laid up tonnage. With so much tonnage chasing limited cargoes fraudsters were no doubt tempted to indulge in unlawful activities.

Broadly frauds can be classified under two headings, i.e. within insurance industry and outside (i.e. beyond the people of insurers) industry. Within the industry the following types generally occur as a result of company's staff/development officer or agent being involved in:

- Granting insurance cover without bringing to books the premium thereon unless and until claim is made by the owner.
- Providing insurance cover after the accident occurred to enable owner to profit by the claim made.
- Allowing in collusion with the owner to recover more than what the owner is entitled under insurance.
- Not disposing off/accounting salvage or other recoveries which would otherwise reduce the loss amount.
- Making fictitious claims with forget claim form, claim bill and other supporting documents to benefit for him/her financially by such claims.

In India the most of the fraudulent claims are related to the second category, i.e. by the claimants under various insurance covers, which are related to different Departments of General Insurance as given below:

Fire department: Issues may relate to:

- Malicious and deliberate intention to set fire particularly when market is falling;
- Making exaggerated claim taking advantage of bona fide accident;
- Offering low salvage value particularly specialized items which are not easily marketable to have benefit of claim and salvage.

Motor department: Issues may relate to:

- Making different claims with same accident relying on one set of evidence such as photographs, etc.
- Falsifying repair bill/suppliers invoice without effecting repairs or purchasing parts.
- Making claims for accident after vehicle is sold without disclosing the sale.

Personal accident: Issue may relate to:

- Preferring claim even though person disabled or dead is different from insured person.

Mediclaim insurance: Issue may relate to:

- Making claim for person undergoing treatment different from insured person.

Householders policy: Issue may relate to:

- Person insuring costly diamond ring under the policy and subsequently claiming for the ring being slipped out of his finger in the toilet while soiling and obviously no surveyor can be sent for finding out of the lost ring from the chamber/sop kit. The claim therefore, may be settled or compromised.

Inland transit: Issue may relate to:

- Utilizing bogus lorry receipt as proof of good sent and making claims for non-delivery, without goods being actually sent.
- Sending worthless goods in containers without sufficient packing so that at destination, contents are damaged or emptied and claims preferred for total loss.
- Sending used and fragile goods which may not withstand long journey and transshipment resulting in damage on delivery and preferring total loss for replacement on insurance cover for exaggerated value.

Transport by Road/Rail

In most cases where a cargo fails to arrive at its destination, advanced planning on the part of the criminals has taken place, unless the consignee laid, and has actually received the cargo, there are four sources that could have supplied the mafia with the required information with regard to incoming shipments:

- The freight forwarders or agents located in Europe, who have access to the necessary documentation (e.g. CMR Notes) as well as shipment timing, route, lorry and driver/ consignor/consignee details.
- Local Customs, most likely located on the CIS Borders, due to the fact they would have access to the documentation above.
- The consignee himself, who is put under pressure by the mafia. If is often the case that the mafia knows each and every company involved in the trade of the commodities they

also deal in. They are then in a position to demand information as well documents for due shipments. It is often not a loss for the consignee, as he may either not yet has paid for the goods or he may be in a position to claim on insurance.

- There may be a leak in the internal system of the insurance company.

Computer and its Related Various Insurance Policies

- Fraud on this insurance is phenomenon of the age we live in. This means wrongful conversion of assets under control of computer system by insertion of fraudulent data/alteration of data, etc., changing financial analysis and confidential information by virtue of which insurance claims are made.

Maritime Fraud

- The biggest insurance fraud, the world is facing today, is maritime fraud, which affects cargo owners, ship-owners, and insurers in various degrees. Historians record the oldest maritime fraud happening over 2000 years ago; frauds at sea have always been a major problem over the centuries. Maritime frauds cost over ₹ 250 million for world insurance market in the last 5 years. Companies trading internationally are increasing target of sophisticated fraudster familiar with way in which business can be manipulated to their advantage. Dishonest firms generally trade honestly for initial period to gain confidence and thereafter show their true colours and make fraud.
- There are Documentary frauds relate to letter of credit and charter party, these documents are forged and negotiated obtaining payment; charter takes vessel on time charter collecting freight charges and then disappears leaving cargo to its own fate and many cases not meeting even wages of crew, etc.
- Scuttling vessels where value of cargo is disproportionately higher than value of ship; vessel nearing end of its useful life is taken out of sea on trading voyage; fraudster seeking out cargo often selecting from development countries. Buyers' pay for same as soon as valid papers like letter of credit, etc. are produced. On high seas, cargo will be removed to other vessels and sold elsewhere and crew transferred. Thereafter that particular vessel is scuttled. There is no shortage of market for cheap cargo across the world. Owners claimed for insured value of ship which is generally more than the market value and also benefited by sale of stolen goods.
- Most maritime frauds are occurring on single vessel owner or with companies in financial difficulties or having complicated network of managers/operators/charter/owner, etc. Fraudsters involved are experts locating right ship, recruiting right crew, finding suckers to buy goods reported to be carried in ship, arranging correct paper work, disposing diverted goods, ensuring proceeds thereof to their bank account and then scuttling that affected ship. The main problem of prosecution is related to jurisdiction. For example, Liberian registered oil tanker with Tunisian crew and Greek officers loads oil for Italian firm at Kuwait sells to Anglo Dutch firm of delivery in France and then diverts to sell second time to South American firm before scuttling ship in West African Coast. The main problem to this case is—who has the jurisdiction.

Conclusion

In Indian market we have seen that the loss ratio in the General insurance Sector highly increases for some of the following fraudulent actions as evident in the market:

1. Failing to report an accurate medical history when applying for Life/Health Insurance at the time of underwriting, is bringing adverse result in our medical policies. An employee of a company who fakes or exaggerates injuries, to avoid work and even sometimes draw workers' compensation payout in the W.C. Policies to a large extent, needs to identified.
2. A motor/other vehicle accident victim who falsified or overstates injuries—or even fakes the accident—to achieve large settlement of award in Motor (Third Party) Claims. Staging automobile accidents which result in inflated injury/false death claim in TP Parlance. Even it happened that the two persons were declared dead under a Motor T.P. Case filed in court in West Bengal but on subsequent enquiry they were found alive thereafter.
3. An insured that draws accident and health insurance benefits because of exaggerated or even fabricated injuries or illness whenever covered under Personal Accident Policies.
4. In general, consumers can often be victimized by unscrupulous agents or brokers and discover only after they file a claim that they are without coverage for their life or any other assets like home or their car. The agents not submitting the premium at all or submitting only the reduced amount—all causes hardship to the consumer.

Huge portion of the insurance procedural aspects are now-a-days are handled by the outsourced agencies. Mainly for the software related operations. Bancassurance and tie-up with other financial institutions lead to the normal customer identification and verification obligations are predicted on the basis that these functions are carried out by officers or employees of the financial institution.

However, having regard to the diversity of the financial sector, there may be many occasions when these functions are performed by the agents or are otherwise outsourced. This is an important issue, because the percentage of financial functions which is being outsourced is increasing, and there is a need to determine whether the agent or other person acting for the financial institution is subject to the same or similar anti-money laundering and the diligence obligations that apply to the institution.

Fraud incidents are also occurring due to the reliance on the insurance intermediaries to operate for procurement of business and also arising out of the roles played by various other third parties to perform identification and verification obligations and processes (other than outsourcing and agency arrangement).

It must be appreciated that service to the client is main motto of insurance industry and this may be judged effectively by prompt settlement of the claims. Insurers generally handle claims as quickly and expeditiously as possible but they do come across few instances of fraud wherein they are really unable to proceed fast until thorough enquiry is completely completed. When they become satisfied that the particular claim is a bona fide one, they then have no hesitation in rejecting that claim. Insurance companies—specially the public sector organizations have serious responsibility in discharging payment to the claimant for which the insurance company is not entitled at all.

Money Laundering is definitely going to hit our life insurance portfolio. As revealed from the global experience the transfer of money flowing from racketeering, drug transactions and other illegal sources into legitimate channels has severely affected the global economy.

Finally we need to focus on the specific Fraud Indicators/Triggers in existence of as the critical areas in insurance operations given as below:

1. Close proximity between issuance of Policy/commencement of Policy and date of accident/ claim.
2. Back dating of coverage period/difference in CN and Policy risk cover period.
3. Same Petitioner/Advocate/Doctor/Police Station/Police IO/Witness/Hospital in more claims.
4. Same Cover Note No. in more than one claim.
5. Insured overtly aggressive in pursuit of a quick settlement.
6. Willing to accept small settlement rather than the documented losses.
7. Documents of doubtful nature.
8. Insured behind in loan re-payment.
9. Accident un-witnessed and not promptly reported.
10. Invisible injury.
11. High value claim without any known casualty.
12. Unexplained/vaguely explained delay in FIR.
13. The driver/vehicle number is not known in FIR, and then there is a subsequent addition/ identification.
14. History in MLC appears to be "fall".
15. History of MLC does not match with discharge card/petition.
16. Over writing in MLC/AR/WC.
17. Criminal case is closed for "mistake of fact."
18. Mismatch in the nature of injury, bills produced and nature of hospital referred.
19. Over writing in Bills, Medical documents, change in hospitalization referred.
20. Exaggerated disability.
21. Duplicate DL prepared after accident & details of original not available.
22. Motor Vehicle Inspection report does not suggest the manner of the accident (No damages to vehicles, despite heavy collisions).
23. Driver escapes unhurt in massive accidents (driver swapping suspected).
24. No corresponding Own damage Claim if it is Pvt. Car comprehensive policy.
25. Petition and police details does not match with information provided at the time of Own damage Claim.
26. Name of driver in police papers not match with OD claim.
27. When all required documents are in order beyond doubt.

28. Close relation between claimant and owner/insured.
29. More than one vehicle with insured, one is insured with us and other is uninsured.
30. Habitual Drivers/offender, Claimant Advocates, Police Stations, Hospitals.
31. Insured and Claimants/injured known to each other as revealed in investigation/during cross.
32. Contradiction of driver in criminal and MACT cases.

Source: *Insurance Times*, March 2015.

16

Insurance Regulatory and Development Authority

IRDA was established in 1999 by an Act called 'Insurance Regulatory and Development Authority' Act, 1999. The relevant provisions are given below:

Section 1. Establishment and Incorporation of Authority

(1) With effect from such date as the Central Government may, by notification, appoint, there shall be established, for the purposes of this Act, an Authority to be called "the Insurance Regulatory and Development Authority".

(2) The Authority shall be a body corporate by the name aforesaid having perpetual succession and a common seal with power, subject to the provisions of this Act, to acquire, hold and dispose of property, both movable and immovable, and to contract and shall, by the said name, sue or be sued.

(3) The head office of the Authority shall be at such place as the Central Government may decide from time to time.

(4) The Authority may establish officers at other places in India.

Section 4. Composition of Authority: The Authority shall consist of the following members, namely:

(a) a chairperson;

(b) not more than five whole-time members;

(c) not more than four part-time members,

to be appointed by the Central Government from amongst persons of ability, integrity and standing who have knowledge or experience in life insurance, general insurance, actuarial science, finance, economic, law, accountancy, administration or any other discipline which would, in the opinion of the Central Government, be useful to the Authority:

Provided that the Central Government shall, while appointing the Chairperson and the whole-time members, ensure that at least one person each is a person having knowledge or experience in life insurance, general insurance or actuarial science, respectively.

Section 5. Tenure of Office of Chairperson and Other Members: (1) The Chairperson and every other whole-time member shall hold office for a term of five years from the date on which he enters upon his office and shall be eligible for reappointment:

Provided that no person shall hold office as a chairperson after he has attained the age of sixty-five years:

Provided further that no person shall hold office as a whole-time member after he has attained the age of sixty-two years.

(2) A part-time member shall hold for a term not exceeding five years from the date on which he enters upon his office.

(3) Notwithstanding anything contained in sub-section (1) or sub-section (2), a member may:

(a) relinquish his office by giving in writing to the Central Government notice of not less than three months; or

(b) be removed from his office in accordance with the provisions of section.

Section 6. Removal From Office: (1) The Central Government may remove from office any member who:

(a) is, or at any time has been, adjudged as an insolvent; or

(b) has become physically or mentally incapable of acting as a member; or

(c) has been convicted of any offence which, in the opinion of the Central Government involves moral turpitude; or

(d) has acquired such financial or other interest as is likely to affect prejudicially his functions as a member; or

(e) has so abused his position as to render his continuation in office detrimental to the public interest.

(2) No such member shall be removed under clause (d) or clause (e) of sub-section (1) unless he has been given a reasonable opportunity of being heard in the matter.

Section 7. Salary and Allowances of Chairperson and Members: (1) The salary and allowances payable to and other terms and conditions of service of, the members other than part-time members shall be such as may be prescribed.

(2) The part-time members shall receive such allowances as may be prescribed.

(3) The salary, allowances and other conditions of service of a member shall not be varied to his disadvantage after appointment.

Section 8. Bar Future Employment of Members: The chairperson and the whole-time members shall not, for a period of two years from the date on which they cease to hold office as such, except with the previous approval of the Central Government, accept:

(a) any employment either under the Central Government or under any State Government; or

(b) any appointment in any company in the insurance sector.

Section 9. Administrative Powers of Chairperson: The Chairperson shall have the powers of general superintendence and direction in respect of all administrative matters of the Authority.

Section 10. Meetings of Authority: (1) The Authority shall meet at such times and places and shall observe such rules and procedures in regard to transaction of business at its meetings (including quorum at such meetings) as may be determined by the regulations.

(2) The Chairperson, or if for any reason he is unable to attend a meeting of the Authority, any other member chosen by the members present from amongst themselves at the meeting shall preside at the meeting.

(3) All questions which come up before any meeting of the Authority shall be decided by a majority of votes by the members present and voting, and in the event of an equality of votes, the Chairperson, or in his absence, the person presiding shall have a second or casting vote.

(4) The Authority may make regulations for the transaction of business at its meetings.

Section 11. Vacancies, etc., Not to invalidate proceedings of Authority: No Act or proceedings of the Authority shall be invalid merely by reason of:

(a) any vacancy in, or any defect in the constitution of the Authority; or

(b) any defect in the appointment of a person acting as a member of the Authority; or

(c) any irregularity in the procedure of the Authority not affecting the merits of the case.

Section 12. Officers and Employees of Authority: (1) The Authority may appoint officers and such other employees as it considered necessary for the efficient discharge of its function under this Act.

(2) The terms and other conditions of service and other employees of the Authority appointed under sub-section (1) shall be governed by regulations made under this Act.

Transfer of Assets, Liabilities etc., of Interim Insurance Regulatory Authority

Section 13. Transfer of Assets, Liabilities, etc., of Interim Insurance Regulatory Authority: On the appointed day,

(a) all the assets and liabilities of the Interim Insurance Regulatory Authority shall stand transferred to and vested in, the Authority.

Explanation: The assets of the Interim Insurance Regulatory Authority shall be deemed to include all rights and powers, and all properties, whether movable or immovable, including, in particular, cash balances, deposits and all other interests and rights in, or arising out of, such properties as may be in the possession of the interim Insurance Regulatory Authority and all books of account and other documents relating to the same; and liabilities shall be deemed to include all debts, liabilities and obligations of whatever kind;

(b) without prejudice to the previous of clause (a), all debts, obligations and liabilities incurred, all contracts entered into and all matters and things engaged to be done by, with or for the Interim Insurance Regulatory Authority immediately before that day, for or in connection with the purpose of the said Regulatory Authority, shall be deemed to have been incurred, entered into or engaged to be done by, with or for, the Authority;

(c) all sums of money due to the Interim Insurance Regulatory Authority immediately before that day may be continued or may be instituted by or against the Authority;

(d) all suits and other legal proceedings instituted or which could have been instituted by or against the Interim Insurance Regulatory Authority immediately before that day may be continued or may be instituted by or against the Authority.

Duties, Powers and Functions of Authority

Section 14. Duties, Powers and Functions of Authority: (1) Subject to the provisions of the Act and any other law for the time being in force, the Authority shall have the duty to regulate, promote and ensure orderly growth of the insurance business and re-insurance business.

(2) Without prejudice to the generality of the provisions continued in sub-section (1), the powers and functions of the Authority shall include:

(a) issue to the applicant a certificate of registration, renew, modify, withdraw, suspends or cancel such registration;

(b) protection of the interests of the policyholders in matters concerning assigning of policy, nomination by policyholders, insurable interest, settlement of insurance claim, surrender value of policy and other terms and conditions of contracts of insurance;

(c) specifying requisite qualifications, code of conduct and practical training for intermediary or insurance intermediaries and agents;

(d) specifying the code of conduct for surveyors and loss assessors;

(e) promoting efficiency in the conduct of insurance business;

(f) promoting and regulating professional organisations connected with the insurance and re-insurance business;

(g) levying fees and other charges for carrying out the purposes of this Act;

(h) calling for information from undertaking Inspection of, conducting enquiries and investigations including audit of the insurers, intermediaries, insurance intermediaries and other organisations concerned with the insurance business;

(i) control and regulation of the rates, advantages, terms and conditions that may be offered by insurers in respect of general insurance business not so controlled and regulated by the Tariff Advisory Committee under section 64U of the Insurance Act, 1938 (4 of 1938);

(j) specifying the form and manner in which books of account shall be maintained and statement of accounts shall be rendered by insurers and other insurance intermediaries;

(k) regulating investment of funds by insurance companies;

(l) regulating maintenance of margin of solvency;

(m) adjudication of disputes between insurers and intermediaries or insurance intermediaries;

(n) supervising the functioning of the Tariff Advisory Committee;

(o) specifying the percentage of premium income of the insurer to finance schemes for promoting and regulating professional organisations referred to in clause (f);

(p) specifying the percentage of life insurance business and general insurance business to be undertaken by the insurer in the rural or social sector; and

(q) existing such other powers as may be prescribed.

Finance, Accounts and Audit

Section 15. Grants by Central Government: The Central Government may, after the appropriation made by Parliament by law in this behalf, made to the Authority grants of such sums of Money as the Government may think fit for the purposes of this Act.

Section 16. Constitution of Funds: (1) There shall be constituted a fund to be called "the Insurance Regulatory and Development Authority Fund" and there shall be credited thereto:

(a) all Government grants, fees and charges received by the Authority;

(b) all sums received by the Authority from such other source as may be decided upon by the Central Government.

(2) The Fund shall be applied for meeting:

(a) the salaries, allowances and other remuneration of the members, officers and other employees of the Authority;

(b) the other expenses of the Authority in connection with the discharge of its functions and for the purposes of this act.

Section 17. Accounts and Audit: (1) The Authority shall maintain proper accounts and other relevant records and prepare an annual statement of accounts in such form as may be prescribed by the Central Government in consultation with the Comptroller and Auditor-General of India.

(2) The accounts of the Authority shall be audited by the Comptroller and Auditor-General of India at such intervals as may be specified by him and any expenditure incurred in connection with such audit shall be payable by the Authority to the Comptroller and Auditor-General.

(3) The Comptroller and Auditor-General of India and any other person appointed by him in connection with the audit of the accounts of the Authority shall have the same rights, privileges and authority in connection with such audit as the Comptroller and Auditor-General generally has in connection with the audit of the Government accounts and, in particular, shall have the right to demand the production of books of account, connected vouchers and other documents and papers and to inspect any of the offices of the Authority.

(4) The accounts of the Authority as certified by the Comptroller and Auditor-General of India or any other person appointed by him in this behalf together with the audit-report thereon shall be forwarded annually to the Central Government and that Government shall cause the same to be laid before each House of Parliament.

Section 18. Power of Central Government to Issue Directions: (1) Without prejudice to the foregoing provisions of this Act, the Authority shall, in exercise of its powers or the performance of is functions under this Act, be bound by such directions on questions of policy, other than those relating to technical and administrative matters, as the Central Government may give in writing to it from time to time:

PROVIDED that the Authority shall, as far as practicable, be given an opportunity to express its views before any direction is given under this sub-section.

(2) The decision of the Central Government, whether a question is one of policy or not, shall be final.

Section 19. Power of Central Government to Supersede Authority: (1) If at any time the Central Government is of the opinion:

(a) that, one account of circumstances beyond the control of the Authority, it is unable to discharge the functions or perform the duties imposed on it by or under the provisions of this Act; or

(b) that the Authority has persistently defaulted in complying with any direction given by the Central Government under this Act or in the discharge of the functions or performance of the duties imposed on it by or under the provisions of this Act and as a result of such default the financial position of the Authority or the administration of the Authority has suffered; or

(c) that circumstances exist which render it necessary in the public interest so to do, the Central Government may, by notification and for reasons to be specified therein, supersede the Authority for such period, not exceeding six months, as may be specified in the notification and appoint a person to be the Controller of Insurance under Section 2B of the Insurance Act, 1938 (4 of 1938), if not already done:

Provided that before issuing any such notification, the Central Government shall give a reasonable opportunity to the Authority to make representations, if any, of the Authority.

(2) Upon the publication of a notification under sub-section (1) superseding the Authority:

(a) the Chairperson and other members shall, as form the date of supersession, vacate their offices as such;

(b) all the powers, functions and duties which may, by or under the provisions of this Act, be exercised or discharged by or on behalf of the Authority shall, until the Authority is reconstituted under sub-section (3), be exercised and discharged by the Controller of Insurance; and

(c) all properties owned or controlled by the Authority shall, until the Authority is reconstituted under sub-section (3), vest in the Central Government.

(3) On or before the expiration of the period of supersession specified in the notification issued under sub-section (1), the Central Government shall constitute the Authority by a fresh appointment of its Chairperson and other members and in such case any person who had vacated his office under clause (a) of sub-section (2) shall not be deemed to be disqualified for reappointment.

(4) The Central Government shall cause a copy of the notification issued under sub-section (1) and a full report to any action to be laid before each House of Parliament at the earliest.

Note: Under Insurance (amendment/Act, 2015, an appeal can be made to the Securities Appellate Tribunal against orders of IRDA.)

Section 20. Furnishing of Returns, etc., To Central Government: (1) The Authority shall furnish to the Central Government at such time and in such form and manner as may be prescribed, or as the Central Government may direct to furnish such returns, statements and other particulars in regard to any proposed or existing programme for the promotion and development existing programme for the promotion and development of the insurance industry as the Central Government may, from time to time, require.

(2) Without prejudice to the provisions of sub-section (1), the Authority shall, within nine months after the close of each financial year, submit to the Central Government a report giving

a true and full account of its activities including the activities for promotion and development of the insurance business during the previous financial year.

(3) Copies of the reports received under sub-section (2) shall be laid, as soon as may be after they are received, before each House of Parliament.

Section 21. Chairperson, Members, Officers and other Employees of Authority to be Public Servants: The Chairperson, members, officers and other employees of Authority shall be deemed, when acting or purporting to act in pursuance of any of the provisions of this Act, to be public servants within the meaning of Section 21 of the Indian Penal Code (45 of 1860).

Section 22. Protection of Action Taken in Good Faith: No suit, prosecution or other legal proceedings shall lie against the Central Government or any officer of the Central Government or any member, officer or other employee of the Authority for anything which is in good faith done or intended to be done under this Act or the rules or regulations made thereunder:

Provided that nothing in this Act shall exempt any person from any suit or other proceedings which might apart from this Act, be brought against him.

Section 23. Delegation of Powers: (1) The Authority may, by general or special order in writing, delegate to the Chairperson or any other member or office of the Authority subject to such condition, if any, as may be specified in the order such of its powers and functions under this Act as it may deem necessary.

(2) The Authority may, by a general or special order in writing, also form committees of the members and delegate to them the powers and functions of the Authority as may be specified by the regulations.

Section 24. Power to make Rules: (1) The Central Government may, be notification, make rules for carrying out the provisions of this Act.

(2) In particular, and without prejudice to the generality of the foregoing power, such rules may provide for all or any of the following matters, namely:

(a) the salary and allowances payable to, and other terms and conditions of service of the members other than part-time members under sub-section (1) of Section 7:

(b) the allowances to be paid to be part-time members under sub-section (2) of Section 7;

(c) such other powers that may be exercised by the Authority under clause (q) of sub-section (2) of Section 14;

(d) the form of annual statement of accounts to be maintained by the Authority under sub-section (1) of Section 17;

(e) the form and the manner in which and the time within which returns and statements and particulars are to be furnished to the Central Government under sub-section (1) of Section 20;

(f) the matters under sub-section (5) of Section 25 on which the Insurance Advisory Committee shall advise the Authority;

(g) any other matter which is required to be, or may be, prescribed or in respect of which provisioned is to be or any be made by rules.

Section 25. Establishment of Insurance Advisory Committee: (1) The Authority may, by notification, establish with effect from such date as it may specify in such notification, a Committee to be known as the Insurance Advisory Committee.

(2) The Insurance Advisory Committee shall consist of not more than twenty-five members excluding ex-officio members to represent the interests of commerce, industry, transport, agriculture, consumer fora, surveyors, agents intermediaries, organisations engaged in safety and loss prevention, research bodies and employees' association in the insurance sector.

(3) The Chairperson and the members of the Authority shall be the ex officio Chairperson and ex officio members of the Insurance Advisory Committee.

(4) The objects of the Insurance Advisory Committee shall be to advise the Authority on matters relating to the making of the regulations under Section 26.

(5) Without prejudice to the provisions of sub-section (4), the Insurance Advisory Committee may advise the Authority on such other matters as may be prescribed.